# Information Retrieval Architecture and Algorithms

Gerald Kowalski

# Information Retrieval Architecture and Algorithms

 Springer

Gerald Kowalski
Ashburn, VA, USA

ISBN 978-1-4899-8216-2      ISBN 978-1-4419-7716-8 (eBook)
DOI 10.1007/978-1-4419-7716-8
Springer New York Dordrecht Heidelberg London

Springer is part of Springer Science+Business Media (www.springer.com)

*This book is dedicated to my grandchildren,*
*Adeline, Bennet, Mollie Kate and Riley who*
*are the future*

Jerry Kowalski

# Preface

Information Retrieval has radically changed over the last 25 years. When I first started teaching Information Retrieval and developing large Information Retrieval systems in the 1980s it was easy to cover the area in a single semester course. Most of the discussion was theoretical with testing done on small databases and only a small subset of the theory was able to be implemented in commercial systems. There were not massive amounts of data in the right digital format for search. Since 2000, the field of Information retrieval has undergone a major transformation driven by massive amounts of new data (e.g., Internet, Facebook, etc.) that needs to be searched, new hardware technologies that makes the storage and processing of data feasible along with software architecture changes that provides the scalability to handle massive data sets. In addition, the area of information retrieval of multimedia, in particular images, audio and video, are part of everyone's information world and users are looking for information retrieval of them as well as the traditional text. In the textual domain, languages other than English are becoming far more prevalent on the Internet.

To understand how to solve the information retrieval problems is no longer focused on search algorithm improvements. Now that Information Retrieval Systems are commercially available, like the area of Data Base Management Systems, an Information Retrieval System approach is needed to understand how to provide the search and retrieval capabilities needed by users. To understand modern information retrieval it's necessary to understand search and retrieval for both text and multimedia formats. Although search algorithms are important, other aspects of the total system such as pre-processing on ingest of data and how to display the search results can contribute as much to the user finding the needed information as the search algorithms.

This book provides a theoretical and practical explanation of the latest advancements in information retrieval and their application to existing systems. It takes a system approach, discussing all aspects of an Information Retrieval System. The system approach to information retrieval starts with a functional discussion of what is needed for an information system allowing the reader to understand the scope of the information retrieval problem and the challenges in providing the needed functions. The book, starting with the Chap. 1, stresses that information retrieval has migrated from textual to multimedia. This theme is carried throughout the book with multimedia search, retrieval and display being discussed as well as all the classic and new textual techniques. Taking a system view of Information Retrieval explores every functional processing step in a system showing how decisions on implementation at each step can add to the goal of information retrieval; providing the user with the information they need minimizing their resources in getting the information (i.e., time it takes). This is not limited to search speed but also how search results are presented can influence how fast a user can locate the information they need. The information retrieval system can be defined as four major processing steps. It starts with "ingestion" of information to be indexed, the indexing process, the search process and finally the information presentation process. Every processing step has algorithms associated with it and provides the opportunity to make searching and retrieval more precise. In addition the changes in hardware and more importantly search architectures, such as those introduced by GOOGLE, are discussed as ways of approaching the scalability issues. The last chapter focuses on how to evaluate an information retrieval system and the data sets and forums that are available. Given the continuing introduction of new search technologies, ways of evaluating which are most useful to a particular information domain become important.

The primary goal of writing this book is to provide a college text on Information Retrieval Systems. But in addition to the theoretical aspects, the book maintains a theme of practicality that puts into perspective the importance and utilization of the theory in systems that are being used by anyone on the Internet. The student will gain an understanding of what is achievable using existing technologies and the deficient areas that warrant additional research. What used to be able to be covered in a one semester course now requires at least three different courses to provide adequate background. The first course provides a complete overview of the Information Retrieval System theory and architecture as provided by this book. But additional courses are needed to go in more depth on the algorithms and theoretical options for the different search, classification, clustering and other related technologies whose basics are provided in this book. Another course is needed to focus in depth on the theory and implementation on the new growing area of Multimedia Information Retrieval and also Information Presentation technologies.

Gerald Kowalski

# Contents

# Chapter 1
# Information Retrieval System Functions

## 1.1 Introduction

Information Retrieval is a very simple concept with everyone having practical experience in it's use. The scenario of a user having an information need, translating that into a search statement and executing that search to locate the information has become ubiquitous to everyday life. The Internet has become a repository of any information a person needs, replacing the library as a more convenient research tool. An Information Retrieval System is a system that ingests information, transforms it into searchable format and provides an interface to allow a user to search and retrieve information. The most obvious example of an Information Retrieval System is GOOGLE and the English language has even been extended with the term "Google it" to mean search for something.

So everyone has had experience with Information Retrieval Systems and with a little thought it is easy to answer the question—"Does it work?" Everyone who has used such systems has experienced the frustration that is encountered when looking for certain information. Given the massive amount of intellectual effort that is going into the design and evolution of a "GOOGLE" or other search systems the question comes to mind why is it so hard to find what you are looking for.

One of the goals of this book is to explain the practical and theoretical issues associated with Information Retrieval that makes design of Information Retrieval Systems one of the challenges of our time. The demand for and expectations of users to quickly find any information they need continues to drive both the theoretical analysis and development of new technologies to satisfy that need. To scope the problem one of the first things that needs to be defined is "information". Twenty-five years ago information retrieval was totally focused on textual items. That was because almost all of the "digital information" of value was in textual form. In today's technical environment most people carry with them most of the time the capability to create images and videos of interest—that is the cell phone. This has made modalities other than text to become as common as text. That is coupled with Internet web sites that allow and are designed for ease of use of uploading and storing those modalities which more than justify the need to include other than text as part of the information retrieval problem. There is a lot of parallelism between the information processing steps for text and for images, audio and video. Although maps are another modality that could be included, they will only be generally discussed.

So in the context of this book, information that will be considered in Information Retrieval Systems includes text, images, audio and video. The term "item" shall be used to define a specific information object. This could be a textual document, a news item from an RSS feed, an image, a video program or an audio program. It is useful to make a distinction between the original items from what is processed by the Information Retrieval System as the basic indexable item. The original item will always be kept for display purposes, but a lot of preprocessing can occur on it during the process of creating the searchable index. The term "item" will refer to the original object. On occasion the term document will be used when the item being referred to is a textual item.

An Information Retrieval System is the hardware and software that facilitates a user in finding the information the user needs. Hardware is included in the definition because specialized hardware is needed to transform certain modalities into digital processing format (e.g., encoders that translate composite video to digital video). As the detailed processing of items is described it will become clear that an information retrieval system is not a single application but is composed of many different applications that work together to provide the tools and functions needed to assist the users in answering their questions. The overall goal of an Information Retrieval System is to minimize the user overhead in locating the information of value. Overhead from a user's perspective can be defined as the time it takes to locate the needed information. The time starts when a user starts to interact with the system and ends when they have found the items of interest. Human factors play significantly in this process. For example, most users have a short threshold on frustration waiting for a response. That means in a commercial system on the Internet, the user is more satisfied with a response less than 3 s than a longer response that has more accurate information. In internal corporate systems, users are willing to wait a little longer to get results but there is still a tradeoff between accuracy and speed. Most users would rather have the faster results and iterate on their searches than allowing the system to process the queries with more complex techniques providing better results. All of the major processing steps are described for an Information Retrieval System, but in many cases only a subset of them are used on operational systems because users are not willing to accept the increase in response time.

The evolution of Information Retrieval Systems has been closely tied to the evolution of computer processing power. Early information retrieval systems were focused on automating the manual indexing processes in libraries. These systems migrated the structure and organization of card catalogs into structured databases. They maintained the same Boolean search query structure associated with the data base that was used for other database applications. This was feasible because all of the assignment of terms to describe the content of a document was done by professional indexers. In parallel there was also academic research work being done on small data sets that considered how to automate the indexing process making all of the text of a document part of the searchable index. The only place that large systems designed to search on massive amounts of text were available was in Government and Military systems. As commercial processing power and storage significantly increased, it became more feasible to consider applying the algorithms and techniques being developed in the Universities to commercial systems. In addition, the creation of the original documents also was migrating to digital format so that they were in a format that could be processed by the new algorithms. The largest change that drove information technologies to become part of everyone's experience was the introduction and growth of the Internet. The Internet became a massive repository of unstructured information and information retrieval techniques were the only approach to effectively locate information on it. This changed the funding and development of search techniques from a few Government funded efforts to thousands of new ideas being funded by Venture Capitalists moving the more practical implementation of university algorithms into commercial systems.

Information Retrieval System architecture can be segmented into four major processing subsystems. Each processing subsystem presents the opportunity to improve the capability of finding and retrieving the information needed by the user. The subsystems are Ingesting, Indexing, Searching and Displaying. This book uses these subsystems to organize the various technologies that are the building blocks to optimize the retrieval of relevant items for a user. That is to say and end to end discussion of information retrieval system architecture is presented.

### 1.1.1 Primary Information Retrieval Problems

The primary challenge in information retrieval is the difference between how a user expresses what information they are looking for and the way the author of the item expressed the information he is presenting. In other words, the challenge is the mismatch between the language of the user and the language of the author. When an author creates an item they will have information (i.e., semantics) they are trying to communicate to others. They will use the vocabulary they are use to express the information. A user will have an information need and will translate the semantics of their information need into the vocabulary they normally use which they present as a query. It's easy to imagine the mismatch of the vocabulary. There are many different ways of expressing the same concept (e.g. car versus automobile). In many cases both the author and the user will know the same vocabulary, but which terms are most used to represent the same concept will vary between them. In some cases the vocabulary will be different and the user will be attempting to describe a concept without the vocabulary used by authors who write about it (see Fig. 1.1). That is why information retrieval systems that focus on a specific domain (e.g., DNA) will perform better than general purpose systems that contain diverse information. The vocabularies are more focused and shared within the specific domain.

There are obstacles to specification of the information a user needs that come from limits to the user's ability to express what information is needed, ambiguities inherent in languages, and differences between the user's vocabulary and that of the authors of the items in the database. In order for an Information Retrieval System

**Fig. 1.1** Vocabulary domains

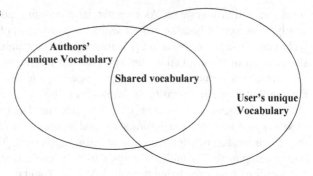

to return good results, it important to start with a good search statement allowing for the correlation of the search statement to the items in the database. The inability to accurately create a good query is a major issue and needs to be compensated for in information retrieval. Natural languages suffer from word ambiguities such as polesemy that allow the same word to have multiple meanings and use of acronyms which are also words (e.g., the word "field" or the acronym "CARE"). Disambiguation techniques exist but introduce system overhead in processing power and extended search times and often require interaction with the user.

Most users have trouble in generating a good search statement. The typical user does not have significant experience with, or the aptitude for, Boolean logic statements. The use of Boolean logic is a legacy from the evolution of database management systems and implementation constraints. Historically, commercial information retrieval systems were based upon databases. It is only with the introduction of Information Retrieval Systems such as FAST, Autonomy, ORACLE TEXT, and GOOGLE Appliances that the idea of accepting natural language queries is becoming a standard system feature. This allows users to state in natural language what they are interested in finding. But the completeness of the user specification is limited by the user's willingness to construct long natural language queries. Most users on the Internet enter one or two search terms or at most a phrase. But quite often the user does not know the words that best describe what information they are looking for. The norm is now an iterative process where the user enters a search and then based upon the first page of hit results revises the query with other terms.

Multimedia items add an additional level of complexity in search specification. Where the source format can be converted to text (e.g., audio transcription, Optical Character Reading) the standard text techniques are still applicable. They just need to be enhanced because of the errors in conversion (e.g. fuzzy searching). But query specification when searching for an image, unique sound, or video segment lacks any proven best interface approaches. Typically they are achieved by grabbing an example from the media being displayed or having prestored examples of known objects in the media and letting the user select them for the search (e.g., images of leaders allowing for searches on "Tony Blair".) In some cases the processing of the multimedia extracts metadata describing the item and the metadata can be searched to locate items of interest (e.g., speaker identification, searching for "notions" in images—these will be discussed in detail later). This type speci-fication becomes more complex when coupled with Boolean or natural language textual specifications.

In addition to the complexities in generating a query, quite often the user is not an expert in the area that is being searched and lacks domain specific vocabulary unique to that particular subject area. The user starts the search process with a gen-eral concept of the information required, but does not have a focused definition of exactly what is needed. A limited knowledge of the vocabulary associated with a particular area along with lack of focus on exactly what information is needed leads to use of inaccurate and in some cases misleading search terms. Even when the user is an expert in the area being searched, the ability to select the proper search terms is constrained by lack of knowledge of the author's vocabulary. The problem comes from synonyms and which particular synonym word is selected by the author and which by the user searching. All writers have a vocabulary limited by their life ex-periences, environment where they were raised and ability to express themselves. Other than in very technical restricted information domains, the user's search vo-cabulary does not match the author's vocabulary. Users usually start with simple queries that suffer from failure rates approaching 50% (Nordlie-99).

Another major problem in information retrieval systems is how to effectively represent the possible items of interest identified by the system so the user can fo-cus in on the ones of most likely value. Historically data has been presented in an order dictated by the order in which items are entered into the search indices (i.e., ordered by date the system ingests the information or the creation date of the item). For those users interested in current events this is useful. But for the majority of searches it does not filter out less useful information. Information Retrieval Systems provide functions that provide the results of a query in order of potential relevance based upon the users query. But the inherent fallacy in the current systems is that they present the information in a linear ordering. As noted before, users have very little patience for browsing long linear lists in a sequential order. That is why they seldom look beyond the first page of the linear ordering. So even if the user's query returned the optimum set of items of interest, if there are too many false hits on the first page of display, the user will revise their search. To optimize the information retrieval process a non-linear way of presenting the search results will optimize the user's ability to find the information they are interested in. The display of the search hits using visualization techniques allows the natural parallel processing capability of the users mind to focus and localize on the items of interest rather than being forced to a sequential processing model.

Once the user has been able to localize on the many potential items of interest other sophisticated processing techniques can aid the users in finding the informa-tion of interest in the hits. Techniques such as summarization across multiple items, link analysis of information and time line correlations of information can reduce the linear process of having to read each item of interest and provide an overall insight into the total information across multiple items. For example if there has been a plane crash, the user working with the system may be able to localize a large number of news reports on the disaster. But it's not unusual to have almost complete redundancy of information in reports from different sources on the same topic. Thus the user will have to read many documents to try and find any new facts. A summarization across the multiple textual items that can eliminate the redundant parts can significantly reduce the user's overhead (time) it takes to find the data the user needs. More importantly it will eliminate the possibility the user gets tired of reading redundant information and misses reading the item that has significant new information in it.

## 1.1.2  Objectives of Information Retrieval System

The general objective of an Information Retrieval System is to minimize the time it takes for a user to locate the information they need. The goal is to provide the information needed to satisfy the user's question. Satisfaction does not necessarily mean finding all information on a particular issue. It means finding sufficient information that the user can proceed with whatever activity initiated the need for information. This is very important because it does explain some of the drivers behind existing search systems and suggests that precision is typically more important than recalling all possible information. For example a user looking for a particular product does not have to find the names of everyone that sells the product or every company that manufactures the product to meet their need of getting that product. Of course if they did have total information then it's possible they could have gotten it cheaper, but in most cases the consumer will never know what they missed. The concept that a user does not know how much information they missed explains why in most cases the precision of a search is more important than the ability to recall all possible items of interest—the user never knows what they missed but they can tell if they are seeing a lot of useless information in the first few pages of search results. That does not mean finding everything on a topic is not important to some users. If you are trying to make decisions on purchasing a stock or a company, then finding all the facts about that stock or company may be critical to prevent a bad investment. Missing the one article talking about the company being sued and possibly going bankrupt could lead to a very painful investment. But providing comprehensive retrieval of all items that are relevant to a users search can have the negative effect of information overload on the user. In particular there is a tendency for important information to be repeated in many items on the same topic. Thus trying to get all information makes the process of reviewing and filtering out redundant information very tedious. The better a system is in finding all items on a question (recall) the more important techniques to present aggregates of that information become.

From the users perspective time is the important factor that they use to gage the effectiveness of information retrieval. Except for users that do information retrieval as a primary aspect of their job (e.g., librarians, research assistants), most users have very little patience for investing extensive time in finding information they need. They expect interactive response from their searches with replies within 3–4 s at the most. Instead of looking through all the hits to see what might be of value they will only review the first one and at most second pages before deciding they need to change their search strategy. These aspects of the human nature of searchers have had a direct effect on the commercial web sites and the development of commercial information retrieval. The times that are candidates to be minimized in an Information Retrieval System are the time to create the query, the time to execute the query, the time to select what items returned from the query the user wants to review in detail and the time to determine if the returned item is of value. The initial research in information retrieval focused on the search as the primary area of interest. But to meet the users expectation of fast response and to maximize the relevant information returned requires optimization in all of these areas. The time to create a query used to be considered outside the scope of technical system support. But systems such as Google know what is in their database and what other users have searched on so as you type a query they provide hints on what to search on. This "vocabulary browse" capability helps the user in expanding the search string and helps in getting better precision.

In information retrieval the term "relevant" is used to represent an item containing the needed information. In reality the definition of relevance is not a binary classification but a continuous function. Items can exactly match the information need or partially match the information need. From a user's perspective "relevant" and "needed" are synonymous. From a system perspective, information could be relevant to a search statement (i.e., matching the criteria of the search statement) even though it is not needed/relevant to user (e.g., the user already knew the information or just read it in the previous item reviewed).

When considering the document space (all items in the information retrieval system), for any specific information request and the documents returned from it based upon a query, the document space can be divided into four quadrants. Documents returned can be relevant to the information request or not relevant. Documents not returned also falls into those two categories; relevant and not relevant (see Fig. 1.2).

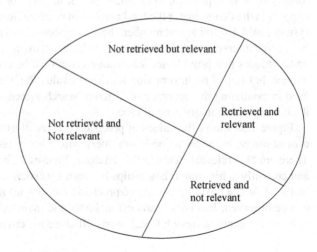

**Fig. 1.2** Relevant retrieval document space

Relevant documents are those that contain some information that helps answer the user's information need. Non-relevant documents do not contain any useful information. Using these definitions the two primary metrics used in evaluating information retrieval systems can be defined. They are Precision and Recall:

$$\text{Precision} = \frac{Number\_Retrieved\_Relevant}{Number\_Total\_Retrieved}$$

$$\text{Recall} = \frac{Number\_Retrieved\_Relevant}{Number\_Possible\_Relevant}$$

The *Number_Possible_Relevant* are the number of relevant items in the database, *Number_Total_Retrieved* is the total number of items retrieved from the query, and *Number_Retrieved_Relevant* is the number of items retrieved that are relevant to the user's search need.

Precision is the factor that most users understand. When a user executes a search and has 80% precision it means that 4 out of 5 items that are retrieved are of interest to the user. From a user perspective the lower the precision the more likely the user is wasting his resource (time) looking at non-relevant items. From a metric perspective the precision figure is across all of the "hits" returned from the query. But in reality most users will only look at the first few pages of hit results before deciding to change their query strategy. Thus what is of more value in commercial systems is not the total precision but the precision across the first 20–50 hits. Typically, in a weighted system where the words within a document are assigned weights based upon how well they describe the semantics of the document, precision in the first 20–50 items is higher than the precision across all the possible hits returned (i.e., further down the hit list the more likely items are not of interest). But when comparing search systems the total precision is used.

Recall is a very useful concept in comparing systems. It measures how well a search system is capable of retrieving all possible hits that exist in the database. Unfortunately it is impossible to calculate except in very controlled environments. It requires in the denominator the total number of relevant items in the database. If the system could determine that number, then the system could return them. There have been some attempts to estimate the total relevant items in a database, but there are no techniques that provide accurate enough results to be used for a specific search request. In Chap. 9 on Information Retrieval Evaluation, techniques that have been used in evaluating the accuracy of different search systems will be described. But it's not applicable in the general case.

Figure 1.3a shows the values of precision and recall as the number of items retrieved increases, under an optimum query where every returned item is relevant. There are "N" relevant items in the database. Figures 1.3b, 1.3c show the optimal and currently achievable relationships between Precision and Recall (Harman-95). In Fig. 1.3a the basic properties of precision (solid line) and recall (dashed line) can be observed. Precision starts off at 100% and maintains that value as long as relevant items are retrieved. Recall starts off close to zero and increases as long as

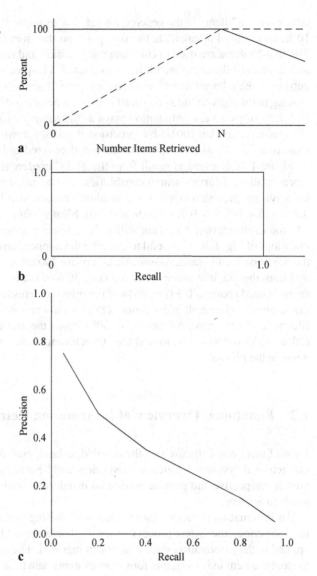

**Fig. 1.3 a** Ideal precision and recall. **b** Ideal precision/recall graph. **c** Achievable precision/recall graph

relevant items are retrieved until all possible relevant items have been retrieved. Once all "N" relevant items have been retrieved, the only items being retrieved are non-relevant. Precision is directly affected by retrieval of non-relevant items and drops to a number close to zero. Recall is not affected by retrieval of non-relevant items and thus remains at 100%.

Precision/Recall graphs show how values for precision and recall change within a search results file (Hit file) assuming the hit file is ordered ranking from the most relevant to least relevant item. As with Fig. 1.3a, 1.3b shows the perfect case where every item retrieved is relevant. The values of precision and recall are recalculated after every "n" items in the ordered hit list. For example if "n" is 10 then the first 10 items are used to calculate the first point on the chart for precision and recall. The first 20 items are used to calculate the precision and recall for the second point and so on until the complete hit list is evaluated. The precision stays at 100% (1.0) until all of the relevant items have been retrieved. Recall continues to increase while moving to the right on the x-axis until it also reaches the 100% (1.0) point. Although Fig. 1.3b stops here. Continuation stays at the same y-axis location (recall never changes and remains 100%) but precision decreases down the y-axis until it gets close to the x-axis as more non-relevant are discovered and precision decreases.

Figure 1.3c is a typical result from the TREC conferences (see Chap. 9) and is representative of current search capabilities. This is called the eleven point interpolated average precision graph. The precision is measured at 11 recall levels (0.0, 0.1, 0.2, 0.3, 0.4, 0.5, 0.6, 0.7, 0.8, 0.9, and 1.0). Most systems do not reach recall level 1.0 (found all relevant items) but will end at a lower number. To understand the implications of Fig. 1.3c, it's useful to describe the implications of a particular point on the precision/recall graph. Assume that there are 200 relevant items in the data base and from the graph at precision of 0.3 (i.e., 30% of the items are relevant) there is an associated recall of 0.5 (i.e., 50% of the relevant items have been retrieved from the database). The recall of 50% means there would be 100 relevant items in the Hit file (50% of 200 items). A precision of 30% means the user would review 333 items (30% of 333 is 100 items) to find the 100 relevant items—thus approximately 333 items in the hit file.

## 1.2   Functional Overview of Information Retrieval Systems

Most of this book is focused on the detailed technologies associated with information retrieval systems. A functional overview will help to better place the technologies in perspective and provide additional insight into what an information system needs to achieve.

An information retrieval system starts with the ingestion of information. Chapter 3 describes the ingest process in detail. There are multiple functions that are applied to the information once it has been ingested. The most obvious function is to store the item in it's original format in an items data base and create a searchable index to allow for later ad hoc searching and retrieval of an item. Another operation that can occur on the item as it's being received is "Selective Dissemination of Information" (SDI). This function allows users to specify search statements of interest (called "Profiles") and whenever an incoming item satisfies the search specification the item is stored in a user's "mail" box for later review. This is a dynamic filtering of the input stream for each user for the subset they want to look at on a daily basis. Since it's a dynamic process the mail box is constantly getting new items of possible interest. Associated with the Selective Dissemination of Information process is the "Alert" process. The alert process will attempt to notify the user whenever any new item meets the user's criteria for immediate action on an item. This helps the user

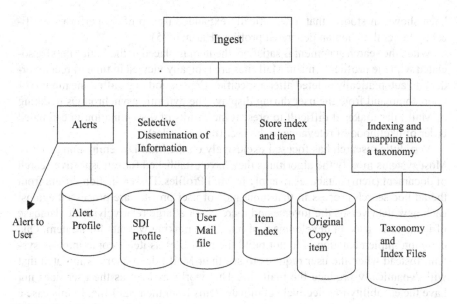

**Fig. 1.4** Functional overview

in multitasking—doing their normal daily tasks but be made aware when there is something that requires immediate attention.

Finally there is automatically adding metadata and creating a logical view of the items into a structured taxonomy. The user can then navigate the taxonomy to find items of interest versus having to search for them. The indexing assigns additional descriptive citational and semantic metadata to an item. Figure 1.4 shows these processes.

## 1.2.1    Selective Dissemination of Information

The Selective Dissemination of Information (Mail) Process (see Fig. 1.4) provides the capability to dynamically compare newly received items to the information system against stored statements of interest of users and deliver the item to those users whose statement of interest matches the contents of the item. The Mail process is composed of the search process, user statements of interest (Profiles) and user mail files. As each item is received, it is processed against every user's profile. A profile typically contains a broad search statement along with a list of user mail files that will receive the document if the search statement in the profile is satisfied. User mail profiles are different than interactive user queries in that they contain significantly more search terms (10–100 times more terms) and cover a wider range of interests. These profiles define all the areas in which a user is interested versus an interactive query which is frequently focused to answer a specific question. It has been shown in studies that automatically expanded user profiles perform significantly better than human generated profiles (Harman-95).

When the search statement is satisfied, the item is placed in the Mail File(s) associated with the profile. Items in Mail files are typically viewed in time of receipt order and automatically deleted after a specified time period (e.g., after one month) or upon command from the user during display. The dynamic asynchronous updating of Mail Files makes it difficult to present the results of dissemination in estimated order of likelihood of relevance to the user (ranked order).

Very little research has focused exclusively on the Mail Dissemination process. Most systems modify the algorithms they have established for retrospective search of document (item) databases to apply to Mail Profiles. Dissemination differs from the ad hoc search process in that thousands of user profiles are processed against each new item versus the inverse and there is not a large relatively static database of items to be used in development of relevance ranking weights for an item. One common implementation is to not build the mail files as items come into the system. Instead when the user requests to see their Mail File, a query is initiated that will dynamically produce the mail file. This works as long as the user does not have the capability to selectively eliminate items from their mail file. In this case a permanent file structure is needed. When a permanent file structure is implemented typically the mail profiles become a searchable structure and the words in each new item become the queries against it. Chapter 2 will describe n-grams which are one method to help in creating a mail search system.

## 1.2.2  Alerts

Alerts are very similar to the processing for mail items. The user defines a set of "alert profiles" that are search statements that define what information a user wants to be alerted on. The profile has additional metadata that may contain a list of e-mail addresses that an alert notice should be mailed. If the user is currently logged onto the alert system a dynamic message could also be presented to the user. Alerts on textual items are simple in that the complete textual item can be processed for the alerts and then the alert notifications with links to the alert item can be sent out. Typically a user will have a number of focused alert profiles rather than the more general Mail profiles because the user wants to know more precisely the cause of the alert versus Mail profiles that are for collecting the general areas of interest to a user. When processing textual items it's possible to process the complete item before the alert profiles are validated against the item because the processing is so fast.

For multimedia (e.g., alerts on television news programs), the processing of the multimedia item happens in real time. But waiting until the end of the complete program to send out the alert could introduce significant delays to allowing the user to react to the item. In this case, periodically (e.g., every few minutes or after "n" alerts have been identified) alert notifications are sent out. This makes it necessary to define other rules to ensure the user is not flooded with alerts. The basic concept that needs to be implemented is that a user should receive only one alert notification for a specific item for each alert profile the user has that the item satisfies. This is enough to get the user to decide if they want to look at the item. When the user looks at the item all instances within the item that has to that point meet the alert criteria should be displayed. For example, assume a user has alert profiles on Natural Disaster, Economic Turmoil and Military Action. When the hurricane hit the US Gulf of Mexico oil platforms, a news video could hit on both Natural Disaster and Economic Turmoil. Within minutes into the broadcast the first hits to those profiles would be identified and the alert sent to the user. The user only needs to know the hits occurred. When the user displays the video, maybe 10 min into the news broadcast, all of the parts of the news program to the current time that satisfied the profiles should be indicated.

### 1.2.3 Items and Item Index

The retrospective item Search Process (see Fig. 1.4) provides the capability for a query to search against all items received by the system. The Item index is the searchable data structure that is derived from the contents of each item. In addition the original item is saved to display as the results of a search. The search is against the Item index by the user entered queries (typically ad hoc queries). It is sometimes called the retrospective search of the system. If the user is on-line, the Selective Dissemination of Information system delivers to the user items of interest as soon as they are processed into the system. Any search for information that has already been processed into the system can be considered a "retrospective" search for information. This does not preclude the search to have search statements constraining it to items received in the last few hours. But typically the searches span far greater time periods. Each query is processed against the total item index. Queries differ from alert and mail profiles in that queries are typically short and focused on a specific area of interest. The Item Database can be very large, hundreds of millions or billions of items. Typically items in the Item Database do not change (i.e., are not edited) once received. The value of information quickly decreases over time. Historically these facts were used to partition the database by time and allow for archiving by the time partitions. Advances in storage and processors now allow all the indices to remain on-line. But for multimedia item databases, the original items are often moved to slower but cheaper tape storage (i.e., using Hierarchical Storage Management systems).

### 1.2.4 Indexing and Mapping to a Taxonomy

In addition to the item there is additional citational metadata that can be determined for the item. Citational metadata typically describes aspects of the item other than the semantics of the item. For example, typical citational metadata that can go into an index of the items received is the date it is received, it's source (e.g. CNN news), the author, etc. All of that information may be useful in locating information but does not describe the information in the item. This metadata can subset the total set of items to be searched reducing the chances for false hits. Automatic indexing can extract the citational information and can also extract additional data from the item that can be used to index the item, but usually the semantic metadata assigned to describe an item is human generated (see Chap. 4). The index of metadata against the entire database of items (called public index) expands the information searchable beyond the index of each item's content to satisfy a users search. In addition to a public index of the items coming in, users can also generate their private index to the items. This can be used to logically define subsets of the received items that are focused on a particular user's interest along with keywords to describe the items. This subsetting can be used to constrain a user's search, thereby significantly increasing the precision of a users search at the expense of recall.

In addition to the indexing, some systems attempt to organize the items by mapping items received to locations within a predefined or dynamically defined taxonomy (e.g., Autonomy system). A Taxonomy (sometimes referred to as Ontology) refers to a hierarchical ordering of a set of controlled vocabulary terms that describe concepts. They provide an alternative mechanism for users to navigate to information of interest. The user will expand the taxonomy tree until they get to the area of interest and then review the items at that location in the taxonomy. This has the advantage that users without an in depth knowledge of an area can let the structured taxonomy help navigate them to the area of interest. A typical use of taxonomy is a wine site that let you navigate through the different wines that are available. It lets you select the general class of wines, then the grapes and then specific brands. In this case there is a very focused taxonomy. But in general information retrieval case there can be a large number of taxonomies on the most important conceptual areas that the information retrieval system users care about. Taxonomies help those users that do not have an in depth knowledge of a particular area select the subset of that area they are interested in.

The data for the taxonomy is often discovered as part of the ingest process and then is applied as an alternative index that users can search and navigate. Some systems as part of their display will take a hit list of documents and create taxonomy of the information content for that set of items. This is an example of the visualization process except the assignment of objects to locations in a static taxonomy (this is discussed in Chap. 7).

## 1.3   Understanding Search Functions

The objective of the search capability is to allow for a mapping between a user's information need and the items in the information database that will answer that need. The search query statement is the means that the user employs to communicate a description of the needed information to the system. It can consist of natural language text in composition style and/or query terms with Boolean logic indicators between them. Understanding the functions associated with search helps in understanding what architectures best allow for those functions to be provided.

The search statement may apply to the complete item or contain additional parameters limiting it to a logical zone within the item (e.g., Title, abstract, references). This restriction is useful in reducing retrieval of non-relevant items by limiting the search to those subsets of the item whose use of a particular word is consistent with the user's search objective. Finding a name in a Bibliography does not necessarily mean the item is about that person. Research has shown that for longer items, restricting a query statement to be satisfied within a contiguous subset of the document (passage searching) provides improved precision (Buckley-95, Wilkinson-95). Rather than allowing the search statement to be satisfied anywhere within a document it may be required to be satisfied within a 100 word contiguous subset of the item (Callan-94). The zoning process is discussed in Chap. 3 Ingest.

Based upon the algorithms used in a system many different functions are associated with the system's understanding the search statement. The functions define the relationships between the terms in the search statement (e.g., Boolean, Natural Language, Proximity, Contiguous Word Phrases, and Fuzzy Searches) and the interpretation of a particular word (e.g., Term Masking, Numeric and Date Range, Contiguous Word Phrases, and Concept/Thesaurus expansion).

One concept for assisting in the location and ordering relevant items, is the "weighting" of search terms. This would allow a user to indicate the importance of search terms in either a Boolean or natural language interface. Given the following natural language query statement where the importance of a particular search term is indicated by a value in parenthesis between 0.0 and 1.0 with 1.0 being the most important:

- Find articles that discuss automobile emissions (0.9) or sulfur dioxide (0.3) on the farming industry.

The system would recognize in it's importance ranking that items about automobile emissions are far more important than items discussing sulfur dioxide problems when in the context of farming (which has an implied weight of 1).

## 1.3.1 Boolean Logic

Boolean logic allows a user to logically relate multiple concepts together to define what information is needed. Typically the Boolean functions apply to processing tokens identified anywhere within an item. The typical Boolean operators are **AND, OR,** and **NOT.** These operations are implemented using set intersection, set union and set difference procedures. A few systems introduced the concept of "exclusive or" but it is equivalent to a slightly more complex query using the other operators and is not generally useful to users since most users do not understand it. Placing portions of the search statement in parentheses are used to overtly specify the order of Boolean operations (i.e., nesting function). If parentheses are not used, the system

**Fig. 1.5** Use of Boolean operators

| SEARCH STATEMENT | SYSTEM OPERATION |
|---|---|
| COMPUTER OR PROCESSOR NOT MAINFRAME | Select all items discussing Computers and/or Processors that do not discuss Mainframes |
| COMPUTER OR (PROCESSOR NOT MAINFRAME) | Select all items discussing Computers and/or items that discuss Processors and do not discuss Mainframes |
| COMPUTER AND NOT PROCESSOR OR MAINFRAME | Select all items that discuss computers and not processors or mainframes in the item |

follows a default precedence ordering of operations (e.g., typically NOT then AND then OR). In the examples of effects of Boolean operators given in Fig. 1.5, no precedence order is given to the operators and queries are processed Left to Right unless parentheses are included. Most commercial systems do not allow weighting of Boolean queries. A technique to allow weighting Boolean queries is described in Chap. 5. Some of the deficiencies of use of Boolean operators in information systems are summarized by Belkin and Croft (Belkin-89). Some search examples and their meanings are given in Fig. 1.5.

A special type of Boolean search is called "M of N" logic. The user lists a set of possible search terms and identifies, as acceptable, any item that contains a subset of the terms. For example, Find any item containing any two of the following terms: "AA," "BB," "CC." This can be expanded into a Boolean search that performs an AND between all combinations of two terms and "OR"s the results together ((AA AND BB) or (AA AND CC) or (BB AND CC)). Most Information Retrieval Systems allow Boolean operations as well as allowing for the natural language interfaces. Very little attention has been focused on integrating the Boolean search functions and weighted information retrieval techniques into a single search result.

## 1.3.2 Proximity

Proximity is used to restrict the distance allowed within an item between two search terms. The semantic concept is that the closer two terms are found in a text the more likely they are related in the description of a particular concept. Proximity is used to increase the precision of a search. If the terms COMPUTER and DESIGN are found within a few words of each other then the item is more likely to be discussing the design of computers than if the words are paragraphs apart. The typical format for proximity is:

TERM1 within "m" "units" of TERM2

The distance operator "m" is an integer number and units are in Characters, Words, Sentences, or Paragraphs. Certain items may have other semantic units that would

**Fig. 1.6** Use of proximity

| SEARCH STATEMENT | SYSTEM OPERATION |
|---|---|
| "Venetian" ADJ "Blind" | would find items that mention a Venetian Blind on a window but not items discussing a Blind Venetian |
| "United" within five words of "American" | would hit on "United States and American interests," "United Airlines and American Airlines" not on "United States of America and the American dream" |
| "Nuclear" within zero paragraphs of "clean-up" | would find items that have "nuclear" and "clean-up" in the same paragraph. |

prove useful in specifying the proximity operation. For very structured items, distances in characters prove useful. Sometimes the proximity relationship contains a direction operator indicating the direction (before or after) that the second term must be found within the number of units specified. The default is either direction. A special case of the Proximity operator is the Adjacent (ADJ) operator that normally has a distance operator of one and a forward only direction. Another special case is where the distance is set to zero meaning within the same semantic unit. Some proximity search statement examples and their meanings are given in Fig. 1.6.

## 1.3.3 Contiguous Word Phrases

A Contiguous Word Phrase (CWP) is both a way of specifying a query term and a special search operator. A Contiguous Word Phrase is two or more words that are treated as a single semantic unit. An example of a CWP is "United States of America." It is four words that specify a search term representing a single specific semantic concept (a country) that can be used with other operators. Thus a query could specify "manufacturing" AND "United States of America" which returns any item that contains the word "manufacturing" and the contiguous words "United States of America."

A contiguous word phrase also acts like a special search operator that is similar to the proximity (Adjacency) operator but allows for additional specificity. If two terms are specified, the contiguous word phrase and the proximity operator using directional one word parameters or the adjacent operator are identical. For contiguous word phrases of more than two terms the only way of creating an equivalent search statement using proximity and Boolean operators is via nested adjacencies which are not found in most commercial systems. This is because Proximity and Boolean operators are binary operators but contiguous word phrases are an "N"ary operator where "N" is the number of words in the CWP.

### 1.3.4   Fuzzy Searches

Fuzzy Searches provide the capability to locate spellings of words that are similar to the entered search term. This function is primarily used to compensate for errors in spelling of words. Fuzzy searching increases recall at the expense of decreasing precision (i.e., it can erroneously identify terms as the search term). In the process of expanding a query term fuzzy searching includes other terms that have similar spellings, giving more weight (in systems that rank output) to words in the database that have similar word lengths and position of the characters as the entered term. A Fuzzy Search on the term "computer" would automatically include the following words from the information database: "computer," "compiter," "conputer," "computter," "compute." An additional enhancement may lookup the proposed alternative spelling and if it is a valid word with a different meaning, include it in the search with a low ranking or not include it at all (e.g., "commuter"). Systems allow the specification of the maximum number of new terms that the expansion includes in the query. In this case the alternate spellings that are "closest" to the query term are included. "Closest" is a heuristic function that is system specific.

Fuzzy searching has it's maximum utilization in systems that accept items that have been Optical Character Read (OCRed). In the OCR process a hardcopy item is scanned into a binary image (usually at a resolution of 300 dots per inch or more). The OCR process also applies to items that are already binary such as JPEG files or video from television. The OCR process is a pattern recognition process that segments the scanned in image into meaningful subregions, often considering a segment the area defining a single character. The OCR process will then determine the character and translate it to an internal computer encoding (e.g., ASCII or some other standard for other than Latin based languages). Based upon the original quality of the hardcopy this process introduces errors in recognizing characters. With decent quality input, systems achieves in the 90–99% range of accuracy. Since these are character errors throughout the text, fuzzy searching allows location of items of interest compensating for the erroneous characters.

### 1.3.5   Term Masking

Term masking is the ability to expand a query term by masking a portion of the term and accepting as valid any processing token that maps to the unmasked portion of the term. The value of term masking is much higher in systems that do not perform stemming or only provide a very simple stemming algorithm. There are two types of search term masking: fixed length and variable length. Sometimes they are called fixed and variable length "don't care" functions.

Variable length "don't cares" allows masking of any number of characters within a processing token. The masking may be in the front, at the end, at both front and

**Fig. 1.7** Term masking

| SEARCH STATEMENT | SYSTEM OPERATION |
|---|---|
| multi-national | Matches"multi-national," multiyna-tional," "multinational" but does not match "multi national" since it is two processing tokens. |
| *computer* | Matches,"minicomputer" "microcompu-ter" or "computer" |
| comput* | Matches "computers," "computing," "computes" |
| *comput* | Matches "microcomputers," "minicom-puting," "compute" |

end, or imbedded. The first three of these cases are called suffix search, prefix search and imbedded character string search, respectively. The use of an imbedded variable length don't care is seldom used. Figure 1.7 provides examples of the use of variable length term masking. If "*" represents a variable length don't care then the following are examples of it's use:

"*COMPUTER"     Suffix Search
"COMPUTER*"     Prefix Search
"*COMPUTER*"    Imbedded String Search

Of the options discussed, trailing "don't cares" (prefix searches) are by far the most common. In operational systems they are used in 80–90% of the search terms (Kracsony-81) and in many cases is a default without the user having to specify it.

Fixed length masking is a single position mask. It masks out any symbol in a particular position or the lack of that position in a word. It not only allows any character in the masked position, but also accepts words where the position does not exist. Fixed length term masking is not frequently used and typically not critical to a system.

## 1.3.6 Numeric and Date Ranges

Term masking is useful when applied to words, but does not work for finding rang-es of numbers or numeric dates. To find numbers larger than "125," using a term "125*" will not find any number except those that begin with the digits "125." Sys-tems, as part of their normalization process, characterize words as numbers or dates. This allows for specialized numeric or date range processing against those words. A user could enter inclusive (e.g., "125–425" or "4/2/93–5/2/95" for numbers and dates) to infinite ranges (">125," "<=233," representing "Greater Than" or "Less Than or Equal") as part of a query.

### 1.3.7    Vocabulary Browse

Vocabulary Browse was a capability used first in databases in the 1980s. The concept was to assist the user in creating a query by providing the user with an alphabetical sorted list of terms in a field along with the number of database records the term was found in. This helped the user in two different ways. The first was by looking at the list surrounding the word the user was interested in, they could discover misspellings they wanted to include in their query. It also would show them the number of records the term was found in allowing them to add additional search terms if there were going to be too many hits.

This concept has been carried over to Information retrieval Systems recently with the expansion capabilities provided by GOOGLE. In this case the system is not trying to show misspellings or the number of items a search term is found in. Instead the system is trying to help the user determine additional modifiers (additional terms) they can add to their query to make it more precise based upon data in the database and what other users search on. It has the effect of dynamically showing the user possible expansions of their search.

### 1.3.8    Multimedia Search

New challenges arise when you are creating queries against multimedia items. There are also challenges associated with the display of the hit list which will be addressed in Chap. 7. The ideal case for users is to enter searches in text form against multimedia items. Historically that has been the primary interface used for searching the Internet. What was being searched is not the actual multimedia item but the text such as file name and hyperlink text that links to the multimedia item. There have been attempts to index the multimedia, primarily images, on the internet. In the few cases where video (television news) has been indexed the closed captioning was used as the index. In the case of image indexing, the user can propose an image and search for others like it. The extra user function associated with searching using an image is the capability to specify a portion of the image and use it for the query versus the complete image.

## 1.4    Relationship to Database Management Systems

There are two major categories of systems available to process items: Information Retrieval Systems and Data Base Management Systems (DBMS). Confusion can arise when the software systems supporting each of these applications get confused with the data they are manipulating. An Information Retrieval System is software that has the features and functions required to manipulate "information" items versus a DBMS that is optimized to handle "structured" data. Information is fuzzy text. The term "fuzzy" is used to imply the results from the minimal standards or controls on the creators of the text items. The author is trying to present concepts, ideas and abstractions along with supporting facts. As such, there is minimal consistency in the vocabulary and styles of items discussing the exact same issue. The searcher has to be omniscient to specify all search term possibilities in the query.

Structured data is well defined data (facts) typically represented by tables. There is a semantic description associated with each attribute within a table that well defines that attribute. For example, there is no confusion between the meaning of "employee name" or "employee salary" and what values to enter in a specific database record. On the other hand, if two different people generate an abstract for the same item, they can be different. One abstract may generally discuss the most important topic in an item. Another abstract, using a different vocabulary, may specify the details of many topics. It is this diversity and ambiguity of language that causes the fuzzy nature to be associated with information items. The differences in the characteristics of the data is one reason for the major differences in functions required for the two classes of systems.

With structured data a user enters a specific request and the results returned provide the user with the desired information. The results are frequently tabulated and presented in a report format for ease of use. In contrast, a search of "information" items has a high probability of not finding all the items a user is looking for. The user has to refine his search to locate additional items of interest. This process is called "iterative search." An Information Retrieval System gives the user capabilities to assist the user in finding the relevant items, such as relevance feedback (Chap. 5). The results from an information system search are presented in relevance ranked order. The confusion comes when DBMS software is used to store "information." This is easy to implement, but the system lacks the ranking and relevance feedback features that are critical to an information system. It is also possible to have structured data used in an information system. When this happens the user has to be very creative to get the system to provide the reports and management information that are trivially available in a DBMS.

From a practical standpoint, the integration of DBMS's and Information Retrieval Systems is very important. Commercial database companies have already integrated the two types of systems. One of the first commercial databases to integrate the two systems into a single view is the INQUIRE DBMS. The most common example is the ORACLE DBMS that now offers an imbedded capability called ORACLE TEXT, which is an informational retrieval system that uses a comprehensive thesaurus which provides the basis to generate "themes" for a particular item. ORACLE TEXT also provides standard statistical techniques that are described in Chap. 4. The SQL query language for structured databases has been expanded to accommodate the functions needed in information retrieval.

## 1.5    Digital Libraries and Data Warehouses

Two other systems frequently described in the context of information retrieval are Digital Libraries and Data Warehouses (or DataMarts). There is significant overlap between these two systems and an Information Storage and Retrieval System. All three systems are repositories of information and their primary goal is to satisfy user information needs. Information retrieval easily dates back to Vannevar Bush's 1945 article on thinking (Bush-45) that set the stage for many concepts in this area. Libraries have been in existence since the beginning of writing and have served as a repository of the intellectual wealth of society. As such, libraries have always been concerned with storing and retrieving information in the media it is created on. As the quantities of information grew exponentially, libraries were forced to make maximum use of electronic tools to facilitate the storage and retrieval process. With the worldwide interneting of libraries and information sources (e.g., publishers, news agencies, wire services, radio broadcasts) via the Internet, more focus has been on the concept of an electronic library. Between 1991 and 1993 significant interest was placed on this area because of the interest in U.S. Government and private funding for making more information available in digital form (Fox-93). During this time the terminology evolved from electronic libraries to digital librar-ies. As the Internet continued it's exponential growth and project funding became available, the topic of Digital Libraries has grown. By 1995 enough research and pilot efforts had started to support the 1st ACM International Conference on Digi-tal Libraries (Fox-96). The effort on digitizing all library assets has continued in both the United States and Europe. The European Digital Libraries Project (i2010 Digital Libraries plans to make all Europe's cultural resources and scientific re-cords—books, journals, films, maps, photographs, music, etc.—accessible to all, and preserve it for future generations. (http://ec.europa.eu/information_society/ activities/digital_libraries/index_en.htm) The effort in the is US managed by the National Science Foundation (NSF) with partnership with many other US Govern-ment entities called the DIGITAL LIBRARIES INITIATIVE—PHASE 2 is not only focusing on significantly increasing the migration of library content into ac-cessible digital form, but also the usability of the distributed information looking at the other functions a library should provide. (http://www.nsf.gov/pubs/1998/ nsf9863/nsf9863.htm)

There remain significant discussions on what is a digital library. Everyone starts with the metaphor of the traditional library. The question is how does the traditional library functions change as they migrate into supporting a digital collection. Since the collection is digital and there is a worldwide communications infrastructure available, the library no longer must own a copy of information as long as it can pro-vide access. The existing quantity of hardcopy material guarantees that we will not have all digital libraries for at least another generation of technology improvements. But there is no question that libraries have started and will continue to expand their focus to digital formats. With direct electronic access available to users the social aspects of congregating in a library and learning from librarians, friends and colleagues will be lost and new electronic collaboration equivalencies will come into existence (Wiederhold-95).

Indexing is one of the critical disciplines in library science and significant effort has gone into the establishment of indexing and cataloging standards. Migration of many of the library products to a digital format introduces both opportunities and challenges. The full text of items available for search makes the index process a value added effort as described in Chap. 4. Another important library service is a source of search intermediaries to assist users in finding information. With the proliferation of information available in electronic form, the role of search intermediary will shift from an expert in search to being an expert in source analysis. Searching will identify so much information in the global Internet information space that identification of the "pedigree" of information is required to understand it's value. This will become the new refereeing role of a library.

Information Storage and Retrieval technology has addressed a small subset of the issues associated with Digital Libraries. The focus has been on the search and retrieval of textual data with no concern for establishing standards on the contents of the system. It has also ignored the issues of unique identification and tracking of information required by the legal aspects of copyright that restrict functions within a library environment. Intellectual property rights in an environment that is not controlled by any country and their set of laws has become a major problem associated with the Internet. The conversion of existing hardcopy text, images (e.g., pictures, maps) and analog (e.g., audio, video) data and the storage and retrieval of the digital version is a major concern to Digital Libraries. Information Retrieval Systems are starting to evolve and incorporate digitized versions of these sources as part of the overall system. But there is also a lot of value placed on the original source (especially printed material) that is an issue to Digital Libraries and to a lesser concern to Information Retrieval systems. Other issues such as how to continue to provide access to digital information over many years as digital formats change have to be answered for the long term viability of digital libraries.

The term Data Warehouse comes more from the commercial sector than academic sources. It comes from the need for organizations to control the proliferation of digital information ensuring that it is known and recoverable. It's goal is to provide to the decision makers the critical information to answer future direction questions. Frequently a data warehouse is focused solely on structured databases. A data warehouse consists of the data, an information directory that describes the contents and meaning of the data being stored, an input function that captures data and moves it to the data warehouse, data search and manipulation tools that allow users the means to access and analyze the warehouse data and a delivery mechanism to export data to other warehouses, data marts (small warehouses or subsets of a larger warehouse), and external systems.

Data warehouses are similar to information storage and retrieval systems in that they both have a need for search and retrieval of information. But a data warehouse is more focused on structured data and decision support technologies. In addition to the normal search process, a complete system provides a flexible set of analytical tools to "mine" the data. Data mining (originally called Knowledge Discovery in

Databases—KDD) is a search process that automatically analyzes data and extract relationships and dependencies that were not part of the database design. Most of the research focus is on the statistics, pattern recognition and artificial intelligence algorithms to detect the hidden relationships of data. In reality the most difficult task is in preprocessing the data from the database for processing by the algorithms. This differs from clustering in information retrieval in that clustering is based upon known characteristics of items, whereas data mining does not depend upon known relationships.

## 1.6 Processing Subsystem Overview

An Information Retrieval System is composed of four major processing subsystems. Each processing subsystem presents the capability to improve the processing of the information to improve the capability of finding and retrieving the information needed by the user. Each of the processing phases will be addressed as a separate chapter to discuss in detail the associated technologies and challenges. The four subsystems are:

- Ingest (Chap. 3): this subsystem is concerned with the ingestion of the information and the initial normalization and processing of the source items. This phase begins with processes to get information into the information retrieval system. It could be via crawling networks (or the Internet) as well as receiving items that are "pushed" to the system. The items undergo normalization which can include format standardization (e.g., Unicode for text, phonemes for audio), defining processing tokens, stemming, and other such processes to get to a canonical format. Once in a standard format many additional pre-indexing analysis techniques can be used to start defining the data that will facilitate the mapping of the user's search vocabulary with the item's author's vocabulary. This includes entity extraction and normalization, categorization and other techniques.
- Index (Chap. 4): this subsystem is concerned with taking the normalized item's processing tokens and other normalized metadata and creating the searchable index from it. There are many different approaches to creating the index from Boolean to weighted and within weighted, Statistical, Concept and Natural Language indexing.
- Search (Chap. 5): This subsystem is concerned with mapping the user search information need to a processable form defined by the searchable index and determining which items are to be returned to the user. Within this process is the identification of the relevancy weights that are used in ordering the display.
- Display (Chap. 7): this subsystem is concerned with how the user can locate the items of interest in the all of the possible results returned. It discusses the options for presenting the "hit lists" of items that are identified by the search process to the user. It will address linear review of hits versus use of visualization techniques. Clustering technologies are core to many of the techniques in visu-

alization and are presented in Chap. 6 to lay a better understanding of displaying items. In addition to the presentation of the hits for users to select which item to review in detail, it discusses optimization techniques associated with individual item review and ways of summarizing information across multiple items. It also will discuss Collaborative Filtering as an augmentation to the review process (i.e., using knowledge of other users reviewing items to optimize the review of the current hit items.

## 1.7 Summary

Chapter 1 places into perspective the functions associated with an information retrieval system. Ten years ago commercial implementation of the algorithms being developed were not realistic, forcing theoreticians to limit their focus to very specific areas. Bounding a problem is still essential in deriving theoretical results. Recent advances in hardware and more importantly software architecture has provided a technical basis for providing information retrieval algorithms against massively large datasets. Advances now allow for all of the functions discussed in this chapter to be provided and have developed heuristics to optimize the search process discussed in Chap. 8. The commercialization of information retrieval functions being driven by the growth of the Internet has changed the basis of development time from "academic years" (i.e., one academic year equals 18 months—the time to define the research, perform it and publish the results) to "Web years" (i.e., one Web year equals three months—demand to get new products up very quickly to be first). The test environment and test databases are changing from small scale academic environments to millions of records with millions of potential users testing new ideas.

The best way for the theoretician or the commercial developer to understand the importance of problems to be solved is to place them in the context of a total vision of a complete system. For example, understanding the differences between Digital Libraries and Information Retrieval Systems will add an additional dimension to the potential future development of systems. The collaborative aspects of digital libraries can be viewed as a new source of information that dynamically could interact with information retrieval techniques. For example, should the weighting algorithms and search techniques discussed later in this book vary against a corpus based upon dialogue between people versus statically published material? During the collaboration, in certain states, should the system be automatically searching for reference material to support the collaboration?

In order to have a basis for discussing algorithms and the tradeoff on alternative approaches, a commonly accepted metric is required. In information retrieval precision and recall provide the basis for evaluating the results of alternative algorithms. In Chap. 9 other evaluative approaches will be presented but precision and recall remain the standard. To understand how to interpret the results of precision and recall results, they need to be placed in the context of what a user considers is important. The understanding that from a user's perspective minimization of the resources the user expends to satisfy his information need needs to be considered in combination with precision and recall. A reduction in precision and recall with a significant improvement in reducing the resources the user has to expend to get information changes the conclusion on what is optimal.

## 1.8  Exercises

1. The metric to be minimized in an Information Retrieval System from a user's perspective is user overhead. Describe the places that the user overhead is encountered from when a user has an information need until when it is satisfied. Is system complexity also part of the user overhead?
2. Under what conditions might it be possible to achieve 100% precision and 100% recall in a system? What is the relationship between these measures and user overhead?
3. Describe how the statement that "language is the largest inhibitor to good communications" applies to Information Retrieval Systems.
4. What is the impact on precision and recall in the use of Stop Lists and Stop Algorithms?
5. What is the difference between the concept of a "Digital Library" and an Information Retrieval System? What new areas of information retrieval research may be important to support a Digital Library?
6. Describe the rationale why use of proximity will improve precision versus use of just the Boolean functions. Discuss it's effect on improvement of recall.
7. Show that the proximity function can not be used to provide an equivalent to a Contiguous Word Phrase.
8. What are the similarities and differences between use of fuzzy searches and term masking? What are the potentials for each to introduce errors?
9. Ranking is one of the most important concepts in Information Retrieval Systems. What are the difficulties in applying ranking when Boolean queries are used?
10. What problems does multimedia information retrieval introduce? What solutions would you recommend to resolve the problems?

# Chapter 2
# Data Structures and Mathematical Algorithms

## 2.1 Data Structures

### 2.1.1 Introduction to Data Structures

There are usually two major data structures in any information system. One structure stores and manages the received items in their normalized form and is the version that is displayed to the user. The process supporting this structure is called the "document manager." The other major data structure contains the processing tokens and associated data (e.g., index) to support search. Figure 2.1 shows the document file creation process which is a combination of the ingest and indexing processes. The results of a search are references to the items that satisfy the search statement, which are passed to the document manager for retrieval. This chapter focuses on data structures used to support the search function. It does not address the document management function nor the data structures and other related theory associated with the parsing of queries.

The Ingest and Indexing processes are described in Chaps. 3 and 4, but some of the lower level data structures to support the indices are described in this chapter. The most common data structure encountered in both data base and information systems is the inverted file system (discussed in Sect. 2.1.2). It minimizes secondary storage access when multiple search terms are applied across the total database. All commercial and most academic systems use inversion as the searchable data structure. A variant of the searchable data structure is the N-gram structure that breaks processing tokens into smaller string units (which is why it is sometimes discussed under stemming) and uses the token fragments for search. N-grams have demonstrated improved efficiencies and conceptual manipulations over full word inversion. PAT trees and arrays view the text of an item as a single long stream versus a juxtaposition of words. Around this paradigm search algorithms are defined based upon text strings. Signature files are based upon the idea of fast elimination of non-relevant items reducing the searchable items to a manageable subset. The subset can be returned to the user for review or other search algorithms may be applied to it to eliminate any false hits that passed the signature filter.

G. Kowalski, *Information Retrieval Architecture and Algorithms*,
DOI 10.1007/978-1-4419-7716-8_2, © Springer Science+Business Media, LLC 2011

**Fig. 2.1** Major data
structures

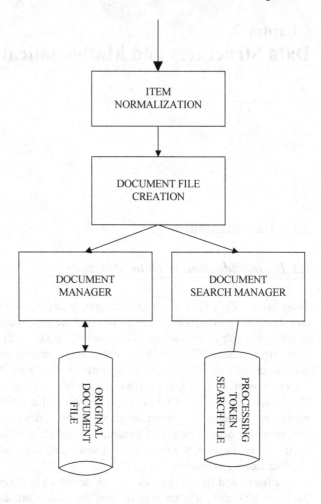

The XML data structure is the most common structure used in sharing information between systems and frequently how it is stored within a system. It is how items are received by the Ingest process and it is typically used if items are exported to other applications and systems. Given the commonality of XML there has been TREC conference experiments on how to optimize search systems whose data structure is XML.

The hypertext data structure is the basis behind URL references on the internet. But more importantly is the logical expansion of the definition of an item when hypertext references are used and its potential impact on searches. The latest Internet search systems have started to make use of hypertext links to expand what information is indexed associated with items. Most commonly it is used when indexing multimedia objects but there is a natural extension to textual items.

There are some mathematical notions that are frequently used in information retrieval systems. Bayesian mathematics has a variety of uses in information retrieval. Another important concept comes from Communications systems and Information Theory based upon the work of Claude Shannon and is the basis behind most of the commonly used weighting algorithms. Hidden Markov models are used in both searching and also are a technical base behind multimedia information item processing. Latent Semantic Indexing is one of the few techniques that has been used commercially to create concept indices. Neural networks and Support Vector Machines are the most common learning algorithms used to automatically construct search structures from user examples used for example in Categorization.

## 2.1.2 *Inverted File Structure*

The most common data structure used in both database management and Information Retrieval Systems is the inverted file structure. Inverted file structures are composed of three basic files: the document file, the inversion lists (sometimes called posting files) and the dictionary. The name "inverted file" comes from its underlying methodology of storing an inversion of the documents: inversion of the documents from the perspective that instead of having a set of documents with words in them, you create a set of words that has the list of documents they are found in. Each document in the system is given a unique numerical identifier. It is that identifier that is stored in the inversion list. The way to locate the inversion list for a particular word is via the Dictionary. The Dictionary is typically a sorted list of all unique words (processing tokens) in the system and a pointer to the location of its inversion list (see Fig. 2.2). Dictionaries can also store other information used in query optimization such as the length of inversion lists. Additional information may be used from the item to increase precision and provide a more optimum inversion list file structure. For example, if zoning is used, the dictionary may be partitioned by zone. There could be a dictionary and set of inversion lists for the "Abstract" zone in an item and another dictionary and set of inversion lists for the "Main Body" zone. This increases the overhead when a user wants to search the complete item versus restricting the search to a specific zone. Another typical optimization occurs when the inversion list only contains one or two entries. Those entries can be stored as part of the dictionary. The inversion list contains the document identifier for each document in which the word is found. To support proximity, contiguous word

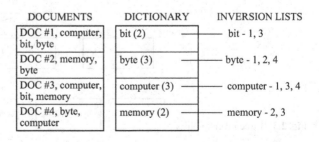

| DOCUMENTS | DICTIONARY | INVERSION LISTS |
|---|---|---|
| DOC #1, computer, bit, byte | bit (2) ———— | bit - 1, 3 |
| DOC #2, memory, byte | byte (3) ———— | byte - 1, 2, 4 |
| DOC #3, computer, bit, memory | computer (3) ——— | computer - 1, 3, 4 |
| DOC #4, byte, computer | memory (2) ——— | memory - 2, 3 |

**Fig. 2.2** Inverted file structure

phrases and term weighting algorithms, all occurrences of a word are stored in the inversion list along with the word position. Thus if the word "bit" was the tenth, twelfth and eighteenth word in document #1, then the inversion list would appear:

   bit—1(10), 1(12), 1(18)

Weights can also be stored in inversion lists. Words with special characteristics are frequently stored in their own dictionaries to allow for optimum internal representation and manipulation (e.g., dates which require date ranging and numbers).

When a search is performed, the inversion lists for the terms in the query are located and the appropriate logic is applied between inversion lists. The result is a final hit list of items that satisfy the query. For systems that support ranking, the list is reorganized into ranked order. The document numbers are used to retrieve the documents from the Document File. Using the inversion lists in Fig. 2.2, the query (bit AND computer) would use the Dictionary to find the inversion lists for "bit" and "computer." These two lists would be logically ANDed: (1,3) AND (1,3,4) resulting in the final Hit list containing (1,3).

Rather than using a dictionary to point to the inversion list, B-trees can be used. The inversion lists may be at the leaf level or referenced in higher level pointers. Fig. 2.3 shows how the words in Fig. 2.1 would appear. A B-tree of order m is defined as:

- A root node with between 2 and 2m keys
- All other internal nodes have between m and 2m keys
- All keys are kept in order from smaller to larger
- All leaves are at the same level or differ by at most one level.

Cutting and Pedersen described use of B-trees as an efficient inverted file storage mechanism for data that undergoes heavy updates (Cutting-90).

The nature of information systems is that items are seldom if ever modified once they are produced. Most commercial systems take advantage of this fact by allowing document files and their associated inversion lists to grow to a certain maximum size and then to freeze them, starting a new structure. Each of these databases of document file, dictionary, inversion lists is archived and made available for a user's query. This has the advantage that for queries only interested in more recent information; only the latest databases need to be searched. Since older items are seldom

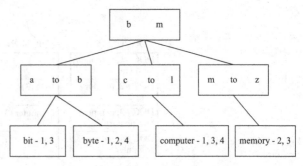

**Fig. 2.3** B-tree inversion lists

deleted or modified, the archived databases may be permanently backed-up, thus saving on operations overhead. Starting a new inverted database has significant overhead in adding new words and inversion lists until the frequently found words are added to the dictionary and inversion lists. Previous knowledge of archived databases can be used to establish an existing dictionary and inversion structure at the start of a new database, thus saving significant overhead during the initial adding of new documents. Other more scalable inversion list techniques are discussed in Chap. 8.

Inversion lists structures are used because they provide optimum performance in searching large databases. The optimality comes from the minimization of data flow in resolving a query. Only data directly related to the query are retrieved from secondary storage. Also there are many techniques that can be used to optimize the resolution of the query based upon information maintained in the dictionary.

Inversion list file structures are well suited to store concepts and their relationships. Each inversion list can be thought of as representing a particular concept. Words are typically used to define an inversion list but in Chap. 3 when categorization and entities are discussed, the inversion lists can easily be extended to include those as additional index for an item. The individual word may not be representative of a concept but by use of a proximity search the user can combine words all within a proximity (e.g., in the same sentence) and thus get closer to a concept. The inversion list is then a concordance of all of the items that contain that concept. Finer resolution of concepts can additionally be maintained by storing locations with an item and weights of the item in the inversion lists. With this information, relationships between concepts can be determined as part of search algorithms. Location of concepts is made easy by their listing in the dictionary and inversion lists. For Natural Language Processing algorithms, other structures may be more appropriate or required in addition to inversion lists for maintaining the required semantic and syntactic information.

### 2.1.3 N-Gram Data Structures

N-Grams can be viewed as a special technique for conflation (stemming) and as a unique data structure in information systems. N-Grams are a fixed length consecutive series of "n" characters. Unlike stemming that generally tries to determine the stem of a word that represents the semantic meaning of the word, n-grams do not care about semantics. Instead they are algorithmically based upon a fixed number of characters. The searchable data structure is transformed into overlapping n-grams, which are then used to create the searchable database. Examples of bigrams, trigrams and pentagrams are given in Fig. 2.4 for the word phrase "sea colony."

For n-grams, with n greater than two, some systems allow interword symbols to be part of the n-gram set usually excluding the single character with interword symbol option. The symbol # is used to represent the interword symbol which is anyone of a set of symbols (e.g., blank, period, semicolon, colon, etc.). Each of the n-grams

**Fig. 2.4** Bigrams, trigrams and pentagrams for "sea colony"

| se ea co ol lo on ny | Bigrams (no interword symbols) |
| sea col olo lon ony | Trigrams (no interword symbols) |
| #se sea ea# #co col olo lon ony ny# | Trigrams (with interword symbol #) |
| #sea# #colo colon olony lony# | Pentagrams (with interword symbol #) |

created becomes separate processing tokens and are searchable. It is possible that the same n-gram can be created multiple times from a single word.

### 2.1.3.1   History

The first use of n-grams dates to World War II when it was used by cryptographers. Fletcher Pratt states that "with the backing of bigram and trigram tables any cryptographer can dismember a simple substitution cipher" (Pratt-42). Use of bigrams was described by Adamson as a method for conflating terms (Adamson-74). It does not follow the normal definition of stemming because what is produced by creating n-grams are word fragments versus semantically meaningful word stems. It is this characteristic of mapping longer words into shorter n-gram fragments that seems more appropriately classified as a data structure process than a stemming process.

Another major use of n-grams (in particular trigrams) is in spelling error detection and correction (Angell-83, McIllroy-82, Morris-75, Peterson-80, Thorelli-62, Wang-77, and Zamora-81). Most approaches look at the statistics on probability of occurrence of n-grams (trigrams in most approaches) in the English vocabulary and indicate any word that contains non-existent to seldom used n-grams as a potential erroneous word. Damerau specified four categories of spelling errors (Damerau-64) as shown in Fig. 2.5.

Using the classification scheme, Zamora showed trigram analysis provided a viable data structure for identifying misspellings and transposed characters. This impacts information systems as a possible basis for identifying potential input errors for correction as a procedure within the normalization process (see Chap. 1). Frequency of occurrence of n-gram patterns also can be used for identifying the language of an item (Damashek-95, Cohen-95).

**Fig. 2.5** Categories of spelling errors

| Error Category | Example |
| --- | --- |
| Single Character Insertion | compuuter |
| Single Character Deletion | compter |
| Single Character Substitution | compiter |
| Transposition of two adjacent characters | computer |

In information retrieval, trigrams have been used for text compression and to manipulate the length of index terms (Schek-78, Schuegraf-76). Some implementations used a variety of different n-grams as index elements for inverted file systems. They have also been the core data structure to encode profiles for the Logicon LMDS system (Yochum-95) used for Selective Dissemination of Information. For retrospective search, the Acquaintance System uses n-grams to store the searchable document file (Damashek-95, Huffman-95) for retrospective search of large textual databases.

### 2.1.3.2 N-Gram Data Structure

As shown in Fig. 2.4, an n-gram is a data structure that ignores words and treats the input as a continuous data, optionally limiting its processing by interword symbols. The data structure consists of fixed length overlapping symbol segments that define the searchable processing tokens. These tokens have logical linkages to all the items in which the tokens are found. Inversion lists, document vectors (described in Chap. 4) and other proprietary data structures are used to store the linkage data structure and are used in the search process. In some cases just the least frequently occurring n-gram is kept as part of a first pass search process (Yochum-85).

The choice of the fixed length word fragment size has been studied in many contexts. Yochum investigated the impacts of different values for "n." Other researchers investigated n-gram data structures using an inverted file system for n = 2 to n = 26. Trigrams (n-grams of length 3) were determined to be the optimal length, trading off information versus size of data structure. The Acquaintance System uses longer n-grams, ignoring word boundaries. The advantage of n-grams is that they place a finite limit on the number of searchable tokens.

$$\text{MaxSeg}_n = (\lambda)^n$$

The maximum number of unique n-grams that can be generated, MaxSeg, can be calculated as a function of $n$ which is the length of the n-grams, and $\lambda$ which is the number of processable symbols from the alphabet (i.e., non-interword symbols).

Although there is a savings in the number of unique processing tokens and implementation techniques allow for fast processing on minimally sized machines, false hits can occur under some architectures. For example, a system that uses trigrams and does not include interword symbols or the character position of the n-gram in an item finds an item containing "retain detail" when searching for "retail" (i.e., all of the trigrams associated with "retail" are created in the processing of "retain detail"). Inclusion of interword symbols would not have helped in this example. Inclusion of character position of the n-gram would have discovered that the n-grams "ret," "eta," "tai," "ail" that define "retail" are not all consecutively starting within one character of each other. The longer the n-gram, the less likely this type error is to occur because of more information in the word fragment. But the longer the n-gram, the more it provides the same result as full word data structures since most words are included within a single n-gram. Another disadvantage of n-grams is the increased size of inversion lists (or other data structures) that store the linkage data structure. In effect, use of n-grams expands the number of processing tokens by a significant factor. The average word in the English language is between six and seven characters in length. Use of trigrams increases the number of processing tokens by a factor of five if interword symbols are not included. Thus the inversion lists increase by a factor of five.

Because of the processing token bounds of n-gram data structures, optimized performance techniques can be applied in mapping items to an n-gram searchable structure and in query processing. There is no semantic meaning in a particular n-gram since it is a fragment of processing token and may not represent a concept. Thus n-grams are a poor representation of concepts and their relationships. But the juxtaposition of n-grams can be used to equate to standard word indexing, achieving the same levels of recall and within 85% precision levels with a significant improvement in performance (Adams-92). Vector representations of the n-grams from an item can be used to calculate the similarity between items. N-grams can be very useful when the items in the database are not typical textual items. For example a database of software programs would be far more searchable using n-grams as the tokenization data structure.

## 2.1.4   PAT Data Structure

Using n-grams with interword symbols included between valid processing tokens equates to a continuous text input data structure that is being indexed in contiguous "n" character tokens. A different view of addressing a continuous text input data structure comes from PAT trees and PAT arrays. The input stream is transformed into a searchable data structure consisting of substrings. The original concepts of PAT tree data structures were described as Patricia trees (Frakes-92) and have gained new momentum as a possible structure for searching text and images and applications in genetic databases. The name PAT is short for PATRICIA Trees (PATRICIA stands for Practical Algorithm To Retrieve Information Coded In Alphanumerics.)

In creation of PAT trees each position in the input string is the anchor point for a sub-string that starts at that point and includes all new text up to the end of the input. All substrings are unique. This view of text lends itself to many different search processing structures. It fits within the general architectures of hardware text search machines and parallel processors. A substring can start at any point in the text and can be uniquely indexed by its starting location and length. If all strings are to the end of the input, only the starting location is needed since the length is the difference from the location and the total length of the item. It is possible to have a substring go beyond the length of the input stream by adding additional null characters. These substrings are called sistring (semi-infinite string). Figure 2.6 shows some possible sistrings for an input text.

**Fig. 2.6** Examples of
sistrings

| Text | Economics for Warsaw is complex. |
|------|----------------------------------|
| sistring 1 | Economics for Warsaw is complex. |
| sistring 2 | conomics for Warsaw is complex. |
| sistring 5 | omics for Warsaw is complex. |
| sistring 10 | for Warsaw is complex. |
| sistring 20 | w is complex. |
| sistring 30 | ex. |

A PAT tree is an unbalanced, binary digital tree defined by the sistrings. The individual bits of the sistrings decide the branching patterns with zeros branching left and ones branching right. PAT trees also allow each node in the tree to specify which bit is used to determine the branching via bit position or the number of bits to skip from the parent node. This is useful in skipping over levels that do not require branching.

The key values are stored at the leaf nodes (bottom nodes) in the PAT Tree. For a text input of size "n" there are "n" leaf nodes and "n − 1" at most higher level nodes. It is possible to place additional constraints on sistrings for the leaf nodes. We may be interested in limiting our searches to word boundaries. Thus we could limit our sistrings to those that are immediately after an interword symbol. Figure 2.7 gives an example of the sistrings used in generating a PAT tree. The example only goes down 9 levels. It shows the minimum binary prefixes that uniquely identify each row. If the binary representations of "h" is (100), "o" is (110), "m" is (001) and "e" is (101) then the word "home" produces the input 100110001101.... Using the sistrings, the full PAT binary tree is shown in Fig. 2.8. A more compact tree where skip (reduced PAT tree) values are in the intermediate nodes is shown in Fig. 2.9. In the compact tree, if only one branch of a tree is being extended by the sistrings, you can skip comparisons on those levels because the values are not optional (i.e., cannot be a 1 or a 0—but just one of those values) and thus there are not branches that you could take. The value in the intermediate nodes (indicated by rectangles) is the number of bits to skip until the next bit to compare that causes differences between similar terms. This final version saves space, but requires one additional comparison whenever you encounter a 1 and zero optional level to validate there were no errors in the positions that were jumped over. In the example provided it is at the leaf level but could occur at any level within the tree (in an oval). In the

| | INPUT | 0110111101101110 |
|---|-------|------------------|
| | sistring 1 | 01101111... |
| | sistring 2 | 1101111... |
| | sistring 3 | 10111.... |
| | sistring 4 | 0111..... |
| | sistring 5 | 1111... |
| | sistring 6 | 1110..... |
| | sistring 7 | 110110... |
| | sistring 8 | 10110... |
| | sistring 9 | 011011110... |

**Fig. 2.7** Sistrings for input
"0110111101101110"

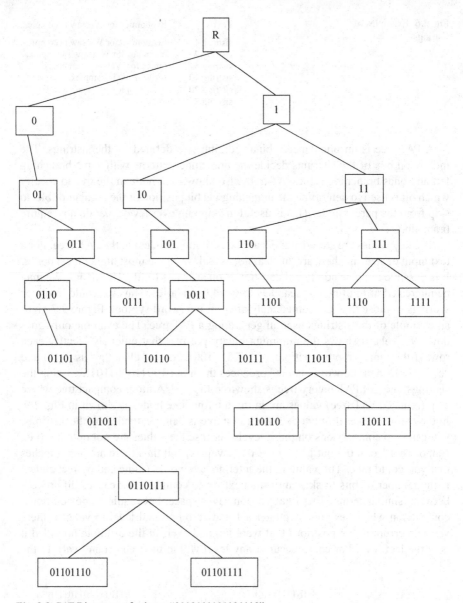

**Fig. 2.8** PAT Binary tree for input "0110111101101110"

reduced PAT tree the node that has "111" in it could have alternatively been shown as a circle with a skip of 1 position.

To search, the search terms are also represented by their binary representation and the PAT trees for the sistrings are traveled down based upon the values in the search term to look for match(es).

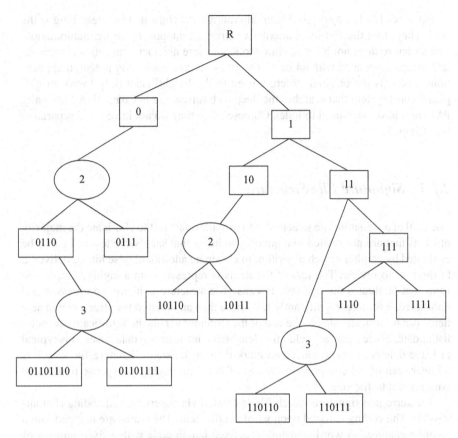

**Fig. 2.9** Reduced PAT tree for "0110111101101110"

As noted in Chap. 1, one of the most common classes of searches is prefix search-es. PAT trees are ideally constructed for this purpose because each sub-tree contains all the sistrings for the prefix defined up to that node in the tree structure. Thus all the leaf nodes after the prefix node define the sistrings that satisfy the prefix search criteria. This logically sorted order of PAT trees also facilitates range searches since it is easy to determine the sub-trees constrained by the range values. If the total in-put stream is used in defining the PAT tree, then suffix, imbedded string, and fixed length masked searches (see Sect. 2.1.5) are all easy because the given characters uniquely define the path from the root node to where the existence of sistrings need to be validated. Fuzzy searches are very difficult because large number of possible sub-trees could match the search term.

A detailed discussion on searching PAT trees and their representation as an array is provided by Gonnet, Baeza-Yates and Snider (Gonnet-92). In their comparison to Signature and Inversion files, they concluded that PAT arrays have more accuracy than Signature files and provide the ability to string searches that are inefficient in inverted files (e.g., suffix searches, approximate string searches, longest repetition).

Pat Trees (and arrays) provide an alternative structure if string searching is the goal. They store the text in an alternative structure supporting string manipulation. The structure does not have facilities to store more abstract concepts and their relationships associated with an item. The structure has interesting potential applications, and was the original structure used in the BrightPlanet (http://www.bright-planet.com) system that searches the deep web (discussed in Chap. 3). Additionally PAT trees have been used to index Chinese since they do not have word separators (see Chap. 3).

## 2.1.5   Signature File Structure

The goal of a signature file structure is to provide a fast test to eliminate the majority of items that are not related to a query. The items that satisfy the test can either be evaluated by another search algorithm to eliminate additional false hits or delivered to the user to review. The text of the items is represented in a highly compressed form that facilitates the fast test. Because file structure is highly compressed and unordered, it requires significantly less space than an inverted file structure and new items can be concatenated to the end of the structure versus the significant inversion list update. Since items are seldom deleted from information data bases, it is typical to leave deleted items in place and mark them as deleted. Signature file search is a linear scan of the compressed version of items producing a response time linear with respect to file size.

The surrogate signature search file is created via superimposed coding (Faloutsos-85). The coding is based upon words in the item. The words are mapped into a "word signature." A word signature is a fixed length code with a fixed number of bits set to "1." The bit positions that are set to one are determined via a hash function of the word. The word signatures are ORed together to create the signature of an item. To avoid signatures being too dense with "1"s, a maximum number of words is specified and an item is partitioned into blocks of that size. In Fig. 2.10 the block size is set at five words, the code length is 16 bits and the number of bits that are allowed to be "1" for each word is five.

TEXT:  Computer Science graduate students study
(assume block size is five words)

| WORD | Signature |
| --- | --- |
| Computer | 0001  0110  0000  0110 |
| Science | 1001  0000  1110  0000 |
| graduate | 1000  0101  0100  0010 |
| students | 0000  0111  1000  0100 |
| study | 0000  0110  0110  0100 |
| Block Signature | 1001  0111  1110  0110 |

**Fig. 2.10** Superimposed coding

The words in a query are mapped to their signature. Search is accomplished by template matching on the bit positions specified by the words in the query.

The signature file can be stored as a signature with each row representing a signature block. Associated with each row is a pointer to the original text block. A design objective of a signature file system is trading off the size of the data structure versus the density of the final created signatures. Longer code lengths reduce the probability of collision in hashing the words (i.e., two different words hashing to the same value). Fewer bits per code reduce the effect of a code word pattern being in the final block signature even though the word is not in the item. For example, if the signature for the word "hard" is 1000 0111 0010 0000, it incorrectly matches the block signature in Fig. 2.10 (false hit). In a study by Faloutous and Christodoulakis (Faloutous-87) it was shown that if compression is applied to the final data structure, the optimum number of bits per word is one. This then takes on the appearance of a binary coded vector for each item, where each position in the vector represents the existence of a word in the item. This approach requires the maximum code length but ensures that there are not any false hits unless two words hash to the same value.

Search of the signature matrix requires $O(N)$ search time. To reduce the search time the signature matrix is partitioned horizontally. One of the earliest techniques hashes the block signature to a specific slot. If a query has less than the number of words in a block it maps to a number of possible slots rather than just one. The number of slots decreases exponentially as the number of terms increases (Gustafson-71). Another approach maps the signatures into an index sequential file, where, for example, the first "n" bits of the signature is used as the index to the block of signatures that will be compared sequentially to the query (Lee-89). Other techniques are two level signatures (Sacks-Davis-83) and use of B-tree structures with similar signatures clustered at leaf nodes (Deppisch-86).

Another implementation approach takes advantage of the fact that searches are performed on the columns of the signature matrix, ignoring those columns that are not indicated by hashing of any of the search terms. Thus the signature matrix may be stored in column order versus row order (Faloutsos-88, Lin-88, Roberts-79), called vertical partitioning. This is in effect storing the signature matrix using an inverted file structure. The major overhead comes from updates, since new "1"s have to be added to each inverted column representing a signature in the new item.

Signature files provide a practical solution for storing and locating information in a number of different situations. Faloutsos summarizes the environments that signature files have been applied as medium size databases, databases with low frequency of terms, WORM devices, parallel processing machines, and distributed environments (Faloutsos-92).

One of the first steps in ingesting items is to detect duplicate and near duplicate items (see Chap. 3). One way of representing the text in items is via signatures which could be used to detect near duplicates.

## 2.1.6   Hypertext and XML Data Structures

The advent of the Internet and its exponential growth and wide acceptance as a new global information network has introduced new mechanisms for representing information. This structure is called hypertext and differs from traditional information storage data structures in format and use. The hypertext is stored in Hypertext Markup Language (HTML) and eXtensible Markup Language (XML). HTML is an evolving standard as new requirements for display of items on the Internet are identified and implemented. Both of these languages provide detailed descriptions for subsets of text similar to the zoning discussed previously. These subsets can be used the same way zoning is used to increase search accuracy and improve display of hit results.

In addition to using the HTML or XML to define zones, it also can be used to identify metadata to be extracted and associated with that item. For example there could be a date field or a source field. HTML also contains display information such as "bolding". That information is also useful to indicate the importance of a word used in ranking (ordering) the hits from a search. Over the past few years a new standard called XHTML has been introduced that merges the XML data description with the HTML presentation.

### 2.1.6.1   Definition of Hypertext Structure

The Hypertext data structure is used extensively in the Internet environment and requires electronic media storage for the item. Hypertext allows one item to reference another item via an imbedded pointer. Each separate item is called a node and the reference pointer is called a link. The referenced item can be of the same or a different data type than the original (e.g., a textual item references a photograph). Each node is displayed by a viewer that is defined for the file type associated with the node.

For example, Hypertext Markup Language (HTML) defines the internal structure for information exchange across the World Wide Web on the Internet. A document is composed of the text of the item along with HTML tags that describe how to display the document. Tags are formatting or structural keywords contained between less-than, greater than symbols (e.g., <title>, <strong> meaning display prominently). The HTML tag associated with hypertext linkages is <a href= …#NAME /a> where "a" and "/a" are an anchor start tag and anchor end tag denoting the text that the user can activate. "href" is the hypertext reference containing either a file name if the referenced item is on this node or an address (Uniform Resource Locator—URL) and a file name if it is on another node. "#NAME" defines a destination point other than the top of the item to go to. The URL has three components: the access method the client used to retrieve the item, the Internet address of the server where the item is stored, and the address of the item at the server (i.e., the file including the directory it is in). For example, the URL for the HTML specification appears:

http://info.cern.ch/hypertext/WWW/MarkUp/HTML.html

**Fig. 2.11** Example of
segment of HTML

```
<CENTER>
<IMG SC="/images/home_iglo.jpg" WIDTH=468 HEIGHT=107
BORDER=0 ALT="WELCOME TO NETSCAPE><BR>
<P>
<DL>
<A HREF="/comprod/mirror/index.html">
<DD>
The beta testing is over: please read our report <A
HREF="http://www.charm.net/doc/charm/report/theme.html"> and
your can find more references at
HREF="http://www.charm.net/doc/charm/results/tests.html">
```

"HTTP" stands for the Hypertext Transfer Protocol which is the access protocol used to retrieve the item in HTML. Other Internet protocols are used for other activities such as file transfer (ftp://), remote logon (telnet://) and collaborative newsgroups (news://). The destination point is found in "info.cern.ch" which is the name of the "info" machine at CERN with "ch" being Switzerland, and "/hypertext/WWW/MarkUP/HTML.html" defines where to find the file HTML.html. Figure 2.11 shows an example of a segment of a HTML document. Most of the formatting tags indicated by < > are not described, being out of the scope of this text, but detailed descriptions can be found in the hundreds of books available on HTML. The <a href= ...> are the previously described hypertext linkages.

An item can have many hypertext linkages. Thus, from any item there are multiple paths that can be followed in addition to skipping over the linkages to continue sequential reading of the item. This is similar to the decision a reader makes upon reaching a footnote, whether to continue reading or skip to the footnote. Hypertext is sometimes called a "generalized footnote." But that can be misleading because quite often the link is to a major extension of the current item.

In a conventional item the physical and logical structure are closely related. The item is sequential with imbedded citations to other distinct items or locations in the item. From the author's perspective, the substantive semantics lie in the sequential presentation of the information. Hypertext is a non-sequential directed graph structure, where each node contains its own information. The author assumes the reader can follow the linked data as easily as following the sequential presentation. A node may have several outgoing links, each of which is then associated with some smaller part of the node called an anchor. When an anchor is activated, the associated link is followed to the destination node, thus navigating the hypertext network. There is text that the reader sees that is associated with the anchor (anchor text). This takes on importance in Information retrieval because it is quite often used as index text for the anchor when it is pointing to a multimedia file versus just another textual page. The organizational and reference structure of a conventional item is fixed at printing time while hypertext nodes and links can be changed dynamically. New linkages can be added and the information at a node can change without modification to the item referencing it.

Conventional items are read sequentially by a user. In a hypertext environment, the user "navigates" through the node network by following links. This is the defining capability that allows hypertext to manage loosely structured information. Each thread through different nodes could represent a different concept with additional detail. In a small and familiar network the navigation works well, but in a large information space, it is possible for the user to become disoriented.

Quite often hypertext references are used to include information that is other than text (e.g., graphics, audio, photograph, video) in a text item. During the ingest process described in Chap. 3, the system can easily identify different multimedia modalities to assist in directing those items to the appropriate ingest and indexing software. The multiple different uses for hypertext references are evolving as more experience is gained with them. When the hypertext is logically part of the item, such as in a graphic, the referenced file is usually resident at the same physical location. When other items created by other users are referenced, they frequently are located at other physical sites. When items are deleted or moved, there is no mechanism to update other items that reference them. Linkage integrity is a major issue in use of hypertext linkages.

Dynamic HTML became available with Navigator 4.0 and Internet Explorer 4.0. It is a collective term for a combination of the latest HTML tags and options, style sheets and programming that will let you create WEB pages that are more animated and responsive to user interaction. Some of the features supported are an object-oriented view of a WEB page and its elements, cascading style sheets, programming that can address most page elements add dynamic fonts. Object oriented views are defined by the Document Object Model—DOM (Micorsoft calls this the Dynamic HTML Object Model while Netscape calls it the HTML Object Model). For example every heading on a page can be named and given attributes of text style and color that can be manipulated by name in a small "program" or script included on the page. A style sheet describes the default style characteristics (page layout, font, text size, etc) of a document or portion of a document. Dynamic HTML allows the specification of style sheets in a cascading fashion (linking style sheets to predefined levels of precedence within the same set of pages). As a result of a user interaction, a new style sheet can be applied changing the appearance of the display. Layering is the use of alternative style sheets to vary the content of a page by providing content layers that overlay and superimpose existing content sections. The existing HTML programming capabilities are being expanded to address the additional data structures.

HTML prior to version 5 was based upon SGML (Standard Generalized Mark-up Language) and was a very simplified subset of it. With the increasing use of XML to define data structures it became sensible to define a new HTML structure that could work well with XML data and provide Internet displays of the XML data. This lead to XHTML (extensible hypertext mark-up language). Since it works with XML it also inherits the "well formed" structural constraints associated with XML. This makes the automated processing easier versus the more complex parsers needed for HTML based upon SGML. The other advantage is XHTML documents could include XML structures from other XML based languages. At this point changes from HTML to XHTML have been kept to a minimum primarily to adhere to the rules of XML. Since Internet Explorer has not accepted XHTML there remains major resistance to its general usage. In July 2009 W3C announced that they will stop work on expanding XHTML and focus on HTML 5 that combines HTML and XHTML.

### 2.1.6.2   Hypertext History

Although information sciences is just starting to address the impact of the hypertext data structure, the concept of hypertext has been around for over 50 years. In 1945 an article written by Vannevar Bush in 1933 was published describing the Memex (memory extender) system (Bush-67). It was a microfilm based system that would allow the user to store much of the information from the scientific explosion of the 1940s on microfilm and retrieve it at multiple readers at the user's desk via individual links. The term "hypertext" came from Ted Nelson in 1965 (Nelson-74). Nelson's vision of all the world's literature being interlinked via hypertext references is part of his Xanadu System. The lack of cost effective computers with sufficient speed and memory to implement hypertext effectively was one of the main inhibitors to its development. One of the first commercial uses of a hypertext system was the mainframe system, Hypertext Editing System, developed at Brown University by Andres van Dam and later sold to Houston Manned Spacecraft Center where it was used for Apollo mission documentation (van Dam-88). Other systems such as the Aspen system at MIT, the KMS system at Carnegie Mellon, the Hyperties system at the University of Maryland and the Notecards system developed at Xerox PARC advanced the hypertext concepts providing hypertext (and hypermedia) systems. HyperCard, delivered with Macintosh computers, was the first widespread hypertext production product. It had a simple metalanguage (HyperTalk) that facilitated authoring hypertext items. It also provided a large number of graphical user interface elements (e.g., buttons, hands,) that facilitated the production of sophisticated items.

Hypertext became more available in the early 1990s via its use in CD-ROMs for a variety of educational and entertainment products. Its current high level of popularity originated with it being part of the specification of the World Wide Web by the CERN (the European Center for Nuclear Physics Research) in Geneva, Switzerland. The Mosaic browser, freely available from CERN on the Internet, gave everyone who had access the ability to receive and display hypertext documents.

## 2.1.7   XML

The eXtensible Markup Language (XML) is also becoming a standard encoding structure for documents on the WEB and as a data exchange format for Web services applications (e.g., used for web services). Its first recommendation (1.0) was issued on February 10, 1998. It is a middle ground between the simplicities but lack of flexibility of HTML and the complexity but richness of SGML (ISO 8879). Its objective is extending HTML with semantic information and removing the display specification from the data specification. The logical data structure within XML is defined by a Data Type Description (DTD) and is not constrained to the 70 defined tags and 50 attributes in the single DTD for HTML. The original DTD did not allow for complex definition of data types within the data structure so it was expanded to other ways of defining XML structures called schemas. The DTD is a very restricted version of an XML schema. Some of the other more common schemas are Schema W3C and RELAX NG. The user can create any tags needed to describe and manipulate their structure. The W3C (World Wide Web Consortium) is redeveloping HTML as a suite of XML tags. The following is a simple example of XML tagging:

<company>Widgets Inc.</company>
<city>Boston</city>
<state>Mass</state>
<product>widgets</product>

The W3C is also developing a Resource Description Format (RDF) for representing properties of WEB resources such as images, documents and relationships between them. This will include the Platform for Internet Content Selection (PICS) for attaching labels to material for filtering (e.g., unsuitable for children).

Hypertext links for XML were being defined in the Xlink (XML Linking Language) but work stopped in this area. Xpoint (XML Pointer language) specifications. This would allow for distinction for different types of links to locations within a document and external to the document. This would allow an application to know if a link is just a repositioning reference within an item or link to another document that is an extension of the existing document. This would help in determining what needs to be retrieved to define the total item to be indexed. But the standards committees could not get a critical mass following interested in implementing this concept.

Finally XML will include an XML Style Sheet Linking definition to define how to display items on a particular style sheet and handle cascading style sheets. This will allow designers to limit what is displayed to the user (saving on display screen space) and allow expansion to the whole item if desired. Cascading Style Sheets provide an easy way to dynamically manage the output display of XML to the user.

## 2.2    Mathematical Algorithms

### 2.2.1    Introduction

There are a number of mathematical concepts that form the basis behind a lot of the weighted indexing techniques used in creating the indices for information retrieval systems. The goal of this section is to provide a brief introduction to the important mathematical concepts. If the student wants to use the concepts in either research or applications they are developing then significant additional reading on the concepts is required. The two most important theories are the Bayesian theory and Shannon' Information theory. Bayesian models are a conditional model associated with probabilities that estimates the probability of one event given another event takes place. This directly maps into the probability that a document is relevant given a specific query. It additionally can be used to define clustering relationships used in automatic creation of taxonomies associated with search results and item databases. Shannon's information model describes the "information value" given the frequency of occurrence of an event. In this case it can be related to how many items contain a particular word and how that affects its importance (if a word is found in every item in the database it does not have much search vale).

Hidden Markov Models are the basis behind the transformation of audio into transcribed text that is one approach to indexing audio and video. In addition it is frequently used in the optical character processing of text in images to computer recognized text. It also has been proposed as a basis behind indexing and search for textual items. Latent semantic indexing is one of the best mathematical techniques to explain how a "concept" index is created and it has been used commercially to create concept indices. It is technique that allows for automatic mapping of millions of words used to create items into a small number (e.g. 300) concept vectors that represent the vocabulary of the language. The concept vectors are then like a meta-language used to express both the items and the queries.

In addition to the algorithms used in creating the index, there is a need in information retrieval for learning algorithms that allow the system to learn what is of interest to a user and then be able to use the dynamically created and updated algorithms to automatically analyze new items to see if they satisfy the existing criteria. This is used in techniques often labeled as "Categorization". The two primary techniques used for the learning algorithms are neural networks and support vector machines.

The goal of this section is to introduce the mathematical basis behind the algorithms used in information retrieval. To really understand the details on how the algorithms are used in information retrieval you should take courses in probability and machine learning.

### 2.2.2  Bayesian Mathematics

The earliest mathematical foundation for information retrieval dates back to the early 1700s when Thomas Bayes developed a theorem that relates the conditional and marginal probabilities of two random events—called Baye's Theorem. It can be used to compute the posterior probability (probability assigned "after" relevant evidence is considered) of random events. For example, it allows to consider the symptoms of a patient and use that information to determine the probability of what is causing the illness. Bayes' theorem relates the conditional and marginal probabilities of events $A$ and $B$, where $B$ cannot equal zero:

$$P(A|B) = \frac{P(B|A)P(A)}{P(B)}.$$

P(A) is called the prior or marginal probability of A. It is called "prior" because it does not take into account any information about B. P(A|B) is the conditional probability of A, given B. It is sometimes named the posterior probability because the probability depends upon the probability of B. P(B|A) is the conditional probability of B given A. P(B) is the prior or marginal probability of B, and normalizes the result.

Putting the terms into words given our example helps in understanding the formula:

- The probability of a patient having the flu given the patient has a high temperature is equal to the probability that if you have a high temperature you have the flu times the probability you will have the flu. This is then normalized by dividing times the probability that you have a high temperature.

To relate Bayesian Theory to information retrieval you need only to consider the search process. A user provides a query, consisting of words, which represent the user's preconceived attempt to describe the semantics needed in an item to be retrieved for it to be relevant. Since each user submits these terms to reflect their own idea of what is important, they imply a preference ordering (ranking) among all of the documents in the database. Applying this to Bayes's Theorem you have:

$$P(\text{An item is relevant}/\text{Query}) = \frac{P(\text{Query}/\text{Relevant item})\,P(\text{An item is relevant})}{P(\text{Query})}$$

The major issues with using this to determine which items are most relevant to the query are Bayes Theorem assumes independence (i.e., each term is independent of every other term), and how to get the probability for some of the terms in the above formula. These issues will be discussed in Chap. 4 on indexing.

A Bayesian network is a directed acyclic graph in which each node represents a random variable and the arcs between the nodes represent a probabilistic dependence between the node and its parents (Howard-81, Pearl-88). Figure 2.12 shows the basic weighting approach for index terms or associations between query terms and index terms.

The nodes $C_1$ and $C_2$ represent "the item contains concept $C_i$," and the F nodes represent "the item has feature (e.g., words) $F_{ij}$." The network could also be inter-

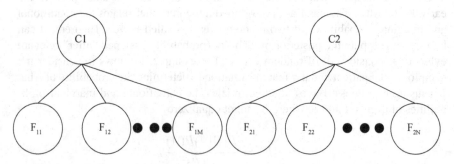

**Fig. 2.12** Two-level Bayesian network

preted as C representing concepts in a query and F representing concepts in an item. The goal is to calculate the probability of $C_i$ given $F_{ij}$. To perform that calculation two sets of probabilities are needed:

1. The prior probability $P(C_i)$ that an item is relevant to concept C
2. The conditional probability $P(F_{ij}/C_i)$ that the features $F_{ij}$ where $j = 1, m$ are present in an item given that the item contains topic $C_i$.

The automatic indexing task is to calculate the posterior probability $P(C_i/F_{i1}, \ldots, F_{im})$, the probability that the item contains concept $C_i$ given the presence of features $F_{ij}$. The Bayes inference formula that is used is:

$$P(C_i/F_{i1}, \ldots, F_{im}) = P(C_i)\, P(F_{i1}, \ldots, F_{im}/C_i)\backslash P(F_{i1}, \ldots, F_{im}).$$

If the goal is to provide ranking as the result of a search by the posteriors, the Bayes rule can be simplified to a linear decision rule:

$$g(C_i/F_{i1}, \ldots, F_{im}) = \Sigma_k I(F_{ik}) w(F_{ik}, C_i)$$

where $I(F_{ik})$ is an indicator variable that equals 1 only if $F_{ik}$ is present in the item (equals zero otherwise) and w is a coefficient corresponding to a specific feature/concept pair. A careful choice of w produces a ranking in decreasing order that is equivalent to the order produced by the posterior probabilities. Interpreting the coefficients, w, as weights corresponding to each feature (e.g., index term) and the function g as the sum of the weights of the features, the result of applying the formula is a set of term weights (Fung-95).

## 2.2.3 Shannon's Theory of Information

In the late 1940s Claude Shannon, a research mathematician at Bell Telephone Laboratories, invented a mathematical theory of communication to be used in the design of telephone systems. The issues to be resolved were how to design telephone systems to carry the maximum amount of information and how to correct for noise on the lines. He approached the problem by defining a simple abstraction of human communication called the channel. Shannon's communication channel consisted of a sender (a source of information), a transmission medium (with noise), and a receiver (whose goal is to reconstruct the sender's messages). In order to analyze the sending of the information through the channel, he defined the concept of the amount of information in a message. In this concept he considered redundant information versus unique information. In this approach a message is very informative (has a high information value) if the chance of its occurrence is small because the loss of the message means the information will be lost. If, in contrast, a message is very predictable, then it has a small amount of information—one is not surprised to receive it and its loss is not as critical because it will be sent again.

Of less importance to information retrieval Shannon also defined the entropy rate that measured the production rate of information production and a measure of the channel capacity to carry information. He showed that if the amount of information you want to send exceeds the capacity you will lose information. If the amount of information you want to send is less than the capacity you can encode the information in a way that it will be received without errors.

Shannon adapted his theory to analyze ordinary human (written) language. He showed that it is quite redundant, using more symbols and words than necessary to convey messages. Presumably, this redundancy is used by us to improve our ability to recognize messages reliably and to communicate different types of information. The formula for the information value of an event is:

$$\text{Info}_k = -\log(p_k)$$

This lead to the interpretation of Shannon's theory that the information value of a word is inversely proportional to how often it is used. A word that is found in every document has no information value because it will always be there. But a word that is found in few documents has high information value when you want to retrieve documents with that word in it. This theory is the basis for the "inverse document formula" (IDF) weighting formula used in many informational retrieval weighting algorithms. It is also used in many other ways such as by the Autonomy product in how it does concept searches—by applying this as a factor on the words it finds when it creates taxonomy for them. This will be discussed in detail in Chap. 4 on Indexing.

### 2.2.4    Latent Semantic Indexing

Latent Semantic Indexing (LSI) was created to support information retrieval and solve the problem of the mismatch between a user's vocabulary and that of the author. Its assumption is that there is an underlying or "latent" structure represented by interrelationships between words (Deerwester-90, Dempster-77, Dumais-95, Gildea-99, Hofmann-99). LSI starts with a "vector/matrix view of a set of documents. Just consider a vector where every position represents one word in a language. Thus it will be a vector that will have millions of positions. A document can be represented by the vector by placing a "weight" in each word location as to the weight of that word in describing the semantics of the document. If you place the vector for each document in the database in rows you will have a matrix representing your documents.

Latent Semantic Indexing uses singular-value decomposition to model the associative relationships between terms similar to eigenvector decomposition and factor analysis (see Cullum-85). This is a form of factor analysis. In SVD, a rectangular matrix is decomposed into the product of three other matrices. One matrix describes the original row entities as vectors of derived orthogonal factor values, another matrix describes the original column entities in the same way, and the final matrix is a diagonal matrix containing scaling values such that when the three components are matrix-multiplied, the original matrix is reconstructed. There is a mathematical proof that any matrix can be so decomposed perfectly, using no more factors than the smallest dimension of the original matrix.

When fewer than the necessary number of factors is used, the reconstructed matrix is a least-squares best fit which minimizes the differences between the original and reduced matrix. One can reduce the dimensionality of the solution simply by deleting coefficients in the diagonal matrix, ordinarily starting with the smallest. Values. By having the values are sorted this will be the bottom rows of the matrix.

Mathematically, the rectangular matrix can be decomposed into the product of three matrices. Let $X$ be a $m \times n$ matrix such that:

$$X = T_0 \cdot S_0 \cdot D_0'$$

where $T_0$ and $D_0$ have orthogonal columns and are $m \times r$ and $r \times n$ matrices, $S_0$ is an $r \times r$ diagonal matrix and $r$ is the rank of matrix $X$. This is the singular value decomposition of $X$. The $k$ largest singular values of $S_0$ are kept along with their corresponding columns/rows in $T_0$ and $D_0$ matrices, the resulting matrix:

$$\bar{X} = T_n \cdot S_n \cdot D_n'$$

is the unique matrix of rank $k$ that is closest in least squares sense to the original $X$. The matrix $\bar{X}$, containing the first $k$ independent linear components of the original $X$ represents the major associations with noise eliminated.

If you consider $X$ to be the term-document matrix (e.g., all possible terms being represented by columns and each item being represented by a row), then truncated singular value decomposition can be applied to reduce the dimensionality caused by all terms to a significantly smaller dimensionality that is an approximation of the original $X$:

$$X = U \cdot SV \cdot V'$$

where $u_1 \ldots u_k$ and $v^1 \ldots v^k$ are left and right singular vectors and $sv_1 \ldots sv_k$ are singular values. A threshold is used against the full SV diagonal matrix to determine the cutoff on values to be used for query and document representation (i.e., the dimensionality reduction). Hofmann has modified the standard LSI approach using additional formalism via Probabilistic Latent Semantic Analysis (Hofmann-99). Chapter 4 will relate this specifically to informational retrieval indexing with examples.

It is instructive to show how to calculate the different matrices. An example of how to calculate the three matrices follows (an online calculator for SVD is available at http://www.bluebit.gr/matrix-calculator/):

Perform Single Value Decomposition on the given matrix A such that $A = USV^T$

$$A = \begin{bmatrix} 1 & 1 & 1 \\ 0 & 1 & 1 \\ 1 & 0 & 0 \\ 0 & 1 & 0 \\ 1 & 0 & 0 \\ 1 & 0 & 1 \\ 1 & 1 & 1 \\ 1 & 1 & 1 \\ 1 & 0 & 1 \\ 0 & 2 & 0 \\ 0 & 1 & 1 \end{bmatrix}$$

**Step 1:** Calculate $A^TA$.

$$A^TA = \begin{bmatrix} 1 & 0 & 1 & 0 & 1 & 1 & 1 & 1 & 1 & 0 & 0 \\ 1 & 1 & 0 & 1 & 0 & 0 & 1 & 1 & 0 & 2 & 1 \\ 1 & 1 & 0 & 0 & 0 & 1 & 1 & 1 & 1 & 0 & 1 \end{bmatrix} \times \begin{bmatrix} 1 & 1 & 1 \\ 0 & 1 & 1 \\ 1 & 0 & 0 \\ 0 & 1 & 0 \\ 1 & 0 & 0 \\ 1 & 0 & 1 \\ 1 & 1 & 1 \\ 1 & 1 & 1 \\ 1 & 0 & 1 \\ 0 & 2 & 0 \\ 0 & 1 & 1 \end{bmatrix}$$

$$= \begin{bmatrix} 7 & 3 & 5 \\ 3 & 10 & 5 \\ 5 & 5 & 7 \end{bmatrix}$$

**Step 2:** Find the determinant such that $|A^TA - CI| = 0$—where I is the identity matrix and C is a scalar—to obtain the *Eigenvalues* and *singular values* which will be used to construct the S matrix.

$$A^TA - CI = \begin{bmatrix} 7 & 3 & 5 \\ 3 & 10 & 5 \\ 5 & 5 & 7 \end{bmatrix} - \left( C * \begin{bmatrix} 1 & 0 & 0 \\ 0 & 1 & 0 \\ 0 & 0 & 1 \end{bmatrix} \right)$$

$$= \begin{bmatrix} 7-c & 3 & 5 \\ 3 & 10-c & 5 \\ 5 & 5 & 7-c \end{bmatrix}$$

$$|A^TA - CI| = (7-c)\left[(10-c)(7-c) - (5*5)\right] - 3\left[3(7-c) - (5*5)\right]$$
$$+ 5\left[(3*5) - 5(10-c)\right]$$
$$= (7-c)(70 - 10c - 7c + c^2 - 25) - 3(21 - 3c - 25)$$
$$+ 5(15 - 50 + 5c)$$
$$= (7-c)(c^2 - 17c + 45) - 3(-3c - 4) + 5(5c - 35)$$
$$= 7c^2 - 119c + 315 - c^3 + 17c^2 - 45c + 9c + 12 + 25c - 175$$
$$= -c^3 + 24c^2 - 130c + 152 = 0$$

$$\left. \begin{array}{l} c_1 = 16.801 \\ c_2 = 5.577 \\ c_3 = 1.622 \end{array} \right\} \text{Eigenvalues}$$

$$|c_1| > |c_2| > |c_3|$$

The singular values would be:

$$s_1 = \sqrt{16.801} = 4.0989$$
$$s_2 = \sqrt{5.577} = 2.3616$$
$$s_3 = \sqrt{1.622} = 1.2736$$

$$S = \begin{bmatrix} s_1 & 0 & 0 \\ 0 & s_2 & 0 \\ 0 & 0 & s_3 \end{bmatrix} = \begin{bmatrix} 4.0989 & 0 & 0 \\ 0 & 2.3616 & 0 \\ 0 & 0 & 1.2736 \end{bmatrix}$$

$$S^{-1} = \begin{bmatrix} 0.244 & 0 & 0 \\ 0 & 0.4234 & 0 \\ 0 & 0 & 0.7852 \end{bmatrix}$$

**Step 3:** Compute the *Eigenvectors* by evaluating $(A^TA - c_iI) X_1 = 0$—where $c_i$ corresponds to each of the Eigenvalues that were computed in the previous step.

*Calculating the Eigenvector for the Eigenvalue $c_1 = 16.801$*

$$A^TA - c_1I = \begin{bmatrix} 7 - 16.801 & 3 & 5 \\ 3 & 10 - 16.801 & 5 \\ 5 & 5 & 7 - 16.801 \end{bmatrix}$$
$$= \begin{bmatrix} -9.801 & 3 & 5 \\ 3 & -6.801 & 5 \\ 5 & 5 & -9.801 \end{bmatrix}$$

$$(A^TA - c_1I)X_1 = \begin{bmatrix} -9.801 & 3 & 5 \\ 3 & -6.801 & 5 \\ 5 & 5 & -9.801 \end{bmatrix} \times \begin{bmatrix} x_1 \\ x_2 \\ x_3 \end{bmatrix} = \begin{bmatrix} 0 \\ 0 \\ 0 \end{bmatrix}$$

$$-9.801x_1 + 3x_2 + 5x_3 = 0 \qquad (1)$$

$$3x_1 - 6.801x_2 + 5x_3 = 0 \qquad (2)$$

$$5x_1 + 5x_2 - 9.801x_3 = 0 \qquad (3)$$

By subtracting Eq. (2) from Eq. (1) we get:

$$-12.801x_1 + 9.801x_2 = 0 \rightarrow x_1 = (-9.801/-12.801) x_2 \rightarrow x_1 = 0.7656\, x_2$$

| $x_1$ | $-1$ |
|---|---|
| $x_2$ | $-1.3061$ |
| $x_3$ | $-1.1765$ |

The Eigenvector for $c_1 = \begin{bmatrix} -1 \\ -1.3061 \\ -1.1765 \end{bmatrix}$

Normalize the vector by the length

$$L = \sqrt{(-1)^2 + (-1.3061)^2 + (-1.1765)^2} = \sqrt{4.0901} = 2.0224$$

The normalized Eigenvector for $c_1 = \begin{bmatrix} -0.4945 \\ -0.6458 \\ -0.5817 \end{bmatrix}$

*Using similar approach for calculating the Eigenvector for the Eigenvalue $c_2 = 5.577$ you get*

The Eigenvector for $c_2 = \begin{bmatrix} 1 \\ -1.1083 \\ 0.3805 \end{bmatrix}$

Normalize the vector by the length

$$L = \sqrt{(1)^2 + (-1.1083)^2 + (0.3805)^2} = \sqrt{2.3731} = 1.5405$$

The normalized Eigenvector for $c_2 = \begin{bmatrix} 0.6491 \\ -0.7194 \\ 0.247 \end{bmatrix}$

And *calculating the Eigenvector for the Eigenvalue $c_3 = 1.622$*

The Eigenvector for $c_3 = \begin{bmatrix} -1 \\ -0.4422 \\ 1.3408 \end{bmatrix}$

Normalize the vector by the length

$$L = \sqrt{(-1)^2 + (-0.4422)^2 + (1.3408)^2} = \sqrt{2.9932} = 1.7301$$

The normalized Eigenvector for $c_3 = \begin{bmatrix} -0.5780 \\ -0.2556 \\ 0.775 \end{bmatrix}$

**Step 4:** Construct the V matrix by using the calculated Eigenvactors as columns in V.

$$V^T = \begin{bmatrix} 0.4945 & 0.6491 & 0.5780 \\ 0.6458 & -0.7194 & 0.2556 \\ -0.5817 & -0.247 & 0.775 \end{bmatrix}$$

**Step 5:** Calculate the U matrix such that $U = AVS^{-1}$.

$$U = \begin{bmatrix} 1 & 1 & 1 \\ 0 & 1 & 1 \\ 1 & 0 & 0 \\ 0 & 1 & 0 \\ 1 & 0 & 0 \\ 1 & 0 & 1 \\ 1 & 1 & 1 \\ 1 & 1 & 1 \\ 1 & 0 & 1 \\ 0 & 2 & 0 \\ 0 & 1 & 1 \end{bmatrix} \times \begin{bmatrix} -0.4945 & 0.6491 & -0.5780 \\ -0.6458 & -0.7194 & -0.2556 \\ -0.5817 & 0.247 & 0.775 \end{bmatrix}$$

$$\times \begin{bmatrix} 0.244 & 0 & 0 \\ 0 & 0.4234 & 0 \\ 0 & 0 & 0.7852 \end{bmatrix}$$

$$U = \begin{bmatrix} 0.4202 & 0.0748 & -0.0461 \\ 0.2995 & -0.2 & 0.4078 \\ 0.1207 & 0.2748 & -0.4539 \\ 0.1576 & -0.3046 & -0.2007 \\ 0.1207 & 0.2748 & -0.4539 \\ 0.2626 & 0.3794 & 0.1546 \\ 0.4202 & 0.0748 & -0.0461 \\ 0.4202 & 0.0748 & -0.0461 \\ 0.2626 & 0.3794 & 0.1546 \\ 0.3152 & -0.6092 & -0.4014 \\ 0.2995 & -0.2 & 0.4078 \end{bmatrix}$$

## 2.2.5 Hidden Markov Models

Hidden Markov Models (HMM) have been applied for the last 20 years to solving problems in speech recognition and to a lesser extent in the areas locating named entities (Bikel-97), optical character recognition (Bazzi-98) and topic identification (Kubala-97). More recently HMMs have been applied more generally to information retrieval search with good results. One of the first comprehensive and practical descriptions of Hidden Markov Models was written by Dr. Lawrence Rabiner (Rabiner-89).

A HMM can best be understood by first defining a discrete Markov process. The easiest way to understand it is by an example. Let's take the example of a three state Markov Model of the Stock Market. The states will be one of the following that is observed at the closing of the market:

State 1 (S1): market decreased
State 2 (S2): market did not change
State 3 (S3): market increased in value

The movement between states can be defined by a state transition matrix with state transitions (this assumes you can go from any state to any other state):

$$A = \{a_{I,i}\} = \begin{matrix} 0.5 & 0.3 & 0.4 \\ 0.1 & 0.6 & 0.3 \\ 0.6 & 0.7 & 0.5 \end{matrix}$$

Given that the market fell on one day (State 1), the matrix suggests that the probability of the market not changing the next day is 0.1. This then allows questions such as the probability that the market will increase for the next 4 days then fall. This would be equivalent to the sequence of SEQ = {S3, S3, S3, S3, S1}. In order to simplify our model, lets assume that instead of the current state being dependent upon all the previous states, lets assume it is only dependent upon the last state (discrete, first order, Markov chain.) This would then be calculated by the formula:

$$
\begin{aligned}
P(SEQ) &= P[S3, S3, S3, S3, S1] \\
&= P[S3] * P[S3/S3] * P[S3/S3] * P[S3/S3] * P[S1/S3] \\
&= S3(init) * a_{3,3} * a_{3,3} * a_{3,3} * a_{1,3} \\
&= (1.0) * (.5) * (.5) * (.5) * (.4) \\
&= .05
\end{aligned}
$$

In the equation we also assume the probability of the initial state of S3 is S3(init) = 1. The Fig. 2.13 depicts the model. The directed lines indicate the state transition probabilities $a_{i,j}$. There is also an implicit loop from every state back to itself. In the example every state corresponded to an observable event (change in the market).

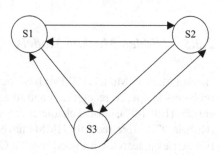

**Fig. 2.13** Diagram of
Markov model

When trying to apply this model to less precise world problems such as in speech recognition, this model was too restrictive to be applicable. To add more flexibility a probability function was allowed to be associated with the state. The result is called the Hidden Markov Model. It gets its name from the fact that there are two stochastic processes with the underlying stochastic process not being observable (hidden), but can only be analyzed by observations which originate from another stochastic process. Thus the system will have as input a series of results, but it will not know the number of states that were associated with generating the results nor the probability of the states. So part of the HMM process is in determining which model of states best explains the results that are being observed.

A more formal definition of a discrete Hidden Markov Model is summarized by consists of the following:

1. $S = \{s_0, \ldots, s_{n-1}\}$ as a finite set of states where $s_0$ always denotes the initial state. Typically the states are interconnected such that any state can be reached from any other state.
2. $V = \{v_0, \ldots, v_{m-1}\}$ is a finite set of output symbols. This will correspond to the physical output from the system being modeled.
3. $A = S \times S$ a transition probability matrix where $a_{i,j}$ represents the probability of transitioning from state i to state j such that $\sum_{j=0}^{n-1} a_{i,j} = 1$ for all $i = 0, \ldots, n-1$. Every value in the matrix is a positive value between 0 and 1. For the case where every state can be reached from every other state every value in the matrix will be non-zero.
4. $B = S \times V$ is an output probability matrix where element $b_{j,k}$ is a function determining the probability and $\sum_{k=0}^{m-1} b_{j,k} = 1$ for all $j = 0, \ldots, n-1$.
5. The initial state distribution.

The HMM will generate an output symbol at every state transition. The transition probability is the probability of the next state given the current state. The output probability is the probability that a given output is generated upon arriving at the next state.

Given the HMM definition, it can be used as both a generator of possible sequences of outputs and their probabilities (as shown in example above), or given a particular out sequence it can model its generation by an appropriate HMM model. The complete specification of a HMM requires specification of the states, the output symbols and three probability measures for the state transitions, output probability functions and the initial states. The distributions are frequently called A, B, and $\pi$, and the following notation is used to define the model:

$$\lambda = (A, B, \pi).$$

One of the primary problems associated with HMM is how to efficiently calculate the probability of a sequence of observed outputs given the HMM model. This can best be looked at as how to score a particular model given a series of outputs. Or another way to approach it is how to determine which of a number of competing models should be selected given an observed set of outputs. This is in effect uncovering the hidden part of the model. They typical approach is to apply an "optimality criterion" to select the states. But there are many such algorithms to choose from. Once you have selected the model that you expect corresponds to the output, then there is the issue of determining which set of state sequences best explains the output. The final issue is how best to tune the $\lambda$ model to maximize the probability of the output sequence given $\lambda$. This is called the training sequence and is crucial to allow the models to adapt to the particular problem being solved. More details can be found in Rabiner's paper (Rabiner-89).

### 2.2.6   Neural Networks

An artificial neural network is based upon biological neural networks and is generally simplified to a directed multilevel network of that uses weighted additive values coupled with non-linear transfer functions and a final output layer. One of the first neural networks created was the Perceptron network created by Frank Rosenblatt in 1958. It had an analogy to how the visual system works. Thus, the first input layer was called the "retina" that distributed inputs to the second layer composed of association units that combined the inputs with weights and triggered a step function that would send the results to the final output layer. The output layer would do the final combination of the inputs and output the results. This model was a simple approximation of the neurons in the human system. But the use of a step function, where a functions value increases in steps versus is continuous and each step would be a different category, made the mathematics very difficult to allow the system to train itself based upon inputs. By 1969 the problems with this model were documented by papers by Marvin Minsky and Seymore Papert. The mathematical approach was revived in 1986 by Rumelhart, Hinton and Williames when they expanded the concept to include a multilayer model that used nonlinear transfer functions in lieu of the step functions.

There are many different types and approaches to neural networks. One of the more common approaches continues with the Perceptron multilayer network which is presented below. The simplest network is a three layer feed forward network that has an input layer, middle layer (often called hidden layer) and an output layer. Figure 2.14 shows the network. In the Input Function (IF), normalizes the

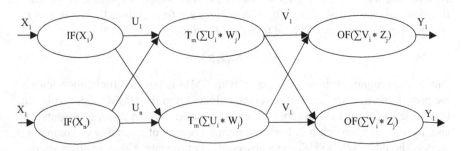

**Fig. 2.14** Neural network

input values by subtracting the median and dividing by the interquartile range and presents the resultant value $U_i$ to the middle layer. The interquartile range (IQR) is a measure of the variability of the distribution and is less sensitive to errors, being equal to the difference between the third and first quartiles. If you divide the sorted list into four parts, the quartiles are the three values from the list that separate each section—the median is the second quartile. Every value goes to very function in the middle layer. Each value is multiplied by a weight W and then summed creating a new vaue that then has the transfer function T applied to it producing the output $V_i$. The V values are then multiplied by a weight Z and summed. The summed value has the Output Transfer function (OF) applied to it producing the final output from the network, Y. This is a feed forward network because none of the values are fed back to previous layers. All neural networks have an Input and Output layer. The number of middle layers can vary. But in general only one middle layer is needed for most problems.

Training is a critical aspect of a neural network. In the training process a set of known data is used that the ideal outputs $(Y_i)$ are known. In the training process the objective is to modify the weight values (W and Z) to match the output as closely as possible. This leads to some of the problems that have to be monitored in the training process. Additional middle layers may help improve the results although as noted above usually one or two middle layers are sufficient. It may be useful to not feed all of the outputs from one layer into all of the nodes at the next layer (the number of nodes at one layer can be different than the previous layer—in the above example they appear to be the same). The biggest issue is to be careful that the solution is not a local maximum versus a more general global maximum that will apply as new inputs are processed causing over fitting of the solution.

Selecting the number of nodes (neurons) at each layer is very complex. If too few are selected it will be difficult to model complex problems. If too many are selected the computation time increases expontentially and the result can more likely be overfitted to the training data. For this reason two sets of test data are used. The first for the training and the second to validate that the system has not been overfitted to just the original data set.

Trying to find the optimum weights is also a very difficult problem. There can be hundreds of weights that need to be estimated. But the estimation is not linear to produce the desired outputs. In the process of finding the weights there will be many cases of local minima and maxima that need to be avoided. To avoid local minima the easiest technique is to try a number of random starting points in the estimation and choose the one that works best. A more sophisticated technique uses widely separated random values and then gradually reduces the widely separated to closer values to produce the weight. By starting with widely varying values the system is more likely to avoid a particular minima that drives to a local solution.

In a typical training scenario Backward propagation is used. The current set of weights will produce a set of outputs. These outputs are then used with the known expected outputs to calculate the error difference. The errors are then averaged across the outputs and then is propagated back through the network in reverse direction where the adjustments to the weights are made to minimize the error.

## 2.2.7 *Support Vector Machines*

Support Vector Machines (SVM) is recently becoming the technical base for learning systems. SVMs are a type of machine learning algorithms used to classify items. A Support Vector Machine (SVM) assigns an item to a category by constructing an *N*-dimensional hyperplane that optimally separates the data into two categories. The SVM approach maps the set of attributes that make up the vector representing an item into a set of features. The features are then used to determine the hyperplane that distinguishes between the two categories an item could go into. One of the challenges is to find an optimal feature representation. The goal of SVM is to find the optimal hyperplane that separates clusters of vector in such a way that items with one category of the target variable are on one side of the plane and items with the other category are on the other side of the plane. The vectors near the hyperplane are the *support vectors*. The optimal hyperplane will have the maximum distance from the support vectors of each category to the plane that classifies them. This will reduce the errors in miss classifying a new item.

To understand the SVM process lets take a simple two dimensional example. Let's assume we have a number of items that are discussing biology and Physics. Let's assume that we have one feature on the X axis and another feature on the Y axis. Figure 2.15a, b shows the graphical layout of each category with circles being Biology and squares being Physics. The SVM process tries to determine a 1-dimensional hyperplane (i.e., a line) that maximally separates the two groups of items. This is sometimes referred to as maximizing the "fatness" and gives the best classification since it has the maximum difference to help in determining which class an items is assigned to. The diagram shows two options—one being a vertical line and the other a line at an angle. It's obvious by observation that the hyperplane

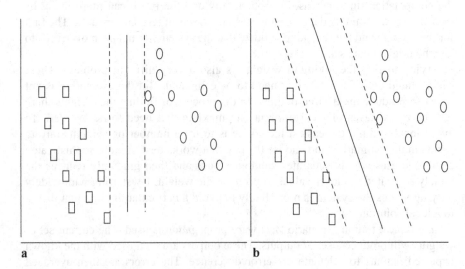

a                                                    b

**Fig. 2.15  a** Vertical separator. **b** Optimal separator

for the diagonal line is better in that it has the maximum distance between items in each group and the hyperplane. The dashed lines in each figure are showing the specific items (support vectors) from each group that are closest to the hyperplane. The distance between the dashed lines is called the margin and the goal is to find the hyperplane that maximizes the margin. The specific items that are closest to the dashed lines are called the support vectors because they drive the size of the margin. Even though they appear as points in the diagram they are called support vectors because each point defines a vector from the original to that point. As the hyperplane changes, the support vectors (items) that drive the margin change. The Support Vector Machine finds the hyperplane that has support vectors that maximize the margin.

In the example we took the simplest case of a two dimension set of items. This can easily expand to a multidimensional case with a multidimensional hyperplane. The more complex case is when the items are not separated by a plane but some sort of non-linear region (e.g. a curved line). In this case SVM uses a kernel function that maps the items into a different space where they can now be separated by a hyperplane. In some cases additional dimensionality needs to be added in the kernel mapping process. SVM models can be related to neural networks. A SVM model using a sigmoid kernel function is equivalent to a two-layer, perceptron neural network.

In addition to the use of mapping to higher dimensionality for the non-linear problem, the real world problem of trying to categorize items based upon text is never statistically pure. There will always be exceptions that come from the variances of language. This is referred to as problems due to the high dimensionality (i.e., lots of unique processing tokens) of text categorization. The approach to solving this is called soft margin classification. In this case instead of trying to raise the dimensionality to account for the data points that are categorized in the wrong category, we ignore them. The way to handle them is to introduce slack variables and by adjusting them minimize the impact by moving those points. The goal is to tradeoff moving points to fit within the current "fat".

## 2.3  Summary

Data structures provide the implementation basis of search techniques in Information Retrieval Systems. They may be searching the text directly, as in use of signature and possibly PAT trees, or providing the structure to hold the searchable data structure created by processing the text in items. The most important data structure to understand is the inverted file system. It has the greatest applicability in information systems. The use of n-grams has also found successes in a limited number of commercial systems. Even though n-grams have demonstrated successes in finding information, it is not a structure that lends itself to representing the concepts in an item. There is no association of an n-gram with a semantic unit (e.g., a word or word stem). Judging the relative importance (ranking) of items is much harder to accomplish under this data structure and the algorithmic options are very limited.

PAT and Signature data file structures have found successful implementations in certain bounded search domains. Both of these techniques encounter significant problems in handling very large databases of textual items. The Hypertext data structure is the newest structure to be considered from an Information Retrieval System perspective. It certainly can be mathematically mapped to linked lists and networks. But the model of how dependencies between items as hyperlinks are resolved is just being considered. The future high usage of this structure in information systems makes its understanding important in finding relevant information on the Internet. Marchionini and Shneiderman believe that hypertext will be used in conjunction with full text search tools (Marchionini-88).

Information retrieval algorithms from basic indexing to learning algorithms for categorization are based upon a number of mathematical models. A general understanding of the models and how they apply to information retrieval provide a foundation for develop of new algorithms. Baysean conditional probabilities, Shannon's Information theory and Latent Semantic Indexing are useful in different approaches to defining the ranked index for items. Hidden Marjkov Models can be used for indices but have greater application in multimedia indexing. Neural networks and Support vector Machines provide a foundation for categorization algorithms and learning how to filter items based upon training examples provided by the users.

## 2.4 Exercises

1. Describe the similarities and differences between term stemming algorithms and n-grams. Describe how they affect precision and recall.
2. a. Compare advantages and disadvantages of Porter Stemming algorithm, Dictionary stemming algorithm and Success Variety stemming algorithm.
   b. Create the symbol tree for the following words (bag, barn, boss, bot any, box, bottle, botch and both). Using successor variety and the Peak and Plateau algorithm, determine if there are any stems for the above set of words.
   c. If there are stems created explain if they make any sense as a stem and why.
3. a. Create the PATRICIA Tree and Reduced PATRICIA for the following binary input. Take it to 9 levels of sistrings: 011100111001111111010
   b. Given the query 111000 show how it would be executed against each tree with the number of decisions.
4. Assuming a term is on the average 6 characters long, calculate the size of the inversion lists for each of the sources in Table 1.1, Distribution of words in TREC Database. Assume that 30% of the words in any item are unique. What is the impact on the calculation if the system has to provide proximity versus no proximity. Assume 4 bytes is needed for the unique number assigned to each item.
5. Describe how a bigram data structure would be used to search for the search term "computer science" (NOTE: the search term is a contiguous word phrase). What are the possible sources of errors that could cause non-relevant items to be retrieved?

6. Perform Single value decomposition on the following matrix:

$$A = \begin{vmatrix} 1 & 3 & 1 \\ 1 & 0 & 2 \\ 0 & 2 & 3 \\ 1 & 2 & 1 \\ 2 & 1 & 1 \\ 0 & 1 & 3 \end{vmatrix}$$

# Chapter 3
# Ingest

## 3.1   Introduction to Ingest

Ingest is the initial process in an information retrieval systems. It is the process that receives the items to be stored and indexed in the system and performs the initial processing of them. The ingest process can be broken down into a number of subprocesses. Each of the subprocesses can add value to the final index and improve the capability of the system to get better results. The ingest subprocess gets the items to be ingested into the system. This process can be either a "pull" or a "catch". A pull process has the system going out to other locations and retrieving items from those locations to ingest (e.g., web/local network crawling or RSS feeds). Catching is where other systems deliver the items by sending them to the ingest process. This is part of an application dependent interface between systems. This typically means that one internal system writes files into an ingest directory or uses the "web services" application interface of the ingest process to deliver new items. Once the item is received it goes through a normalization process for processing purposes. The original item is usually kept as part of the document repository to ensure no information is lost in the normalization process. One of the first checks in many systems is to validate if this item has already been ingested into their system. This is a very common check when crawling the Internet or/and internal network. Copies of items are often distributed across many locations and duplicate detection can save a lot of redundant processing. Next the item is processed to determine what will be indexed in the item. This process is referred to as generation of processing tokens. In addition some normalization can be done on the processing tokens to map them into a canonical value—called entity identification. The result of these steps is the data that is ready to be passed to the Indexing process. One final process called Categorization can also be applied to expand the processing tokens for an item.

G. Kowalski, *Information Retrieval Architecture and Algorithms,*
DOI 10.1007/978-1-4419-7716-8_3, © Springer Science+Business Media, LLC 2011

## 3.2    Item Receipt

Item receipt is the process associated with first getting items into the system. The major way items are received for processing is by the system actively going across the network it has access to read items called "pulling" items. The best example of pulling is crawling the Internet or a local network or getting items from an RSS feed. The following describes the crawling process on the Internet or a local network. Crawling a network has to start with a list of addresses that can be used as a starting point for the crawling. This is called the "seed list" and defines the maximum subset of the network from which items can be part of the information system. The maximum subset is not limited to the seed list but includes all of the other locations that are linked to from the items found from the initial seed. Each item (e.g., web page) pointed to by the seed list is retrieved from its web site to be indexed. When the page is retrieved to be indexed, all the links (i.e., Universal Resource Locators—URLs) on that page that link to other pages on that site or a different site are extracted and added to the list of crawlable locations. The data structure used to store the new URLs to be crawled is called the URL Frontier. As pages are crawled from the URL frontier they are marked as crawled along with a date time of crawl. The list of all items to retrieve is continually growing. At some point you will have a list of all possible items and all those items will only point back to items already on the list. The set of all URLs in the original seed list along with those added to the URL Frontier is the maximum subset of the network that is indexed based upon the initial seed list. The term "black web" is used to describe that subset of the Internet that is not retrieved and indexed. A study by Lawrence and Giles (Lawrence and Giles-2000) showed that no search engine indexes more than 16% of the Web. The same can be true when crawling an internal network.

The two major approaches to crawling a network is breath first or depth first. Depth first says you select pages from the URL Frontier following pages to the same site to retrieve as much of the site as you can. Breath first says you significantly limit the number of pages retrieved from a site, going on to other sites that you have not retrieved—thus giving you a better sample of many sites versus in depth of a fewer number of sites. Depth first has the possible negative aspect of hitting the same site often in a limited interval which could cause the site administrator to lock your crawler out. This is called "politeness" of crawling and the general rule is to have at least two seconds before the system retrieves another page from a site. The software that takes the URLs from the Seed list or URL Frontier and retrieves the linked page is called a web crawler, spider or robot. The software must be scalable allowing for many crawlers to work concurrently. They also have to communicate in that you do not want multiple crawlers crawling the same page. There also is required a structure that quickly identifies if a URL on a retrieved page is already on the URL Frontier so that it is not redundantly added. Design and optimization of the crawlers and the URL Frontier is one of the first challenges in a retrieval system. Web sites can contain a file caller "Robot.txt" that defines what if any of the web site the crawler is allowed to retrieve pages from.

One technique frequently used on the internet that makes some sites appear to be infinite is their generation of dynamic pages with dynamically generated URLs. Instead of having a priori statically defined pages stored that are retrieved by a URL, many web sites dynamically generate the page when it is requested. This allows for providing the most recent information requested and can save on storage of static web pages. But when these dynamic pages are created they can also create slightly different URLs to the page references on the dynamic page retrieved. Even though it's the same pages that were retrieved last time that page was retrieved, to the system it will appear as new URLs. Many crawlers will not index dynamic pages for this reason.

One issue associated with crawling a site is that the crawler cannot retrieve from the same web site too frequently or it will alert a system administrator who could block that crawler from future access to its site. A system design decision is how often to retrieve web pages that have already been crawled to get latest information. For a current event news site it might be multiple times a day where the seed home page changes with the latest information. This decision is usually based upon how often a web site is updated where the more often a web sites changes the more frequent the recrawl occurs. How deep you go on a web site or if it is better to have some data across lots of sites or go in depth on a site reflect the design and goal of an information retrieval System. There is also a question if the pages can be stored in the document repository or just links to the pages on the Web because of copyright protection. Commercial systems such as Google will in most cases only visit the same pages on a site to see if they have changed once every 30 days. But some sites that have daily frequent changes (e.g., news sites) they will revisit many times a day to get the latest information. In many cases permission is requested ahead of time for frequent crawling of a site since it may be of value to the site to have the most recent information on the site indexed.

Another challenge to crawling the Internet is the amount of data that is kept in databases at web sites. When a user accesses the site, the database is used as a source of information to be placed on dynamically generated web page. Static web pages are pages that have been preconstructed and are resident on a web site. The databases that are used to dynamically create web pages are often referred to as the hidden web. The "hidden web" is estimated to be 500 times larger than the visible "static" web. There are two ways of indexing information in the hidden web. The first is there is an agreement with the site and that site will dynamically generate most of the database into pages to be indexed. For example Amazon.com could expand its content with specific commercial search engines to index the products on its web site using a database to generate the pages for a crawler. The other way is by employing a subsystem that is focused on crawling hidden web sites. Bright Planet is an example of a system that focuses on this issue. In this case the software knows the structure of the search page on the web site and will have a number of terms that it is interested in. By entering the terms and then following the hits it is in effect navigating a subset of the database hidden at the site.

Another pulling process for getting items is by subscribing to an RSS feeds. RSS stands for either Really Simple Syndication or Rich Site Summary. An RSS feeds include a specifications on how a web site can publish information to a user. Publishes means that the user "subscribes" to the RSS feed and when requested by an RSS client, the RSS feed will deliver a document in XML format that contains the information that is available at the RSS site. RSS is an Internet (or internal network) feed used to publish frequently updated works such as blog entries, news headlines, audio, and video in a standardized format. The RSS document includes the item plus metadata such as dates and authorship. The RSS client then can determine which items from the RSS site to download and which ones it has already retrieved. The RSS is designed to help the publisher get their new information quickly out to a large group of users who are interested in it. From the user's perspective they do not have to constantly be manually checking for new information but will periodically (user defines how often to check) get the all the new information as it is published by the RSS feed.

RSS feeds are read using software called an RSS reader or an aggregator. The RSS reader or aggregator reduces the time and effort needed to manually check websites for updates. Once subscribed to a feed, an aggregator is able to check for new content at user-determined intervals and retrieve the update. The content is sometimes described as being pulled to the user. A standardized XML file format allows the user application to easily ingest the downloaded information the user subscribes to a feed by entering the feed's link into the reader (aggregator) The RSS reader checks the user's subscribed feeds regularly for new items, downloads any updates that it finds. An example of the XML is:

```xml
<?xml version="1.0"?>
<rss version="2.0">
  <channel>
    <title>Flood News</title>
    <link>http://weather.nasa.gov/</link>
    <description>Flood hits US.</description>
    <language>en-us</language>
    <pubDate>Tue, 10 Jun 2009 07:00:00 GMT</pubDate>
    <lastBuildDate>Tue, 10 Jun 2009 11:41:01 GMT</lastBuildDate>
    <docs>http://blogs.weather.harvard.edu/tech/rss</docs>
    <generator>Weblog Editor 2.0</generator>
    <managingEditor>editor@example.com</managingEditor>
    <webMaster>webmaster@example.com</webMaster>
    <ttl>5</ttl>

    <item>
      <title>Washington Flood</title>
      <link>http://weather.nasa.gov/news/2009/news-washington.asp</link>
      <description>The flood destroyed most of washington except the
      monuments.</description>
      <pubDate>Tue, 03 Jun 2009 09:39:21 GMT</pubDate>
      <guid>http://weather.nasa.gov/2009/06/03.html#item573</guid>
    </item>
```

```
<item>
    <title>Flood hits Baltimore</title>
    <link>http://weather.nasa.gov/</link>
    <description>In addition to Washington the flood hit Baltimore.
    </description>
    <pubDate>Fri, 30 May 2009 11:06:42 GMT</pubDate>
    <guid>http://weather.nasa.gov/2003/05/30.html#item572</guid>
</item>
</channel>
</rss>
```

The XML lends itself to extracting the citation metadata as well as identifying the main text of the item to process.

The "catch" process is usually associated with internal systems. Within the internal generation of new information there is a step where new items are written to a queue that is monitored by the indexing process. In this case there is no crawling but more a push of information to the indexer who then only needs to process the item it has received.

So how does the architecture and decisions on crawling effect how well an information retrieval system performs. The value of an information retrieval system is limited by the information in the system and its interest to the users. The crawler is designed to retrieve and update a collection of pages that defines what a user can find. The retrieved database needs to balance completeness and currency. These two goals compete, because when a crawler completes processing its current page, the crawler must decide between downloading a new page, not currently indexed, or refreshing a page that is probably outdated in the index. There is a trade-off between quantity (more objects) and quality (more up-to-date objects). The same is true of RSS feeds in determining how many feeds and if you filter what comes in on the feed.

The first decision that affects an information retrieval systems performance in terms of precision and recall is what data will be ingested and indexed. The more focused on likely items of potential interest the ingest can be, the higher the performance. Information retrieval Systems that focus what they retrieve to a specific area are called "vertical" index systems. Decisions on constraining what is collected and filtering out items that have a low chance of being of value before you start the processing of the item can make improvements in the overall system performance from a user's perspective.

## 3.3   Duplicate Detection

As items are received to be processed for an Information retrieval system, the first process that can make search and retrieval more effective is to eliminate duplicate information. Some estimates are as high as 30% of the Internet is duplicate information. For example, whenever there are multiple different sources feeding the input to a system there is a strong possibility that duplicate information will come from the feeds. It's easy to see the duplicate information on the internet. For example stories from news agencies like Reuters usually appear as copies or near-copies in hundreds of newspapers on the Internet. If you are crawling those web sites or receiving the different news sources via RSS feeds you will be getting a large number of duplicate items. Even in private networks there are a lot of times a copy of an item will be made on many different locations because of sharing of information between users. The duplicates cause a lot of wasted system overhead in indexing the same item. But more importantly when you run a search you will get multiple hits displaying exactly the same data wasting entries in your hit list and the time for the user to look at the item and discover it is a duplicate of what they have seen before (Chowdhury et al.-2002, Cho et al.-1999, Grossman and Frieder-2004).

The process of detecting a duplicate at first seems straight forward. The standard approach is to create a signature unique key that represents the contents of an item. The most common methodology is to create a hash for the complete file (e.g., Message Digital Algorithm 2—MD2 or MD5). These hashes have the characteristics most desired for hashing items of variable lengths, they have low probability of collisions (two different items creating the same hash number), they are fast to compute and can work on variable length documents. The problem with this approach is it is a hash on every character in the item. If there is just a few characters different (e.g., a copy is made of an article but a system assigns a unique ID it places on the article or it places a current date on the article) you will get two different hash values and not detect it as a duplicate. When a new item is received, the system can determine if there already exists a previous copy by seeing if there exists a signature is already stored. This works best when a complete copy of a file is saved by another user such as copies of multimedia files. But if a user copies the content of an item and places it in a new web page, then there can be minor differences in the header information that would cause a different signature value and make it appear as if it's not a duplicate. It could be something as simple as the current date is dynamically added to the top of the item. This is also why use of dynamic HTML, where small modifications can easily be merged with the substantive data, can make it difficult for a crawler to know if a page has really been changed.

This problem can be addressed by heuristic algorithms that try to detect when the substantive text begins and the header information ends. It is at that point that the text is used to create the CRC. A similar issue can be with dynamic information at the end of an item. The generation and maintenance of the heuristic algorithms can be very expensive.

An automated algorithm is needed to work with the ingest system to look for items that are basically the same. This is called the "near duplicate detection" process. There are two ways of defining near duplicate. One is where the text in the two items is almost identical. The second is where the semantics of both items is identical but the text used to express the semantics is different. Although eliminating items that are semantically the same could significantly reduce the number of items that require indexing, the technology is not yet accurate enough to detect semantic equivalence. Thus the standard approach is to look for items that have a significant amount of text in common. The first question is when is one document a near duplicate of another. Pugh used a definition that "two documents are considered near duplicates if they have more than $r$ features in common." Conrad et al., avoided the more abstract features definition and said two documents are near duplicates if they share more than 80% terminology and their length difference is not more than +20% (Conrad and Schriber-2004). The larger portion of text that is a copy the more likely they are to be duplicates. This approach in duplication was proposed by Broder in 1997 using the concept of "resemblance" (Broder et al.-1997). He defined the resemblance between two documents as:

$$R(D_1, D_2) = \frac{(S(D_1) \text{ AND } S(D_2))}{(S(D_1) \text{ OR } S(D_2))}$$

The formula specifies that the resemblance is measured by ratio of the intersection of the features divided by the union of the features. So using terms as the feature then if two documents are both 50 words in length and there are 20 words that are common to both documents, the resemblance would be $(20)/(50 + 50 - 20) = 20/70$. Many attempts have been made to define a resemblance threshold that would find near duplicates. The "resemblance" formula is similar to the Jaccard similarity formula that is discussed in Chap. 5. The problems encountered when trying to use this approach have been with the determination of which features to use and if the algorithms are scalable to large collections of items.

The simplest definition would be based upon looking at items as "bags of words". If two items have almost all the same words they could be defined as near duplicates (see Conrad's definition above). Although a simpler process it introduces to many errors. The second approach is to break the items up into shorter segments and create signatures for each of the segments. The shorter segments are called "shingles". The idea there is if there are differences at the start or end of an item, the text in the rest of the items will be identical. A fixed number of words is defined for each segment and the segments partition the original item. The issue with this approach comes if the segments don't start on the same boundary. If one item is off by one word from the other, then all the segments will be off by one word. The signature codes will be different for each segment in each item. The only way this could work is if a logical semantic boundary is defined for the segments. For example if each sentence is selected as a segment, then once past the portions of each item that are different, the segments will be identical and the signatures will be identical. This technique would work but requires more sophisticated parsing to accurately define the segments and the process would vary by language. An alternative is to define each segment as a fixed number of words but overlap the segments to ensure the majority of them are in both items. This is similar to the N-Gram process defined in Chap. 2. But instead of using a fixed number of characters for the "n", a fixed number of words will be used. Thus if "n" is selected as 4 words, then the process would be the following: the first four words of the item would be the first signature, words 2–5 will be the second signature, words 3–7 will be the third signature and

**Fig. 3.1** Shingles and
signatures

Item 1: w1 w5 w3 w1 w7 w4 w5 w1 w6
Item 2: w7 w3 w1 w7 w4 w5 w1 w8 w6

Shingles item 1: w1 w5 w3 = 75, w5 w3 w1 = 22, w3 w1 w7 = 24
w1 w7 w4 = 82, w7 w4 w5 = 12, w4 w5 w1 = 33, w5 w1 w6 = 18

Shingles item 2: w7 w3 w1 = 77, w3 w1 w7 = 24, w1 w7 w4 = 82,
w7 w4 w5 = 12, w4 w5 w1 = 33, w5 w1 w8 = 99, w1 w8 w6 = 55

so on. Thus there will be as many signatures created as there are words in the item. This process is called "sliding window shingling". Some systems simplify this by eliminating any duplicate signatures created (i.e., where the same four words are found more than once in an item).

There will be a very large number of signatures in each item and it will take significant processing to compare the signatures between the current item and all the items so far ingested into the system. The process of creating signatures inherently will randomize the segments from an item since the signatures are inherently random numbers. By having an algorithm that selects a subset of the signatures that will be the same for each item will be selecting random subsets from each item. Since we are looking for near duplicates, the expectation is the random subset of segments should have significant overlap. Figure 3.1 shows how this process works using 3 word shingles.

If we then use a rule that we only compare the lowest 4 signatures from any items we would have from Item 1 signatures: 12, 18, 22 and 24 and for Item 2 it would be 12, 24, 33, and 55. Notice also that "12" comes from close to the end of the phase (w7 w4 w5) while 24 comes from the start (w3 w1 w7) which shows the random selection that comes even when you use a structured rule for selecting the subset of signatures to compare. Using Broder's formula for resemblance which is the number of signatures in common in the numerator and the total number of unique signatures in the denominator:

$$\text{Resemblance (Item1, Item2)} = \frac{2}{8-2} = \frac{2}{6}$$

This first technique to reduce the number of comparisons is taking the lowest "n" signatures for comparison. Other examples of rules for selection of the signatures could be all those that are divisible by "25". This was a rule first used by Broder in the Alta Vista search engine crawler where he also limited the number of shingles per document to 400. He was able to process 30 million web pages in 10 days using this technique. Another approach to reduce the magnitude of the comparison problem is to take the shingles created and create super shingles by combining a number of shingles into larger shingles. The biggest issue with this technique is that it will get poorer results for shorter item that do not have that many shingles to combine into bigger shingles.

To avoid the problem that comes from defining word segments, another approach is to use a similarity approach between documents as a measure if they are near duplicates. The advantage is that similarity measures are looking across all of the words in the document to determine those that add the most in defining the semantics of the document. Similarity of items is discussed in detail in Chaps. 5 and 6 on search and clustering respectively. The problem is that it's necessary to compare pairwise all existing items to the latest item received to detect if it is similar and thus may be a near duplicate. One approach around this issue is used by AURORIA that clusters items as they are received and thus all of the items in the same cluster may be near duplicates. But in all of the discussion of near duplicates, the process is errorful enough that in general systems do not use it to select items to not be processed and indexed. It is more used to help a user at search time.

## 3.4 Item Normalization

To start the indexing process the substantive text from the non-duplicate item must be extracted. Any of the data fielded that should be treated as metadata needs to be extracted and placed in the appropriate metadata field associated with that item. This could be the capture date and time that comes from the local computer time or structured fields in the HTML/XML such as Source or Title. All of the formatting and other HTML structure needs to be removed just leaving continuous text. In cases such as PDF files the text needs to be separated from the other objects.

As you retrieve items from multiple sources, it's possible that the encoding formats from different sources can vary. The first step in processing the items is to normalize the format to a standard format. This simplifies the processing of the item since all the items will have a standard encoding. For example there are many different encoding formats used for a language and you can have different languages that also have their own encoding. The first step in processing a textual item is to detect the language(s) that the item is in. In many cases the language and encoding will be part of the metadata (HTML/XML/etc.) that is at the start of an item. In some cases the item can be in multiple languages so language detection needs to be at a text segment level as well as the item level. You must know the language to perform the follow-on processing (e.g., morphological rules, stemming rules, dictionary look-up, etc. are all language dependent). Once determined, the language should be added as a metadata field using the ISO-639 standard for language identification. Once the language is determined the text can be put into UNICODE, then all of the different formats will be normalized to a single format. UNICODE is an industry standard that has over 100,000 characters and all major languages map to a subset to the Unicode characters. UTF-8 is the most common Unicode format used. It is a variable length format that uses one byte to represent ASCII characters and up to 4 bytes to represent the characters in other languages. UTF-16 may also be used but since HTML uses UTF-8 most applications use the UTF-8 encoding. There are convertors that convert between UTF-8 and UTF-16.

Once you have standardized the characters to a single format, then there is a next step some systems use called character normalization. The issue is that some characters can be used both syntactically and semantically associated with a word. For example, consider accented characters or the use of an apostrophe which could mean possessive or be part of a person's name. The character normalization process can disambiguate these cases making sure when the character is part of a semantic unit (person's name) it is kept but in other cases it can be eliminated in the next steps of normal processing. In other cases where there is both the unique character and a transliteration, both may be made available for search. For example finding documents containing *schoen* when searching for *schön*, diacritic removal finding documents containing *ç* when searching for *c or* ligature expansion finding documents containing *Æ* when searching for *ae*.

For multimedia objects you may also need to normalize to a standard format to make the development of algorithms more efficient. For example you may decide to use MPEG-2 OR MPEG-4 as your standard processing format for video and thus you would transcode the windows media, MPEG-1, FLASH or real media video into MPEG-2 before processing of it to create an index. Most multimedia search engines accept the major different formats for its modality.

## 3.5   Zoning and Creation of Processing Tokens

Once an item has been normalized and selected to be indexed, the next step in the process is to zone the document and identify processing tokens for indexing. The item is parsed into logical sub-divisions that have meaning to the user. This process, called "Zoning," is visible to the user and used to increase the precision of a search and optimize the display. A typical item is sub-divided into zones, which may overlap and can be hierarchical, such as Title, Author, Abstract, Main Text, Conclusion, and Bibliography. The term "Zone" was selected over field because of the variable length nature of the data identified and because it is a logical sub-division of the total item, whereas the term "fields" has a connotation of independence. There may be other source-specific zones such as "Country" and "Keyword." The zoning information is passed to the processing token identification operation to store the zone location information, allowing searches to be restricted to a specific zone. For example, if the user is interested in articles discussing "Einstein" then the search should not include the Bibliography, which could include references to articles written by "Einstein." Zoning differs for multi-media based upon the source structure. For a television news broadcast, zones may be defined as each news story in the input. For speeches or other programs, there could be different semantic boundaries that make sense from the user's perspective. For images the total image can be segmented into portions that contain text, logos, etc. This could be viewed as zoning but is more related to the internal preprocessing for the index process.

Another use of zones is when a user wants to display the results of a search. A major limitation to the user is the size of the display screen which constrains the number of items that are visible for review. To optimize the number of items reviewed per display screen, the user wants to display the minimum data required from each item to allow determination of the possible relevance of that item. Quite often the user will only display zones such as the Title or Title and Abstract. This allows multiple items to be displayed per screen. The user can expand those items of potential interest to see the complete text.

Once the standardization and zoning has been completed, information (i.e., words) that are used in creating the index to be searched needs to be identified in the item. The term "processing token" is used because a "word" is not the most efficient unit on which to base search structures. The first step in identification of a processing token consists of determining a word. Systems determine words by dividing input symbols into three classes: valid word symbols, inter-word symbols, and special processing symbols. A word is defined as a contiguous set of word symbols bounded by inter-word symbols. In most systems inter-word symbols are non-searchable and should be carefully selected. Examples of word symbols are alphabetic characters and numbers. Examples of possible inter-word symbols are blanks, periods and semicolons. The exact definition of an inter-word symbol is dependent upon the aspects of the language domain of the items to be processed by the system. For example, an apostrophe may be of little importance if only used for the possessive case in English, but might be critical to represent foreign names in the database. Based upon the required accuracy of searches and language charac- teristics, a trade off is made on the selection of inter-word symbols. There are some symbols that may require special processing. A hyphen can be used many ways, often left to the taste and judgment of the writer (Bernstein-84). At the end of a line it is used to indicate the continuation of a word. In other places it links independent words to avoid absurdity, such as in the case of "small business men." To avoid interpreting this as short males that run businesses, it would properly be hyphenated "small-business men." Thus when a hyphen (or other special symbol) is detected a set of rules are executed to determine what action is to be taken generating one or more processing tokens. Finally some languages that are glyph or ideogram based (e.g., CJK—Chinese, Japanese, and Korean) do not have any interword symbols between the characters. An ideogram is a character or symbol representing an idea or a thing without expressing the pronunciation of a particular word or words for it. Unlike most languages where the characters and words reflect the phonetic pro- nunciation of the word from which the meaning is derived, for the glyph based languages the glyph (or contiguous set of glyphs) represents the idea not the sound. In this case special processing is used to break the contiguous characters (glyphs) into words. These are typically one, two and three sequences of characters. Details of how this is done can be found in many papers on the internet. They typically use a combination of an existing dictionary and also using frequency of occurrence of 2 and 3 combinations of the glyphs. Understanding this difference is critical when designing multimedia information retrieval systems that take the audio output and transcribe it to words. For most languages seeing the speech to text output along with hearing the audio is useful in understanding what is being spoken and trans- lating it. But for the CJK languages it is very confusing for a user to concurrently process both and only the audio or the speech to text output should be processed. There is no correlation of the written glyphs to the spoken word.

Some systems will expand the items to be indexed by also creating a translated version of the item. This helps the users that do not have the ability to read and understand multiple different languages. This also introduces an additional processing step that will introduce errors coming from the translation process. It's not unusual that multiple different translation systems are used since some are better for some languages than others. The additional advantage of the translation process is that when results from a search are displayed, the translated version can be displayed. Examples of the most common machine translation systems used are Language Weaver and Systran. But based upon the languages you are indexing, other translation software may be needed. Keeping both the vernacular index and the translated index will double the resources required for the index. An alternative solution is to just keep the original text as indexed and dynamically translate a user's query and the resultant hits (e.g., the way GOOGLE works). The disadvantage to this process is that translating a query can be very errorful because users do not type in complete syntactically correct search statements. Thus there can be a lot of errors in translating the search. This is less likely to happen when translating the text which is syntactically correct. This will be discussed in more detail in Chap. 5 on search.

Processing tokens for multimedia items also exist. The three modalities we will discuss indexing are images, audio and video. Images are the most difficult because the processing tokens are the pixels and their characteristics in an image (e.g., intensity and color). Pixels and indexing images is discussed in detail in Chap. 4. For audio the processing token is the phoneme. The phoneme is a basic, theoretical unit of sound that can distinguish words (i.e. changing one phoneme in a word can produce another word). Every language has a different number of phonemes and the phonemes from one language are different than the phonemes from another language. Some Native American (Indian) languages only have 3 phonemes while English has 40–46 (there is disagreement on the actual number). Some languages spoken in Southern Africa have as many as 141 phonemes. When processing audio the first task is to recognize the source language and then once recognized it can be parsed into meaningful phonemes. Audio is broken into smaller segments of audio which are then combined to determine the phonemes. But these smaller units can first be used to determine which language is being spoken. Because of the distribution of the smaller sound units (which are combined to make the phonemes) are unique to each language its possible with a very small sample of sound to first determine what language is being spoken. Then the appropriate model can be applied to determine the phonemes for that language. The phonemes can be used to determine what words are spoken or used directly for indexing (see Chap. 4 on indexing). In addition to determining phonemes for searching for words, other sounds can be modeled and detected that might be of search interest, for example the sound of gun fire. Video is really a combination of audio and images and thus the video stream can be broken into those two substreams and the processing token identification mentioned above can be used. In addition there can be closed captioning or teletext in the video stream.

The next step in defining processing tokens is identification of any specific word characteristics. The characteristic is used in systems to assist in disambiguation of a particular word. Morphological analysis of the processing token's part of speech is included here. Thus, for a word such as "plane," the system understands that it could mean "level or flat" as an adjective, "aircraft or facet" as a noun, or "the act of smoothing or evening" as a verb. Other characteristics may classify a token as a member of a higher class of tokens such as "European Country" or "Financial Institution." Another example of characterization is if upper case should be preserved. In most systems upper/lower case is not preserved to avoid the system having to expand a term to cover the case where it is the first word in a sentence. For proper names, acronyms and organizations, the upper case represents a completely different use of the processing token versus it being found in the text. "Pleasant Grant" should be recognized as a person's name versus a "pleasant grant" that provides funding. Other characterizations that are typically treated separately from text are numbers and dates. Most of the categorized words such as proper names and organizations are excluded from the following processes to ensure their integrity. This also helps in the process of entity identification described in Sect. 3.6. Numbers and dates may also go through their own specialized processing to keep their format to allow for searching on them.

Now that the potential list of processing tokens has been defined, some can be removed by a Stop List or a Stop Algorithm. The objective of the Stop function is to save system resources by eliminating from the set of searchable processing tokens those that have little value to the system or the user. Given the significant increase in available cheap memory, storage and processing power, the need to apply the Stop function to processing tokens is decreasing. Nevertheless, Stop Lists are commonly found in most systems and consist of words (processing tokens) whose frequency and/or semantic use make them of no value as a searchable token. For example, any word found in almost every item would have no discrimination value during a search. Parts of speech, such as articles (e.g., "the"), have no search value and are not a useful part of a user's query. By eliminating these frequently occurring words the system saves the processing and storage resources required to incorporate them as part of the searchable data structure. Stop Algorithms go after the other class of words, those found very infrequently.

Ziph (Ziph-49) postulated that, looking at the frequency of occurrence of the unique words across a corpus of items, the majority of unique words are found to occur a few times. The rank-frequency law of Ziph is:

$$Frequency * Rank = constant$$

where Frequency is the number of times a word occurs and rank is the rank order of the word (i.e. number of unique words that is found with that frequency). The law was later derived analytically using probability and information theory (Fairthorne-69). Table 1.1 shows the distribution of words in the first TREC test database (Harman-93), a database with over one billion characters and 500,000 items. In Table 3.1, WSJ is Wall Street Journal (1986–1989), AP is AP Newswire (1989), ZIFF—Information from Computer Select disks, FR—Federal Register (1989), and DOE—Short abstracts from Department of Energy.

**Table 3.1** Distribution of words in TREC Database. (From TREC-1 Conference Proceedings, Harmon-93)

| Source | WSJ | AP | ZIFF | FR | DOE |
|---|---|---|---|---|---|
| Size in MB | 295 | 266 | 251 | 258 | 190 |
| Median number terms/record | 182 | 353 | 181 | 313 | 82 |
| Average number terms/record | 329 | 375 | 412 | 1017 | 89 |
| Number unique terms | 156,298 | 197,608 | 173,501 | 126,258 | 186,225 |
| Number of terms occurring once | 64,656 | 89,627 | 85,992 | 58,677 | 95,782 |
| Average number terms occurrences > 1 | 199 | 174 | 165 | 106 | 159 |

The highly precise nature of the words only found once or twice in the database reduce the probability of their being in the vocabulary of the user and the terms are almost never included in searches. Numbers are also an example of this class of words where the number does not represent something else such as a date. Part numbers and serial numbers are often found in items. Eliminating these words saves on storage and access structure (e.g., dictionary) complexities. The best technique to eliminate the majority of these words is via a Stop algorithm versus trying to list them individually. Examples of Stop algorithms are:

- Stop all numbers greater than "999,999" (this was selected to allow dates to be searchable)
- Stop any processing token that has numbers and characters intermixed

The algorithms are typically source specific, usually eliminating unique item identifiers that are frequently found in systems and have no search value.

At this point the textual processing tokens have been identified and stemming may be applied.

## 3.6 Stemming

One of the last transformations often applied to data before placing it in the searchable data structure is stemming. Stemming reduces the diversity of representations of a concept (word) to a canonical morphological representation. The risk with stemming is that concept discrimination information may be lost in the process, causing a decrease in precision and the ability for ranking to be performed. On the positive side, stemming has the potential to improve recall. A related operation is called lemmatization. Lemmatization is typically accomplished via dictionary look-up which is also one of the possible techniques for stemming. Lemmatization not only addresses endings that can be modified or dropped as in stemming but maps one word to another. For example it could map "eat" to "ate" or "tooth" and "teeth". It handles inflectional variations. It in most cases expands the item by adding in the variants unlike stemming which redefines the current processing token to its stemmed version. Lemmatization can take the context of the word into account when it does its normalization, stemming does not. But stemming is usually faster than lemmatization. There is also an option to do lemmization at query time by expanding the query versus expanding the search index. This is similar to synonym expansion.

The concept of stemming has been applied to information systems from their initial automation in the 1960s. The original goal of stemming was to improve performance and require less system resources by reducing the number of unique words that a system has to contain. With the continued significant increase in storage and computing power, use of stemming for performance reasons is no longer as important. Stemming should now be traded off for the potential improvements it can make in recall versus its associated decline in precision. A system designer can trade off the increased overhead of stemming in creating processing tokens versus reduced search time overhead of processing query terms with trailing "don't cares" (see Sect. 2.1.5 Term Masking) to include all of their variants. The stemming process creates one large index for the stem versus Term Masking which requires the merging (ORing) of the indexes for every term that matches the search term.

## 3.6.1 Introduction to the Stemming Process

Stemming algorithms are used to improve the efficiency of the information system and to improve recall. Conflation is the term frequently used to refer to mapping multiple morphological variants to a single representation (stem). The premise is that the stem carries the meaning of the concept associated with the word and the affixes (endings) introduce subtle modifications to the concept or are used for syntactical purposes. Languages have precise grammars that define their usage, but also evolve based upon human usage. Thus exceptions and non-consistent variants are always present in languages that typically require exception look-up tables in addition to the normal reduction rules.

At first glance, the idea of equating multiple representations of a word as a single stem term would appear to provide significant compression, with associated savings in storage and processing. For example, the stem "comput" could associate "computable, computability, computation, computational, computed, computing, computer, computerese, computerize" to one compressed word. But upon closer examination, looking at an inverted file system implementation, the savings is only in the dictionary since weighted positional information is typically needed in the inversion lists. In an architecture with stemming, the information is in the one inversion list for the stem term versus distributed across multiple inversion lists for each unstemmed term. Since the size of the inversion lists are the major storage factor, the compression of stemming does not significantly reduce storage requirements. For small test databases such as the Cranfield collection,

Lennon reported savings of 32% (Lennon-81). But when applied to larger databases of 1.6 MB and 50 MB, the compression reduced respectively to 20% and 13.5% (Harman-91). Harman also points out that misspellings and proper names reduce the compression even more. In a large text corpus, such as the TREC database, over 15% of the unique words are proper nouns or acronyms that should not be stemmed.

Another major use of stemming is to improve recall. As long as a semantically consistent stem can be identified for a set of words, the generalization process of stemming does help in not missing potentially relevant items. Stemming of the words "calculate, calculates, calculation, calculations, calculating" to a single stem ("calculat") insures whichever of those terms is entered by the user, it is translated to the stem and finds all the variants in any items they exist. In contrast, stemming cannot improve, but has the potential for decreasing precision. The precision value is not based on finding all relevant items but just minimizing the retrieval of non-relevant items. Any function that generalizes a user's search statement can only increase the likelihood of retrieving non-relevant items unless the expansion guarantees every item retrieved by the expansion is relevant.

It is important for a system to be able to categorize a word prior to making the decision to stem it. Certain categories such as proper names and acronyms should not have stemming applied because their morphological basis is not related to a common core concept. Stemming can also cause problems for Natural Language Processing (NLP) systems by causing the loss of information needed for aggregate levels of natural language processing (discourse analysis). The tenses of verbs may be lost in creating a stem, but they are needed to determine if a particular concept (e.g., economic support) being indexed occurred in the past or will be occurring in the future. Time is one example of the type of relationships that are defined in Natural Language Processing systems (see Chap. 5).

The most common stemming algorithm removes suffixes and prefixes, sometimes recursively, to derive the final stem. Other techniques such as table lookup and successor stemming provide alternatives that require additional overheads. Successor stemmers determine prefix overlap as the length of a stem is increased. This information can be used to determine the optimal length for each stem from a statistical versus a linguistic perspective. Table lookup requires a large data structure. A system such as RetrievalWare (recently purchased by the FAST system) that is based upon a very large thesaurus/concept network has the data structure as part of its basic product and thus uses table look-up. The Kstem algorithm used in the INQUERY System combines a set of simple stemming rules with a dictionary to determine processing tokens.

The affix removal technique removes prefixes and suffixes from terms leaving the stem. Most stemmers are iterative and attempt to remove the longest prefixes and suffixes (Lovins-68, Salton-68, Dawson-74, Porter-80 and Paice-90). The Porter algorithm is the most commonly accepted algorithm, but it leads to loss of precision and introduces some anomalies that cause the user to question the integrity of the system. Stemming is applied to the user's query as well as to the incoming text. If the transformation moves the query term to a different semantic meaning, the user will not understand why a particular item is returned and may begin questioning the integrity of the system in general.

## 3.6.2   Porter Stemming Algorithm

The Porter Algorithm is based upon a set of conditions of the stem, suffix and prefix and associated actions given the condition. Some examples of stem conditions are:

1. The measure, m, of a stem is a function of sequences of vowels (a, e, i, o, u, y) followed by a consonant. If V is a sequence of vowels and C is a sequence of consonants, then m is:

$$C(VC)^m V$$

where the initial C and final V are optional and m is the number VC repeats.

| Measure | Example |
|---------|---------|
| m = 0 | free, why |
| m = 1 | frees, whose |
| m = 2 | prologue, compute |

2. *<X>—stem ends with letter X
3. *v*—stem contains a vowel
4. *d—stem ends in double consonant
5. *o—stem ends with consonant-vowel-consonant sequence where the final consonant is not w, x, or y

Suffix conditions take the form current_suffi = = pattern
Actions are in the form old_suffix -> new_suffix

Rules are divided into steps to define the order of applying the rules. The following are some examples of the rules:

| Step | Condition | Suffix | Replacement | Example |
|------|-----------|--------|-------------|---------|
| 1a | NULL | sses | ss | stresses->stress |
| 1b | *v* | ing | NULL | making->mak |
| 1b1[1] | Null | at | ate | inflat(ed)->inflate |
| 1c | *v* | y | i | happy->happi |
| 2 | m > 0 | aliti | al | formaliti->formal |
| 3 | m > 0 | icate | ic | duplicate->duplic |
| 4 | m > 1 | able | Null | adjustable->adjust |
| 5a | m > 1 | e | Null | inflate->inflat |
| 5b | m > 1 and *d and *<L> | NULL | single letter | controll->control |

[1] 1b1 rules are expansion rules to make correction to stems for proper conflation

Given the word "duplicatable," the following are the steps in the stemming process:

duplicat     rule 4
duplicate    rule 1b1
duplic       rule 3

The application of another rule in step 4, removing "ic," cannot be applied since only one rule from each step is allowed be applied.

### 3.6.3  Dictionary Look-Up Stemmers

An alternative to solely relying on algorithms to determine a stem is to use a dictionary look-up mechanism. In this approach, simple stemming rules still may be applied. The rules are taken from those that have the fewest exceptions (e.g., removing pluralization from nouns). But even the most consistent rules have exceptions that need to be addressed. The original term or stemmed version of the term is looked up in a dictionary and replaced by the stem that best represents it.

The INQUERY system at the University of Massachusetts used a stemming technique called Kstem. Kstem is a morphological analyzer that conflates word variants to a root form (Kstem-95). It tries to avoid collapsing words with different meanings into the same root. For example, "memorial" and "memorize" reduce to "memory." But "memorial" and "memorize" are not synonyms and have very different meanings. Kstem, like other stemmers associated with Natural Language Processors and dictionaries, returns words instead of truncated word forms. Generally, Kstem requires a word to be in the dictionary before it reduces one word form to another. Some endings are always removed, even if the root form is not found in the dictionary (e.g., 'ness', 'ly'). If the word being processed is in the dictionary, it is assumed to be unrelated to the root after stemming and conflation is not performed (e.g., 'factorial' needs to be in the dictionary or it is stemmed to 'factory'). For irregular morphologies, it is necessary to explicitly map the word variant to the root desired (for example, "matrices" to "matrix").

The Kstem system uses the following six major data files to control and limit the stemming process:

- Dictionary of words (lexicon)
- Supplemental list of words for the dictionary
- Exceptions list for those words that should retain an "e" at the end (e.g., "suites" to "suite" but "suited" to "suit")
- Direct_Conflation—allows definition of direct conflation via word pairs that override the stemming algorithm
- Country_Nationality—conflations between nationalities and countries ("British" maps to "Britain")
- Proper Nouns—a list of proper nouns that should not be stemmed.

The strength of the FAST (previously Retrievalware) System lies in its Thesaurus/ Semantic Network support data structure that contains over 400,000 words. The dictionaries that are used contain the morphological variants of words. New words that are not special forms (e.g., dates, phone numbers) are located in the dictionary to determine simpler forms by stripping off suffixes and respelling plurals as defined in the dictionary.

## 3.6.4  Successor Stemmers

Successor stemmers are based upon the length of prefixes that optimally stem expansions of additional suffixes. The algorithm is based upon an analogy in structural linguistics that investigated word and morpheme boundaries based upon the distribution of phonemes, the smallest unit of speech that distinguish one word from another (Hafer-74). The process determines the successor varieties for a word, uses this information to divide a word into segments and selects one of the segments as the stem.

The successor variety of a segment of a word in a set of words is the number of distinct letters that occupy the segment length plus one character. For example, the successor variety for the first three letters (i.e., word segment) of a five-letter word is the number of words that have the same first three letters but a different fourth letter plus one for the current word. A graphical representation of successor variety is shown in a symbol tree. Figure 3.2 shows the symbol tree for the terms bag, barn, bring, both, box, and bottle. The successor variety for any prefix of a word is the number of children that are associated with the node in the symbol tree representing that prefix. For example, the successor variety for the first letter "b" is three. The successor variety for the prefix "ba" is two.

The successor varieties of a word are used to segment a word by applying one of the following methods:

1. Cutoff method: a cutoff value is selected to define stem length. The value varies for each possible set of words.
2. Peak and Plateau: a segment break is made after a character whose successor variety exceeds that of the character immediately preceding it and the character immediately following it.
3. Complete word method: break on boundaries of complete words.

A cutoff value is selected and a boundary is identified whenever the cutoff value is reached. Hafer and Weiss experimented with the techniques, discovering that combinations of the techniques performed best, which they used in defining their stemming process. Using the words in Fig. 3.1 plus the additional word "boxer," the successor variety stemming is shown in Fig. 3.3.

If the cutoff method with value four was selected then the stem would be "boxe." The peak and plateau method can not apply because the successor variety monotonically decreases. Applying the complete word method, the stem is "box." The example given does not have enough values to apply the entropy method. The ad-

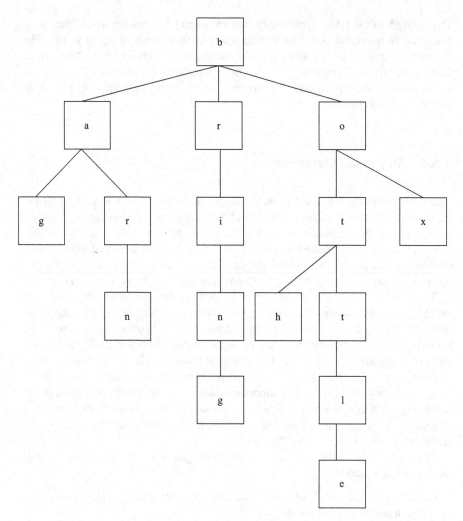

**Fig. 3.2** Symbol tree for terms bag, barn, bring, box, bottle, both

**Fig. 3.3** Successor variety
stemming

| PREFIX | Successor Variety | Branch Letters |
|---|---|---|
| b | 3 | a, r, o |
| bo | 2 | t, x |
| box | 1 | e |
| boxe | 1 | r |
| boxer | 1 | blank |

vantage of the peak and plateau and the complete word methods is that a cutoff
value does not have to be selected (Frakes-92).

After a word has been segmented, the segment to be used as the stem must be
selected. Hafer and Weiss used the following rule:

if (first segment occurs in <= 12 words in database)
first segment is stem
else (second segment is stem)

The idea is that if a segment is found in more than 12 words in the text being analyzed, it is probably a prefix. Hafer and Weiss noted that multiple prefixes in the
English language do not occur often and thus selecting the first or second segment
in general determines the appropriate stem.

### 3.6.5 Conclusions on Stemming

Frakes summarized studies of various stemming studies (Frakes-92). He cautions
that some of the authors failed to report test statistics, especially sizes, making interpretation difficult. Also some of the test sample sizes were so small as to make their
results questionable. Frakes came to the following conclusions:

- Stemming can affect retrieval(recall) and where effects were identified they were
  positive. There is little difference between retrieval effectiveness of different full
  stemmers with the exception of the Hafer and Weiss stemmer.
- Stemming is as effective as manual conflation.
- Stemming is dependent upon the nature of the vocabulary.

To quantify the impact of stemmers, Paice has defined a stemming performance
measure called Error Rate Relative to Truncation (ERRT) that can be used to compare stemming algorithms (Paice-94). The approach depends upon the ability to
partition terms semantically and morphologically related to each other into "concept groups." After applying a stemmer that is not perfect, concept groups may still
contain multiple stems rather than one. This introduces an error reflected in the under stemming Index (UI). Also it is possible that the same stem is found in multiple
groups. This error state is reflected in the Overstemming Index (OI). The worst case
stemming algorithm is where words are stemmed via truncation to a word length
(words shorter than the length are not truncated). UI and OI values can be calculated
based upon truncated word lengths. The perfect case is where UI and OI equal zero.
ERRT is then calculated as the distance from the origin to the (UI, OI) coordinate of
the stemmer being evaluated (OP) versus the distance from the origin to the worst
case intersection of the line generated by pure truncation (OT) (see Fig. 3.4).

The values calculated are biased by the initial grouping of the test terms. Larger
ERRT values occur with looser grouping. For the particular test runs, the UI of the
Porter Algorithm was greater than the UI of the Paice/Husk algorithms (Paice-90).
The OI was largest for the Paice and the least for Porter. Finally, the ERRT of the
Porter was greater than the Paice algorithm. These results suggest that the Paice algorithm appeared significantly better than the Porter algorithm. But the differences
in objectives between the stemmers (Porter being a light stemmer—tries to avoid
overstemming leaving understemming errors and Paice being the opposite, a heavy
stemmer) makes comparison less meaningful. While this approach to stemmer
evaluation requires additional work to remove imprecisions and provide a common

**Fig. 3.4** Computation of
ERRT value

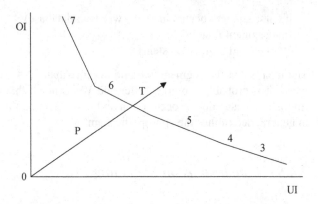

comparison framework, it provides a mechanism to develop a baseline to discuss future developments.

The comparisons by Frakes and Paice support the intuitive feeling that stemming as a generalization of processing tokens for a particular concept (word) can only help in recall. In experiments, stemming has never been proven to significantly improve recall (Harman-91). Stemming can potentially reduce precision. The impact on precision can be minimized by the use of ranking items based upon all the terms in the query, categorization of terms and selective exclusion of some terms from stemming. Unless the user is very restrictive in the query, the impact of the other search terms and those expanded automatically by the system ameliorates the effects of generalization caused by stemming. Stemming in large databases should not be viewed as a significant compression technique to save on storage. Its major advantage is in the significant reduction of dictionary sizes and therefore a possible reduction in the processing time for each search term.

## 3.7 Entity Processing

As noted in Chap. 1 the core problem in getting good search results is the mismatch between the vocabulary of the author and the vocabulary of the user. In addition to basic differences in the words used to represent the same idea, there is an issue with the many variants on how an entity can be specified. An entity can be any real world discrete object from people to organizations, URLs, phone numbers, etc. There are many different ways that a person's name may be expressed as well as transliteration issues on exactly how a person from one country (language group) is expressed in the language of the index. For example the following are just a subset of the ways of expressing Libiyan leader's name: Muammar el Qaddafi, Ghaddafi, Kaddafi, Muammar al-Gathafi, Col. Mu'ammar al-Qadhafi. Yet they all refer to the same person (entity). Also within the text, pronouns are often used instead of using the person's name. For example a search using proximity would not find that George Bush is from Texas because in the text of the item George Bush may be in one sentence and then a little later the text specified "he is from Texas". The association of an entity to a pronoun is called the coreference problem. Entity processing attempts to disambiguate many of these issues before the searchable index is created.

## 3.7.1   Entity Identification

Entity Identification can be broken down into three major processes. The first process is identifying if a word or words belongs to an entity class. For example you can have entity classes such as people, places, organizations, telephone numbers, Internet URLs, etc., and this process would associate the processing token with one or more of those classes. This in a sense "tags" some of the processing tokens with additional metadata to help define its semantics. If the processing token "bush" is in the text it could be a plant. But if it is identified and tagged to be in the Person Entity category than you know it's a person's name.

The technical approaches of entity identification and normalization fall into three major classes. The first is a matching enumeration process where all of the different possible values for an entity are identified and then whenever any of those values are found, that processing token is associated with the appropriate entity class and single value representing that instance of an entity (normalization step). This is in a sense a dictionary look-up type process and in most cases users can add additional terms to the dictionary. The original SEMIO product (now owned by Entrieva) used this approach. The second approach is a rule based approach. The user can generate "production rules" that help identify what entity class a processing token applies to and also which entity value to assign it to. The SRA NetOwl is an example of a commercial product that uses production rules for entity identification and extraction. It also uses some linguistic analysis. It comes with an extensive list of predefined rules and the users can add additional rules. The rules are typically regular expressions that help in identifying specific types of entities. For example a regular expression for identifying a "Company" entity might contain the logic:

- Word starts with upper case and is followed by any of the following strings (Inc., LLC, Ltd) is a company

The final approach is a linguistic approach using the morphological rules associated with a specific language. In this case the processing token may only be assigned to an entity class and the normalization process may not occur. The Inxight Product (started by Zerox PARC and currently owned by SAP AG) uses the Thingfinder entity identifier. The linguistic approach is the only approach to find entities associated with the coreference problem. There are some approaches where linguistic rules unique to a language are used to identify different variant spellings for a specific entity. These are very useful when names from one language are being transliterated into another language.

A special class of entity identification is for geographic references. Many entity identification products do some level of geographic processing. But the MetaCarta product with its geotagger is the most commonly used product to extract geographic entity information from text. The geotagger parses content, extracts geographic references, and resolves the geographic meaning intended by the author. Often a gazetteer is used to locate the processing tokens associated with geographic locations. This creates latitude and longitude coordinates and country code tags for places mentioned within documents. It also generates a confidence score for every identified location. The confidence score is a number between zero and one that is the probability that the author intended the geographic meaning represented by the coordinates.

### 3.7.2  Entity Normalization

The second process is entity normalization. In this process different variants of the same entity instance are mapped to a common name. As noted above in some of the approaches to identify and entity, the normalization can also occur. For example George Bush, President Bush, George W. Bush, and Bush might all be mapped to a single value that represents that one person (that instance). A more complex extension is associating pronouns with specific entities. This is called coreference which means the identification of an anaphoric relation. An anaphoric relation indicates the relation between two textual elements that denote the same object. For example:

• George Bush is the president. He is from Texas

In this case George Bush and "He" refer to the same object. This also could be the mapping of different spellings of the same name to a single value such as in the Muammar el Qaddafi example above. In a sense you are applying two different values to the same processing token. One is the actual value in the text and the other is the single value that represents that entity instance. The single value of the instance becomes another processing token that maps to all the locations of the different variants of the entity exist in the text. You can create an additional inversion list represented by the single value that has all of the instances of all of the variants in it. This expansion of the processing token list allows for the search a specific value or a search for all variants of an entity. This helps resolve the difference in vocabularies between the author and the searcher.

The products that use the enumeration method of listing all variants manually or by linguistic rules associated with names can handle mapping various name variants. But they do not handle the issue of coreference. The products that use linguistic rules are more apt to be able to handle the coreference issue—but quite often do not because it's not accurate enough and is too complex.

### 3.7.3  Entity Resolution

The third process is entity resolution. As processing tokens are associated with an entity instance, it's possible they will be assigned to the wrong entity instance. As the processing tokens are sequentially processed and assigned, entity resolution allows the system to reconsider some of the mappings based upon additional information as it processes the item. For example the first time a processing token George Bush is encountered it might be mapped to George W. Bush. But as the item continues processing it might find that all the other processing tokens are referring to George H. Bush and thus the first processing token should also refer to George H. Bush. Entity resolution also refers to when entities and attributes about the entities are identified across multiple items. When the entities with their attributes are merged into the searchable database its possible that there are inconsistencies between the entities and their attributes. The merging and resolution of the conflicts is also called entity resolution.

There are two major approaches to entity resolution. Many applications focus on a particular entity class and specific rules are defined to resolve conflicts against that class. Stanford University in its SREF project is taking a more generic approach to developing a framework for entity resolution that can be applied to a variety of problems. In addition to the resolution process looking for conflicts it includes a method to show the logic executed by the system that came to the entity resolution proposal (Garcia-Molina-2007).

### 3.7.4   Information Extraction

Entity identification is some times related to the more general Information Extraction process. All systems use some level of information extraction in order to extract the "citation" metadata information about an item to augment the processing tokens to make that searchable. There are two processes associated with information extraction: determination of facts to go into structured fields in a database and extraction of text that can be used to summarize an item. In the first case only a subset of the important facts in an item may be identified and extracted. In summarization all of the major concepts in the item should be represented in the summary.

The process of extracting facts to go into indexes is called Automatic File Build. Its goal is to process incoming items and extract index terms that will go into a structured database. This differs from indexing in that its objective is to extract specific types of information versus understanding all of the text of the document. An Information Retrieval System's goal is to provide an in-depth representation of the total contents of an item (Sundheim-92). An Information Extraction system only analyzes those portions of a document that potentially contain information relevant to the extraction criteria. The objective of the data extraction is in most cases to update a structured database with additional facts. The updates may be from a controlled vocabulary or substrings from the item as defined by the extraction rules. The term "slot" is used to define a particular category of information to be extracted. Slots are organized into templates or semantic frames. Information extraction requires multiple levels of analysis of the text of an item. It must understand the words and their context (discourse analysis). The processing is very similar to the natural language processing described under indexing.

In establishing metrics to compare information extraction, the previously defined measures of precision and recall are applied with slight modifications to their meaning. Recall refers to how much information was extracted from an item versus how much should have been extracted from the item. It shows the amount of correct and relevant data extracted versus the correct and relevant data in the item. Precision refers to how much information was extracted accurately versus the total information extracted.

Additional metrics used are overgeneration and fallout. Overgeneration measures the amount of irrelevant information that is extracted. This could be caused by templates filled on topics that are not intended to be extracted or slots that get filled with non-relevant data. Fallout measures how much a system assigns incorrect slot fillers as the number of potential incorrect slot fillers increases (Lehnert-91).

These measures are applicable to both human and automated extraction processes. Human beings fall short of perfection in data extraction as well as automated systems. The best source of analysis of data extraction is from the Message Understanding Conference Proceedings. Conferences (similar to TREC) were held in 1991, 1992, 1993 and 1995. The conferences are sponsored by the Advanced Research Project Agency/Software and Intelligent Systems Technology Office of the Department of Defense. Large test databases are made available to any organization interested in participating in evaluation of their algorithms. In MUC-5 (1993), four experienced human analysts performed detailed extraction against 120 documents and their performance was compared against the top three information extraction systems. The humans achieved a 79% recall with 82% precision. That is, they extracted 79% of the data they could have found and 18% of what they extracted was erroneous. The automated programs achieved 53% recall and 57% precision. The other mediating factor is the costs associated with information extraction. The humans required between 15 and 60 min to process a single item versus the 30 s to 3 min required by the computers. Thus the existing algorithms are not operating close to what a human can achieve, but they are significantly cheaper. A combination of the two in a computer-assisted information extraction system appears the most reasonable solution in the foreseeable future.

## 3.8 Categorization

The categorization process is focused on finding additional descriptors for the content of an item. It is attempting to get to the more complex issue of finding index values that define the more abstract references for an item. In this case the processing tokens for an item are expanded by the terms associated with each category found for an item. For example, there may be a category for Environment Protection. When an item comes in that discusses oil spills, it will also have the term Environment Protection assigned to it, even though neither those words nor any variants of those words were included in the item.

As discussed in Chap. 2 the primary approaches to categorization are use of learning algorithms such as neural nets or support vector machines. The systems allow users or system administrators to create a new category. When the category is created the user needs to find 20–30 examples of existing items that should be assigned to that category to be used to train the system on the category. In some systems the user is also asked to find 5–10 examples of items that are close to the topic but which should not be assigned to the category. These examples are then used to train the system on that particular category. When a new item is ingested it will be processed against all of the category definitions. The result of the categorization process is a "confidence" value that the item should be part of that category. This is typically a value between 0 and 1 or 0 to 100. In some systems a threshold is set and if the confidence value does not exceed it, the category value is not added to the index. In other systems that are based upon weighting algorithms, the category and its associated confidence level will always be added as additional processing tokens. The confidence values created by one categorization process is unique to that process and cannot be compared to confidence levels assigned to an item by a different categorization tool, even if they use the same training data. Thus the cutoff thresholds are unique to a particular system and use of multiple different categorization processes does not improve the capability to accurately determine what categories an item should be assigned. This is because there are heuristics and feedback tuning parameters that are part of the configuration of each categorization product and quite often proprietary in nature (part of the intellectual property of the product) that ensures there is no consistency in values between products. Thus one product may assign a value of 65 for Environmental Protection and it should be applied whereas another product may have a value of 80 which for that product may still be too low to assign the value.

Most of the approaches allow the user to add more items to the training set as they use the system. In some cases they allow the user to select a subset of an item (e.g., select a subset of the text from an item) as training material. This is extremely useful when the items have the possibility to discuss multiple topics or provide background on a general topical area.

Another common approach to categorization uses Naïve Bayes as an algorithmic approach. It is called Naïve because it assumes every word is independent of every other word. But that simplification seems to not cause serious miss categorization of items. The goal is to define which category and item belongs to and the data that is available is a training set of documents to estimate the effects of different words on the inclusion of the item in a particular class. Starting with a Bayesian approach the classification problem can be defined as:

$$P(C/I) = (P(I/C) * P(C))/P(I)$$

which is saying the probability of a particular Category given a particular Item equals the probability of an Item given the Category times the probability the category occurs divided by the probability an Item occurs. The first simplification is that the denominator can be dropped without effecting the overall evaluation. The goal is to select if an item should be in a category and the denominator is the same for all calculations and is just a normalization factor that does not effect the decision information which is in the numerator. The P(C) factor is useful because if a category does not occur very often and the conditional probability P(I/C) marginally suggests it should be assigned to the category, then it could change the decision to not assigning the category to the item (or vice versa).

The next step is to determine how to calculate the factor P(I/C). An item is a set of processing tokens (words) that are meaningful (i.e., stop words need to be eliminated). Thus the formula can be estimated to be P(set of words in I) given a Category. The concept of using a training set is that you will have a set of Items identified as those in the Category and those not in the Category. From the training set an estimate for each unique word can be calculated how much that word contributes to the decision that an item should be in the category. This simply becomes the ratio of the number of times a word occurs in the Items of the training set assigned to the category divided by the total number of words in the category. The formula now becomes:

$$P(C/I) \propto P(C) * \prod P(t_k/C)$$

Where $P(t_k/C)$ uses each word found in the Item as an independent (the assumption noted above) estimator contributing to the decision if the Item should be assigned to the Category. Sometimes in operational systems the Log function is used to be sure that if a particular word would have a value close to or equal to zero it would not zero out this function by changing it to an addition of Logs versus a multiplication of factors.

$$P(C/I) \propto \log(p(C)) + \sum \log p(t_k/C)$$

The $p(t_k/C)$ factor is the number of times that a word is found in the training data set for a particular Category divided by the total number of words. This approach can lead to problems if certain terms are not found in the training set so Laplace smoothing can be added to eliminate zeros. Thus the factor $p(t_k/C)$ is changed to:

$$p(t_k/C) = (t_k + 1)/ \sum (t_k + 1) = (t_k + 1)/ \left(\sum (t_k) + N\right)$$

where "N" is the number of unique processing tokens in the training set. Thus to calculate the factor that each processing token contributes to an item being considered for a category we sum up the number of times that word is found in items in the training set for that category plus one and divide it by total number of processing tokens in the training data set plus the number of unique processing tokens in the training set. In addition from the training set a factor the P(C) can be estimated although this factor can be easily changed as operational Items are assigned to the Category.

This factor from the training set of $p(t_k/C)$ for each $t_k$ is used for each occurrence of that term in a new Item to determine if it should be assigned the Category multiplied times the probability the category will occur. Then to calculate the probability

Item 1 = computer physics computer computer      is in computer category

Item 2 = computer mathematics physics physics      is in computer category

Item 3 = computer computer biology      is in computer category

Item 4 = computer computer computer physics      is in computer category

Item 5 = computer physics physics      is not in computer category

Item 6 = physics biology physics physics      is not in computer category

$P(\text{computer/category}) = (9 + 1)/(15 + 4) = 10/19 = .526$

$P(\text{physics/category}) = (4 + 1)/(15 + 4) = 5/19 = .263$

$P(\text{mathematics/category}) = P(\text{biology/category}) = (1 + 1)/(15 + 4) = 2/19 = .105$

$P(\text{computer/not category}) = (1 + 1)/(7 + 4) = 2/11 = .182$

$P(\text{physics/not category}) = (5 + 1)/(7 + 4) = 6/11 = .546$

$P(\text{mathematics/not category}) = (0 + 1)/(7 + 4) = 1/11 = .091$

$P(\text{biology/not category}) = (1 + 1)/(7 + 4) = 2/11 = .182$

**Fig. 3.5** Naïve Bayes example

that an item is not a member of the category you use the same formula on the training items that the category does not apply to. This then gives you an estimate if the Item should be in the Category or if the Item should not be assigned to the Category.

In the example from Fig. 3.5, given the following 6 Items in the training data set, the factors for each of two categories are calculated. The P(computer category) is $4/6 = 0.667$ and the P(not computer is $2/6$) $= 0.333$ which is the number of times Items in the training data set are in the Category or not in the Category. The issue with that assumption is that it's hard to get a training set that adequately reflects what will be what is observed in the operational data for this factor. Thus this factor is adjusted as the system assigns new Items to the Categories. Dynamic adjustments for word frequencies and new words are part of the proprietary heuristics that each product using this approach creates.

If a new Item is to be categorized and the system is calculating if it should be in the "computer" category then the data above would be used. For example if a new item is:

Item 7 = computer physics computer mathematics
Then the P(computer/Item 7) = (0.667) * (0.526 * 0.263 * 0.526 * 0.105) = 0.0051
and the P(not computer/Item 7) = (0.333) * (0.182 * 0.546 * 0.182 * 0.091) = 0.0005

Thus the Item 7 would be assigned the category "computer".

This example is a good opportunity to see why the term "probability" is used often in Information Retrieval but really in almost all cases it is not a probability because of the simplifications and the estimates used for the various data. You might think that the P(Computer/Item 7) + the P(not in Computer/Item 7) should equal 1, which it is not even close. That is because these are not real probabilities. The concept of "confidence" or relative value is what is used in Information Retrieval because you are getting estimates but the goal is to make a relative decision compared to other items such as should it be in a Category or which should be displayed first. In the example above the decision would be to assign Item 7 to Category "Computer". But given the estimates a threshold is many times applied where even if the calculation for the assignment to a Category suggests it should be assigned, if it is not above a threshold, it still is not assigned.

As with Entity identification, there is also a rule based approach to categorization. In rule based you could have a rule like "Chicago" and "Seattle" would classify an item talking about locations. There are likely subsets of categories that can be defined by rules where there are clear boundaries on what should be in a category. But the rule based approach as with the added dictionary discussed above are techniques to enhance a more automated statistical classification scheme to either add specific results that can be defined and are important or to define exceptions to eliminate some recurring errors that the statistical classifier is producing.

## 3.9   Citational Metadata

Most of the above discussion is focused on creating processing tokens from the content of an item. But there is additional indexable data that is associated with where the item came from. This information can help limit the users search to a subset of the items in the database, thereby improving precision. Examples of citational information are the date the item was ingested by the search system, the date the item was created by the user, the source of the item (e.g., web site name, news agency for RS feeds, etc.), author of the item, and language an item is in. The advantage of this data is that it is more4 facts than subjective information and can help narrow a search down if it is an aspect of what the information need of the user is.

## 3.10   Summary

The Ingest process is the first process in the creation of an Information retrieval system. It is the first level filter to try and eliminate items that would expand the database without providing useful information to the user. The less extraneous information the more precision will come from searches. In addition to the filtering process, it performs different types of normalization. Zoning of an item is useful to improve the precision of a search. This is accomplished by defining a logical subset of the item to search and in some cases assign a higher weight if a search "hits" in a particular subset (e.g., on the Title). The stemming process helps eliminate mismatches between the users search and the text by attempting to map processing token to the canonical form that best represents the concept the word is addressing. The entity identification process has the most value in disambiguating the received processing tokens and disambiguating between different variants of the same entity. The additional processing tokens generated by the entity identification process can be used to resolve many of the ambiguities of a search. In most searches users are searching for specific entities and this process while keep the resultant set focused improving both precision and recall. Categorization is also useful in expanding the processing tokens identifying an item. Although the author and the user use different vocabularies, use of learning algorithms driven by examples that the user identifies is using the author's vocabulary to learn how to find the specific categories that the user is interested in and mapping it to the category label.

## 3.11 Exercises

1. Discuss the additional complexities and metadata that might be useful when you are crawling "BLOGS" versus normal static web pages. If you were crawling "FACEBOOK" how would you modify to optimize the ingest process (HINT: discuss it both from a metadata perspective and a multimedia information retrieval perspective).
2. Given the following two items compare how well the shingle process works between looking at the 3 lowest signatures versus the 6 lowest signatures—use Borders resemblance formula. Discuss the results.

   Item 1: w2 w4 w2 w6 w6 w2 w7 w5 w4 w2 w6
   Item 2: w5 w4 w2 w6 w2 w4 w2 w6 w6 w2 w7

3. Consider other types of information—images, and audio. Compare the processing of them to create a searchable index versus the processing of text. For example when you think of processing text you start with symbols and interword symbols that build up to defining words. Then words are processed to defining processing tokens. What parallels do you see for images and audio?
4. Describe the similarities and differences between term stemming algorithms and n-grams. Describe how they affect precision and recall.
5. Apply the Porter stemming steps to the following words: irreplaceable, informative, activation, and triplicate.
6. Assuming the database has the following words: act, able, arch, car, court, waste, wink, write, writer, wrinkle. Show the successor variety for the word "writeable." Apply the cutoff method, peak and plateau method and complete word method to determine possible stems for the word. Explain your rationale for the cutoff method.

# Chapter 4
# Indexing

## 4.1 What is Indexing

Chapter 3 focused on the initial processing (ingest) of an item. It concluded with having identified the processing tokens that would be used to create the searchable index for the item. Before the specific indexing techniques are discussed it's useful to understand what an index is and what its goal is. One of the most critical aspects of an information retrieval system that determines its effectiveness is how it represents concepts (semantics) in items. The transformation from the received item to the searchable data structure is called Indexing. This process historically was manual but is now primarily automatic, creating the basis for search of items. The index is what really defines an item more than its original content. This is because the primary mechanism to get to an item is based upon search of the index. If information is not in the index, then the user will never know the item exists. For example, if a new term to describe a process is unique and found in one item, it's possible that the stop algorithm process will eliminate the processing token before it gets to the indexing phase. If a user searches for that unique word it will appear as if there are no items in the database that contain that term. Indexing is the process of mapping from the contents of an item to the searchable structure used to find items. If there are concepts in the item that are not reflected in the index, then a user will not find that item when searching for those concepts. In addition to mapping the concepts to the searchable data structure, the automatic indexing process may attempt to assign a weight on how much that item discusses a particular concept. This is used in the display phase for ranking the outputs, attempting to get the items more likely to be relevant higher in the hit list. To better understand the indexing process a discussion of manual indexing process sheds some insights into the automatic indexing process.

Once the processing tokens have been identified they can be used to create the searchable index for the item. The index that is created defines how well an information retrieval system will perform. Users do not browse all of the items in the database unless there is Taxonomy and they follow the taxonomy tree. But in a sense that is also a search where each level in the taxonomy can be defined by a search. Since the users can only find items of interest by searching, if the semantics of what is important within an item is not reflected in the searchable index, users will never find the item.

G. Kowalski, *Information Retrieval Architecture and Algorithms,*
DOI 10.1007/978-1-4419-7716-8_4, © Springer Science+Business Media, LLC 2011

Before introducing the actual indexing methodologies, reviewing the history of indexing puts into perspective the importance of indexing and how it evolved. Through most of the 1980s the goals of commercial Information Retrieval Systems were constrained to facilitating the manual indexing paradigm. In the 1990s, exponential growth in computer processing capabilities with a continuing decrease in cost of computer systems has allowed Information Retrieval Systems to implement previously theoretical functions, introducing a new information retrieval paradigm where the text of the item could be the index. In the 2000s the technology had evolved where it was not only scalable to billions of items being indexed, but also other support technologies such as entity identification, duplicate removal and categorization can be used to enhance both precision and recall. But there still there remains a place for manual indexing.

### 4.1.1   History

Indexing (originally called Cataloging) is the oldest technique for identifying the contents of items to assist in their retrieval. The objective of cataloging is to give access points to a collection that are expected and most useful to the users of the information. The basic information required on an item, what is the item and what it is about, has not changed over the centuries. As early as the third-millennium, in Babylon, libraries of cuneiform tablets were arranged by subject (Hyman-89). Up to the nineteenth century there was little advancement in cataloging, only changes in the methods used to represent the basic information (Norris-69). In the late 1800s subject indexing became hierarchical (e.g., Dewey Decimal System). In 1963 the Library of Congress initiated a study on the computerization of bibliographic surrogates. From 1966–1968 the Library of Congress ran its MARC I pilot project. MARC (MAchine Readable Cataloging) standardizes the structure, contents and coding of bibliographic records. The system became operational in 1969 (Avram-75). The earliest commercial cataloging system is DIALOG, which was developed by Lockheed Corporation in 1965 for NASA. It became commercial in 1978 with three government files of indexes to technical publications. By 1988, when it was sold to Knight-Ridder, DIALOG contained over 320 index databases used by over 91,000 subscribers in 86 countries.

Indexing (cataloging), until recently, was accomplished by creating a bibliographic citation in a structured file that references the original text. These files contain citation information about the item, keywording the subject(s) of the item and, in some systems a constrained length free text field used for an abstract/summary. The indexing process is typically performed by professional indexers associated with library organizations. Throughout the history of libraries, this has been the most important and most difficult processing step. Most items are retrieved based upon what the item is about. The user's ability to find items on a particular subject is limited by the indexer creating index terms for that subject. But libraries and library indexing has always assumed the availability of the library staff to act if needed as a human intermediary for users having problems in locating information. Users looking for well-defined data (e.g., people by name and titles) have good success by themselves. But when users are searching for topics they fail on 70% of single query requests and 45% of the time they never find the data they need. But when the users consult with a librarian the failure rates drop to 10% (Nordlie-99.) Thus library based indexing was never under significant pressure to invent user interfaces, support material and augmented search engines that would assure users could find the material they needed. They could rely on human interaction to resolve the more complex information needs.

The initial introduction of computers to assist the cataloguing function did not change its basic operation of a human indexer determining those terms to assign to a particular item. The standardization of data structures (e.g., MARC format) did allow sharing of the indexes between libraries. It reduced the manual overhead associated with maintaining a card catalog. By not having to make physical copies of the index card for every subject index term, it also encouraged inclusion of additional index terms. Also it allowed for Boolean logic to further refine the user's request (e.g., author and subject). But the process still required the indexer to enter index terms that quite often were redundant with the words in the referenced item. The user, instead of searching through physical cards in a card catalog, now performed a search on a computer and electronically displayed the card equivalents. It allows the user to search on multiple index terms using Boolean logic allowing for more precise retrieval.

In the 1990s, the significant reduction in cost of processing power and memory in modern computers, along with access to the full text of an item from the publishing stages in electronic form, allowed use of the full text of an item as an alternative to the indexer-generated subject index. The searchable availability of the text of items has changed the role of indexers and allowed introduction of new techniques to facilitate the user in locating information of interest. The indexer is no longer required to enter index terms that are redundant with words in the text of an item. The searcher is no longer presented a list of potential item of interest, but is additionally informed of the likelihood that each item satisfies his search goal. Additional new automated tools such as entity identification, categorization have moved the processing closer to full automation, but manual indexing still holds value (e.g., Yahoo).

### 4.1.2  Objectives

The objective of indexing has not changed from the earliest days of libraries. The index needs to represent the semantics of the item that is of potential interest to users. If there are semantics (ideas) in the item that are not reflected in the index, users will not be able to find the item. This is true from the days of using physical rooms to index, to adding index terms in card catalogs and making copies of the index cards to the automatic indexing algorithms discussed in this chapter.

How indexing occurs and the roles played by machines and humans have changed with the evolution of Information Retrieval Systems. Availability of the full text of the item in searchable form alters the manual indexing needs historically used in determining guidelines for manual indexing. In the new environment where all of the processing tokens in all items are indexed, all of the words within the item are potential index descriptors of the subject(s) of the item. Chapter 3 discusses the ingest process that takes all possible words in an item and transforms them into processing tokens used in defining the searchable representation of an item. In addition to determining the processing tokens, current systems have the ability to automatically weight the processing tokens based upon their potential importance in defining the concepts in the item and assigning items to locations in taxonomy that describes the overall subject of the information database.

The first reaction of many people is to question the need for manual indexing at all, given that total document indexing is available for search. If one can search on any of the words in a document why does one need to add additional index terms? Previously, indexing defined the source and major concepts of an item and provided a mechanism for standardization of index terms (i.e., use of a controlled vocabulary). A controlled vocabulary is a finite set of index terms from which all index terms must be selected (the domain of the index). In a manual indexing environment, the use of a controlled vocabulary makes the indexing process slower, but potentially simplifies the search process. The extra processing time comes from the indexer trying to determine the appropriate index terms for concepts that are not specifically in the controlled vocabulary set. Controlled vocabularies aide the user in knowing the domain of terms that the indexer had to select from and thus which terms best describe the information needed. Thus controlled vocabularies significantly reduce the miss match between the vocabulary of the author and the vocabulary of the searcher. Uncontrolled vocabularies have the opposite effect, making indexing faster but the search process much more difficult.

The availability of items in electronic form changes the objectives of manual indexing. The source information (frequently called citation data) can automatically be extracted. The use of entity identification and availability of electronic thesauri and other reference databases can compensate for diversity of language/vocabulary use and thus eliminate the need for controlled vocabularies. The primary use of manual subject indexing now shifts to abstraction of concepts and judgments on the value of the information. The automatic text analysis algorithms cannot consistently perform abstraction on all concepts that are in an item. They cannot correlate the facts in an item in a cause/effect relationship to determine additional related concepts to be indexed. An item that is discussing the increase in water temperatures at factory discharge locations could also be providing information on "economic stability" of a country that has fishing as its major industry. It requires the associative capabilities of a human being to make the connection. A computer system would typically not be able to correlate the changes in temperature to economic stability (e.g., use of categorization tool with economic stability as a category). The additional index terms added if manual indexing (tagging) is allowed will enhance the recall capability of the system. For certain queries it may also increase the precision.

The words used in an item do not always reflect the value of the concepts being presented. It is the combination of the words and their semantic implications that contain the intelligence value of the concepts being discussed. The utility of a concept is also determined by the user's need. The Public File indexer needs to consider the information needs of all users of the library system. Individual users of the system have their own domains of interest that bound the concepts in which they are interested. It takes a human being to evaluate the quality of the concepts being discussed in an item to determine if that concept should be indexed. The difference in "user need" between the library class of indexers and the individual users is why Private Index files are an essential part of any good information system. It allows the user to logically subset the total document file into folders of interest including only those documents that, in the user's judgment, have future value. It also allows the user to judge the utility of the concepts based upon his need versus the system need and perform concept abstraction. Selective indexing based upon the value of concepts increases the precision of searches.

Availability of full document indexing saves the indexer from entering index terms that are identical to words in the document. In most private corporate systems users are given the opportunity to add additional index terms or their opinions on the information which is available to all other users. Sometimes the index terms are entered by professional indexers and in most other cases they are added by other users of the system. This distinction is important because the system needs to protect the index data added by the professionals while allowing changes to that added by the users. There is overlap between the Private and Public index terms added. One of the changes that has come with the Internet is where some web sites are allowing any user to enter indexing. In this case there are users responsible for the integrity of subsets of the site that review what other users enter and make adjustments as needed (Wikipedia). This concept of collaborative indexing has significantly expanded the knowledge base available for search systems and users.

## 4.2 Manual Indexing Process

When an organization with multiple indexers decides to create a public or private index some procedural decisions on how to create the index terms assist the indexers and end users in knowing what to expect in the index file. The first decision is the scope of the indexing to define what level of detail the subject index will contain. This is based upon usage scenarios of the end users. The other decision is the need to link index terms together in a single index for a particular concept.

### 4.2.1 Scope of Indexing

When manual indexing is allowed to augment the automated indexing, the process of reliably and consistently determining the bibliographic terms that represent the concepts in an item is extremely difficult. Problems arise from interaction of two sources: the author and the indexer. The vocabulary domain of the author may be different than that of the indexer, causing the indexer to misinterpret the emphasis and possibly even the concepts being presented. The indexer is not an expert on all areas and has different levels of knowledge in the different areas being presented in the item. This results in different quality levels of indexing. The indexer must determine when to stop the indexing process.

There are two factors involved in deciding on what level to index the concepts in an item: the exhaustivity and the specificity of indexing desired. Exhaustivity of indexing is the extent to which the different concepts in the item are indexed. For example, if two sentences of a 10-page item on microprocessors discuss on-board caches, should this concept be indexed? Specificity relates to the preciseness of the index terms used in indexing. For example, whether the term "processor" or the term "microcomputer" or the term "Pentium" should be used in the index of an item is based upon the specificity decision. Indexing an item only on the most important concept in it and using general index terms yields low exhaustivity and specificity. This approach requires a minimal number of index terms per item and reduces the cost of generating the index. For example, indexing this paragraph would only use the index term "indexing." High exhaustivity and specificity indexes almost every concept in the item using as many detailed terms as needed. Under these parameters this paragraph would have "indexing," "indexer knowledge," "exhaustivity" and "specificity" as index terms. Low exhaustivity has an adverse effect on both precision and recall. If the full text of the item is indexed, then low exhaustivity is used to index the abstract concepts not explicit in the item with the expectation that the typical query searches both the index and the full item index. Low specificity has an adverse effect on precision, but no effect to a potential increase in recall.

Another decision on indexing is what portions of an item should be indexed. The simplest case is to limit the indexing to the Title or Title and Abstract zones. This indexes the material that the author considers most important and reduces the costs associated indexing an item. This leads to loss of recall.

Weighting of index terms is not common in manual indexing systems. Weighting is the process of assigning an importance to an index term's use in an item. The weight should represent the degree to which the concept associated with the index term is represented in the item. The weight should help in discriminating the extent to which the concept is discussed in items in the database.

### 4.2.2   Precoordination and Linkages

Another decision on the indexing process is whether linkages are available between index terms for an item. Linkages are used to correlate related attributes associated with concepts discussed in an item. This process of creating term linkages at index creation time is called precoordination. When index terms are not coordinated at index time, the coordination occurs at search time. This is called post coordination that is coordinating terms after (post) the indexing process. Post coordination is implemented by "AND"ing index terms together, which only find indexes that have all of the search terms.

Factors that must be determined in the linkage process are the number of terms that can be related, any ordering constraints on the linked terms, and any additional descriptors are associated with the index terms (Vickery-70). The range of the number of index terms that can be linked is not a significant implementation issue and primarily affects the design of the indexer's user interface. When multiple terms are being used, the possibility exists to have relationships between the terms. For example, the capability to link the source of a problem, the problem and who is affected by the problem may be desired. Each term must be caveated with one of these three categories along with linking the terms together into an instance of the relationships describing one semantic concept. The order of the terms is one technique for providing additional role descriptor information on the index terms. Use of the order of the index terms to implicitly define additional term descriptor information limits the number of index terms that can have a role descriptor. If order is not used, modifiers may be associated with each term linked to define its role. This technique allows any number of terms to have the associated role descriptor. Figure 4.1 shows the different types of linkages. It assumes that an item discusses the drilling of oil wells in Mexico by CITGO and the introduction of oil refineries in Peru by the U.S. When the linked capability is added, the system does not erroneously relate Peru and Mexico since they are not in the same set of linked items. It still does not have the ability to discriminate between which country is introducing oil refineries into the other country. Introducing roles in the last two examples of Fig. 4.1 removes this ambiguity. Positional roles treat the data as a vector allowing only one value per position. Thus if the example is expanded so that the U.S. was introducing oil refineries in Peru, Bolivia and Argentina, then the positional role technique would require three entries, where the only difference would be in the value in the "affected country" position. When modifiers are used, only one entry would be required and all three countries would be listed with three "MODIFIER"s.

| INDEX TERMS | Methodology |
| --- | --- |
| oil, wells, Mexico, CITGO, refineries, Peru, BP, drilling | No linking of terms |
| (oil wells, Mexico, drilling, CITGO) | linked (Pre-coordination) |
| (U.S., oil refineries, Peru, introduction) | |
| (CITGO, drill, oil wells, Mexico) | linked (Pre-coordination) |
| (U.S., introduction, oil refineries, Peru) | with position indicating role |
| (SUBJECT: CITGO; ACTION: drilling; OBJECT: oil, wells MODIFIER: in Mexico) | linked (Pre-coordination) with modifier indicating role |
| (SUBJECT:U.S.; ACTION: introduces; OBJECT: oil refineries; MODIFIER: in Peru) | |

Fig. 4.1 Linkage of index terms

## 4.3   Automatic Indexing of Text

Automatic indexing is the capability for the system to automatically determine the index terms to be assigned to an item. The simplest case is when all words in the document are used as possible index terms (total document indexing). More complex processing is required when the objective is to emulate a human indexer and determine a limited number of index terms for the major concepts in the item. As discussed, the advantages of human indexing are the ability to determine concept abstraction and judge the value of a concept. The disadvantages of human indexing over automatic indexing are cost, processing time and consistency. Once the initial hardware cost is amortized, the costs of automatic indexing are absorbed as part of the normal operations and maintenance costs of the computer system. There are no additional indexing costs versus the salaries and benefits regularly paid to human indexers.

Processing time of an item by a human indexer varies significantly based upon the indexer's knowledge of the concepts being indexed, the exhaustivity and specificity guidelines and the amount and accuracy of preprocessing via Automatic File Build. Even for relatively short items (e.g., 300–500 words) it normally takes at least 5 min per item. A significant portion of this time is caused by the human interaction with the computer (e.g., typing speeds, cursor positioning, correcting spelling errors, and taking breaks between activities). Automatic indexing requires only a few seconds or less of computer time based upon the size of the processor and the complexity of the algorithms to generate the index.

Another advantage to automatic indexing is the predictably of algorithms. If the indexing is being performed automatically, by an algorithm, there is consistency in the index term selection process. Human indexers typically generate different indexing for the same document. In an experiment on consistency in TREC-2, there was, on the average, a 20% difference in judgment of the same item's topics between the original and a second independent judge of over 400 items (Harman-95). Since the judgments on relevance are different, the selection of index terms and their weighting to reflect the topics is also different. In automatic indexing, a sophisticated researcher understands the automatic process and be able to predict its utility and deficiencies, allowing for compensation for system characteristics in a search strategy. Even the end user, after interacting with the system, understands for certain classes of information and certain sources, the ability of the system to find relevant items is worse than other classes and sources. For example, the user may determine that searching for economic issues is far less precise than political issues in a particular newspaper based information system. The user may also determine that it is easier to find economic data in an information database containing *Business Weekly* than the newspaper source.

Automatic indexing is the process of analyzing an item to extract the information to be permanently kept in an index. This process is associated with the generation of the searchable data structures associated with an item. The first step in automatic indexing is associated with the Ingest process described in Chap. 3 where the structure of the item (e.g., zoning) and the processing tokens to be used in the indexing process are determined. In addition to the structure that is associated the document, in order to improve precision some systems automatically divide the document up into fixed length passages or localities, which become the item unit that is indexed (Kretser-99.) Having shorter logical documents limits the number of words that are associated with that item and thus avoids false hits that come from words separated by distances (e.g., paragraphs apart) that are unrelated still causing the retrieval of an item. The shorter items are only for search purposes in all cases the original item is retrieved. Figure 4.2 shows the indexing process and the associated search and retrieval process. After the searchable index is created the user will issue a search statement. The Hit List generated from the search will have pointers to the original documents so they can be displayed upon request from the user.

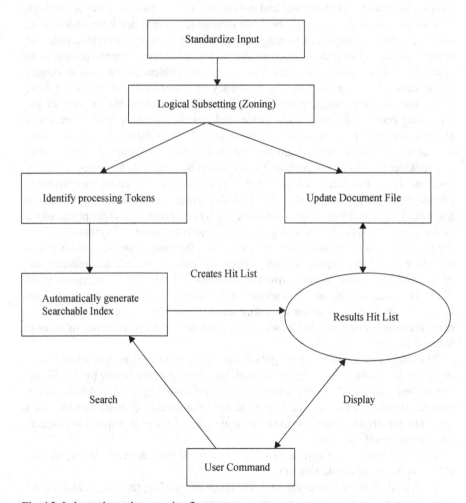

**Fig. 4.2** Index and search processing flow

Indexes resulting from automated indexing fall into two classes: weighted and unweighted. In an unweighted indexing system, the existence of an index term in a document and sometimes its word location(s) are kept as part of the searchable data structure. No attempt is made to discriminate between the values of the index terms in representing concepts in the item (i.e., they are all the same weight). Looking at the index, it is not possible to tell the difference between the main topics in the item and a casual reference to a concept. This architecture is typical of the commercial systems through the 1980s. Queries against unweighted systems are based upon Boolean logic and the items in the resultant Hit file are considered equal in value. The last item presented in the Hit file is as likely as the first item to be relevant to the user's information need.

To understand how automatic weighting occurs the first thing to consider is what information is available to the system to do the automatic indexing. There are three things available; the current item and the processing tokens in it, there is the database so far built and there could be other databases of reference information (e.g., in-link/out-links of web sites to judge a sites importance). In a weighted indexing system, an attempt is made to place a value on the index term's representation of its associated concept in the document. The most direct evidence to be used in weighting an item is the item itself and the frequency of occurrence of words in the item. Luhn, one of the pioneers in automatic indexing, introduced the concept of the "resolving power" of a term. Luhn postulated that the significance of a concept in an item is directly proportional to the frequency of use of the word associated with the concept in the document (Luhn-58, Salton-75). This is reinforced by the studies of Brookstein, Klein and Raita that show "content bearing" words are not randomly distributed (i.e., Poisson distributed), but that their occurrence "clump" within items (Brookstein-95). Typically, values for the index terms are normalized between zero and one. The higher the weight, the more the term represents a concept discussed in the item. The weight can be adjusted to account for other information such as the number of items in the database that contain the same concept. Although this process was initially applied to each processing token as if each was independent of its neighbors, some systems also consider word phases (i.e., Contiguous Word Phrases) as a searchable unit and apply similar techniques to weighting them. This initial weight is then adjusted by information across the database (such as how often the word occurs in other items and/or the other external databases of support information).

The query process uses the weights along with any weights assigned to terms in the query to determine a scalar value (rank value) used in predicting the likelihood that an item satisfies the query. Thresholds or a parameter specifying the maximum number of items to be returned is used to bind the number of items returned to a user. The results are presented to the user in order of the rank value from highest number to lowest number.

There are three major approaches to generation of the searchable index; statistical, natural language, and concept.

Statistical strategies cover the broadest range of indexing techniques and are the most prevalent in commercial systems. The basis for a statistical approach is use of frequency of occurrence of events. The events usually are related to occurrences of processing tokens (words/phrases) within documents and within the database. The words/phrases are the domain of searchable values. The statistics that are applied to the event data are probabilistic, Bayesian, and vector space. The static approach stores a single statistic, such as how often each word occurs in an item that is used in generating relevance scores after a standard Boolean search. Probabilistic indexing stores the information that are used in calculating a probability that a particular item satisfies (i.e., is relevant to) a particular query. Bayesian and vector approaches store information used in generating a relative confidence level of an item's relevance to a query. In addition the Bayesian approach is probabilistic, but to date the developers of this approach are more focused on a good relative relevance value than producing and absolute probability. Neural networks are dynamic learning structures that are also discussed under concept indexing where they are used to determine concept classes.

Natural Language approaches perform similar processing token identification as in statistical techniques, but then additionally perform varying levels of natural language parsing of the item. This parsing disambiguates the context of the processing tokens and generalizes to more abstract concepts within an item (e.g., present, past, future actions). This additional information is stored within the index to be used to enhance the search precision.

Concept indexing uses the words within an item to correlate to concepts discussed in the item. This is a mapping of the specific words to a new set of "concept words" used to index the item. When generating the concept words automatically, there is not a name applicable to the concept but just a statistical significance.

Finally, there is an extension of what is being indexed associated with the existence of hypertext linkages. These linkages provide virtual threads of concepts between items versus directly defining the concept within an item.

### 4.3.1 Statistical Indexing

Statistical indexing uses frequency of occurrence of events to calculate a number that is used to indicate the potential relevance of an item. One approach used in search of older systems does not use the statistics to aid in the initial selection, but uses them to assist in calculating a relevance value of each item for ranking. The documents are found by a normal Boolean search and then statistical calculations are performed on the Hit file, ranking the output (e.g., term frequency algorithms).

Probabilistic systems attempt to calculate a probability value that should be invariant to both calculation method and text corpora. This allows easy integration of the final results when searches are performed across multiple databases and use different search algorithms. A probability of 50% would mean that if enough items are reviewed, on the average one half of the reviewed items are relevant. The Bayesian and Vector approaches calculate a relative relevance value (i.e., confidence level) that a particular item is relevant. Quite often term distributions across the searchable database are used in the calculations. An issue that continues to be researched is how to merge results, even from the same search algorithm, from multiple databases. The problem is compounded when an attempt is made to merge the results from different search algorithms. This would not be a problem if true probabilities versus confidence levels were calculated.

### 4.3.1.1 Probabilistic Weighting

The probabilistic approach is based upon direct application of the theory of probability to information retrieval systems. This has the advantage of being able to use the developed formal theory of probability to direct the algorithmic development. It also leads to an invariant result that facilitates integration of results from different databases. The use of probability theory is a natural choice because it is the basis of evidential reasoning (i.e., drawing conclusions from evidence). This is summarized by the Probability Ranking Principle (PRP) and its Plausible Corollary (Cooper-94):

- HYPOTHESIS: If a reference retrieval system's response to each request is a ranking of the documents in the collection in order of decreasing probability of usefulness to the user who submitted the request, where the probabilities are estimated as accurately as possible on the basis of whatever data is available for this purpose, then the overall effectiveness of the system to its users is the best obtainable on the basis of that data.
- PLAUSIBLE COROLLARY: The most promising source of techniques for estimating the probabilities of usefulness for output ranking in IR is standard probability theory and statistics.

There are several factors that make this hypothesis and its corollary difficult (Gordon-92, Gordon-91, Robertson-77). Probabilities are usually based upon a binary condition; an item is relevant or not. But in information systems the relevance of an item is a continuous function from non-relevant to absolutely useful. A more complex theory of expected utility (Cooper-78) is needed to address this characteristic. Additionally, the output ordering by rank of items based upon probabilities, even if accurately calculated, may not be as optimal as that defined by some domain specific heuristic (Stirling-77). The domains in which probabilistic ranking are suboptimal are so narrowly focused as to make this a minor issue. But these issues mentioned are not as compelling as the benefit of a good probability value for ranking that would allow integration of results from multiple sources. There is an assumption in probability theory that terms are independent of each other, but proximity of terms in textual items affects their potential aggregate weight in representing a concept which is the ultimate goal.

The source of the problems that arise in application of probability theory come from a lack of accurate data and simplifying assumptions that are applied to the mathematical model. If nothing else, these simplifying assumptions cause the results of probabilistic approaches in ranking items to be less accurate than other approaches. The advantage of the probabilistic approach is that it can accurately identify its weak assumptions and work to strengthen them. In many other approaches, the underlying weaknesses in assumptions are less obvious and harder to identify and correct. Even with the simplifying assumption, results from comparisons of approaches in the TREC conferences have shown that the probabilistic approaches, while not scoring highest, are competitive against all other approaches.

There are many different areas in which the probabilistic approach may be applied. The method of logistic regression is described as an example of how a probabilistic approach is applied to information retrieval (Gey-94). The approach starts by defining a "Model 0" system which exists before specific probabilistic models are applied. In a retrieval system there exist query terms $q_i$ and document terms $d_i$, which have a set of attributes $(v_1, \ldots, v_n)$ from the query (e.g., counts of term frequency in the query), from the document (e.g., counts of term frequency in the document) and from the database (e.g., total number of documents in the database divided by the number of documents indexed by the term).

The logistic reference model uses a random sample of query-document-term triples for which binary relevance judgments have been made from a training sample. Log O is the logarithm of the odds (logodds) of relevance for term $t_k$ which is present in document $D_j$ and query $Q_i$:

$$\log(O(R|Q_i, D_j, t_k)) = c_0 + c_1 v_1 + \cdots + c_n v_n$$

The logarithm that the ith Query is relevant to the jth Document is the sum of the logodds for all terms:

$$\log(O(R|Q_i, D_j)) = \sum_{k=1}^{q} [\log(O(R|Q_i, D_j, t_k)) - \log(O(R))]$$

where $O(R)$ is the odds that a document chosen at random from the database is relevant to query $Q_i$. The coefficients $c$ are derived using logistic regression which fits an equation to predict a dichotomous independent variable as a function of independent variables that show statistical variation (Hosmer-89). The inverse logistic transformation is applied to obtain the probability of relevance of a document to a query:

$$P(R|Q_i, D_j) = 1 \backslash (1 + e^{-\log(O(R|Q_i, D_j))})$$

The coefficients of the equation for logodds is derived for a particular database using a random sample of query-document-term-relevance quadruples and used to predict odds of relevance for other query-document pairs.

Gey applied this methodology to the Cranfield Collection (Gey-94). The collection has 1,400 items and 225 queries with known results. Additional attributes of relative frequency in the query (QRF), relative frequency in the document (DRF) and relative frequency of the term in all the documents (RFAD) were included, producing the following logodds formula:

$$Z_j = \log(O(R|t_j)) = c_0 + c_1 \log(QAF) + c_2 \log(QRF) + c_3 \log(DAF)$$
$$+ c_4 \log(DRF) + c_5 \log(IDF) + c_6 \log(RFAD)$$

where QAF, DAF, and IDF were previously defined, QRF = QAF\(total number of terms in the query), DRF = DAF\(total number of words in the document) and RFAD = (total number of term occurrences in the database)\(total number of all words in the database). Logs are used to reduce the impact of frequency information; then smooth out skewed distributions. A higher maximum likelihood is attained for logged attributes.

The coefficients and log (O(R)) were calculated creating the final formula for ranking for query vector $\vec{Q}$, which contains q terms:

$$\log(O(R|\vec{Q})) = -5.138 + \sum_{k=1}^{q} (Z_j + 5.138)$$

The logistic inference method was applied to the test database along with the Cornell SMART vector system which uses traditional term frequency, inverse document frequency and cosine relevance weighting formulas (see Sect. 5.2.2). The logistic inference method outperformed the vector method.

Thus the index that supports the calculations for the logistic reference model contains the O(R) constant value (e.g., −5.138) along with the coefficients $c_0$ through $c_6$. Additionally, it needs to maintain the data to support DAF, DRF, IDF and RFAD. The values for QAF and QRF are derived from the query.

Attempts have been made to combine the results of different probabilistic techniques to get a more accurate value. The objective is to have the strong points of different techniques compensate for weaknesses. To date this combination of probabilities using averages of Log-Odds has not produced better results and in many cases produced worse results (Hull-96).

The Okapi weighting model that started with TREC in the 1990s tries to adjust the standard probability models to account for the variances in textual documents that were causing many of the errors in a probabilistic approach. It is probably the best developed probabilistic approach to information retrieval.

### 4.3.1.2   Baysean Indexing

Another Probabilistic model that has been most successful in this area is the Bayesian approach. This approach is natural to information systems and is based upon the theories of evidential reasoning (drawing conclusions from evidence). One way of overcoming the restrictions inherent in a vector model is to use a Bayesian approach to maintaining information on processing tokens. The Bayesian model provides a conceptually simple yet complete model for information systems. In its most general definition, the Bayesian approach is based upon conditional probabilities (e.g., Probability of Event 1 given Event 2 occurred). This general concept can be applied to the search function as well as to creating the index to the database. The objective of information systems is to return relevant items. Thus the general case, using the Bayesian formula, is P (REL/$DOC_i$, $Query_j$) which is interpreted as the probability of relevance (REL) to a search statement given a particular document and query.

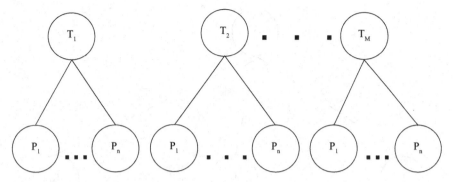

**Fig. 4.3** Bayesian term weighting

In addition to search, Bayesian formulas can be used in determining the weights associated with a particular processing token in an item. The objective of creating the index to an item is to represent the semantic information in the item. A Bayesian network can be used to determine the final set of processing tokens (called topics) and their weights. Figure 4.3 shows a simple view of the process where $T_i$ represents the relevance of topic "i" in a particular item and $P_j$ represents a statistic associated with the event of processing token "j" being present in the item.

The "m" topics would be stored as the final index to the item. The statistics associated with the processing token are typically frequency of occurrence. But they can also incorporate proximity factors that are useful in items that discuss multiple topics. There is one major assumption made in this model:

• Assumption of Binary Independence: the topics and the processing token statistics are independent of each other. The existence of one topic is not related to the existence of the other topics. The existence of one processing token is not related to the existence of other processing tokens.

In most cases this assumption is not true. Some topics are related to other topics and some processing tokens related to other processing tokens. For example, the topics of "Politics" and "Economics" are in some instances related to each other (e.g., an item discussing Congress debating laws associated with balance of trade) and in many other instances totally unrelated. The same type of example would apply to processing tokens. There are two approaches to handling this problem. The first is to assume that there are dependencies, but that the errors introduced by assuming the mutual independence do not noticeably effect the determination of relevance of neither an item nor its relative rank associated with other retrieved items. This is the most common approach used in system implementations. A second approach can extend the network to additional layers to handle interdependencies. Thus an additional layer of Independent Topics (ITs) can be placed above the Topic layer and a layer of Independent Processing Tokens (IPs) can be placed above the processing token layer. Figure 4.4 shows the extended Bayesian network. Extending the network creates new processing tokens for those cases where there are dependencies between processing tokens. The new set of Independent Processing Tokens can then be used to define the attributes associated with the set of topics selected to represent the semantics of an item.

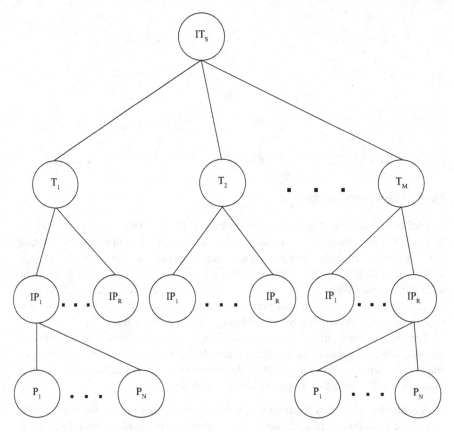

**Fig. 4.4** Extended Bayesian network

To compensate for dependencies between topics the final layer of Independent Topics is created. The degree to which each layer is created depends upon the error that could be introduced by allowing for dependencies between Topics or Processing Tokens. Although this approach is the most mathematically correct, it suffers from losing a level of precision by reducing the number of concepts available to define the semantics of an item.

### 4.3.1.3 Vector Weighting

One of the earliest systems that investigated statistical approaches to information retrieval was the SMART system at Cornell University (Buckley-95, Salton-83). The system is based upon a vector model. The semantics of every item are represented as a vector. A vector is a one-dimensional set of values, where the order/ position of each value in the set is fixed and represents a particular domain. In information retrieval, each position in the vector typically represents a process-

|          | Petroleum | Mexico | Oil | Taxes | Refineries | Shipping |
|----------|-----------|--------|-----|-------|------------|----------|
| Binary   | 1         | 1      | 1   | 0     | 1          | 0        |
| Weighted | 2.8       | 1.6    | 3.5 | .3    | 3.1        | .1       |

**Fig. 4.5** Binary and vector representation of an item

ing token. There are two approaches to the domain of values in the vector: binary and weighted. Under the binary approach, the domain contains the value of one or zero, with one representing the existence of the processing token in the item. In the weighted approach, the domain is typically the set of all real positive numbers. The value for each processing token represents the relative importance of that processing token in representing the semantics of the item. Figure 4.5 shows how an item that discusses petroleum refineries in Mexico would be represented. In the example, the major topics discussed are indicated by the index terms for each column (i.e., Petroleum, Mexico, Oil, Taxes, Refineries and Shipping).

Binary vectors require a decision process to determine if the degree that a particular processing token represents the semantics of an item is sufficient to include it in the vector. In the example for Fig. 4.5, a five-page item may have had only one sentence like "Standard taxation of the shipment of the oil to refineries is enforced." For the binary vector, the concepts of "Tax" and "Shipment" are below the threshold of importance (e.g., assume threshold is 1.0) and they not are included in the vector.

A weighted vector acts the same as a binary vector but it provides a range of values that accommodates a variance in the value of the relative importance of a processing token in representing the semantics of the item. The use of weights also provides a basis for determining the rank of an item.

The vector approach allows for a mathematical and a physical representation using a vector space model. Each processing token can be considered another dimension in an item representation space. In Chap. 5 it is shown that a query can be represented as one more vector in the same n-dimensional space. Figure 4.6 shows a

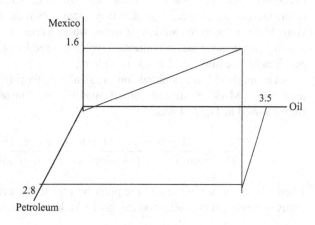

**Fig. 4.6** Vector
representation

three-dimensional vector representation assuming there were only three processing tokens, Petroleum, Mexico and Oil.

The original document vector is typically extended by additional information such as citations/references and some times categorization and entity extracted values to add more information for search and clustering purposes. The citation information is not weighted because it's more like database facts (e.g., date of publication).

There are many algorithms that can be used in calculating the weights used to represent a processing token. Part of the art in information retrieval is deriving changes to the basic algorithms to account for normalization (e.g., accounting for variances in number of words in items). The following subsections present the major algorithms starting with the most simple term frequency algorithm.

## Simple Term Frequency Algorithm

An automatic indexing process implements an algorithm to determine the weight to be assigned to a processing token for a particular item. Looking at a typical textual item, the data elements that are potentially available for calculating a weight are the frequency of occurrence of the processing token in an existing item (i.e., term frequency—TF), the frequency of occurrence of the processing token in the existing database (i.e., total frequency—TOTF) and the number of unique items in the database that contain the processing token (i.e., item frequency—IF, frequently labelled in other publications as document frequency—DF). As discussed previously, the premises by Luhn and later Brookstein that the resolving power of content-bearing words is directly proportional to the frequency of occurrence of the word in the item is used as the basis for most automatic weighting techniques. Weighting techniques usually are based upon positive weight values.

All algorithms start with the approach to have the weight equal to the term frequency. This approach emphasizes the use of a particular processing token within an item. Thus if the word "computer" occurs 15 times within an item it has a weight of 15. The simplicity of this technique encounters problems of normalization between items and use of the processing token within the database. The longer an item is, the more often a processing token may occur within the item. Use of the absolute value biases weights toward longer items, where a term is more likely to occur with a higher frequency. One normalization typically used in weighting algorithms compensates for the number of words in an item.

An example of this normalization in calculating term-frequency is the algorithm used in the SMART System at Cornell (Buckley-96). The term frequency weighting formula used in TREC 4 was:

$$\frac{(1 + \log(TF))/1 + \log(\text{average }(TF))}{(1 - \text{slope}) * \text{pivot} + \text{slope} * \text{number of unique terms}}$$

where slope was set at 0.2 and the pivot was set to the average number of unique terms occurring in the collection (Singhal-95). In addition to compensating for document length, they also want the formula to be insensitive to anomalies introduced by stemming or misspellings.

Although initially conceived of as too simple, experiments by the SMART system using the large databases in TREC demonstrated that use of the simpler algorithm with proper normalization factors is far more efficient in processing queries and return hits similar to more complex algorithms.

There are many approaches to account for different document lengths when normalizing the value of Term Frequency to use (e.g., an items that is only 50 words may have a much smaller term frequency then and item that is 1,000 words on the same topic). In the first technique, the term frequency for each word is divided by the maximum frequency of the word in any item. This normalizes the term frequency values to a value between zero and one. This technique is called "maximum term frequency". The problem with this technique is that the maximum term frequency in just one item in the database can be so large that it decreases the value of term frequency in short items to too small a value and loses significance. Additionally as new items are added to the database there is a question what to do with all of the currently processed items if one of them has a new larger maximum term frequency. A simpler version of this takes the maximum term frequency of any word within an item and divides all the term frequencies in the item by it—thus getting relative values between zero and one. Once again this can be distorted if on word has a very large term frequency within an item.

Another option is to use logaritmetic term frequency. In this technique the log of the term frequency plus a constant is used to replace the term frequency. The log function will perform the normalization when the term frequencies vary significantly due to size of documents. Along this line the COSINE function used as a similarity measure (see Chap. 5) can be used to normalize values in a document. This is accomplished by treating the index of a document as a vector and divide the weights of all terms by the length of the vector. This will normalize to a vector of maximum length one. This uses all of the data in a particular item to perform the normalization and will not be distorted by any particular term. The problem occurs when there are multiple topics within an item. The COSINE technique will normalize all values based upon the total length of the vector that represents all of topics. If a particular topic is important but briefly discussed, its normalized value could significantly reduce its overall importance in comparison to another document that only discusses the topic.

Another approach recognizes that the normalization process may be over penalizing long documents (Singhal-95). Singhal did experiments that showed longer documents in general are more likely to be relevant to topics then short documents. Yet normalization was making all documents appear to be the same length. To compensate, a correction factor was defined that is based upon document length that maps the Cosine function into an adjusted normalization function. The function determines the document length crossover point for longer documents where the probability of relevance equals the probability of retrieval. (given a query set). This value called the "pivot point" is used to apply an adjustment to the normalization process. The theory is based upon straight lines so it is a matter of determining slope of the lines.

$$\text{New normalization} = (\text{slope}) * (\text{old normalization}) + K$$

K is generated by the rotation of the pivot point to generate the new line and the old normalization = the new normalization at that point. The slope for all higher values will be different. Substituting pivot for both old and new value in the above formula we can solve for K at that point. Then using the resulting formula for K and substituting in the above formula produces the following formula:

$$\text{Pivoted function} = (\text{slope}) * (\text{old normalization}) + (1.0 - \text{slope}) * (\text{pivot})$$

Slope and pivot are constants for any document/query set. Another problem is that the Cosine function favors short documents over long documents and also favors documents with a large number of terms. This favoring is increased by using the pivot technique. If log(TF) is used instead of the normal frequency then TF is not a significant factor. In documents with large number of terms the Cosine factor is approximated by the square root of the number of terms. This suggests that using the ratio of the logs of term frequencies would work best for longer items in the calculations:

$$(1 + \log(TF))/(1 + \log(\text{average}(TF)))$$

This leads to the final algorithm that weights each term by the above formula divided by the pivoted normalization:

$$(1 + \log(TF))/(1 + \log(\text{average}(TF)))/(\text{slope})$$
$$(\text{No. unique terms}) + (1 - \text{slope}) * (\text{pivot})$$

Singhal demonstrated the above formula works better against TREC data then TF/MAX(TF) or vector length normalization. The effect of a document with a high term frequency is reduced by the normalization function by dividing the TF by the average TF and by use of the log function. The use of pivot normalization adjusts for the bias towards shorter documents increasing the weights of longer documents.

Inverse Document Frequency

Once the frequency within an item has been normalized the weighting can be improved by taking into consideration the frequency of occurrence of the processing token in the database. One of the objectives of indexing an item is to discriminate the semantics of that item from other items in the database. If the token "computer" occurs in every item in the database, its value representing the semantics of an item may be less useful compared to a processing token that occurs in only a subset of the items in the database. The term "computer" represents a concept used in an item, but it does not help a user find the specific information being sought since it returns the complete database. This leads to the general statement enhancing weighting algorithms that the weight assigned to an item should be inversely proportional to the frequency of occurrence of an item in the database. This is referred to as Shannon's information theory law. The algorithm based upon this idea is called inverse document frequency (IDF). The un-normalized weighting formula is:

$$\text{WEIGHT}_{ij} = \text{TF}_{ij} * [\text{Log}_2(n) - \text{Log}_2(\text{IF}_j) + 1]$$

where $\text{WEIGHT}_{ij}$ is the vector weight that is assigned to term "j" in item "i," $\text{TF}_{ij}$ (term frequency) is the frequency of term "j" in item "i", "n" is the number of items in the database and $\text{IF}_j$ (item frequency or document frequency) is the number of items in the database that have term "j" in them. A negative log is the same as dividing by the log value, thus the basis for the name of the algorithm. Figure 5.4 demonstrates the impact of using this weighting algorithm. The term "refinery" has the highest frequency in the new item (10 occurrences). But it has a normalized weight of 20 which is less than the normalized weight of "Mexico." This change in relative importance between "Mexico" and "refinery" from the unnormalized to normalized vectors is due to an adjustment caused by "refinery" already existing in 50% of the database versus "Mexico" which is found in 6.25% of the items.

The major factor of the formula for a particular term is $(\text{Log}_2(n) - \text{Log}_2(\text{IF}_j))$. The value for IF can vary from "1" to "n." At "n," the term is found in every item in the database and the factor becomes $(\text{Log}_2(n) - \text{Log}_2(n)) = 1$. As the number of items a term is found in decreases, the value of the denominator decreases eventually approaching the value $\text{Log}_2(1)$ which is close to 1. The weight assigned to the term in the item varies from $\text{Tf}_{i,j} * (1 + 1)$ to $\text{Tf}_{i,j} * (\sim\text{Log}_2(n))$. The effect of this factor can be too great as the number of items that a term is found in becomes small. To compensate for this, the INQUERY system at the University of Massachusetts normalizes this factor by taking an additional log value.

The value of "n" and $\text{IF}_i$ vary as items are added and deleted from the database. To implement this algorithm in a dynamically changing system, the physical index only stores the frequency of occurrence of the terms in an item (usually with their word location) and the IDF factor is calculated dynamically at retrieval time. The required information can easily be determined from an inversion list for a search term that is retrieved and a global variable on the number of items in the database. The following example shows how inverse document frequency works.

Assume that the term "oil" is found in 128 items, "Mexico" is found in 16 items and "refinery" is found in 1,024 items. If a new item arrives with all three terms in it, "oil" found 4 times, "Mexico" found 8 times, and "refinery" found 10 times and there are 2,048 items in the total database, Fig. 5.4 shows the weight calculations using inverse document frequency.

Using a simple unnormalized term frequency, the item vector is (4, 8, 10)
Using inverse document frequency the following calculations apply:

$$\text{Weight}_{oil} = 4 * (\text{Log}_2(2048) - \text{Log}_2(128) + 1) = 4 * (11 - 7 + 1) = 20$$
$$\text{Weight}_{Mexico} = 8 * (\text{Log}_2(2048) - \text{Log}_2(16) + 1) = 8 * (11 - 4 + 1) = 64$$
$$\text{Weight}_{refinery} = 10 * (\text{Log}_2(2048) - \text{Log}_2(1024) + 1) = 10 * (11 - 10 + 1) = 20$$

with the resultant inverse document frequency item vector = (20, 64, 20)

**Fig. 4.7** Item distribution for
SAW and DRILL

| Item Distribution | SAW | DRILL |
|---|---|---|
| A | 10 | 2 |
| B | 10 | 2 |
| C | 10 | 18 |
| D | 10 | 10 |
| E | 10 | 18 |

## Signal Weighting

Inverse document frequency adjusts the weight of a processing token for an item based upon the number of items that contain the term in the existing database. What it does not account for is the term frequency distribution of the processing token in the items that contain the term. The distribution of the frequency of processing tokens within an item can affect the ability to rank items. For example, assume the terms "SAW" and "DRILL" are found in 5 items with the following frequencies defined in Fig. 4.7.

Both terms are found a total of 50 times in the five items. The term "SAW" does not give any insight into which item is more likely to be relevant to a search of "SAW". If precision is a goal (maximizing relevant items shown first), then the weighting algorithm could take into consideration the non-uniform distribution of term "DRILL" in the items that the term is found, applying even higher weights to it than "SAW." The theoretical basis for the algorithm to emphasize precision is Shannon's work on Information Theory (Shannon-51).

In Information Theory, the information content value of an object is inversely proportional to the probability of occurrence of the item. An instance of an event that occurs all the time has less information value than an instance of a seldom occurring event. This is represented as INFORMATION $= -\log_2(p)$, where p is the probability of occurrence of event "p." The information value for an event that occurs 0.5% of the time is:

$$\text{INFORMATION} = -\text{Log}_2(.005)$$
$$= -(-7.64)$$
$$= 7.64$$

The information value for an event that occurs 50% of the time is:

$$\text{INFORMATION} = -\text{Log}_2(.50)$$
$$= -(-1)$$
$$= 1$$

If there are many independent occurring events then the calculation for the average information value across the events is:

$$\text{AVE\_INFO} = -\sum_{k=1}^{n} p_k \, \text{Log}_2(p_k)$$

The value of AVE_INFO takes its maximum value when the values for every $p_k$ is the same. Its value decreases proportionally to increases in variances in the values of $p_k$. The value of $p_k$ can be defined as $TF_{ik}/TOTF_k$, the ratio of the frequency of occurrence of the term in an item to the total number of occurrences of the item in the data base. Using the AVE_INFO formula, the terms that have the most uniform distribution in the items that contain the term have the maximum value. To use this information in calculating a weight, the formula needs the inverse of AVE_INFO, where the minimum value is associated with uniform distributions and the maximum value is for terms that have large variances in distribution in the items containing the term. The following formula for calculating the weighting factor called **Signal** can be used:

$$Signal_k = Log_2(TOTF) - AVE\_INFO$$

producing a final formula of:

$$Weight_{ik} = TF_{ik} * Signal_k$$

$$Weight_{ik} = TF_{ik} * \left[ Log_2(TOTF_k) - \sum_{i=1}^{n} -TF_{ik}/TOTF_k Log_2(TF_{ik}/TOTF_k) \right]$$

An example of use of the weighting factor formula is given for the values in Fig. 5.5:

$$Signal_{SAW} = LOG_2(50) - [5 * \{10/50 LOG_2(10/50)\}]$$
$$= 5.64 - (5 * (0.2 * (2.32))) = 5.64 - 2.32 = 2.68$$

$$Signal_{DRILL} = LOG_2(50) - \left[ 2/50 LOG_2(2/50) + 2/50 LOG_2(2/50) \right.$$
$$+ 18/50 LOG_2(18/50) + 10/50 LOG_2(10/50)$$
$$+ \left. 18/50 LOG_2(18/50) \right]$$
$$= 5.64 - (0.04 * (4.64) + 0.04 * (4.64) + 0.36(1.47) + (0.2 * (2.32)$$
$$+ (0.36(1.47)))) = 5.64 - (0.186 + 0.186 + 0.053 + 0.464 + 0.053)$$
$$= 5.64 - 0.942 = 4.058$$

The weighting factor for term "DRILL" that does not have a uniform distribution is larger than that for term "SAW" and gives it a higher weight.

This technique could be used by itself or in combination with inverse document frequency or other algorithms. The overhead of the additional data needed in an index and the calculations required to get the values have not been demonstrated to produce better results than other techniques and are not used in any systems at this time. It is a good example of use of Information Theory in developing information retrieval algorithms. Effectiveness of use of this formula can be found in results from Harman and also from Lockbaum and Streeter (Harman-86, Lochbaum-89).

Discrimination Value

Another approach to creating a weighting algorithm is to base it upon the discrimination value of a term. To achieve the objective of finding relevant items, it is important that the index discriminates among items. The more all items appear the same, the harder it is to identify those that are needed. To use this approach a "similarity" function is needed that can compare two Items and determine how similar they are. When the function is applied to the two Items the results should be a value between zero and one, where zero would mean there is no similarity between the Items and 1 suggests that the items are the same. Examples of these functions are in Chap. 5. Salton and Yang (Salton-73) proposed a weighting algorithm that takes into consideration the ability for a search term to discriminate among items. They proposed use of a discrimination value for each term "i":

$$DISCRIM_i = AVESIM_i - AVESIM$$

where AVESIM is the average similarity between every item in the database and $AVESIM_i$ is the same calculation except that term "i" is removed from all items. AVESIM is calculated by summing the similarity between every Item and every other Item in the database and then divide by a normalization number. There are three possibilities with the $DISCRIM_i$ value being positive, close to zero or negative. A positive value indicates that removal of term "i" has increased the similarity between items. In this case, leaving the term in the database assists in discriminating between items and is of value. A value close to zero implies that the term's removal or inclusion does not change the similarity between items. If the value of $DISCRIM_i$ is negative, the term's effect on the database is to make the items appear more similar since their average similarity decreased with its removal. Once the value of $DISCRM_i$ is normalized as a positive number, it can be used in the standard weighting formula as:

$$Weight_{ik} = TF_{ik} * DISCRIM_k$$

Problems with Weighting Schemes

Often weighting schemes use information that is based upon processing token distributions across the database. The two weighting schemes, inverse document frequency and signal, use total frequency and item frequency factors which makes them dependent upon distributions of processing tokens within the database. Information databases tend to be dynamic with new items always being added and to a lesser degree old items being changed or deleted. Thus these factors are changing dynamically. There are a number of approaches to compensate for the constant changing values.

1. Ignore the variances and calculate weights based upon current values, with the factors changing over time. Periodically rebuild the complete search database.

2. Use a fixed value while monitoring changes in the factors. When the changes reach a certain threshold, start using the new value and update all existing vectors with the new value.

3. Store the invariant variables (e.g., term frequency within an item) and at search time calculate the latest weights for processing tokens in items needed for search terms.

In the first approach the assumption minimizes the system overhead of maintaining currency on changing values, with the effect that term weights for the same term vary from item to item as the aggregate variables used in calculating the weights based upon changes in the database vary over time. Periodically the database and all term weights are recalculated based upon the most recent updates to the database. For large databases in the millions of items, the overhead of rebuilding the database can be significant. In the second approach, there is recognition that for the most frequently occurring items, the aggregate values are large. As such, minor changes in the values have negligible effect on the final weight calculation. Thus, on a term basis, updates to the aggregate values are only made when sufficient changes not using the current value will have an effect on the final weights and the search/ranking process. This process also distributes the update process over time by only updating a subset of terms at any instance in time. The third approach is the most accurate. The weighted values in the database only matter when they are being used to determine items to return from a query or the rank order to return the items. This has more overhead in that database vector term weights must be calculated dynamically for every query term. If the system is using an inverted file search structure, this overhead is minor.

An interesting side effect of maintaining currency in the database for term weights is that the same query over time returns a different ordering of items. A new word in the database undergoes significant changes in its weight structure from initial introduction until its frequency in the database reaches a level where small changes do not have significant impact on changes in weight values.

Another issue is the desire to partition an information database based upon time. The value of many sources of information vary exponentially based upon the age of an item (older items have less value). This leads to physically partitioning the database by time (e.g., starting a new database each year), allowing the user to specify the time period to search. There are issues then of how to address the aggregate variables that are different for the same processing token in each database and how to merge the results from the different databases into a single Hit file.

The best environment would allow a user to run a query against multiple different time periods and different databases that potentially use different weighting algorithms, and have the system integrate the results into a single ranked Hit file.


Problems with the Vector Model

In addition to the general problem of dynamically changing databases and the effect on weighting factors, there are problems with the vector model on assignment of a weight for a particular processing token to an item. Each processing token can be viewed as a new semantic topic. A major problem comes in the vector model when there are multiple topics being discussed in a particular item. For example, assume that an item has an in-depth discussion of "oil" in "Mexico" and also "coal" in "Pennsylvania." The vector model does not have a mechanism to associate each energy source with its particular geographic area. There is no way to associate correlation factors between terms (i.e., precoordination discussed in Chap. 3) since each dimension in a vector is independent of the other dimensions. Thus the item results in a high value in a search for "coal in Mexico."

Another major limitation of a vector space is in associating positional information with a processing term. The concept of proximity searching (e.g., term "a" within 10 words of term "b") requires the logical structure to contain storage of positional information of a processing term. The concept of a vector space allows only one scalar value to be associated with each processing term for each item. Restricting searches to subsets of an item has been shown to provide increased precision. In effect this capability overcomes the multi-topical item problem by looking at subsets of an item and thus increasing the probability that the subset is discussing a particular semantic topic.

## 4.3.2   Natural Language

The goal of natural language processing is to use the semantic information in addition to the statistical information to enhance the indexing of the item. This improves the precision of searches, reducing the number of false hits a user reviews. The semantic information is extracted as a result of processing the language rather than treating each word as an independent entity. The simplest output of this process results in generation of phrases that become indexes to an item. More complex analysis generates thematic representation of events rather than phrases. Statistical approaches use proximity as the basis behind determining the strength of word relationships in generating phrases. For example, with a proximity constraint of adjacency, the phrases "venetian blind" and "blind Venetian" may appear related and map to the same phrase. But syntactically and semantically those phrases are very different concepts. Word phrases generated by natural language processing algorithms enhance indexing specification and provide another level of disambiguation. Natural language processing can also combine the concepts into higher level concepts sometimes referred to as thematic representations. One example represents them as concept-relationship-concept triples (Liddy-93).

### 4.3.2.1   Index Phrase Generation

The goal of indexing is to represent the semantic concepts of an item in the information system to support finding relevant information. Single words have conceptual context, but frequently they are too general to help the user find the desired information. Term phrases allow additional specification and focusing of the concept to provide better precision and reduce the user's overhead of retrieving non-relevant items. Having the modifier "grass" or "magnetic" associated with the term "field" clearly disambiguates between very different concepts. One of the earliest statistical approaches to determining term phrases proposed by Salton was use of a COHE-SION factor between terms (Salton-83):

$$COHESION_{k,h} = SIZE\text{-}FACTOR * (PAIR\text{-}FREQ_{k,h}/(TOTF_k * TOTF_H))$$

where SIZE-FACTOR is a normalization factor based upon the size of the vocabulary and PAIR-FREQ$_{k,h}$ is the total frequency of co-occurrence of the pair Term$_k$, Term$_h$ in the item collection. Co-occurrence may be defined in terms of adjacency, word proximity, sentence proximity, etc. This initial algorithm has been modified in the SMART system to be based on the following guidelines (Buckley-95):

- any pair of adjacent non-stop words is a potential phrase
- any pair must exist in 25 or more items
- phrase weighting uses a modified version of the SMART system single term algorithm
- normalization is achieved by dividing by the length of the single-term subvector.

Natural language processing can reduce errors in determining phrases by determining inter-item dependencies and using that information to create the term phrases used in the indexing process. Statistical approaches tend to focus on two term phrases. A major advantage of natural language approaches is their ability to produce multiple-term phrases to denote a single concept. If a phrase such as "industrious intelligent students" was used often, a statistical approach would create phrases such as "industrious intelligent" and "intelligent student." A natural language approach would create phrases such as "industrious student," "intelligent student" and "industrious intelligent student."

The first step in a natural language determination of phrases is a lexical analysis of the input. In its simplest form this is a part of speech tagger that, for example, identifies noun phrases by recognizing adjectives and nouns. Precise part of speech taggers exist that are accurate to the 99% range. Additionally, proper noun identification tools exist that allow for accurate identification of names, locations and organizations since these values should be indexed as phrases and not undergo stemming. Greater gains come from identifying syntactic and semantic level dependencies creating a hierarchy of semantic concepts. For example, "nuclear reactor fusion" could produce term phrases of "nuclear reactor" and "nuclear fusion." In the ideal case all variations of a phrase would be reduced to a single canonical form that represents the semantics for a phrase. Thus, where possible the phrase detection process should output a normalized form. For example, "blind Venetian" and "Venetian who is blind" should map to the same phrase. This not only increases the precision of searches, but also increases the frequency of occurrence of the common phrase. This, in turn, improves the likelihood that the frequency of occurrence of the common phrase is above the threshold required to index the phrase. Once the phrase is indexed, it is available for search, thus participating in an item's selection for a

**Fig. 4.8** Part of speech tags

| CLASS | EXAMPLES |
| --- | --- |
| determiners | a, the |
| singular nouns | paper, notation, structure |
| plural nouns | operations, data, processes |
| preposition | in, by, of, for |
| adjective | high, concurrent |
| present tense verb | presents, associates |
| present participal | multiprogramming |

search and the rank associated with an item in the Hit file. One solution to finding a common form is to transform the phrases into an operator-argument form or a header-modifier form. There is always a category of semantic phrases that comes from inferring concepts from an item that is non-determinable. This comes from the natural ambiguity inherent in a language that is discussed in Chap. 1.

A good example of application of natural language to phrase creation is in the natural language information retrieval system at New York University developed in collaboration with GE Corporate Research and Development. The text of the item is processed by a fast syntactical process and extracted phrases are added to the index in addition to the single word terms. Statistical analysis is used to determine similarity links between phrases and identification of subphrases. Once the phrases are statistically noted as similar, a filtering process categorizes the link onto a semantic relationship (generality, specialization, antonymy, complementation, synonymy, etc.).

The Tagged Text Parser (TTP), based upon the Linguistic String Grammar, produces a regularized parse tree representation of each sentence reflecting the predicate-argument structure. The tagged text parser contains over 400 grammar production rules. Some examples of the part of speech tagger identification are given in Fig. 4.8.

The TTP parse trees are header-modifier pairs where the header is the main concept and the modifiers are the additional descriptors that form the concept and eliminate ambiguities. Figure 4.9 gives an example of a regularized parse tree structure generated for the independent clause.

This structure allows for identification of potential term phrases usually based upon noun identification. To determine if a header-modifier pair warrants indexing, Strzalkowski calculates a value for Informational Contribution (IC) for each element in the pair. Higher values of IC indicate a potentially stronger semantic relationship between terms. The basis behind the IC formula is a conditional probability between the terms. The formula for IC between two terms (x, y) is:

$$IC(x, [x, y]) = \frac{f_{x,y}}{Nx + Dx - 1}$$

where $f_{x,y}$ is the frequency of (x, y) in the database, $n_x$ is the number of pairs in which "x" occurs at the same position as in (x, y) and $D(x)$ is the dispersion parameter

**Fig. 4.9** TTP parse tree

The former Soviet President has been a local hero
ever since a Russian tank invaded Wisconsin

```
|assert
 perf[HAVE]
  verb[BE]
   subject
    np
     noun[President]
     t_pos[The]
     adj[former]
     adj[Soviet]
   object
    np
     noun[hero]
     t_pos[a]
     adj[local]
   adv[ever]
   sub_ord
    [since]
     verb[invade]
      subject
       np
        noun[tank]
        t_pos[a]
        adj[Russian]
      object
       np
        noun[Wisconsin]
```

which is the number of distinct words with which x is paired. When IC = 1, x occurs only with y ($f_{x,y} = n_x$ and $d_x = 1$).

Nominal compounds are the source of many inaccurate identifications in creating header-modifier pairs. Use of statistical information on frequency of occurrence of phrases can eliminate some combinations that occur infrequently and are not meaningful.

The next challenge is to assign weights to term phrases. The most popular term weighting scheme uses term frequencies and inverse document frequencies with normalization based upon item length to calculate weights assigned to terms. Term phrases have lower frequency occurrences than the individual terms. Using natural language processing, the focus is on semantic relationships versus frequency relationships. Thus weighting schemes such as inverse document frequency require adjustments so that the weights are not overly diminished by the potential lower frequency of the phrases. For example, the weighting scheme used in the New York University system uses the following formula for weighting phrases:

$$\text{weight}(\text{Phrase}_i) = (C_i * \log(\text{termf}) + C_2 * \alpha(N, i)) * \text{IDF}$$

where $\alpha(N,i)$ is 1 for i < N and 0 otherwise and $C_1$ and $C_2$ are normalizing factors. The N assumes the phrases are sorted by IDF value and allows the top "N" highest

IDF (inverse document frequency) scores to have a greater effect on the overall weight than other terms.

### 4.3.2.2 Natural Language Processing

Section 4.3.2.1 discussed generation of term phrases as indexes. Lexical analysis determining verb tense, plurality and part of speech is assumed to have been completed prior to the following additional processing. Natural language processing not only produces more accurate term phrases, but can provide higher level semantic information identifying relationships between concepts.

The DR-LINK system (Liddy-93) and its commercial implementation via Textwise System adds the functional processes Relationship Concept Detectors, Conceptual Graph Generators and Conceptual Graph Matchers that generate higher level linguistic relationships including semantic and discourse level relationships. This system has evolved into the CINDOR system that expanded to natural language (http://www.textwiselabs.com/government/index.html) and cross language retrieval. This system is representative of natural language based processing systems. During the first phase of this approach, the processing tokens in the document are mapped to Subject Codes as defined by the codes in the Longman's Dictionary of Common English (LDOCE). Disambiguation uses *a priori* statistical term relationships and the ordering of the subject codes in the LDOCE, which indicates most likely assignment of a term to a code. These codes equate to index term assignment and have some similarities to the concept-based systems discussed in Sect. 5.4.

The next phase is called the Text Structurer, which attempts to identify general discourse level areas within an item. Thus a news story may be subdivided into areas associated with EVALUATION (opinions), Main event (basic facts), and Expectations (Predictions). These have been updated to include Analytical Information, Cause/Effect Dimension and Attributed Quotations in the more recent versions of DR-LINK (see http://199.100.96.2 on the Internet). These areas can then be assigned higher weighting if the user includes "Preference" in a search statement. The system also attempts to determine TOPIC statement identifiers. Natural language processing is not just determining the topic statement(s) but also assigning semantic attributes to the topic such as time frame (past, present, and future). To perform this type analysis, a general model of the predicted text is needed. For example, news items likely follow a model proposed by van Dijk (Dijk-88). Liddy reorganized this structure into a News Schema Components consisting of Circumstance, Consequence, Credentials, Definition, Error, Evaluation, Expectation, History, Lead, Main Event, No Comment, Previous Event, References and Verbal reaction. Each sentence is evaluated and assigned weights associated with its possible inclusion in the different components. Thus, if a query is oriented toward a future activity, then, in addition to the subject code vector mapping, it would weight higher terms associated with the Expectation component.

The next level of semantic processing is the assignment of terms to components, classifying the intent of the terms in the text and identifying the topical statements. The next level of natural language processing identifies inter-relationships between the concepts. For example, there may be two topics within an item "national elections" and "guerrilla warfare." The relationship "as a result of" is critical to link the order of these two concepts. This process clarifies if the elections were caused by the warfare or the warfare caused by the elections. Significant information is lost by not including the connector relationships. These types of linkages are generated by general linguistic cues (words in text) that are fairly general and domain independent.

The final step is to assign final weights to the established relationships. The relationships are typically envisioned as triples with two concepts and a relationship between them. Although all relationships are possible, constructing a system requires the selection of a subset of possible relationships and the rules to locate the relationships. The weights are based upon a combination of statistical information and values assigned to the actual words used in establishing the linkages. Passive verbs would receive less weight than active verbs.

The additional information beyond the indexing is kept in additional data structures associated with each item. This information is used whenever it is implicitly included in a search statement that is natural language based or explicitly requested by the user.

## *4.3.3  Concept Indexing*

Natural language processing starts with a basis of the terms within an item and extends the information kept on an item to phrases and higher level concepts such as the relationships between concepts. In the DR-LINK system, terms within an item are replaced by an associated Subject Code. Use of subject codes or some other controlled vocabulary is one way to map from specific terms to more general terms. Often the controlled vocabulary is defined by an organization to be representative of the concepts they consider important representations of their data. Concept indexing takes the abstraction a level further. Its goal is to gain the implementation advantages of an index term system but use concepts instead of terms as the basis for the index, producing a reduced dimension vector space. By reducing the dimensionality (think of it as the number of words in the "concept language"), different synonyms for the same word/concept will be mapped to a single new word (concept vector). This then helps solve the difference in vocabularies that is one of the core problems in information retrieval.

Rather than *a priori* defining a set of concepts that the terms in an item are mapped to, concept indexing can start with a number of unlabeled concept classes and let the information in the items define the concepts classes created. The process of automatic creation of concept classes is similar to the automatic generation of thesaurus classes that will be described in Chap. 6. The process of mapping from a specific term to a concept that the term represents is complex because a term may represent multiple different concepts to different degrees. A term such as "automobile" could be associated with concepts such as "vehicle," "transportation," "mechanical device," "fuel," and "environment." The term "automobile" is strongly related to "vehicle," lesser to "transportation" and much lesser the other terms. Thus a term in an item needs to be represented by many concept codes with different weights for a particular item.

An early example of applying a concept approach is the Convectis System from HNC Software Inc. (Caid-93) approaches for decision software. The basis behind the generation of the concept approach is a neural network model (Waltz-85). If a vector approach is envisioned, then there is a finite number of concepts that provide coverage over all of the significant concepts required to index a database of items. The goal of the indexing is to allow the user to find required information, minimizing the reviewing of items that are non-relevant. In an ideal environment there would be enough vectors to account for all possible concepts and thus they would be orthogonal in an "N" dimensional vector-space model. It is difficult to find a set of concepts that are orthogonal with no aspects in common. Additionally, implementation trade offs naturally limit the number of concept classes that are practical. These limitations increase the number of classes to which a processing token is mapped.

The Convectis system uses neural network algorithms and terms in a similar context (proximity) of other terms as a basis for determining which terms are related and defining a particular concept. A term can have different weights associated with different concepts as described. The definition of a similar context is typically defined by the number of non-stop words separating the terms. The farther apart terms are, the less coupled the terms are associated within a particular concept class. Existing terms already have a mapping to concept classes. New terms can be mapped to existing classes by applying the context rules to the classes that terms near the new term are mapped. Special rules must be applied to create a new concept class. Example Fig. 4.10 demonstrates how the process would work for the term "automobile."

Using the concept representation of a particular term, phrases and complete items can be represented as a weighted average of the concept vectors of the terms

| TERM: automobile | Weights for associated concepts |
|---|---|
| Vehicle | .65 |
| Transportation | .60 |
| Environment | .35 |
| Fuel | .33 |
| Mechanical Device | .15 |

**Fig. 4.10** Concept vector for automobile

Vector Representation Automobile: (.65, ... , .60, ... , .35, .33, ... , .15)

in them. The algorithms associated with vectors (e.g., inverse document frequency) can be used to perform the merging of concepts.

Latent Semantic Indexing (LSI) is another approach to defining concept vectors and it is the more common approach in commercial systems. GOOGLE, when it acquired Applied Semantics, recognized that to better deliver what a user is looking for, the limitation of only returning results based upon the users query terms is too restrictive. Another major commercial company (Autonomy and their IDOL system) also claim to be using concept indexing, but it is based upon an Naïve Baysean approach. Latent Semantic Indexing's assumption is that there is an underlying or "latent" structure represented by interrelationships between words (Deerwester-90, Dempster-77, Dumais-95, Gildea-99, Hofmann-99). The index contains representations of the "latent semantics" of the item. The large term-document matrix is decomposed into a small set (e.g., 100–300) of orthogonal factors which use linear combinations of the factors (concepts) to approximate the original matrix. Latent Semantic Indexing uses singular-value decomposition to model the associative relationships between terms similar to eigenvector decomposition and factor analysis (see Cullum-85).

As described in Chap. 2, a rectangular matrix can be decomposed into the product of three matrices. Let $X$ be a $m \times n$ matrix such that:

$$X = T_0 \cdot S_0 \cdot D_0'$$

where $T_0$ and $D_0$ have orthogonal columns and are $m \times r$ and $r \times n$ matrices, $S_0$ is an $r \times r$ diagonal matrix and $r$ is the rank of matrix $X$. This is the singular value decomposition of $X$. The $k$ largest singular values of $S_0$ are kept along with their corresponding columns in $T_0$ and $D_0$ matrices, the resulting matrix:

$$\bar{X} = T_n \cdot S_n \cdot D_n'$$

is the unique matrix of rank $k$ that is closest in least squares sense to $X$. The matrix $\bar{X}$, containing the first $k$ independent linear components of the original $X$ represents the major associations with noise eliminated.

If you consider X to be the term-document matrix (e.g., all possible terms being represented by columns and each item being represented by a row), then truncated singular value decomposition can be applied to reduce the dimmensionality caused by all terms to a significantly smaller dimensionality that is an approximation of the original X:

$$X = U \cdot SV \cdot V'$$

where $u_1 \ldots u_k$ and $v^1 \ldots v^k$ are left and right singular vectors and $sv_1 \ldots sv_k$ are singualr values. A threshold is used against the full SV diagonal matrix to determine the cutoff on values to be used for query and document representation (i.e., the dimensionality reduction). Hofmann has modified the standard LSI approach using addional formalism via Probabilistic Latent Semantic Analysis (Hofmann-99).

With so much reduction in the number of words, closeness is determined by patterns of word usage versus specific co-locations of terms. This has the effect of a thesaurus in equating many terms to the same concept. Both terms and documents (as collections of terms) can be represented as weighted vectors in the $k$ dimensional space. The selection of $k$ is critical to the success of this procedure. If $k$ is too small, then there is not enough discrimination between vectors and too many false hits are returned on a search. If $k$ is too large, the value of Latent Semantic Indexing is lost and the system equates to a standard vector model.

The details of how to create the vectors for Latent Semantic Indexing was described in detail in Chap. 2. We will now use that derivation and relate it to creating a textual index. We will redefine the original matrix A from Chap. 2 to be a matrix representing a textual input and use an example shown in Grossman and Fieder book on Information Retrieval (Grossman and Fieder 2004). In Chap. 5 we will show how a query operates against the index.

D1: "Shipment of gold damaged in a fire"
D2: "Delivery of silver arrived in a silver truck"
D3: "Shipment of gold arrived in a truck"

That produces the matrix we used in the LSI example in Chap. 2:

|          | D1 | D2 | D3 |
|----------|----|----|----|
| a        | 1  | 1  | 1  |
| arrived  | 0  | 1  | 1  |
| damaged  | 1  | 0  | 0  |
| delivery | 0  | 1  | 0  |
| fire     | 1  | 0  | 0  |
| gold     | 1  | 0  | 1  |
| in       | 1  | 1  | 1  |
| of       | 1  | 1  | 1  |
| Shipment | 1  | 0  | 1  |
| silver   | 0  | 2  | 0  |
| truck    | 0  | 1  | 1  |

The goal is to reduce the dimensionality of the information space and that is accomplished by dropping the lowest singular values of the S matrix. The S matrix calculated in Chap. 2 was:

$$ S = \begin{bmatrix} s_1 & 0 & 0 \\ 0 & s_2 & 0 \\ 0 & 0 & s_3 \end{bmatrix} = \begin{bmatrix} 4.0989 & 0 & 0 \\ 0 & 2.3616 & 0 \\ 0 & 0 & 1.2736 \end{bmatrix} $$

There are only three values so in this example the lowest value (1.2737) is dropped. The U matrix can be thought of as a mapping of the original vocabulary (rows) to the new concept vector vocabulary (columns). Instead of each column representing a document each column represents a concept vector and the rows are mapping how much each processing token in the original document space is represented in each of the concept vectors. The column associated with the lowest singular value is dropped. In the Singular value diagonal matrix the row in this example (or rows) with lowest values are dropped. The V matrix can be considered a mapping of the documents to the concept vectors which are like the new vocabulary with the concept vectors being the rows. Thus the bottom row in this case is dropped. This yields the following index space starting with

$$
U: \begin{bmatrix}
0.4202 & 0.0748 & -0.0461 \\
0.2995 & -0.2 & 0.4078 \\
0.1207 & 0.2748 & -0.4539 \\
0.1576 & -0.3046 & -0.2007 \\
0.1207 & 0.2748 & -0.4539 \\
0.2626 & 0.3794 & 0.1546 \\
0.4202 & 0.0748 & -0.0461 \\
0.4202 & 0.0748 & -0.0461 \\
0.2626 & 0.3794 & 0.1546 \\
0.3152 & -0.6092 & -0.4014 \\
0.2995 & -0.2 & 0.4078
\end{bmatrix}
\text{ to }
\begin{bmatrix}
0.4202 & 0.0748 \\
0.2995 & -0.2 \\
0.1207 & 0.2748 \\
0.1576 & -0.3046 \\
0.1207 & 0.2748 \\
0.2626 & 0.3794 \\
0.4202 & 0.0748 \\
0.4202 & 0.0748 \\
0.2626 & 0.3794 \\
0.3152 & -0.6092 \\
0.2995 & -0.2
\end{bmatrix}
$$

The Singular Value diagonal matrix has reduced:

$$
\begin{bmatrix}
4.0989 & 0 & 0 \\
0 & 2.3616 & 0 \\
0 & 0 & 1.2736
\end{bmatrix}
\text{ to }
\begin{bmatrix}
4.0989 & 0 \\
0 & 2.3616
\end{bmatrix}
$$

And the V new index has reduced to:

$$
\begin{bmatrix}
0.4945 & 0.6491 & 0.5780 \\
0.6458 & -0.7194 & 0.2556 \\
-0.5817 & -0.247 & 0.775
\end{bmatrix}
\text{ to }
\begin{bmatrix}
0.4945 & 0.6491 & 0.5780 \\
0.6458 & -0.7194 & 0.2556
\end{bmatrix}
$$

The new U matrix will be used to transform a user's query into a query in the concept vectors. That will then be searched against the reduced V matrix to get document answers.

## 4.4 Automatic Indexing of Multimedia

The study of Information Retrieval Systems is not complete unless a basic understanding of items that are multimedia are also considered. They are becoming too common in the electronic communications and processes due to major advances and simplifications in new technologies. The users will expect to be able to get similar accuracy in searching for multimedia items that they get in textual items. There is a growing commercial need for such tools to help users to organize and find information in the large qualities of multimedia they are storing on their local systems as well as finding it on the Internet. A good example is the new capability to have your iPhone listen to a few seconds of music and the system will then tell you the song and author (and of course how to purchase it). The demands for accurate multimedia information retrieval will continue to grow as a new commercial area with pressure in developing better search techniques.

### 4.4.1   Introduction to Mutlimedia Indexing

Indexing associated with multimedia differs from the previous discussions of indexing. The automated indexing takes place in multiple transitions of the information versus just a direct conversion to the indexing structure. In some cases (e.g., analog video, audio) the input modality needs to be converted to a digital format before the ingestion process can begin as the first transition. Once digital, algorithms are applied to the digital structure to extract the unit of processing of the different modalities that will be used to represent the item. In an abstract sense this could be considered the location of a processing token in the modality. This unit will then undergo the final processing that will extract the searchable features that represent the item.

There are many different modalities other than text that could be discussed for indexing. This book will focus on the three major modalities that are most common to all users; audio, video and images. Modalities such as maps and geographic objects, although becoming more common because of GOOGLE Earth, are not as prevalent as the three that will be discussed. Image search has been around for a long time. The first sophisticated search techniques were funded by the Government to focus on satellite imagery. When the Internet started to become popular attempts were made to be able to search for images on the Internet (e.g., IBM, Virage and Alta Vista). But it was quickly found that searching the text associated with images was more accurate than in searching the images themselves. Now searching the images is starting to become more feasible and will provide better results that just the text. When audio is discussed what is of interest is primarily when there is speech in the audio or other sounds of interest. Although the earliest commercial information retrieval for audio was focused on validating how often advertisements or songs were played to be sure contract commitments were met. Searching for what is being spoken, for example on news Internet broadcasts is now becoming important. When video is discussed what is being considered is a modality that has time synchronized video and audio subtracks. There also could be closed captioning and Teletext that imbedded in the video that will be discussed. In current television news video there are additional independent information streams of text on other topics running at the bottom of many news sources imbedded in the video. Video is a super set of audio and images because it is composed of an audio track and the video which uses image search technologies. Search of audio and search of images will be discussed first. The techniques discussed for them will be applicable to video with additional constraints possible.

## 4.4.2 Audio Indexing

Indexing of audio may first have to start with conversion of an analog audio into digital format to be processed. This first conversion is critical because any noise introduced in the conversion process can affect the capability to process the digital form and identify the spoken word or other sounds of interest. The voice range goes up to 16 KHz and typically 16 bit sampling is required as a minimum. Thus the analog audio is converted to a minimum 256 Kbits/s (16 KHz times 16 bits) as the minimum encoding. It is very import that the audio levels are watched so that they do not "overdrive" the encoding process. If the audio levels are too strong it will force the audio signal to be outside the encoders range and the signal can be "clipped" or cut off losing the shape and distinction between samples. The other issue is that the digitization processors can introduce noise into the audio (e.g., think of it as a buzz sound) that can make it harder to recognize the original sounds. Thus care is needed in the initial first phase of converting the audio to digital format.

Audio indexing is based upon phonemes and uses Hidden Markov models when speech to text (automatic speech recognition—ASR) is the search approach. When search of a phonetic index is used then the Hidden Markov Model is not so important. To be able to build an audio index the first step is to train a system on a particular audio source (i.e. language/dialect). The first step in the training process is to define the phonemes for the language to the system. The phonemes for a language are equivalent to the alphabet for a written language. There is an international standard (International Phonetic Alphabet—IPA) that is used to define the phonemes for a language, but there is usually disagreement on the exact number of phonemes for a language. Phonemes are the smallest sounds that are needed to differentiate between words in a language. For English there are 42–46 phonemes (there is not a consensus on the exact number). One of the languages with the most number of phonemes is an African language spoken in Botswana that has over 112 phonemes. One of the languages with the fewest number of phonemes is Rutukas spoken in New Guinea that has only 11 phonemes. Ideally you would like for a system to learn the phonemes from the training data. But typically the phonemes are defined are manually defined before the training data is used to develop the Hidden Markov Model. Statistical language models are used that look at the probabilities of the juxtaposition of phonemes, which sounds are likely to follow which sounds, and the probability of occurrence of words and their juxtaposition.

Once the audio arrives at the indexer, it will match the audio input to the language the system has been trained on. The training data set is typically 60 to 100 h of audio along with a transcription of the audio. There are training data sets available at the Linguistic Data Consortium (LDC) at the University of Pennsylvania. But for new languages, they need to be developed (e.g., Appen from Australia will do it). The transcription of the 60–100 h of audio is a marked up transcription of the words spoken. Marked up in the sense it shows the start and stop time in the audio track for each word (although modern systems can now automatically determine the stop time). When the process first started many years ago all sounds were included in the marked up transcription (e.g., breathing, "hems", clear throat, ect.). Over time models for all these other sounds have been developed that can be used in processing new languages, so they are no longer needed. The training data serves two major purposes. First, by having the words correlated to the audio locations for the words and having the theoretical phonetic definitions that map phonemes to characters (or glyphs) in the vernacular language, the system can improve the mapping (model) of the particular glyph to the actual audio sounds for that phoneme. This will improve the accuracy as new unmarked data is processed. Second is that it allows the system to automatically develop a statistical model of the frequency of occurrence of phonemes in the language. In addition to the frequency of occurrence of the phonemes it also develops the frequency of occurrence of the trinemes (three phonemes together) and quinemes (four phonemes together) that are used in many of the word detection algorithms used in Automatic Speech Recognition. When ASR is the goal, in addition to the training to recognize phonemes by an audio training set, it is also useful to get a large corpus of items in the vernacular. That large corpus (preferable millions of words) is used to develop a model of when one word follows another.

There are two major indexing approaches to searching the audio called text based Continuous Speech Recognition (CSR) also called Automatic Speech Recognition (ASR) and Phonetic Search. In text based ASR, the audio is processed and the words are recognized in the audio source and a textual transcription in the vernacular of the audio source is made. Once the audio has been transformed into text, it can be processed using all the algorithms discussed above for text. The training data will be used to create a Hidden Markov Model (HMM—see Chap 2) that represents the audio model of the language constructed from the training data. The HMM is mapped to a dictionary of words so that the sounds which are considered the observable output of the HMM are used with knowledge of probability of the phonemes, trinemes and quinemes that define the state transitions and probability of the set of states to estimate which word is in the audio. As each word is identified, the physical location of the word is also output typically in an XML data stream to be used in the results display interface (see Chap. 7).

The text will contain a significant number of word errors. Audio transcription maps the phonemes that are in an audio item to the words most closely approximating those phonemes in a dictionary. Good audio transcription of broadcast news still has 10% of the words in error and conversational speech has 40% or more of the words in error. These will be valid words but the wrong word. One mechanism to reduce the impact of the missing words in conversational speech is to use the existing database to expand the document. This is accomplished by using the transcribed document as a query against the existing database, selecting a small number of the highest ranked results, determining the most important (highest frequency) words across those items and adding those words to the original document. The new document will then be normalized and reweighted based upon the added words (Singhal-99). This technique reduced the losses in retrieval effectiveness from 15–27% to 7–13% when the audio transcriptions had high errors (40% or more). It has marginal benefit when the transcription has errors in the 15% range. Thus it is useful when working with conversational speech but marginally useful against broadcast news and professional speakers.

The Phonetic Indexing approach works with sounds by identifying the phonemes in the in the audio stream. It then creates an index based upon the phonetic sounds of each word. The proprietary aspect of a phonetic search system is how the phoneme index is created, stored and searched. A Phonetic dictionary is required to take the search input typically, in textual form from a user, and convert it to a phonetic search string.

The comparison of the two approaches shows each has its major advantages and disadvantages. Both approaches are sensitive to the training data provided. Since the training data is used to adjust the acoustic model of the phonemes, the developed system will work more accurately against similar audio (e.g., from that source or a similar source) then from new sources. Thus in the training data diversity of speakers and examples of the types of audio to be processed can make an improvement in the overall accuracy of the operational system. In most systems using either approach accuracies of around 90% recognition can be achieved for broadcast news and 65% for conversational speech. The accuracy is very sensitive to dialects and individuals. Conversational speech is difficult for both methods because of the typical overlap of speakers (both people speaking at the same time) and dialects and accents of the speakers. Also people have a tendency to speak faster when in conversation versus when doing formal speaking.

In terms of processing performance, the Phonetic Index approach can process 10 or more different sources on a single processor and the phonetic index is about 10% the size of the audio input. ASR can now handle 6 or more different audio streams on a single processor. The size of the index is based upon the text produced versus the size of the audio input. The ASR approach converts the audio to text which then uses standard text indexing methods. Since it is based upon the dictionary created during the training process it has always suffered from a problem called "out of vocabulary—OOV" words that were not part of the initial dictionary. This deficiency of being limited to the vocabulary in the training set has the serious limitation on new names of people and organizations that will be mapped to the wrong word. More recently ASR systems are allowing the user to dynamically enter new vocabulary terms which are not merged into the HMM model but made recognizable as an adjunct data set. Phonetic search is based upon phonemes and not words. Thus new words or names are indexed as well as those in the training data set. This is one of strongest advantages of phonetic search over text based ASR. Since Phonetic search is based upon phonemes, shorter words that have fewer phonemes suffer from false hits where the acoustic model of the few phonemes of the search term is a subset of a phonetic model of longer words. For example if you have a search term "ray" you will possibly get hits on the word "tray". ASR creates a text word based system that avoids that issue. The other major issue of a phonetic search system is related to how the output (hit list) is shown. For the text ASR system the hit list can contain textual snippets of the text around the hit term which places each hit in context. For a phonetic search system only the search term and the position in the audio can be shown. Thus the user does not have the textual context of the hit to determine if the hit is in error or something they want to listen too. Thus the user has to open the item and listen to the audio to determine if the audio meets their information need. This will be discussed more in Chap. 7.

In addition to recognizing words in a language, audio models can be used to recognize other information. Audio models can recognize what language a particular audio input is in. This is a precursor to feeding that audio to a particular indexer that has that audio language model. With a little amount of training a system can recognize who is speaking (speaker identification). The only issue comes with the number of speakers that have been modeled. As the number gets into the hundreds (e.g., over 300) the error rates begin to grow because of too many similar models. Also other unique sounds can be modeled and identified. For example gunfire and explosions have been identified that assist in alerting a user when those sounds are discovered in news sources.

For audio the processing tokens are either the phonemes if you are using a phonetic search system or the transcribed words if you are using an ASR system.

### 4.4.3   Image Indexing

Images are typically in digital form. Images are made up of pixels (picture elements—always wondered why they are not called picels). A pixel is the smallest processing aspect of the image. A pixel has a location and has attributes such as color and intensity (e.g., grey scale). The number of bits per pixel defines the display options. For example 2 bits allow for just black/white, 8 bits are used to define gray scale or super VGA color scale, and 24 bit for true color (3 8-bit subpixels for red, green and blue.) The processing tokens for indexing images can be accomplished at the raw data level (e.g., the aggregation of raw pixels), the feature level distinguishing primitive attributes such as color and luminance, and at the semantic level where meaningful objects are recognized (e.g., an airplane in the image/video frame or recognizing text within the image). In the aggregation of pixel information the image is partitioned into sub-areas and all of the pixel information in a sub-area will be combined to create a single value for that sub-area. The heuristics is in the way that the pixel information is used to create a value for the sub-area. It could be combined using Fourier transforms or it could use averaging techniques such as Shannon's entropy law. The smaller the size of the sub-area the more detailed the indexing locating more detailed features but the more complex the search. At the primitive attribute level the processing tokens will define a vector that represents the different features associated with that frame. Each dimension of the vector represents a different feature level aspect of the frame. The vector then becomes the unit of processing in the search system. The three primary primitive aspects are the color, the "texture" and shapes within the image. Colors are an attribute of each pixel and the processing tokens can be created by defining a color histogram for different portions of the image. Texture is a more difficult aspect of the image. There is no universal definition of texture and the actual value of texture is a relative value. It is sometimes described as the two dimensional grey level variations between adjacent pixels and can be discussed in terms of contrast, coarseness and directionality. The texture can be defined in terms of "texels—texture elements" associated with a 3-dimension consideration of the image (i.e., texture overlay on the 3-dimensional definition of the two dimensional image). Texture or texels are relative because the nearness of the viewer (e.g., focal point) can redefine the visibility of the texture. If you get up close to an image you can see a lot more detail of the adjacent pixels and thus can see a lot more texture. As you move further away the textures start to blend together as you lose the distinction. The texture can be defined statistically as grey tone spatial distributions or its possible to set up a series of "production rules" that define structural texels. Like the color the texels can be grouped as arrays and defined as elements in a vector describing the image.

The final primitive feature of an image is basic shapes. They can be localized by adjacent pixels that vary in color or grayness. It's possible by looking at variations to define the basic shapes that are found in the image. These also can be made part of the vector. The resultant vector and its individual elements become the processing tokens that define the image and can be used to search for other images that have the same characteristics. Those that are similar could be copies or the same information in the current image. This leads to a lot of errors in search.

The semantic level tries to get closer to indexing the actual content of the image rather than just the characteristics of the image. The major semantic aspects of an image are the actual objects in the image and the text within an image. Text is far more important when inputs such as video and television news are considered where text plays a major role in defining what is being shown or providing additional news. For example television usually places in text the name of an important person that the news is showing. It also has streams of text on other subjects across the bottom of the display. There are two approaches for indexing the text in an image by segment. Both start with the initial process of identifying text in the image. This is accomplished by recognizing the overall shape of text and segmenting that portion of the image for additional processing. The first approach given the text has been segmented is to segment it down to the character level and then applying Optical Character Recognition (OCR) or (Optical Writing Recognition) algorithms to translate the image to text that is then searchable. The text is extracted and associated with that image. The second approach is to do more extensive shape definition for that textual portion and store it as part of the processing tokens for that image. Then when a user searches for Text in an image the users textual search is treated similarity as an image and thus the matching is image of text against image of text. This has achieved very high recognition rates (e.g., See the PixServe system).

The other semantic level indexing comes from better recognition of semantic items in the image. It is an extension of the shapes that have been recognized as basic elements in defining semantic (thematic) objects. For example the image can be broken into foreground and background. Specific objects can be defined by a meta-language defining the shapes. A flower is an oval/circular colorful object connected by a rectangular/long oval shape major object typically greenish in color.

These semantic objects can then be used as part of the processing tokens associated with an image and can be specified by the users query.

When working with the primitive elements that are extracted as processing tokens a vector—or specific fielded data architecture can be used as the index. When the semantic information is being used as processing tokens the searchable index is stored as an XML structure that can be loaded into memory and searched.

### 4.4.4   Video Indexing

Video can be a simple construct that only contains the video and audio associated with that video. But when looking at television broadcasting there are additional data that can be imbedded in the television signal. In particular there is closed captioning and Teletext. Teletext is often an independent textual stream that has information not related to the audio and video and as such it can be extracted and treated as a new input textual stream. Teletext was developed based upon requirements of the British Broadcasting Corporation (BBC) in 1970 as a mechanism to include subtitles in television transmission. Teletext information is broadcast in the vertical blanking interval (i.e., vbi is the time between frames in a raster scan TV signal when the scan is being reset back to the top to start the next scan) between image frames in a broadcast television signal.

Closed captioning is an attempt by a human transcriber to capture what is being said in the audio portion of the video. It is encoded also in the vertical blanking interval. It is similar to the automatic speech recognition described above for audio except it is being done by a human. This makes it errorful in an unpredictable fashion (i.e., whereas it is possible to predict many of the types of errors in ASR). But it is closely correlated to the audio and the video, similar to ASR. The correlation between the audio, the video and the closed captioning is the relative time within the video. It is possible to have all three independent but correlated channels of information from a television broadcast. More recently television news channels have been running within the image another independent banner of text at the bottom of the screen that describes additional items of interest that have nothing to do with what is currently being shown and discussed. Recognizing that video stream and extracting it as an independent text channel of information is a new technology currently being developed. Although there is occasionally text on images, text also plays a major role in television where usually an important person who is shown will have their name in text underneath them. Also text is used in the images to describe what is going on (e.g., "terrorist Alert"). All of that text provides a real rich information searchable area different than in just searching the image itself. Another useful thing found in television is the display of logos which indicate what organization is being discussed and what television station is broadcasting.

Each of the channels has its own index as described in this chapter. The video is really a series of images. Image indexing software described above can be set to periodically (e.g., once a second) capture a frame (which is equivalent to an image) and index that image. The audio can be processed as described in audio indexing. The closed captioning can be captured as a stream of text.

The audio indexing carries with the index an offset into where the text being transcribed or indexed exists within the video. The same is true of the indexing of the image. Both of these are done to help in the display of search results to allow a user to jump to the location of a hit search term in the television stream. Closed captioning can also come with offsets into the television stream. Where there has been minimal research is how to do a multi-modality search across all three of these channels (image, audio and closed captioning) and determine a hit from it. In this case the user could create a query with search terms against all three of the channels. The system would correlate the hits in each channel to when they occurred in relative time since the start of the video. Then if the hits were within a time window (e.g., with 3 s of each other) the hit would be reported. Thus you could set up a query that is looking for a Burning building (image search) where the closed captioning or audio transcription are discussing "terrorism". Since it is typically a different company/product that creates the search index for each of the channels, there has been minimal commercial effort and little research in the academic community on this more complex integrated search capability.

Another example of a multimedia integrated search would be for textual items that have multimedia links or images within them. There are two main mechanisms that are used, positional and temporal. Positional is used when the modalities are interspersed in a linear sequential composition. For example a document that has images or audio inserted can be considered a linear structure and the only relationship between the modalities will be the juxtaposition of each modality. This would allow for a query that would specify location of an image of a boat within one paragraph of "Cuba and refugees". In this case position is used in lieu of time as the mechanism that is used to synchronize the different modalities. To accomplish either type of integrated search the index must include a time-offset parameter versus a physical displacement. The above examples use proximity to increase precision based upon time concurrency (or ranges) or physical proximity.

## 4.5   Summary

Automatic indexing is the preprocessing stage allowing search of items in an Information Retrieval System. Its role is critical to the success of searches in finding relevant items. If the concepts within an item are not located and represented in the index during this stage, the item is not found during search. Some techniques allow for the combinations of data at search time to equate to particular concepts (i.e. postcoordination). But if the words are not properly identified at indexing time and placed in the searchable data structure, the system can not combine them to determine the concept at search time. If an inefficient data structure is selected to hold the index, the system does not scale to accommodate large numbers of items.

The steps in the identification of the processing tokens used in the index process were generally discussed in Chap. 3. This chapter focused on the specific characteristics of the processing tokens to support the different search techniques. There are many ways of defining the techniques. All of the techniques have statistical algorithmic properties. But looking at the techniques from a conceptual level, the approaches are classified as statistical, natural language and concept indexing. Hypertext linkages are placed in a separate class because an algorithm to search items that include linkages has to address dependencies between items. Normally the indexing of processing tokens is restricted to an item. The next item may use some corpus statistics that changed by previous items, but does not consider a tight coupling between items. Hypertext linkage could in effect indicate that one item may be considered an extension of another, which should affect the concept identification and representation process.

Of all the statistical techniques, an accurate probabilistic technique would have the greatest benefit in the search process. Unfortunately, identification of consistent statistical values used in the probabilistic formulas has proven to be a formidable task. The assumptions that must be made significantly reduce the accuracy of the search process. Vector techniques have very powerful representations and have been shown to be successful. But they lack the flexibility to represent items that contain many distinct but overlapping concepts. Bayesian techniques are a way to relax some of the constraints inherent in a pure vector approach, allowing dependencies between concepts within the same item to be represented. Most commercial systems do not try to calculate weighted values at index time. It is easier and more flexible to store the basic word data for each item and calculate the statistics at search time. This allows tuning the algorithms without having to re-index the database. It also allows the combination of statistical and traditional Boolean techniques within the same system.

Natural language systems attempt to introduce a higher level of abstraction indexing on top of the statistical processes. Making use of rules associated with language assist in the disambiguation of terms and provides an additional layer of concepts that are not found in purely statistical systems. Use of natural language processing provides the additional data that could focus searches, reducing the retrieval of non-relevant items. The tendency of users to enter short queries may reduce the benefits of this approach.

Concept indexing is a statistical technique whose goal is to determine a canonical representation of the concepts. It has been shown to find relevant items that other techniques miss. In its transformation process, some level of precision is lost. The analysis of enhanced recall over potential reduced precision is still under investigation.

Indexing of multimedia introduces an initial first step that is needed to transform the original multimedia into a format from which indexable data can be derived.

At the end of the indexing process the indexing terms and the weights assigned to them are finalized. The weights used are very important because there are two possible reasons items are missed. The first is that the index term that represents semantics is not associated with an item. The second issue is that the weight associated with a concept is not high enough that it will be ranked sufficiently to have the user ever see the item. Users quite looking at hits after a couple of pages so if the weight is not appropriate the item will still realistically never be seen by the user even if it's in the hit list.

## 4.6   Exercises

1. What is the goal of the "index" that is created for documents. What is the impact if it is not sufficient exhaustive. What is the impact of high specificity.
2. Discuss the advantages and disadvantages of using a statistical vector approach, a natural language approach and a concept indexing approach to creating the index. Where are the limits for each technique in finding query results.
3. a. Given the following Weighted term Document matrix, calculate the new document vectors using Normalized TF (using maximum value per row), Inverse Document Frequency, and Signal Show how you came up with the weights for the different algorithms for each term (T1–T6).

|     | T1 | T2 | T3 | T4 | T5 | T6 |
|-----|----|----|----|----|----|----|
| D1  | 4  | 2  | 2  | 1  | 6  | 0  |
| D2  | 3  | 2  | 1  | 12 | 0  | 0  |
| D3  | 0  | 2  | 0  | 4  | 2  | 0  |
| D4  | 2  | 2  | 0  | 5  | 2  | 0  |
| D5  | 4  | 2  | 0  | 8  | 4  | 2  |

   b. Discuss the advantages of each approach and indicate where they are seen in the new document vectors.
   c. Can you combine multiple of these techniques into a combined weighting scheme—which ones would you combine, what would the effect be—show it by calculating new document vectors and discussing results.

4. Discuss the tradeoffs between Automatic Speech Recognition (ASR) and Phonetic search. Which is the most flexible and what are limits to each approach.
5. Is image search more difficult than audio search. Justify your answer.

# Chapter 5
# Search

## 5.1 Introduction

The information retrieval processes of ingest and indexing lead up to the next process which is executing a search against the index. To understand the search process, it is first necessary to look at the different binding levels of the search statement entered by the user to the database being searched. The selection and ranking of items is accomplished via similarity measures that calculate the similarity between the user's search statement and the weighted stored representation of the semantics in an item. Relevance feedback can help a user enhance search by making use of results from previous searches. This technique uses information from items judged as relevant and non-relevant to determine an expanded search statement. Hyperlinked items introduce new concepts in search originating from the dynamic nature of the linkages between items.

Search statements are the statements of an information need generated by users to specify the concepts they are trying to locate in items. As discussed in Chap. 1, the search statement uses traditional Boolean logic and/or Natural Language. The typical search statement is a few words that the user selected to represent the information they are looking for. In generation of the search statement, the user may have the ability to weight (assign an importance) to different concepts in the statement. At this point the binding of the search is to the vocabulary and past experiences of the user. Binding in this sense is when a more abstract form is redefined into a more specific form. The search statement is the user's attempt to specify the conditions needed to subset logically the total item space to that cluster of items that contains the information needed by the user.

The next level of binding comes when the search statement is parsed for use by a specific search system. The search system translates the query to its own meta-language. This process is similar to the indexing of item processes described in Chap. 4. For example, statistical systems determine the processing tokens of interest and the weights assigned to each processing token based upon frequency of occurrence from the search statement. Natural language systems determine the syntactical and discourse semantics using algorithms similar to those used in in-

G. Kowalski, *Information Retrieval Architecture and Algorithms*,
DOI 10.1007/978-1-4419-7716-8_5, © Springer Science+Business Media, LLC 2011

**Fig. 5.1** Examples of query binding

| INPUT | Binding |
|---|---|
| "Find me information on the impact of the oil spills in Alaska on the price of oil" | User search statement using vocabulary of user |
| impact, oil (petroleum), spills (accidents), Alaska, price (cost, value) | Statistical system binding extracts processing tokens |
| impact (.308), oil (.606), petroleum (.65), spills (.12), accidents (.23), Alaska (.45), price (.16), cost (.25), value (.10) | Weights assigned to search terms based upon inverse document frequency algorithm and database |

dexing. Concept systems map the search statement to the set of concepts used to index items. The final level of binding comes as the search is applied to a specific database. This binding is based upon the statistics of the processing tokens in the database and the semantics used in the database. This is especially true in statistical and concept indexing systems. Some of the statistics used in weighting are based upon the current contents of the database. Some examples are Document Frequency and Total Frequency for a specific term. Frequently in a concept indexing system, the concepts that are used as the basis for indexing are determined by applying a statistical algorithm against a representative sample of the database versus being generic across all databases. Natural Language indexing techniques tend to use the most corpora-independent algorithms. Figure 5.1 illustrates the three potential different levels of binding. Parenthesis is used in the second binding step to indicate expansion by a thesaurus.

The length of search statements directly affects the ability of Information Retrieval Systems to find relevant items. The longer the search query, the easier it is for the system to find items. Profiles used as search statements for Selective Dissemination of Information systems are usually very long, typically 75–100 terms. In large systems used by research specialists and analysts, the typical ad hoc search statement is approximately 7 terms. The typical search statement on the Internet is one or two words.

## 5.2 Similarity Measures and Ranking

Searching is concerned with calculating the similarity between a user's search statement and the items in the database. Thinking about a query and a document, as was observed in Chap. 4, they both can be considered a vector where each element (position) represents a different processing token. The most obvious measure of how similar two items are would be a measure on how many processing tokens they both have. With that thought in mind it is fairly obvious that the concept to use in defining similarity measures between two vectors is the co-occurrence of the same element (processing token) in each vector. It is generally a goal to have the similarity value be a number between 0 and 1 to facilitate the ranking of the results. But as a minimum its best to have a zero value mean the two vectors are not similar and then a monotonically increasing positive value to indicate how similar they are. That data allows the ordering (sorting) of the results based upon the similarity measure for each item. Although many of the older systems are unweighted, the newer classes of Information Retrieval Systems have logically stored weighted values for the indexes to an item. The same arguments that went into how to derive the "weighted" index in Chap. 4 apply to calculating similarity in this chapter. That is to say there will be a main formula that drives the similarity measure and then other factors that are used to normalize the similarity to make it easier to use. The other difference from Chap. 4 is instead of looking at a single item and using other information from the database to normalize, in this case there will be two vectors that will drive the similarity process and the normalization comes from characteristics of those two vectors. If you are working from weighted vectors then you want the similarity to be sensitive to how strongly the shared processing tokens are weighted in each item. Based upon this idea the basic formula for the similarity between two items (vectors) is:

$$\text{SIM}(\text{Item}_i, \text{Item}_j) = \sum (\text{Term}_{i,k})(\text{Term}_{j,k})$$

Use of the multiplication function has the desired effect in calculating similarity values. If one of the items does not contain a processing token it will have zero as a weight. When multiplied, that factor is zero and will not add to the final similarity. When there are weighted values in both for the same processing token, the higher the values the larger the result for that factor.

There are some intrinsic errors that come from this approach. First is if the author and the user do not select the same processing token to search on (e.g., one uses car and the other automobile) then there will be no hit even though there are discussing the same concept. The other problem comes when a long item is considered where there are different concepts being presented. The aggregate weight across the whole item may assign a weight to a processing token that does not reflect how much it contributes to each of the different concepts that are indexed. To resolve this issue the similarity may be applied to the total item or constrained to logical passages in the item. For example, every paragraph may be defined as a passage or every 100 words. Rather limiting the definition of a passage to a fixed length size, locality based similarity allows variable length passages (neighborhoods) based upon similarity of content (Kretser-99). This then leads to the ability to define locality based searching and retrieval of the precise locations of information that satisfies the query. The highest similarity for any of the passages is used as the similarity measure for the item. Restricting the similarity measure to passages gains significant precision with minimal impact on recall. In results presented at TREC-4, it was discovered that passage retrieval makes a significant difference when search statements are long (hundreds of terms) but does not make a major difference for short queries. The lack of a large number of terms makes it harder to find shorter passages that contain the search terms expanded from the shorter queries. More recently in the TREC experiments on GENOME search, passage level retrieval has proven to significantly improve the accuracy of the retrieval (Frieder-09).

Once items are identified as possibly relevant to the user's query, it is best to present the most likely relevant items first. This process is called "ranking." Usually the output of the use of a similarity measure in the search process is a scalar number that represents how similar an item is to the query.

### 5.2.1  Similarity Measures

A variety of different similarity measures can be used to calculate the similarity between the item and the search statement. A characteristic of a similarity formula is that the results of the formula increase as the items become more similar. The value is zero if the items are totally dissimilar. An example of a simple "sum of the products" similarity measure is the basis behind many similarity measures and was mentioned above:

$$SIM(Item_i, Item_j) = \sum (Term_{i,k})(Term_{j,k})$$

This formula uses the summation of the product of the various terms of two items when treating the index as a vector. If $Item_j$ is replaced with $Query_j$ then the same formula generates the similarity between every Item and $Query_j$. The problem with this simple measure is in the normalization needed to account for variances in the length of items. Additional normalization is also used to have the final results come between zero and +1 (some formulas use the range $-1$ to +1). The similarity measure will be used for both search in this chapter and as a basis for clustering items in the Chap. 6. Many of the similarity measures discussed below are less useful in the search process because the number of terms in the query can be very low (e.g., 1–3 terms). But they do start to have more meaning if operations such as relevance feedback are used which significantly expands the number of search terms.

Before we get into the complexities of similarity measures for weighted systems, a discussion of similarity measures for binary system can help in understanding the formulas. Most of the formulas were first developed for a binary environment and then expanded for the weighted vector case. Since the vectors are binary containing either a value of 0 or a value for 1 for each position, simpler interpretations of the formulas can apply. The basis behind these formulas becomes the number of dimensions (processing tokens) that are in common to both vectors since the values are either 0 which means it does not exist or 1 meaning it is there. Mathematically this is the cardinality of the set that is created using Boolean logic between vectors. The formula sometimes called Matching Coefficient is:

$$Similarity\ (X, Y) = |X \cap Y|$$

This calculates the number of processing tokens in common between the two items, X and Y. The formula is the basic similarity value and next additional normalization factors can be added. The DICE Coefficient normalizes the length by dividing by the total number of non-zero components (elements) in both items. Thus the number of unique processing tokens in each item. To get a value between zero and 1 it is multiplied by 2. Consider if every element in X is in Y and assuming "n" elements then $|X \cap Y| = n$ and $|X| + |Y| = n + n = 2n$ thus the need for the 2 in the numerator.

$$\text{Dice Coefficient} = \frac{2|X \cap Y|}{|X| + |Y|}$$

The DICE formula is useful when there are not a lot of elements in common between the two vectors. The next formula is useful when there are fewer processing tokens in common.

$$\text{Jaccard (Tanimoto) coefficient} = \frac{|X \cap Y|}{|X \cup Y|}$$

The JACCARD coefficient penalizes when there is a small number of shared entries as a proportion of all shared entries more than the DICE penalizes. Both measures range from 0 to 1, but the Jaccard gives lower values to low overlap cases. For example two vectors with 10 non-zero entries and one common entry get a DICE score of 2 * 1/(10 + 10) = 0.1 while a Jaccard score of 1/(10 + 10 − 1) = 0.05.

The Overlap coefficient is used when the vectors are very large to reduce the impact of the denominator on causing the value to be too small.

$$\text{Overlap coefficient} = \frac{|X \cap Y|}{\text{Min}(|X|, |Y|)}$$

As can be observed the above techniques are primarily focusing on the denominator to get a normalization to account for different characteristics of the two vectors.

### 5.2.1.1 Weighted Vector Similarity Measures

Now let's expand the discussion to include weighted vectors and we will add a few more similarity measures for them. One of the originators of the theory behind statistical indexing and similarity functions was Robertson and Spark Jones (Robertson-76). Their model suggests that knowledge of terms in relevant items retrieved from a query should adjust the weights of those terms in the weighting process. They used the number of relevant documents versus the number of non-relevant documents in the database and the number of relevant documents having a specific query term versus the number of non-relevant documents having that term to devise four formulas for weighting. This assumption of the availability of relevance information in the weighting process was later relaxed by Croft and Harper (Croft-79). Croft expanded this original concept, taking into account the frequency of occurrence of terms within an item producing the following similarity formula (Croft-83):

$$SIM(DOC_i, QUERY_j) = \sum_{i=1}^{Q} ((C + IDF_i) * f_{i,j})$$

where C is a constant used in tuning, $IDF_i$ is the inverse document frequency for term "i" in the collection and

$$f_{i,j} = K + (K - 1)TF_{i,j}/maxfreq_j$$

where K is a tuning constant, $TF_{i,j}$ is the frequency of $term_i$ "i" $item_j$ and $maxfreq_j$ is the maximum frequency of any term in item "j." The best values for K seemed to range between 0.3 and 0.5.

The most obvious starting point for a similarity measure between two vectors is the distance between the vectors. If the two vectors are identical then the distance is zero. A more general starting point for distance metrics is using the Minkowski metric which is:

$$D(x, y) = \left( \sum_{k=1}^{n} (x_i - y_i)^k \right)^{1/k}$$

The sensitivity to the parameter $k$ affects the distance metric exponentially in that the distance quickly decreases towards zero as $k$ increases. When $k$ is equal to 1 it is the classic Hamming distance and using absolute value for the difference ensures the distance measure is equal to or greater than zero. When $k$ equals 2 then the formula is the Euclidian distance measure between two vectors used in Euclidean based mathematics and the similarity measure most likely to be used for Information retrieval.

$$D(x, y) = \left( \sum_{k=1}^{n} (x_i - y_i)^2 \right)^{1/2}$$

A simpler version of the form called the Canberra measure is used in calculating distances (similarity) such as between color vectors and is useful because it detects small changes near zero:

$$D(x, y) = \sum_{i=1}^{n} ((|x_i - y_i|)/(|x_i| + |y_i|))$$

Which is just the absolute value of the subtraction of each position divided by the absolute value of each position added together. It is much easier to calculate than the distance similarity formula. It is also a useful check to validate if one vector is a multiple of another vector.

The binary similarity measures above that were based upon the cardinality can now be adjusted to account for weighted vectors. The Matching coefficient becomes the sum of products when looking at a Query vector and the Document vectors:

$$\text{SIM}(\text{Doc}_i, \text{Query}_j) = \sum (\text{Doc}_{i,k})(\text{Query}_{j,k})$$

As described above in the binary case, two commonly used measures discussed above are the Jaccard and the Dice similarity measures (Rijsbergen-79). Both change the normalizing factor in the denominator to account for different characteristics of the data. In the Jaccard similarity measure, the denominator becomes dependent upon the number of terms in common. As the common elements increase, the similarity value quickly decreases but the final value is no longer restricted to be between −1 and +1 but can be larger negative values:

$$\text{SIM}(\text{DOC}_i, \text{QUERY}_j) = \frac{\sum_{k=1}^{n} (DOC_{i,k} * QTERM_{j,k})}{\sum_{k=1}^{n} DOC_{i,k} + \sum_{k=1}^{n} QTERM_{j,k} - \sum_{k=1}^{n} (DOC_{i,k} * QTERM_{j,k})}$$

The overlap similarity measure can be restated as:

$$\text{SIM}(\text{DOC}_i, \text{QUERY}_j) = \frac{\sum_{k=1}^{n} (DOC_{i,k} * QTERM_{j,k})}{\text{MIN}\left( \sum_{k=1}^{n} DOC_{i,k}, \sum_{k=1}^{n} QTERM_{j,k} \right)}$$

The Dice measure simplifies the denominator from the Jaccard measure. The normalization in the Dice formula is also invariant to the number of terms in common. The results for weighted vectors is no longer restricted to a value between 0 and 1 but can have larger values.

$$\text{SIM}(\text{DOC}_i, \text{QUERY}_j) = \frac{2 * \sum_{k=1}^{n} (DOC_{i,k} * QTERM_{j,k})}{\sum_{k=1}^{n} DOC_{i,k} + \sum_{k=1}^{n} QTERM_{j,k}}$$

Another early similarity formula was used by Salton in the SMART system (Salton-83). Salton treated the index and the search query as n-dimensional vectors (see Chap. 4). To determine the "weight" an item has with respect to the search statement, the Cosine formula is used to calculate the distance between the vector for the item and the vector for the query:

$$\text{SIM}(\text{DOC}_i, \text{QUERY}_j) = \frac{\sum_{k=1}^{n} (DOC_{i,k} * QTERM_{j,k})}{\sqrt{\sum_{k=1}^{n} (DOC_{i,k})^2 * \sum_{k=1}^{n} (QTERM_{j,k})^2}}$$

where $DOC_{i,k}$ is the $k^{th}$ term in the weighted vector for Item "i" and $QTERM_{j,k}$ is the $k^{th}$ term in query "j." The Cosine formula calculates the Cosine of the angle between the two vectors. As the Cosine approaches "1," the two vectors become coincident (i.e., the item and the query represent the same concept). If the two are totally unrelated, then they will be orthogonal and the value of the Cosine is "0." What is not taken into account is the length of the vectors. For example, if the following vectors are in a three dimensional (three term) system:

Item = (4, 8, 0)
Query 1 = (1, 2, 0)
Query 2 = (3, 6, 0)

then the Cosine value is identical for both queries even though Query 2 has significantly higher weights in the terms in common which if a distance function is used would make them more similar. The denominator in the Cosine formula is invariant to the number of terms in common and produces very small numbers when the vectors are large and the number of common elements is small.

To improve the formula, Salton and Buckley (Salton-88) changed the term factors in the query to:

$$QTERM_{i,k} = (0.5 + (0.5TF_{i,k}/maxfreq_k)) * IDF_i$$

where $TF_{i,k}$ is the frequency of term "i" in query "k," $maxfreq_k$ is the maximum frequency of any term in query "k" and $IDF_i$ is the inverse document frequency for term "i" (see Chap. 4 for the formula). In an evolution of the formula, the IDF factor has been dropped (Buckley-96).

The final correlation to be introduced is the Pearson $R$ correlation measure. It is known also as the Pearson product-moment correlation coefficient and is obtained by dividing the covariance by the standard deviation. It was developed by Francis Galton but named after Karl Pearson. It measures the relationship over an interval when two vectors have a linear relationship which is looking for the case described above under the Cosine measure. The measure between a document $D_i$ and query $Q_j$ is:

$$SIM(D_i, Q_j) = \frac{\sum_{k=1}^{n} (D_{i,k} - AVED) * (QTERM_{j,k} - AVEQ)}{\sqrt{\sum_{k=1}^{n} (D_{i,k} - AVED)^2} * \sqrt{\sum (QTERM_{j,k} - AVEQ)^2}}$$

Where AVED is the average of the $DOC_i$ elements and AVEQ is the average of the $QTERM_j$ elements that are not zero. If you included all elements of the vector then the average would be close to zero since typically so few of the elements in the vector are non-zero. Since the zero value implies the term is not in the item, zero elements should be left with a zero value ensuring they will not have an effect on the similarity value calculated (i.e., do not subtract the average from them). The Cosine similarity is related to Pearson correlation which represents the angular separation between two normalized data vectors measured from the mean while the Cosine measures the separation of two data vectors measured from zero.

|         | D1  | D2   | D3     | D4    |
|---------|-----|------|--------|-------|
| DICE    | 3   | 4.5  | 1.875  | 1.375 |
| Jaccard | −3  | −1.8 | 15     | 2.2   |
| Cosine  | 1   | 1    | 0.43   | 0.86  |
| Pearson | 1   | 1    | − 0.45 | 0     |
| Canberra | 0  | 1/2  | 24/33  | 1/2   |

**Fig. 5.2** Similarity measure comparison table

Figure 5.2 is a table that shows how the similarity measure values vary for the different algorithms. Notice that as long as the vector values are same, independent of their order, the Cosine, Pearson and Dice normalization factors do not change. Also notice that when there are a number of terms in common between the query and the document, that the Jaccard formula can produce a negative normalization factor. Also notice that for the Canberra measure that the document that is closest to the query scores better than one that is on the same vector but just a multiple so its further away from the query. The results in Fig. 5.2 are based upon the following Query and Documents:

$Q = (3, 0, 4, 2, 2)$
$D1 = (3, 0, 4, 2, 2)$
$D2 = (9, 0, 12, 6, 6)$
$D3 = (0, 6, 0, 8, 7)$
$D4 = (1, 1, 1, 1, 1)$

**DICE**

$$Sim(D_1, Q_1) = 2 * \sum_{k=1}^{n} (D_{1,k} * Q_{1,k}) / \sum_{k=1}^{n} D_{1,k} + \sum_{k=1}^{n} Q_{1,k}$$

$$Sim(D_1, Q_1) = 2 * ((3 * 3) + (4 * 4) + (2 * 2) + (2 * 2))/3 + 0 + 4 + 2 + 2 + 3$$
$$+ 0 + 4 + 2 + 2$$

$$Sim(D_1, Q_1) = (2 * 33)/22 = 3$$
$$Sim(D_2, Q_1) = (2 * 99)/44 = 4.5$$
$$Sim(D_3, Q_1) = (2 * 30)/32 = 1.875$$
$$Sim(D_4, Q_1) = (2 * 11)/16 = 1.375$$

**Jaccard**

$$Sim(D_1, Q_1) = \sum_{k=1}^{n} (D_{1,k} * Q_{1,k}) / \sum_{k=1}^{n} D_{1,k} + \sum_{k=1}^{n} Q_{1,k} - \sum_{k=1}^{n} (D_{1,k} * Q_{1,k})$$

$$Sim(D_1, Q_1) = (3 * 3) + (4 * 4) + (2 * 2) + (2 * 2)/(3 + 4 + 2 + 2 + 3 + 4$$
$$+ 2 + 2) - ((3 * 3) + (4 * 4) + (2 * 2) + (2 * 2))$$

$$Sim(D_1, Q_1) = 33/(22 - 33) = -3$$
$$Sim(D_2, Q_1) = 99/(44 - 99) = -1.8$$
$$Sim(D_3, Q_1) = 30/(32 - 30) = 15$$
$$Sim(D_4, Q_1) = 11/(16 - 11) = 2.2$$

**Cosine**

$$Sim(D_1, Q_1) = \frac{\sum\limits_{k=1}^{n} (D_{1,k} * Q_{1,k})}{\sqrt{\sum\limits_{k=1}^{n} D_{1,k}^2 * \sum\limits_{k=1}^{n} Q_{1,k}^2}}$$

$Sim(D_1, Q_1)$

$$= \frac{(3 * 3) + (4 * 4) + (2 * 2) + (2 * 2)}{\sqrt{((3 * 3) + (4 * 4) + (2 * 2) + (2 * 2)) * ((3 * 3) + (4 * 4) + (2 * 2) + (2 * 2))}}$$

$$Sim(D_1, Q_1) = \frac{33}{\sqrt{33 * 33}} = 1$$

$$Sim(D_2, Q_1) = \frac{99}{\sqrt{297 * 33}} = 1$$

$$Sim(D_3, Q_1) = \frac{30}{\sqrt{149 * 33}} = 0.43$$

$$Sim(D_3, Q_1) = \frac{11}{\sqrt{5 * 33}} = 0.86$$

**Pearson**

$$Sim(D_1, Q_1) = \frac{\sum\limits_{k=1}^{n} (D_{1,k} - AveD) * (Q_{1,k} - AveQ)}{\sqrt{\sum\limits_{k=1}^{n} (D_{1,k} - AveD)^2} * \sqrt{\sum\limits_{k=1}^{n} (Q_{1,k} - AveQ)^2}}$$

$$Sim(D_1, Q_1) = \frac{\begin{array}{c}((3 - 2.75) * (3 - 2.75)) + ((4 - 2.75) * (4 - 2.75)) \\ + ((2 - 2.75) * (2 - 2.75)) + ((2 - 2.75) * (2 - 2.75))\end{array}}{\sqrt{(3 - 2.75)^2 + (4 - 2.75)^2 + (2 - 2.75)^2 + (2 - 2.75)^2} \\ * \sqrt{(3 - 2.75)^2 + (4 - 2.75)^2 + (2 - 2.75)^2 + (2 - 2.75)^2}}$$

$$Sim(D_1, Q_1) = \frac{2.75}{\sqrt{2.75} * \sqrt{2.75}} = 1$$

$$Sim(D_2, Q_1) = \frac{8.25}{\sqrt{24.75} * \sqrt{2.75}} = 1$$

$$Sim(D_3, Q_1) = \frac{-0.75}{\sqrt{1} * \sqrt{2.75}} = -0.45$$

$$Sim(D_4, Q_1) = \frac{0}{\sqrt{0} * \sqrt{2.75}} = 0$$

**Canberra**

$$D(x, y) = \sum_{i=1}^{n} \left( (|x_i - y_i|) / \sum_{i=1}^{n} (|x_i| + |y_i|) \right)$$

$$Sim(D_1, Q_1) = \frac{|3 - 3| + |0 - 0| + |4 - 4| + |2 - 2| + |2 - 2|}{(|3| + |3|) + (|0| + |0|) + (|4| + |4|) + (|2| + |2|) + (|2| + |2|)}$$

$Sim(D_1, Q_1) = 0/22 = 0$
$Sim(D_2, Q_1) = 22/44 = 1/2$
$Sim(D_3, Q_1) = 24/33$
$Sim(D_4, Q_1) = 8/16 = 1/2$

Use of a similarity algorithm returns the complete data base as search results. Many of the items have a similarity close or equal to zero (or minimum value the similarity measure produces). For this reason, thresholds are usually associated with the search process. The threshold defines the items in the resultant Hit file from the query. Thresholds are either a value that the similarity measure must equal or exceed or a number that limits the number of items in the Hit file. A default is always the case where the similarity is greater than zero. Figure 5.3 illustrates the threshold process.

The simple "sum of the products" similarity formula is used to calculate similarity between the query and each document. If no threshold is specified, all three documents are considered hits. If a threshold of 4 is selected, then only DOC1 is returned.

Vector: (American, geography, lake, Mexico, painter, oil, reserve, subject)

DOC1 = geography *of* Mexico *suggests* oil reserves *are available*
vector (0, 1, 0, 2, 0, 3, 1, 0)

DOC2 = American geography *has* lakes *available everywhere*
vector (1, 3, 2, 0, 0, 0, 0, 0)

DOC3 = painters *suggest* Mexico lakes *as* subjects
vector (0, 0, 1, 3, 3, 0, 0, 2)

QUERY = oil reserves *in* Mexico
vector (0, 0, 0, 1, 0, 1, 1, 0)

**Fig. 5.3** Query threshold process

SIM(Q, DOC1) = 6, SIM(Q, DOC2) = 0, SIM(Q, DOC3) = 3

## 5.3   Hidden Markov Models Techniques

Use of Hidden Markov Models (HMMs) for searching textual corpora has introduced a new paradigm for search. In most of the previous search techniques, the
query is thought of as another "document" and the system tries to find other documents similar to it. In HMMs the documents are considered unknown statistical
processes that can generate output that is equivalent to the set of queries that would
consider the document relevant. Another way to look at it is by taking the general
definition that a HMM is defined by output that is produced by passing some unknown key via state transitions through a noisy channel. The observed output is the
query, and the unknown keys are the relevant documents. The noisy channel is the
mismatch between the author's way of expressing ideas and the user's ability to
specify his query. Leek, Miller and Schwartz (Leek-99) computed for each document the probability that D was the relevant document in the users mind given that
Q was the query produced, i.e., P(D is R/Q).

The development for a HMM approach begins with applying Bayes rule to the
conditional probability:

$$P(D \text{ is } R/Q) = P(Q/D \text{ is } R) * P(D \text{ is } R)/P(Q)$$

Since we are performing the analysis from the document's perspective, the P(Q)
will be the same for every document and thus can be ignored. P(D is R) is also
almost an impossible task in a large diverse corpora. Relevant documents sets
seem to be so sensitive to the specific queries, that trying to estimate P(D is
R) does not return any noticeable improvements in query resolution. Thus the
probability that a document is relevant given a specific query can be estimated
by calculating the probability of the query given the document is Relevant, i.e.,
P(Q/D is R).

As described in Chap. 2, a Hidden Markov Model is defined by a set of states,
a transition matrix defining the probability of moving between states, a set of
output symbols and the probability of the output symbols given a particular state.
The set of all possible queries is the output symbol set and the Document file
defines the states. States could for example be any of the words or stems of the
words in the documents. Thus the HMM process traces itself through the states of
a document (e.g., the words in the document) and at each state transition has an
output of query terms associated with the new state. State transitions are associated with ways that words are combined to make documents. Given the query, it
is possible to calculate the probability that any particular document generated the
query.

The biggest problem in using this approach is to estimate the transition probability matrix and the output (queries that could cause hits) for every document in the
corpus. If there was a large training database of queries and the relevant documents
they were associated with that included adequate coverage, then the problem could
be solved using Estimation-Maximization algorithms (Dempster-77, Bryne-93.)
But given the lack of data, Leek et al. recommend making the transition matrix

independent of specific document sets and applying simple unigram estimation for output distributions (Leek-99).

## 5.4   Ranking Algorithms

A by-product of use of similarity measures for selecting Hit items is a value that can be used in ranking the output. Ranking the output implies ordering the output from most likely items that satisfy the query to least likely items. This reduces the user overhead by allowing the user to display the most likely relevant items first. The original Boolean systems returned items ordered by date of entry into the system versus by likelihood of relevance to the user's search statement. With the inclusion of statistical similarity techniques into commercial systems and the large number of hits that originate from searching diverse corpora, such as the Internet, ranking has become a common feature of modern systems. A summary of ranking algorithms from the research community is found in an article written by Belkin and Croft (Belkin-87).

In most of the commercial systems, heuristic rules are used to assist in the ranking of items. Generally, systems do not want to use factors that require knowledge across the corpus (e.g., inverse document frequency) as a basis for their similarity or ranking functions because it is too difficult to maintain current values as the database changes and the added complexity has not been shown to significantly improve the overall weighting process.

In most commercial search systems the ranking is based upon location and frequency. For example if some or all of the search terms are in the Title of an item, then that would be ranked higher than an item where the terms occur only in the text. Even within the text of an item location matters because if the search terms are closer to the start of the item they are ranked more importantly than those terms towards the end of the item. Of course how often terms occur in an item is also a gage of how high it should be ranked on a list of hits. Those items with the terms occurring more frequently will be ranked higher than those with fewer occurrences. In addition to positive information that can be associated with an item, because of spamming on the Internet, a negative weight can be associated with an item where the computer detects the creator is trying to "fix the system". For example if the user repeats the same word hundreds of times.

When looking at a hyperlink environment such as the Internet a completely different approach can be used in determining the rank of an item. Instead of only considering the specific search, it's possible via link analysis to determine the "authority" of the page (this is one of the concepts introduced by GOOGLE). This is called the page ranking approach. Page ranking is discussed in Chap. 7 because it is an example of collaborative filtering that is used in determining weights.

Although ranking creates a ranking score, most systems try to use other ways of indicating the rank value to the user as Hit lists are displayed. The scores have a tendency to be misleading and confusing to the user. The differences between the values may be very close or very large. It has been found to be better to indicate the general relevance of items than to be over specific (see Chap. 8).

## 5.5 Relevance Feedback

As discussed in the early chapters in this text, one of the major problems in finding relevant items lies in the difference in vocabulary between the authors and the user. Thesauri and semantic networks provide utility in generally expanding a user's search statement to include potential related search terms. But this still does not correlate to the vocabulary used by the authors that contributes to a particular database. There is also a significant risk that the thesaurus does not include the latest jargon being used, acronyms or proper nouns. In an interactive system, users can manually modify an inefficient query or have the system automatically expand the query via a thesaurus. The user can also use relevant items that have been found by the system (irrespective of their ranking) to improve future searches, which is the basis behind relevance feedback. Relevant items (or portions of relevant items) are used to reweight the existing query terms and possibly expand the user's search statement with new terms.

The first major work on relevance feedback was published in 1965 by Rocchio (republished in 1971: Rocchio-71). Rocchio was documenting experiments on reweighting query terms and query expansion based upon a vector representation of queries and items. The concepts are also found in the probabilistic model presented by Robertson and Sparck Jones (Robertson-76). The relevance feedback concept was that the new query should be based on the old query modified to increase the weight of terms in relevant items and decrease the weight of terms that are in non-relevant items. This technique not only modified the terms in the original query but also allowed expansion of new terms from the relevant items. The formula used is:

$$Q_n = Q_o + \frac{1}{r} \sum_{i=1}^{r} DR_I - \frac{1}{nr} \sum_{j=1}^{nr} DNR_j$$

where

$Q_n$ = the revised vector for the new query
$Q_o$ = the original query
$r$ = number of relevant items
$DR_i$ = the vectors for the relevant items
$nr$ = number of non-relevant items
$DNR_j$ = the vectors for the non-relevant items.

The factors $r$ and $nr$ were later modified to be constants that account for the number of items along with the importance of that particular factor in the equation. Additionally a constant was added to $Q_o$ to allow adjustments to the importance of the weight assigned to the original query. This led to the revised version of the formula:

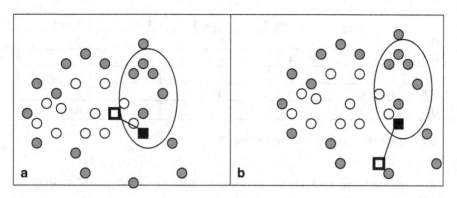

**Fig. 5.4** Impact of relevance feedback. **a** Positive feedback **b** Negative feedback

$$Q_n = \alpha Q_o + \beta \sum_{i=1}^{r} DR_I - \gamma \sum_{j=1}^{nr} DNR_j$$

where $\alpha$, $\beta$, and $\gamma$ are the constants associated with each factor (usually $1/n$ or $1/nr$ times a constant). The factor $\beta \sum_{i=1}^{r} DR_I$ is referred to as positive feedback because it is using the user judgments on relevant items to increase the values of terms for the next iteration of searching. The factor $\gamma \sum_{j=1}^{nr} DNR_j$ is referred to as negative feedback since it decreases the values of terms in the query vector. Positive feedback is weighted significantly greater than negative feedback. Many times only positive feedback is used in a relevance feedback environment. Positive feedback is more likely to move a query closer to a user's information needs. Negative feedback may help, but in some cases it actually reduces the effectiveness of a query. Figure 5.4 gives an example of the impacts of positive and negative feedback. The filled circles represent non-relevant items; the other circles represent relevant items. The oval represents the items that are returned from the query. The solid box is logically where the query is initially. The hollow box is the query modified by relevance feedback (positive only or negative only in the Fig. 5.4).

Positive feedback moves the query to retrieve items similar to the items retrieved and thus in the direction of more relevant items. Negative feedback moves the query away from the non-relevant items retrieved, but not necessarily closer to more relevant items.

Figure 5.5 shows how the formula is applied to three items (two relevant and one non-relevant). If we use the factors $\alpha = 1$, $\beta = \frac{1}{4}$ ($\frac{1}{2}$ times a constant $\frac{1}{2}$), $\gamma = \frac{1}{4}$ ($1/1$ times a constant $\frac{1}{4}$) in the foregoing formula we get the following revised query (NOTE: negative values are changed to a zero value in the revised Query vector):

$$Q_n = (3, 0, 0, 2, 0) + \frac{1}{4}(2 + 1, 4 + 3, 0 + 0, 0 + 0, 2 + 0) - \frac{1}{4}(0, 0, 4, 3, 2)$$
$$= (3\frac{3}{4}, 1\frac{3}{4}, 0\{-1\}, 1\frac{1}{4}, 0)$$

|         | Term 1 | Term 2 | Term 3 | Term 4 | Term 5 |
|---------|--------|--------|--------|--------|--------|
| $Q_0$   | 3      | 0      | 0      | 2      | 0      |
| $DOC1_r$ | 2     | 4      | 0      | 0      | 2      |
| $DOC2_r$ | 1     | 3      | 0      | 0      | 0      |
| $DOC3_{nr}$ | 0  | 0      | 4      | 3      | 3      |
| $Q_n$   | 3¾     | 1¾     | 0      | 1¼     | 0      |

**Fig. 5.5** Query modification via relevance feedback

Using the unnormalized similarity formula $SIM(Q_k, DOC_1) = \sum_{i=1}^{5} TERM_{k,i} *$ $TERM_{1,I}$ produces the results shown in Fig. 5.6.

In addition to showing the benefits of relevance feedback, this example illustrates the problems of identifying information. Although DOC3 is not relevant to the user, the initial query produced one of the highest similarity measures for it. This was caused by a query term (Term 4) of interest to the user that has a significant weight in DOC3. The fewer the number of terms in a user query, the more likely a specific term to cause non-relevant items to be returned. The modification to the query by the relevance feedback process significantly increased the similarity measure values for the two relevant items (DOC1 and DOC2) while decreasing the value of the non-relevant item. It is also of interest to note that the new query added a weight to Term 2 that was not in the original query. One reason that the user might not have initially had a value to Term 2 is that it might not have been in the user's vocabulary. For example, the user may have been searching on "PC" and "word processor" and not been aware that many authors use the specific term "Macintosh" rather than "PC."

Relevance feedback, in particular positive feedback, has been proven to be of significant value in producing better queries. Some of the early experiments on the SMART system (Ide-69, Ide-71, Salton-83) indicated the possible improvements that would be gained by the process. But the small collection sizes and evaluation techniques put into question the actual gains by using relevance feedback. One of the early problems addressed in relevance feedback is how to treat query terms that are not found in any retrieved relevant items. Just applying the algorithm would have the effect of reducing the relative weight of those terms with respect to other query terms. From the user's perspective, this may not be desired because the term may still have significant value to the user if found in the future iterations of the search process. Harper and van Rijisbergen addressed this issue in their proposed EMIM weighting scheme (Harper-78, Harper-80). Relevance feedback has become a common feature in most information systems. When the original query is modified based upon relevance feedback, the systems ensure that the original query

|         | DOC1 | DOC2 | DOC3 |
|---------|------|------|------|
| $Q_o$   | 6    | 3    | 6    |
| $Q_n$   | 14½  | 9.0  | 3.75 |

**Fig. 5.6** Effect of relevance feedback

terms are in the modified query, even if negative feedback would have eliminated them. In some systems the modified query is presented to the user to allow the user to readjust the weights and review the new terms added.

Recent experiments with relevance feedback during the TREC sessions have shown conclusively the advantages of relevance feedback. Queries using relevance feedback produce significantly better results than those being manually enhanced. When users enter queries with a few number of terms, automatic relevance feedback based upon just the rank values of items has been used. This concept in information systems called pseudo-relevance feedback, blind feedback or local context analysis (Xu-96) does not require human relevance judgments. The highest ranked items from a query are automatically assumed to be relevant and applying relevance feedback (positive only) used to create and execute an expanded query. The system returns to the user a Hit file based upon the expanded query. This technique also showed improved performance over not using the automatic relevance feedback process. In the automatic query processing tests from TREC (see Chap. 10) most systems use the highest ranked hits from the first pass to generate the relevance feedback for the second pass.

## 5.6 Selective Dissemination of Information Search

Selective Dissemination of Information, frequently called dissemination systems, are becoming more prevalent with the growth of the Internet. A dissemination system is sometimes labeled a "push" system while a search system is called a "pull" system. The differences are that in a search system the user proactively makes a decision that he needs information and directs the query to the information system to search. In a dissemination system, the user defines a profile (similar to a stored query) and as new information is added to the system it is automatically compared to the user's profile. If it is considered a match, it is asynchronously sent to the user's "mail" file (see Chap. 1).

One concept that ties together the two search statements (query and profile) is the introduction of a time parameter associated with a search statement. As long as the time is in the future, the search statement can be considered active and disseminating as items arrive. Once the time parameter is past, the user's need for the information is no longer exists except upon demand (i.e., issuing the search statement as an ad hoc query).

The differences between the two functions lie in the dynamic nature of the profiling process, the size and diversity of the search statements and number of simultaneous searches per item. In the search system, an existing database exists. As such, corpora statistics exist on term frequency within and between terms. These can be used for weighting factors in the indexing process and the similarity comparison (e.g., inverse document frequency algorithms). A dissemination system does not necessarily have a retrospective database associated with it. Thus its algorithms need to avoid dependency upon previous data or develop a technique to estimate terms for their formula. This class of system is also discussed as a binary classification system because there is no possibility for real time feedback from the user to assist in search statement refinement. The system makes a binary decision to reject or file the item (Lewis-95).

Profiles are relatively static search statements that cover a diversity of topics. Rather than specifying a particular information need, they usually generalize all of the potential information needs of a user. They are focused on current information needs of the user. Thus profiles have a tendency to contain significantly more terms than an ad hoc query (hundreds of terms versus a small number). The size tends to make them more complex and discourages users from wanting to change them without expert advice.

One of the first commercial search techniques for dissemination was the Logicon Message Dissemination System (LMDS). The system originated from a system created by Chase, Rosen and Wallace (CRW Inc.). It was designed for speed to support the search of thousands of profiles with items arriving every 20 s. It demonstrated one approach to the problem where the profiles were treated as the static database and the new item acted like the query. It uses the terms in the item to search the profile structure to identify those profiles whose logic could be satisfied by the item. The system uses a least frequently occurring trigraph (three characters) algorithm that quickly identifies which profiles are not satisfied by the item. The potential profiles are analyzed in detail to confirm if the item is a hit.

Another example of a dissemination approach is the Personal Library Software (PLS) system. It uses the approach of accumulating newly received items into the database and periodically running user's profiles against the database. This makes maximum use of the retrospective search software but loses near real time delivery of items. More recent examples of a similar approach are the Retrievalware and the InRoute software systems. In these systems the item is processed into the searchable form. Since the Profiles are relatively static, some use is made in identifying all the terms used in all the profiles. Any words in the items that are members of this list can not contribute to the similarity process and thus are eliminated from the search structure. Every profile is then compared to the item. Retrievalware uses a statistical algorithm but it does not include any corpora data. Thus not having a database does not affect its similarity measure. InRoute, like the INQUERY system used against retrospective database, uses inverse document frequency information. It creates this information as it processes items, storing and modifying it for use as future items arrive. This would suggest that the values would be continually changing as items arrive until sufficient items have arrived to stabilize the inverse document frequency weights. Relevance feedback has been proven to enhance the search capabilities of ad hoc queries against retrospective databases. Relevance feedback can also be applied to dissemination systems. Unlike an ad hoc query situation, the dissemination process is continuous, and the issue is the practicality of archiving all of the previous relevance judgments to be used in the relevance feedback process. Allan performed experiments on the number of items that have to arrive and be judged before the effects of relevance feedback stabilize (Allan-96). Previous work has been done on the number of documents needed to generate a new query and the amount of training needed (Buckley-94, Aalbersberg-92, Lewis-94). The two major choices are to save relevant items or relevance statistics for words. By saving dissimilar items, Allan demonstrated that the system sees a 2–3% loss in effectiveness by archiving 10% of the relevance judgments. This still requires significant storage space. He was able to achieve high effectiveness by storing information on as few as 250 terms.

Another approach to dissemination uses a statistical classification technique and explicit error minimization to determine the decision criteria for selecting items for a particular profile (Schutze-95). In this case, the classification process is related to assignment for each item into one of two classes: relevant to a user's profile or non-relevant. Error minimization encounters problems in high dimension spaces. The dimensionality of an information space is defined by the number of unique terms where each term is another dimension. This is caused by there being too many dimensions for a realistic training set to establish the error minimization parameters. To reduce the dimensionality, a version of latent semantic indexing (LSI) can be used. The process requires a training data set along with its associated profiles. Relevance feedback is an example of a simple case of a learning algorithm that does not use error minimization. Other examples of algorithms used in linear classifiers that perform explicit error minimization are linear discriminant analysis, logistic regression and linear neural networks.

Schutze et al. used two approaches to reduce the dimensionality: selecting a set of existing features to use or creating a new much smaller set of features that the original features are mapped into. A $\chi^2$ measure was used to determine the most important features. The test was applied to a table that contained the number of relevant ($N_r$) and non-relevant ($N_{nr}$) items in which a term occurs plus the number of relevant and non-relevant items in which the term does not occur ($N_{r-}$, $N_{nr-}$ respectively). The formula used was:

$$\chi^2 = \frac{N(N_r N_{nr-} - N_{r-} N_{nr})^2}{(N_r + N_{r-})(N_{nr} + N_{nr-})(N_r + N_{nr})(N_{r-} + N_{nr-})}$$

To focus the analysis, only items in the local region defined by a profile were analyzed. The chi-squared technique provides a more effective mechanism than frequency of occurrence of terms. A high $\chi^2$ score indicates a feature whose frequency has a significant dependence on occurrence in a relevant or non-relevant item.

An alternative technique to identify the reduced feature (vector) set is to use a modified latent semantic index (LSI) technique to determine a new reduced set of concept vectors. The technique varies from the LSI technique described in Chap. 5 by creating a separate representation of terms and items by each profile to create the "local" space of items likely to be relevant (i.e., Local LSI). The results of the analysis go into a learning algorithm associated with the classification technique (Hull-94). The use of the profile to define a local region is essential when working with large databases. Otherwise the number of LSI factors is in the hundreds and the ability to process them is currently unrealistic. Rather than keeping the LSI factors separate per profile, another approach is to merge the results from all of the queries into a single LSI analysis (Dumais-93). This increases the number of factors with associated increase in computational complexity.

Once the reduced vector set has been identified, then learning algorithms can be used for the classification process. Linear discriminate analysis, logistic regression and neural networks are three possible techniques that were compared by Schutze et al. Other possible techniques are classification trees (Tong-94, Lewis-94a), Bayesian networks (Croft-94), Bayesian classifiers (Lewis-92), rules induction (Apte-94), nearest neighbor techniques (Masand-92, Yang-94), and least square methods (Fuhr-89). Linear discrimination analysis uses the covariance class for each document class to detect feature dependence (Gnanadesikan-79). Assuming a sample of data from two groups with $n_1$ and $n_2$ members, mean vectors $\bar{x}_1$ and $\bar{x}_2$ and covariance matrices $C_1$ and $C_2$ respectively, the objective is to maximize the separation between the two groups. This can be achieved by maximizing the distance between the vector means, scaling to reflect the structure in the pooled covariance matrix. Thus choose $a$ such that:

$$a^* = \arg_a \max \frac{a^T(\bar{x}_1 - \bar{x}_2)}{\sqrt{a^T C_a}}$$

is maximized where T is the transpose and $(n_1 + n_2 - 2)C = (n_1 - 1)C_1 + (n_2 - 1)C_2$. Since C is positive, the Cholesky decomposition of $C = R^T$. Let $b = Ra$; then the formula becomes;

$$a^* = \arg_b \max \frac{b^T R^{T-1}(\bar{x}_1 - \bar{x}_2)}{\sqrt{b^T b}}$$

which is maximized by choosing $b \propto R^{T-1}(\bar{x}_1 - \bar{x}_2)$. This means:

$$a^* = R^{-1}b = C^{-1}(\bar{x}_1 - \bar{x}_2)$$

The one dimensional space defined by $y = a^{*T}x$ should cause the group means to be well separated. To produce a non-linear classifier, a pair of shrinkage parameters is used to create a very general family of estimators for the group covariance matrix (Friedman-89). This process called Regularized Discriminant Analysis looks at a weighted combination of the pooled and unpooled covariance matrices. The optimal values of the shrinkage parameters are selected based upon the cross validation over the training set. The non-linear classifier produced by this technique has not been shown to make major improvements in the classification process (Hull-95).

A second approach is to use logistic regression (Cooper-94a). It models a binary response variable by a linear combination of one or more predictor variables, using a logit link function:

$$g(\pi) = \log(\pi/(1 - \pi))$$

and modeling variance with a binomial random variable. This is achieved by modeling the dependent variable $\log(\pi/(1 - \pi))$ as a linear combination of independent variables using a form $g(\pi) = x_i\beta$. In this formula $\pi$ is the estimated response probability (probability of relevance), $x_i$ is the feature vector (reduced vector) for document $I$, and $\beta$ is the weight vector which is estimated from the matrix of feature vectors. The optimal value of $\beta$ can be calculated using the maximum likelihood and the Newton-Raphson method of numerical optimization (McCullagh-89). The major difference from previous experiments using logistic regression is that Schutze et al. do not use information from all the profiles but restrict the analysis for each profile.

A third technique is to use neural networks for the learning function. A neural network is a network of input and output cells (based upon neuron functions in the brain) originating with the work of McCulloch and Pitts (McCulloch-43). Each input pattern is propagated forward through the network. When an error is detected it is propagated backward adjusting the cell parameters to reduce the error, thus achieving learning. This technique is very flexible and can accommodate a wide range of distributions. A major risk of neural networks is that they can overfit by learning the characteristics of the training data set and not be generalized enough for the normal input of items. In applying training to a neural network approach, a validation set of items is used in addition to the training items to ensure that overfitting has not occurred. As each iteration of parameter adjustment occurs on the training set, the validation set is retested. Whenever the errors on the validation set increase, it indicates that overfitting is occurring and establishes the number of iterations on training that improve the parameter values while not harming generalization.

The linear and non-linear architectures for an implementation of neural nets is shown in Fig. 5.7.

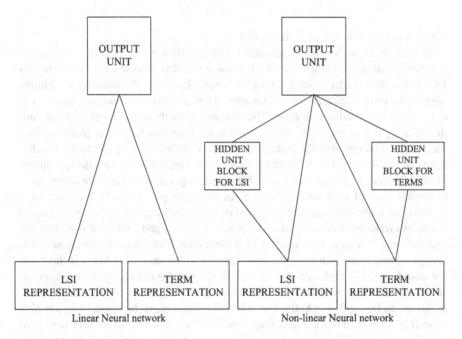

**Fig. 5.7** Linear and non-linear networks

In the non-linear network, each of the hidden blocks consists of three hidden units. A hidden unit can be interpreted as feature detectors that estimate the probability of a feature being present in the input. Propagating this to the output unit can improve the overall estimation of relevance in the output unit. The networks show input of both terms and the LSI representation (reduced feature set). In both architectures, all input units are directly connected to the output units. Relevance is computed by setting the activations of the input units to the document's representation and propagating the activation through the network to the output unit, then propagating the error back through the network using a gradient descent algorithm (Rumelhart-95). A sigmoid was chosen as:

$$f(x) = \frac{e^x}{1 + e^x}$$

as the activation function for the units of the network (Schutze-95). In this case backpropagation minimizes the same error as logistic regression (Rumelhart-95a). The cross-entropy error is:

$$L = -\sum (t_i \log \sigma_i + 1 - t_i) \log(1 - \sigma_i)$$

where $t_i$ is the relevance for document $I$ and $\sigma_I$ is the estimated relevance (or activation of the output unit) for document $i$. The definition of the sigmoid is equivalent to:

$$x = \log\left(\frac{f(x)}{1 - f(x)}\right)$$

which is the same as the logit link function.

Schutze et al. performed experiments with the Tipster test database to compare the three algorithms. They show that the linear classification schemes perform 10–15% better than the traditional relevance feedback. To use the learning algorithms based upon error minimization and numerical computation one must use some technique of dimensionality reduction. Their experiments show that local latent semantic indexing is best for linear discrimination analysis and logistic regression since they have no mechanism for protecting against overfitting. When there are mechanisms to avoid overfitting such as in neural networks, other less precise techniques of dimension reduction can be used. This work suggests that there are alternatives to the statistical classification scheme associated with profiles and dissemination.

An issue with Mail files is the logical reorganization associated with display of items. In a retrospective query, the search is issued once and the hit list is a static file that does not change in size or order of presentation. The dissemination function is always adding items that satisfy a user's profile to the user's Mail file. If the items are stored sorted by rank, then the relative order of items can always be changing as new items are inserted in their position based upon the rank value. This constant re-ordering can be confusing to the user who remembers items by spatial relationships as well as naming. Thus the user may remember an item next to another item is of significant interest. But in trying to retrieve it at a later time, the reordering process can make it significantly harder to find.

## 5.7 Weighted Searches of Boolean Systems

The two major approaches to generating queries are Boolean and natural language. Natural language queries are easily represented within statistical models and are usable by the similarity measures discussed. Issues arise when Boolean queries are associated with weighted index systems. Some of the issues are associated with how the logic (AND, OR, NOT) operators function with weighted values and how weights are associated with the query terms. If the operators are interpreted in their normal interpretation, they act too restrictive or too general (i.e., AND and OR operators respectively). Salton, Fox and Wu showed that using the strict definition of the operators will suboptimize the retrieval expected by the user (Salton-83a). Closely related to the strict definition problem is the lack of ranking that is missing from a pure Boolean process. Some of the early work addressing this problem recognized the fuzziness associated with mixing Boolean and weighted systems (Brookstein-78, Brookstein-80).

To integrate the Boolean and weighted systems model, Fox and Sharat proposed a fuzzy set approach (Fox-86). Fuzzy sets introduce the concept of degree of membership to a set (Zadeh-65). The degree of membership for AND and OR operations are defined as:

$$DEG_{A \cap B} = min(DEG_A, DEG_B)$$
$$DEG_{A \cup B} = max(DEG_A, DEG_B)$$

where A and B are terms in an item. DEG is the degree of membership. The Mixed Min and Max (MMM) model considers the similarity between query and document to be a linear combination of the minimum and maximum item weights. Fox proposed the following similarity formula:

$$SIM(QUERY_{OR}, DOC) = C_{OR1} * max(DOC1_1, DOC_2, \ldots, DOC_n)$$
$$+ C_{OR2} * min(DOC_1, DOC_2, \ldots, DOC_n)$$
$$SIM(QUERY_{AND}, DOC) = C_{AND1} * min(DOC_1, DOC_2, \ldots, DOC_n)$$
$$+ C_{AND2} * max(DOC1_1, DOC_2, \ldots, DOC_n)$$

where $C_{OR1}$ and $C_{OR2}$ are weighting coefficients for the OR operation and $C_{AND1}$ and $C_{AND2}$ are the weighting coefficients for the AND operation. Lee and Fox found in their experiments that the best performance comes when $C_{AND1}$ is between 0.5 to 0.8 and $C_{OR1}$ is greater than 0.2.

The MMM technique was expanded by Paice (Paice-84) considering all item weights versus the maximum/minimum approach. The similarity measure is calculated as:

$$SIM(QUERY\ DOC) = \sum_{i=1}^{n} r^{i-1} d_i / \sum_{i=1}^{n} r^{i-1}$$

where the $d_i$'s are inspected in ascending order for AND queries and descending order for OR queries. The $r$ terms are weighting coefficients. Lee and Fox showed that the best values for $r$ are 1.0 for AND queries and 0.7 for OR queries (Lee-88). This technique requires more computation since the values need to be stored in ascending or descending order and thus must be sorted.

An alternative approach is using the P-norm model which allows terms within the query to have weights in addition to the terms in the items. Similar to the Cosine similarity technique, it considers the membership values $(d_{A1}, \ldots, d_{An})$ to be coordinates in an "n" dimensional space. For an OR query, the origin (all values equal zero) is the worst possibility. For an AND query the ideal point is the unit vector where all the $D_i$ values equal 1. Thus the best ranked documents will have maximum distance from the origin in an OR query and minimal distance from the unit vector point. The generalized queries are:

$$Q_{OR} = (A_1, a_1) \text{ OR } (A_2, a_2) \text{ OR} \ldots \text{OR} (A_n, a_n)$$
$$Q_{AND} = (A_1, a_1) \text{ AND } (A_2, a_2) \text{ AND} \ldots \text{AND} (A_n, a_n)$$

The operators (AND and OR) will have a strictness value assigned that varies from 1 to infinity where infinity is the strict definition of the Boolean operator. The $a_i$ values are the query term weights. If we assign the strictness value to a parameter labeled "S" then the similarity formulas between queries and items are:

$$SIM(Q_{OR}, DOC) = \sqrt[S]{(a_1^S d_{A1}^S + \cdots + a_n^S d_{An}^S)/(a_1^S + a_2^S + \cdots + a_n^S)}$$

$$SIM(Q_{AND}, DOC)$$
$$= 1 - \sqrt[S]{(a_1^S(1 - d_{A1})^S + \cdots + a_n^S(1 - d_{An})^S)/(a_1^S + a_2^S + \cdots + a_n^S)}$$

$$SIM(Q_{not}, DOC) = 1 - SIM(Q, DOC)$$

Another approach suggested by Salton provides additional insight into the issues of merging the Boolean queries and weighted query terms under the assumption that there are no weights available in the indexes (Salton-83). The objective is to perform the normal Boolean operations and then refine the results using weighting techniques. The following procedure is a modification to his approach for defining search results. The normal Boolean operations produce the following results:

"A OR B" retrieves those items that contain the term A or the term B or both
"A AND B" retrieves those items that contain both terms A and B
"A NOT B" retrieves those items that contain term A and not contain term B.

If weights are then assigned to the terms between the values 0.0–1.0, they may be interpreted as the significance that users are placing on each term. The value 1.0 is assumed to be the strict interpretation of a Boolean query. The value 0.0 is interpreted to mean that the user places little value on the term. Under these assumptions, a term assigned a value of 0.0 should have no effect on the retrieved set. Thus

**Fig. 5.8** VENN diagram

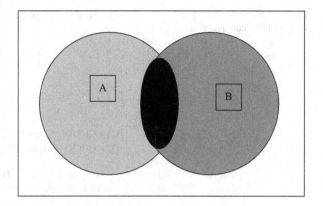

"$A_1$ OR $B_0$" should return the set of items that contain A as a term
"$A_1$ AND $B_0$" will also return the set of items that contain term A
"$A_1$ NOT $B_0$" also return set A.

This suggests that as the weight for term B goes from 0.0 to 1.0 the resultant set changes from the set of all items that contains term A to the set normally generated from the Boolean operation. The process can be visualized by use of the VENN diagrams shown in Fig. 5.8. Under the strict interpretation "$A_1$ OR $B_1$" would include all items that are in all the areas in the VENN diagram. "$A_1$ OR $B_0$" would be only those items in A (i.e., the white and black dotted areas) which is everything except items in "B NOT A" (the grey area.) Thus as the value of query term B goes from 0.0 to 1.0, items from "B NOT A" are proportionally added until at 1.0 all of the items will be added.

Similarly, under the strict interpretation "$A_1$ AND $B_1$" would include all of the items that are in the black dotted area. "$A_1$ AND $B_0$" will be all of the items in A as described above. Thus, as the value of query term B goes from 1.0 to 0.0 items will be proportionally added from "A NOT B" (white area) until at 0.0 all of the items will be added.

Finally, the strict interpretation of "$A_1$ NOT $B_1$" is grey area while "$A_1$ NOT $B_0$" is all of A. Thus as the value of B goes from 0.0 to 1.0, items are proportionally added from "A AND B" (black dotted area) until at 1.0 all of the items have been added.

The final issue is the determination of which items are to be added or dropped in interpreting the weighted values. Inspecting the items in the totally strict case (both terms having weight 1.0) and the case where the value is 0.0 there is a set of items that are in both solutions (invariant set). In adding items they should be the items most similar to the set of items that does not change in either situation. In dropping items, they should be the items least similar to those that are in both situations.

Thus the algorithm follows the following steps:

1. Determine the items that are satisfied by applying strict interpretation of the Boolean functions
2. Determine the items that are part of the set that is invariant

**Fig. 5.9** Example of weighted boolean query

| | Computer | program | cost | sale |
|---|---|---|---|---|
| D1 | 0 | 4 | 0 | 8 |
| D2 | 0 | 2 | 0 | 0 |
| D3 | 4 | 0 | 2 | 4 |
| D4 | 0 | 6 | 4 | 6 |
| D5 | 0 | 4 | 6 | 4 |
| D6 | 6 | 0 | 4 | 0 |
| D7 | 0 | 0 | 0 | 0 |
| D8 | 4 | 2 | 0 | 2 |

$$Q1 = QUERY_1 = Computer_{1.0} \ OR \ program_{.333}$$
$$Q2 = QUERY_2 = cost_{.75} \ AND \ sale_{1.0}$$

$Q1_{strict \ interpretation} = (D1, D2, D3, D4, D5, D6, D8)$
$Q2_{strict \ interpretation} = (D3, D4, D5)$

$Q1_{invariant} = (D8)$
$Q2_{invariant} = (D3, D4, D5)$

$Q1_{optional} = (D1, D2, D3, D4, D5, D6)$ thus $\lceil .333 \ times \ 6 \ items \rceil = 2 \ items$
$Q2_{optional} = (D1, D8)$ which means $\lceil (1 - .75) \ times \ 2 \ items \rceil = 1 \ item$

3. Determine the Centroid of the invariant set
4. Determine the number of items to be added or deleted by multiplying the term weight times the number of items outside of the invariant set and rounding up to the nearest whole number
5. Determine the similarity between items outside of the invariant set and the Centroid
6. Select the items to be included or removed from the final set

Figure 5.9 gives an example of solving a weighted Boolean query.

QUERY$_1$ ends up with a set containing all of the items that contain the term "Computer" and two items from the set "computer" NOT "program." The symbol ⌈ ⌉ stands for rounding up to the next integer. In QUERY$_2$ the final set contains all of set "cost" AND "sale" plus 0.25 of the set of "sale" NOT "cost." Using the simple similarity measure:

$$SIM(Item_i, Item_j) = \sum (Term_{i,k})(Term_{j,k})$$

leads to the following set of similarity values based upon the centroids:

CENTROID (Q1) = (D8) = (4, 2, 0, 2)
CENTROID (Q2) = (D3, D4, D5) = 1/3(4 + 0 + 0, 0 + 6 + 4, 2 + 4 + 6, 4 + 6 + 4)
SIM(CENTROID$_{Q1}$, D1) = (0 + 8 + 0 + 16) = 24
SIM(CENTROID$_{Q1}$, D2) = (0 + 4 + 0 + 0) = 4
SIM(CENTROID$_{Q1}$, D3) = (16 + 0 + 0 + 8) = 24
SIM(CENTROID$_{Q1}$, D4) = (0 + 12 + 0 + 12) = 24
SIM(CENTROID$_{Q1}$, D5) = (0 + 8 + 0 + 8) = 16
SIM(CENTROID$_{Q1}$, D6) = (24 + 0 + 0 + 0) = 24

$$\text{SIM(CENTROID}_{Q2}, D1) = 1/3(0 + 40 + 0 + 112) = 1/3(152)$$
$$\text{SIM(CENTROID}_{Q2}, D8) = 1/3(16 + 20 + 0 + 28) = 1/3(64)$$

For Q1, two additional items are added to the invariant set $(D8) \cup (D1, D3)$, by choosing the lowest number items because of the tie at 24, giving the answer of (D1, D3, D8). For Q2, one additional item is added to the invariant set $(D3, D4, D5) \cup (D1)$ giving the answer (D1, D3, D4, D5).

## 5.8   Multimedia Searching

As described in Chap. 4 there are many approaches to indexing multimedia items that are based upon how the semantics from the multimedia is transformed into a searchable index. Always associated with a multimedia item is some level of textual information that can be structured and unstructured. The structured metadata could be the file name of the item that quite describes what it is about. When audio and video is being index the source of audio or video also holds potential to help in filtering what the user is looking for (e.g., CNN News versus Cartoon Network). When the multimedia item is found as part of a textual item as a reference or attachment, then most systems use the surrounding text and hypertext link anchor text as additional descriptive unstructured metadata for what the multimedia item is about. When the multimedia item is video there are the possibilities of closed captioning that may add more information on the audio track of a video. All of the above metadata is useful in allowing a user to enter a textual query specifying what they are interested in and determining which multimedia items to return.

The more complex challenge is to index the multimedia item via determining semantically important information in it. Audio items are the easiest modality to index because in most cases it's the speech within the audio that is of interest to the user. For the cases where it's the actual audio it is typically to identify specific songs in music and thus the indexing algorithms can be focused on that goal. Since the speech is the most important aspect, once a mapping from the analog audio to specific words is accomplished all of the techniques associated with text search are now applicable.

The most difficult modality is images or video which is just a number of images shown 24–30 times per second. The indexing of the image is very difficult to extract the semantics and recognize the semantics that needs to be searchable. The easiest approach is not to recognize specific objects in the image but focus on an aggregate measure of the characteristics of the pixels (e.g. color) over a grouping of pixels. That representation will be a set of values in a vector that represents that image or a portion of the image. The next layer of extraction detects categories of images and backgrounds. This is done by specific algorithms focused on detecting shapes (e.g., lines, oval, and rectangles) along with their combinations into semantically meaningful image definitions. Thus an image that is of a map could be estimated by an image that has a lot of lines in it. An image of a crowd of people would be an image with a large number of small ovals in it (people's faces). Pornography has frequently been defined as image with a few number of ovals with specific colors in the ovals. The most complex searching for images/video images is when the user provides an example of what they are looking for and the system searches for similar images. The users search image is decomposed into whatever the indexing base is for a specific search system and then those components are used to search the vectors representing the indexed items. There are no universal generic algorithms that define how a similarity measure is created between the search vector and the vectors representing the indexed items. The specific algorithms tend to be heuristically optimized for the proprietary indexing scheme of the images. But the end result is a ranked list of references to the items. Since the index representation is typically a vector, a distance measure of some sort between the users query in vector form and the items in vector form is the basis behind the search along with the system specific heuristics.

## 5.9   Summary

Creating the index to an Information Retrieval System defines the searchable concepts that represent the items received by a system. The user search process is the mechanism that correlates the user's search statement with the index via a similarity function. There are a number of techniques to define the indexes to an item. It is typically more efficient to incur system overhead at index creation time than search time. An item is processed once at index time, but there will be millions of searches against the index. Also, the user is directly affected by the response time of a search but, in general, is not aware of how long it takes from receipt of an item to its being available in the index. The selection and implementation of similarity algorithms for search must be optimized for performance and scaleable to accommodate very large databases.

It is typical during search parsing that the user's initial search statement is expanded via a thesaurus or semantic net to account for vocabulary differences between the user and the authors. But excessive expansion takes significantly more processing and increases the response time due to the number of terms that have to be processed. Most systems have default limits on the number of new terms added to a search statement. Chapter 7 describes some of the basic algorithms that can be used as similarity measures. These algorithms are still in a state of evolution and are continually being modified to improve their performance. The search algorithms in a probabilistic indexing and search system are much more complex than the similarity measures described. For systems based upon natural language processing, once the initial similarity comparisons are completed, there is an additional search processing step to make use of discourse level information, adding additional precision to the final results.

Relevance feedback is an alternative to thesaurus expansion to assist the user in creating a search statement that will return the needed information. Thesaurus and semantic net expansions are dependent upon the user's ability to use the appropriate vocabulary in the search statement that represents the required information. If the user selects poor terms, they will be expanded with many more poor terms. Thesaurus expansion does not introduce new concepts that are relevant to the users information need, it just expands the description of existing concepts. Relevance feedback starts with the text of an item that the user has identified as meeting his information need; incorporating it into a revised search statement. The vocabulary in the relevant item text has the potential for introducing new concepts that better reflect the user's information need along with adding additional terms related to existing search terms and adjusting the weights (importance) of existing terms.

Selective Dissemination of Information search is different from searches against the persistent information database in that it is assumed there is no information from a large corpus available to determine parameters in determining a temporary index for the item to use in the similarity comparison process (e.g., inverse document frequency factors.) An aspect of dissemination systems that helps in the search process is the tendency for the profiles to have significantly more terms than ad hoc queries. The additional information helps to identify relevant items and increase the precision of the search process. Relevance feedback can also be used with profiles with some constraints. Relevance feedback used with ad hoc queries against an existing database tends to move the terminology defining the search concepts towards the information need of the user that is available in the current database. Concepts in the initial search statement will eventually lose importance in the revised queries if they are not in the database. The goal of profiles is to define the coverage of concepts that the user cares about if they are ever found in new items. Relevance feedback applied to profiles aides the user by enhancing the search profile with new terminology about areas of interest. But, even though a concept has not been found in any items received, that area may still be of critical importance to the user if it ever is found in any new items. Thus weighting of original terms takes on added significance over the ad hoc situation.

Searching the Internet for information has brought into focus the deficiencies in the search algorithms developed to date. The ad hoc queries are extremely short (usually less than three terms) and most users do not know how to use the advanced features associated with most search sites. Until recently research had focused on a larger more sophisticated query. With the Internet being the largest most available information system supporting information retrieval search, algorithms are in the process of being modified to account for the lack of information provided by the users in their queries. Intelligent Agents are being proposed as a potential mechanism to assist users in locating the information they require. The requirements for autonomy and the need for reasoning in the agents will lead to the merging of information retrieval algorithms and the learning processes associated with Artificial Intelligence. The use of hyperlinks is adding another level of ambiguity in what should be defined as an item. When similarity measures are being applied to identify the relevance weight, how much of the hyperlinked information should be considered part of the item? The impacts on the definition of information retrieval boundaries are just starting to be analyzed while experimental products are being developed in Web years and immediately being made available.

## 5.10 Exercises

1. Discuss the sources of potential errors in the final set of search terms from when a user first identifies a need for information to the creation of the final query. (HINT: you may also want to use information from Chap. 1)
2. Why are there three levels of binding in the creation of a search?
3. Why does the numerator remain basically the same in all of the similarity measures.? Discuss other possible approaches and their impact on the formulas.
4. Given the following set of retrieved documents with relevance judgments

| TERM | T1 | T2 | T3 | T4 | T5 | T6 |
|------|----|----|----|----|----|----|
| QUERY | 0 | 0 | 4 | 2 | 6 | 0 |
| REL D1 | 0 | 4 | 4 | 0 | 2 | 0 |
| REL D2 | 0 | 2 | 6 | 0 | 1 | 0 |
| NOT REL D3 | 6 | 0 | 0 | 6 | 1 | 0 |
| NOT REL D4 | 4 | 0 | 1 | 2 | 0 | 10 |

  a. Calculate a new query using a factor of 1/2 for positive feedback and 1/4 for negative feedback
  b. Determine which documents would be retrieved by the original and by the new query
  c. Discuss the differences in documents retrieved by the original versus the new query.

5. Is the use of positive feedback always better than using negative feedback to improve a query?
6. Given the following documents, determine which documents will be returned by the query ($A_{1.0}$ and $B_{0.5}$)

| TERM | A | B | C | D |
|------|---|---|---|---|
| D1 | 2 | 0 | 2 | 1 |
| D2 | 0 | 2 | 0 | 3 |
| D3 | 3 | 2 | 1 | 0 |
| D4 | 2 | 1 | 2 | 0 |
| D5 | 1 | 0 | 3 | 3 |
| D6 | 3 | 0 | 1 | 2 |
| D7 | 1 | 4 | 0 | 4 |
| D8 | 4 | 0 | 0 | 3 |
| D9 | 0 | 4 | 1 | 2 |
| D10 | 0 | 2 | 0 | 0 |
| D11 | 2 | 0 | 6 | 2 |
| D12 | 4 | 0 | 0 | 3 |

7. How would you define an item on the Internet with respect to a search statement and similarity function?

# Chapter 6
# Document and Term Clustering

## 6.1 Introduction to Clustering

Chapter 5 introduced indexing whose goal is to represent the semantics of an item.
In all of the techniques discussed in Chap. 5, our information database can be
viewed as being composed of a number of independent items indexed by a series
of index terms. In addition there are relationships that can be found between the
items. These relationships can be detected by using clustering techniques. They fall
into two classes: clustering index terms to create a statistical thesaurus and clustering items to create document clusters. In the first case the results of the clustering
can be used to increase recall by expanding searches with related terms. Document
clustering can be used to determine similar documents. The clustering process is
not precise and care must be taken on use of clustering techniques to minimize the
negative impact misuse can have. These issues are discussed in Sect. 6.1 along with
some general guidelines of clustering.

Section 6.2 discusses a variety of specific techniques to create thesaurus clusters. The techniques can be categorized as those that use the complete database to
perform the clustering and those that start with some initial structure. Section 6.3
looks at the same techniques as they apply to item (document) clustering. A class of
clustering algorithms creates a hierarchical output. The hierarchy of clusters usually
reflects more abstract concepts in the higher levels and more detailed specific items
in the lower levels. Hierarchical clustering and its associated performance improvements are described in Sect. 6.4.

The concept of clustering has been around as long as there have been libraries.
One of the first uses of clustering was an attempt to cluster items discussing the
same subject. The goal of the clustering was to assist in the location of information.
This eventually led to indexing schemes used in organization of items in libraries
and standards associated with use of electronic indexes. One of the first uses for
clustering of words was with the generation of thesauri. Thesaurus, coming from
the Latin word meaning "treasure," is similar to a dictionary in that it stores words.
Instead of definitions, it provides the synonyms and antonyms for the words. Its
primary purpose is to assist authors in selection of vocabulary. The goal of clustering is to provide a grouping of similar objects (e.g., terms or items) into a "class"

G. Kowalski, *Information Retrieval Architecture and Algorithms,*
DOI 10.1007/978-1-4419-7716-8_6, © Springer Science+Business Media, LLC 2011

under a more general title. The term class is frequently used as a synonym for the term cluster. They are used interchangeably in this chapter. The process of clustering follows the following steps:

1. Define the domain for the clustering effort. If a thesaurus is being created, this equates to determining the scope of the thesaurus such as "medical terms." If document clustering is being performed, it is determination of the set of items to be clustered. This can be a subset of the database or the complete database. Defining the domain for the clustering identifies those objects to be used in the clustering process and reduce the potential for erroneous data that could induce errors in the clustering process.
2. Once the domain is determined, determine the attributes of the objects to be clustered. If a thesaurus is being generated, determine the specific words in the objects to be used in the clustering process. Similarly, if documents are being clustered, the clustering process may focus on specific zones within the items (e.g., Title and abstract only, main body of the item but not the references, etc.) that are to be used to determine similarity. The objective, as with the first step (1.) is to reduce erroneous associations.
3. Determine the strength of the relationships between the attributes whose co-occurrence in objects suggest those objects should be in the same class. For thesauri this is determining which words are synonyms and the strength of their term relationships. For documents it may be defining a similarity function based upon word co-occurrences that determine the similarity between two items.
4. At this point, the total set of objects and the strengths of the relationships between the objects have been determined. The final step is applying some algorithm to determine the class(es) to which each item will be assigned.

There are guidelines (not hard constraints) on the characteristics of the classes:

- A well-defined semantic definition should exist for each class. There is a risk that the name assigned to the semantic definition of the class could also be misleading. In some systems numbers are assigned to classes to reduce the misinterpretation that a name attached to each class could have. A clustering of items into a class called "computer" could mislead a user into thinking that it includes items on main memory that may actually reside in another class called "hardware."
- The size of the classes should be within the same order of magnitude. One of the primary uses of the classes is to expand queries or expand the resultant set of retrieved items. If a particular class contains 90% of the objects, that class is not useful for either purpose. It also places in question the utility of the other classes that are distributed across 10% of the remaining objects.
- Within a class, one object should not dominate the class. For example, assume a thesaurus class called "computer" exists and it contains the objects (words/word phrases) "microprocessor," "286-processor," "386-processor" and "pentium." If the term "microprocessor" is found 85% of the time and the other terms are used 5% each, there is a strong possibility that using "microprocessor" as a synonym for "286-processor" will introduce too many errors. It may be better to place "microprocessor" into its own class.

- Whether an object can be assigned to multiple classes or just one must be decided at creation time. This is a tradeoff based upon the specificity and partitioning capability of the semantics of the objects. Given the ambiguity of language in general, it is better to allow an object to be in multiple classes rather than constrained to one. This added flexibility comes at a cost of additional complexity in creating and maintaining the classes.

There are additional important decisions associated with the generation of thesauri that are not part of item clustering (Aitchison-72):

- Word coordination approach: specifies if phrases as well as individual terms are to be clustered (see discussion on precoordination and postcoordination in Chap. 3).
- Word relationships: when the generation of a thesaurus includes a human interface (versus being totally automated), a variety of relationships between words are possible. Aitchison and Gilchrist (Aitchison-72) specified three types of relationships: equivalence, hierarchical and non-hierarchical. Equivalence relationships are the most common and represent synonyms. The definition of a synonym allows for some discretion in the thesaurus creation, allowing for terms that have significant overlap but differences. Thus the terms photograph and print may be defined as synonyms even though prints also include lithography. The definition can even be expanded to include words that have the same "role" but not necessarily the same meaning. Thus the words "genius" and "moron" may be synonyms in a class called "intellectual capability." A very common technique is hierarchical relationships where the class name is a general term and the entries are specific examples of the general term. The previous example of "computer" class name and "microprocessor," "pentium," etc. is an example of this case. Non-hierarchical relationships cover other types of relationships such as "object"-"attribute" that would contain "employee" and "job title."

  - Another word relationship scheme (Wang-85) classified relationships as Parts-Wholes, Collocation, Paradigmatic, Taxonomy and Synonymy, and Antonymy. The only two of these classes that require further amplification are collocation and paradigmatic. Collocation is a statistical measure that relates words that co-occur in the same proximity (sentence, phrase, paragraph). Paradigmatic relates words with the same semantic base such as "formula" and "equation."
  - In the expansion to semantic networks other relationships are included such as contrasted words, child-of (sphere is a child-of geometric volume), parent-of, part-of (foundation is part of a building), and contains part-of (bicycle contains parts-of wheel, handlebars) (RetrievalWare-95).

- Homograph resolution: a homograph is a word that has multiple, completely different meanings. For example, the term "field" could mean an electronic field, a field of grass, etc. It is difficult to eliminate homographs by supplying a unique meaning for every homograph (limiting the thesaurus domain helps). Typically the system allows for homographs and requires that the user interact with the system to select the desired meaning. It is possible to determine the correct meaning of the homograph when a user enters multiple search terms by analyzing the other terms entered (hay, crops, and field suggest the agricultural meaning for field).

- Vocabulary constraints: this includes guidelines on the normalization and specificity of the vocabulary. Normalization may constrain the thesaurus to stems versus complete words. Specificity may eliminate specific words or use general terms for class identifiers. The previous discussion in Chap. 3 on these topics applies to their use in the thesauri.

As is evident in these guidelines, clustering is as much an arcane art as it is a science. Good clustering of terms or items assists the user by improving recall. But typically an increase in recall has an associated decrease in precision. Automatic clustering has the imprecision of information retrieval algorithms, compounding the natural ambiguities that come from language. Care must be taken to ensure that the increases in recall are not associated with such decreases in precision as to make the human processing (reading) of the retrieved items unmanageable. The key to successful clustering lies in steps 3. and 4., selection of a good measure of similarity and selection of a good algorithm for placing items in the same class. When hierarchical item clustering is used, there is a possibility of a decrease in recall discussed in Sect. 6.4. The only solution to this problem is to make minimal use of the hierarchy.

## 6.2   Thesaurus Generation

Manual generation of clusters usually focuses on generating a thesaurus (i.e., clustering terms versus items) and has been used for hundreds of years. As items became available in electronic form, automated term statistical clustering techniques became available. Automatically generated thesauri contain classes that reflect the use of words in the corpora. The classes do not naturally have a name, but are just groups of statistically similar terms. The optimum technique for generating the classes requires intensive computation. Other techniques starting with existing clusters can reduce the computations required but may not produce optimum classes.

There are three basic methods for generation of a thesaurus; hand crafted, co-occurrence, and header-modifier based. Using manually made thesauri only helps in query expansion if the thesauri are domain specific for the domain being searched. General thesaurus (e.g., WordNet) does not help as much because of the many different meanings for the same word (Voorhees-93, Voorhees-94). Techniques for co-occurrence creation of thesauri are described in detail below. In header-modifier based thesauri term relationships are found based upon linguistic relationships. Words appearing in similar grammatical contexts are assumed to be similar (Hindle-90, Greffenstette-94, Jing-94, Ruge-92). The linguistic parsing of the document discovers the following syntactical structures: Subject-Verb, Verb-Object,

Adjective-Noun, and Noun-Noun. Each noun has a set of verbs, adjectives and nouns that it co-occurs with, and a mutual information value is calculated for each using typically a log function (see Mandala-99). Then a final similarity between words is calculated using the mutual information to classify the terms.

## 6.2.1 Manual Clustering

The manual clustering process follows the steps described in Sect. 6.1 in the generation of a thesaurus. The first step is to determine the domain for the clustering. Defining the domain assists in reducing ambiguities caused by homographs and helps focus the creator. Usually existing thesauri, concordances from items that cover the domain and dictionaries are used as starting points for generating the set of potential words to be included in the new thesaurus. A concordance is an alphabetical listing of words from a set of items along with their frequency of occurrence and references of which items in which they are found. The art of manual thesaurus construction resides in the selection of the set of words to be included. Care is taken to not include words that are unrelated to the domain of the thesaurus or those that have very high frequency of occurrence and thus hold no information value (e.g., the term Computer in a thesaurus focused on data processing machines). If a concordance is used, other tools such as KWOC, KWIC or KWAC may help in determining useful words. A Key Word Out of Context (KWOC) is another name for a concordance. Key Word In Context (KWIC) displays a possible term in its phrase context. It is structured to identify easily the location of the term under consideration in the sentence. Key Word And Context (KWAC) displays the keywords followed by their context. Figure 6.1 shows the various displays for "computer design contains memory chips" (NOTE: the phrase is assumed to be from doc4; the other frequency and document ids for KWOC were created for this example.) In the Fig. 6.1 the character "/" is used in KWIC to indicate the end of the phrase.

|  | KWOC | | |
|---|---|---|---|
|  | TERM | FREQ | ITEM Ids |
|  | chips | 2 | doc2, doc4 |
|  | computer | 3 | doc1, doc4, doc10 |
|  | design | 1 | doc4 |
|  | memory | 3 | doc3, doc4, doc8, doc12 |
|  | KWIC | | |
|  | chips/ | | computer design contains memory |
|  | computer | | design contains memory chips/ |
|  | design | | contains memory chips/ computer |
|  | memory | | chips/ computer design contains |
|  | KWAC | | |
|  | chips | | computer design contains memory chips |
|  | computer | | computer design contains memory chips |
|  | design | | computer design contains memory chips |
|  | memory | | computer design contains memory chips |

**Fig. 6.1** Example of KWOC, KWIC and KWAC

The KWIC and KWAC are useful in determining the meaning of homographs. The term "chips" could be wood chips or memory chips. In both the KWIC and KWAC displays, the editor of the thesaurus can read the sentence fragment associated with the term and determine its meaning. The KWOC does not present any information that would help in resolving this ambiguity.

Once the terms are selected they are clustered based upon the word relationship guidelines and the interpretation of the strength of the relationship. This is also part of the art of manual creation of the thesaurus, using the judgment of the human analyst. The resultant thesaurus undergoes many quality assurance reviews by additional editors using some of the guidelines already suggested before it is finalized.

## 6.2.2   Automatic Term Clustering

There are many techniques for the automatic generation of term clusters to create statistical thesauri. They all use as their basis the concept that the more frequently two terms co-occur in the same items, the more likely they are about the same concept. They differ by the completeness with which terms are correlated. The more complete the correlation, the higher the time and computational overhead to create the clusters. The most complete process computes the strength of the relationships between all combinations of the "n" unique words with an overhead of $O(n^2)$. Other techniques start with an arbitrary set of clusters and iterate on the assignment of terms to these clusters. The simplest case employs one pass of the data in creation of the clusters. When the number of clusters created is very large, the initial clusters may be used as a starting point to generate more abstract clusters creating a hierarchy.

The steps described in Sect. 6.1 apply to the automatic generation of thesauri. The basis for automatic generation of a thesaurus is a set of items that represents the vocabulary to be included in the thesaurus. Selection of this set of items is the first step of determining the domain for the thesaurus. The processing tokens (words) in the set of items are the attributes to be used to create the clusters. Implementation of the other steps differs based upon the algorithms being applied. In the following sections a term is usually restricted to be included in only one class. It is also possible to use a threshold instead of choosing the highest value, allowing a term to be assigned to all of the classes that it could be included in above the threshold. The automated method of clustering documents is based upon the polythetic clustering (Rijsbergen-79) where each cluster is defined by a set of words and phrases. Inclusion of an item in a cluster is based upon the similarity of the item's words and phrases to those of other items in the cluster.

### 6.2.2.1   Complete Term Relation Method

In the complete term relation method, the similarity between every term pair is calculated as a basis for determining the clusters. The easiest way to understand

| | Term 1 | Term 2 | Term 3 | Term 4 | Term 5 | Term 6 | Term 7 | Term 8 |
|---|---|---|---|---|---|---|---|---|
| Item 1 | 0 | 4 | 0 | 0 | 0 | 2 | 1 | 3 |
| Item 2 | 3 | 1 | 4 | 3 | 1 | 2 | 0 | 1 |
| Item 3 | 3 | 0 | 0 | 0 | 3 | 0 | 3 | 0 |
| Item 4 | 0 | 1 | 0 | 3 | 0 | 0 | 2 | 0 |
| Item 5 | 2 | 2 | 2 | 3 | 1 | 4 | 0 | 2 |

Fig. 6.2  Vector example

this approach is to consider the vector model. The vector model is represented by a matrix where the rows are individual items and the columns are the unique words (processing tokens) in the items. The values in the matrix represent how strongly that particular word represents concepts in the item. Figure 6.2 provides an example of a database with 5 items and 8 terms.

To determine the relationship between terms, a similarity measure is required. The measure calculates the similarity between two terms. In Chap. 7 a number of similarity measures are presented. The similarity measure is not critical in understanding the methodology so the following simple measure is used:

$$SIM(Term_i, Term_j) = \sum (Term_{k,i})(Term_{k,j})$$

where "k" is summed across the set of all items. In effect the formula takes the two columns of the two terms being analyzed, multiplying and accumulating the values in each row. The results can be placed in a resultant "m" by "m" matrix, called a Term-Term Matrix (Salton-83), where "m" is the number of columns (terms) in the original matrix. This simple formula is reflexive so that the matrix that is generated is symmetric. Other similarity formulas could produce a non-symmetric matrix. Using the data in Fig. 6.2, the Term-Term matrix produced is shown in Fig. 6.3. There are no values on the diagonal since that represents the auto-correlation of a word to itself. The next step is to select a threshold that determines if two terms are considered similar enough to each other to be in the same class. In this example, the threshold value of 10 is used. Thus two terms are considered similar if the similarity value between them is 10 or greater. This produces a new binary matrix called the

| | Term 1 | Term 2 | Term 3 | Term 4 | Term 5 | Term 6 | Term 7 | Term 8 |
|---|---|---|---|---|---|---|---|---|
| Term 1 | | 7 | 16 | 15 | 14 | 14 | 9 | 7 |
| Term 2 | 7 | | 8 | 12 | 3 | 18 | 6 | 17 |
| Term 3 | 16 | 8 | | 18 | 6 | 16 | 0 | 8 |
| Term 4 | 15 | 12 | 18 | | 6 | 18 | 6 | 9 |
| Term 5 | 14 | 3 | 6 | 6 | | 6 | 9 | 3 |
| Term 6 | 14 | 18 | 16 | 18 | 6 | | 2 | 16 |
| Term 7 | 9 | 6 | 0 | 6 | 9 | 2 | | 3 |
| Term 8 | 7 | 17 | 8 | 9 | 3 | 16 | 3 | |

Fig. 6.3  Term-Term matrix

|        | Term 1 | Term 2 | Term 3 | Term 4 | Term 5 | Term 6 | Term 7 | Term 8 |
|--------|--------|--------|--------|--------|--------|--------|--------|--------|
| Term 1 |        | 0      | 1      | 1      | 1      | 1      | 0      | 0      |
| Term 2 | 0      |        | 0      | 1      | 0      | 1      | 0      | 1      |
| Term 3 | 1      | 0      |        | 1      | 0      | 1      | 0      | 0      |
| Term 4 | 1      | 1      | 1      |        | 0      | 1      | 0      | 0      |
| Term 5 | 1      | 0      | 0      | 0      |        | 0      | 0      | 0      |
| Term 6 | 1      | 1      | 1      | 1      | 0      |        | 0      | 1      |
| Term 7 | 0      | 0      | 0      | 0      | 0      | 0      |        | 0      |
| Term 8 | 0      | 1      | 0      | 0      | 0      | 1      | 0      |        |

Fig. 6.4 Term relationship matrix

Term Relationship matrix (Fig. 6.4) that defines which terms are similar. A one in the matrix indicates that the terms specified by the column and the row are similar enough to be in the same class. Term 7 demonstrates that a term may exist on its own with no other similar terms identified. In any of the clustering processes described below this term will always migrate to a class by itself.

The final step in creating clusters is to determine when two objects (words) are in the same cluster. There are many different algorithms available. The following algorithms are the most common: cliques, single link, stars and connected components.

Cliques require all items in a cluster to be within the threshold of all other items. The methodology to create the clusters using cliques is:

0. Let $i = 1$
1. Select $term_i$ and place it in a new class
2. Start with $term_k$ where $r = k = i + 1$
3. Validate if $term_k$ is within the threshold of all terms within the current class
4. If not, let $k = k + 1$
5. If $k > m$ (number of words)
   then $r = r + 1$
      if $r = m$ then go to 6 else
         $k = r$
         create a new class with $term_i$ in it
         go to 3
   else go to 3

6. If current class only has $term_i$ in it and there are other classes
   with $term_i$ in them
      then delete current class
         else $i = i + 1$
7. If $i = m + 1$ then go to 8
   else go to 1
8. Eliminate any classes that duplicate or are subsets of other classes.

Applying the algorithm to Fig. 6.4, the following classes are created:

Class 1 (Term 1, Term 3, Term 4, Term 6)
Class 2 (Term 1, Term 5)

Class 3 (Term 2, Term 4, Term 6)
Class 4 (Term 2, Term 6, Term 8)
Class 5 (Term 7)

Notice that Term 1, Term 4 and Term 6 are in more than one class. A characteristic of this approach is that terms can be found in multiple classes.

In single link clustering the strong constraint that every term in a class is similar to every other term is relaxed. The rule to generate single link clusters is that any term that is similar to any term in the cluster can be added to the cluster. It is impossible for a term to be in two different clusters. This in effect partitions the set of terms into the clusters. The algorithm is:

1. Select a term that is not in a class and place it in a new class
2. Place in that class all other terms that are related to it
3. For each term entered into the class, perform step 2
4. When no new terms can be identified in step 2, go to step 1.

Applying the algorithm for creating clusters using single link to the Term Relationship Matrix, Fig. 6.4, the following classes are created:

Class 1 (Term 1, Term 3, Term 4, Term 5, Term 6, Term 2, Term 8)
Class 2 (Term 7)

There are many other conditions that can be placed on the selection of terms to be clustered. The Star technique selects a term and then places in the class all terms that are related to that term (i.e., in effect a star with the selected term as the core). Terms not yet in classes are selected as new seeds until all terms are assigned to a class. There are many different classes that can be created using the Star technique. If we always choose as the starting point for a class the lowest numbered term not already in a class, using Fig. 6.4, the following classes are created:

Class 1 (Term 1, Term 3, Term 4, Term 5, Term 6)
Class 2 (Term 2, Term 4, Term 8, Term 6)
Class 3 (Term 7)

This technique allows terms to be in multiple clusters (e.g., Term 4). This could be eliminated by expanding the constraints to exclude any term that has already been selected for a previous cluster.

The String technique starts with a term and includes in the class one additional term that is similar to the term selected and not already in a class. The new term is then used as the new node and the process is repeated until no new terms can be added because the term being analyzed does not have another term related to it or the terms related to it are already in the class. A new class is started with any term not currently in any existing class. Using the additional guidelines to select the lowest number term similar to the current term and not to select any term already in an existing class produces the following classes:

Class 1 (Term 1, Term 3, Term 4, Term 2, Term 6, Term 8)
Class 2 (Term 5)
Class 3 (Term 7)

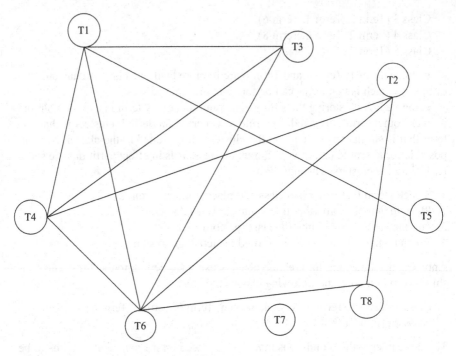

**Fig. 6.5** Network diagram of term similarities

A technique to understand these different algorithms for generating classes is based upon a network diagram of the terms. Each term is considered a node and arcs between the nodes indicate terms that are similar. A network diagram for Fig. 6.4 is given in Fig. 6.5. To determine cliques, sub-networks are identified where all of the items are connected by arcs. From this diagram it is obvious that Term 7 (T7) is in a class by itself and Term 5 (T5) is in a class with Term 1 (T1). Other common structures to look for are triangles and four sided polygons with diagonals. To find all classes for an item, it is necessary to find all subnetworks, where each subnetwork has the maximum number of nodes, that the term is contained. For Term 1 (T1), it is the subnetwork T1, T3, T4, and T6. Term 2 (T2) has two subnetworks: T2, T4, T6 and the subnetwork T2, T6, T8. The network diagram provides a simple visual tool when there are a small number of nodes to identify classes using any of the other techniques.

The clique technique produces classes that have the strongest relationships between all of the words in the class. This suggests that the class is more likely to be describing a particular concept. The clique algorithm produces more classes than the other techniques because the requirement for all terms to be similar to all other terms will reduce the number of terms in a class. This will require more classes to include all the terms. The single link technique partitions the terms into classes. It produces the fewest number of classes and the weakest relationship between terms (Salton-72, Jones-71, Salton-75). It is possible using the single link algorithm that two terms that have a similarity value of zero will be in the same class. Classes will not be associated with a concept but cover a diversity of concepts. The other techniques lie between these two extremes.

The selection of the technique is also governed by the density of the term relationship matrix and objectives of the thesaurus. When the Term Relationship Matrix is sparse (i.e., contains a few number of ones), then the constraint dependencies between terms need to be relaxed such as in single link to create classes with a reasonable number of items. If the matrix is dense (i.e., lots of ones implying relationships between many terms), then the tighter constraints of the clique are needed so the number of items in a class does not become too large.

Cliques provide the highest precision when the statistical thesaurus is used for query term expansion. The single link algorithm maximizes recall but can cause selection of many non-relevant items. The single link assignment process has the least overhead in assignment of terms to classes, requiring $O(n^2)$ comparisons (Croft-77)

### 6.2.2.2  Clustering Using Existing Clusters

An alternative methodology for creating clusters is to start with a set of existing clusters. This is called K-means algorithm. This methodology reduces the number of similarity calculations required to determine the clusters. The initial assignment of terms to the clusters is revised by revalidating every term assignment to a cluster. The process stops when minimal movement between clusters is detected. To minimize calculations, centroids are calculated for each cluster. A centroid is viewed in Physics as the center of mass of a set of objects. In the context of vectors, it will equate to the average of all of the vectors in a cluster.

One way to understand this process is to view the centroids of the clusters as another point in the N-dimensional space where N is the number of items. The first assignment of terms to clusters produces centroids that are not related to the final clustering of terms. The similarity between all existing terms and the centroids of the clusters can be calculated. The term is reallocated to the cluster(s) that has the highest similarity. This process is iterated until it stabilizes. Calculations using this process are of the order $O(n)$. The initial assignment of terms to clusters is not critical in that the iterative process changes the assignment of terms to clusters.

A graphical representation of terms and centroids illustrates how the classes move after the initial assignment. The solid black box represents the centroid for each of the classes. In Fig. 6.6b the centroids for the first three arbitrary classes are shown. The ovals in Fig. 6.6b show the ideal cluster assignments for each term. During the next iteration the similarity between every term and the clusters is performed reassigning terms as needed. The resulting new centroid for the new clusters are again shown as black squares in Fig. 6.6a. The new centroids are not yet perfectly associated with the ideal clusters, but they are much closer. The process continues until it stabilizes.

**Fig. 6.6** **a** Centroids after reassigning terms. **b** Initial centroids for clusters

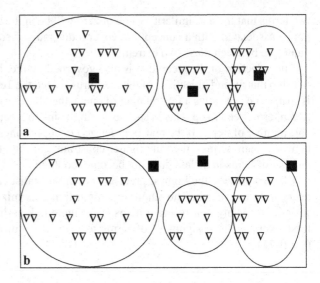

The following example of this technique uses Fig. 6.2 as our weighted environment, and assumes we arbitrarily placed Class 1=(Term 1 and Term 2), Class 2=(Term 3 and Term 4) and Class 3=(Term 5 and Term 6). This would produce the following centroids for each class:

Class 1= (0+4)/2, (3+1)/2, (3+0)/2, (0+1)/2, (2+2)/2
       =4/2, 4/2, 3/2, 1/2, 4/2
Class 2=0/2, 7/2, 0/2, 3/2, 5/2
Class 3=2/2, 3/2, 3/2, 0/2, 5/2

Each value in the centroid is the average of the weights of the terms in the cluster for each item in the database. For example in Class 1 the first value is calculated by averaging the weights of Term 1 and Term 2 in Item 1. For Class 2 and 3 the numerator is already the sum of the weights of each term. For the next step, calculating similarity values, it is often easier to leave the values in fraction form.

Applying the simple similarity measure defined in Sect. 6.2.2.1 between each of the 8 terms and 3 centroids just calculated comes up with the following assignment of similarity weights and new assignment of terms to classes in the row Assign shown in Fig. 6.7.

|         | Term 1  | Term 2  | Term 3  | Term 4  | Term 5  | Term 6  | Term 7  | Term 8  |
|---------|---------|---------|---------|---------|---------|---------|---------|---------|
| **Class 1** | 29/2    | 29/2    | 24/2    | 27/2    | 17/2    | 32/2    | 15/2    | 24/2    |
| **Class 2** | 31/2    | 20/2    | 38/2    | 45/2    | 12/2    | 34/2    | 6/2     | 17/2    |
| **Class 3** | 28/2    | 21/2    | 22/2    | 24/2    | 17/2    | 30/2    | 11/2    | 19/2    |
|         |         |         |         |         |         |         |         |         |
| **Assign** | Class 2 | Class 1 | Class 2 | Class 2 | Class 3 | Class 2 | Class 1 | Class 1 |

**Fig. 6.7** Iterated class assignments

| | Term 1 | Term 2 | Term 3 | Term 4 | Term 5 | Term 6 | Term 7 | Term 8 |
|---|---|---|---|---|---|---|---|---|
| **Class 1** | 23/3 | 45/3 | 16/3 | 27/3 | 15/3 | 36/3 | 23/3 | 34/3 |
| **Class 2** | 67/4 | 45/4 | 70/4 | 78/4 | 33/4 | 72/4 | 17/4 | 40/4 |
| **Class 3** | 12/1 | 3/1 | 6/1 | 6/1 | 11/1 | 6/1 | 9/1 | 3/1 |
| **Assign** | Class 2 | Class 1 | Class 2 | Class 2 | Class 3 | Class 2 | Class 3 | Class 1 |

**Fig. 6.8** New centroids and cluster assignments

In the case of Term 5, where there is tie for the highest similarity, either class could be assigned. One technique for breaking ties is to look at the similarity weights of the other items in the class and assign it to the class that has the most similar weights. The majority of terms in Class 1 have weights in the high 20's/2, thus Term 5 was assigned to Class 3. Term 7 is assigned to Class 1 even though its similarity weights are not in alignment with the other terms in that class. Figure 6.8 shows the new centroids and results of similarity comparisons for the next iteration.

Class 1 = 8/3, 2/3, 3/3, 3/3, 4/3
Class 2 = 2/4, 12/4, 3/4, 3/4, 11/4
Class 3 = 0/1, 1/1, 3/1, 0/1, 1/1

In this iteration of the process, the only change is Term 7 moves from Class 1 to Class 3. This is reasonable, given it was not that strongly related to the other terms in Class 1.

Although the process requires fewer calculations than the complete term relationship method, it has inherent limitations. The primary problem is that the number of classes is defined at the start of the process and cannot grow. It is possible for there to be fewer classes at the end of the process. Since all terms must be assigned to a class, it forces terms to be allocated to classes, even if their similarity to the class is very weak compared to other terms assigned. It also does not guarantee to get an optimal clustering solution. The example that shows the potential suboptimal nature of this technique is to consider a two dimensional space with four items to cluster. Consider each item located at a point on a rectangle where the height is greater than the width. If the starting points are midpoint one the two lines connecting the height then the clustering will end up with the two points on each line for the height being clustered. This is independent of how much higher the rectangle is versus wide. But the two points on the width would be better clusters minimizing the distance between clustered points (distance metric for evaluating how well cluster works is discussed later in this chapter).

One technique for choosing the initial cluster points to try and keep their locations away from each other is to selects the first starting point. Then from the remaining points select the next cluster point with probability proportional to the square of the distance from the closest existing cluster point. This takes additional processing initially but over the total clustering process is more likely to be faster and yield better results than random selection.

### 6.2.2.3   One Pass Assignments

This technique has the minimum overhead in that only one pass of all of the terms is used to assign terms to classes. The first term is assigned to the first class. Each additional term is compared to the centroids of the existing classes. A threshold is chosen. If the item is greater than the threshold, it is assigned to the class with the highest similarity. A new centroid has to be calculated for the modified class. If the similarity to all of the existing centroids is less than the threshold, the term is the first item in a new class. This process continues until all items are assigned to classes. Using the system defined in Fig. 6.3, with a threshold of 10 the following classes would be generated:

> Class 1 = Term 1, Term 3, Term 4
> Class 2 = Term 2, Term 6, Term 8
> Class 3 = Term 5
> Class 4 = Term 7

NOTE: the centroid values used during the one-pass process:

> Class 1 (Term 1, Term 3) = 0, 7/2, 3/2, 0, 4/2
> Class 1 (Term 1, Term 3, Term 4) = 0, 10/3, 3/3, 3/3, 7/3
> Class 2 (Term 2, Term 6) = 6/2, 3/2, 0/2, 1/2, 6/2

Although this process has minimal computation on the order of $O(n)$, it does not produce optimum clustered classes. The different classes can be produced if the order in which the items are analyzed changes. Items that would have been in the same cluster could appear in different clusters due to the averaging nature of centroids.

## 6.3   Item Clustering

Clustering of items is very similar to term clustering for the generation of thesauri. Manual item clustering is inherent in any library or filing system. In this case someone reads the item and determines the category or categories to which it belongs. When physical clustering occurs, each item is usually assigned to one category. With the advent of indexing, an item is physically stored in a primary category, but it can be found in other categories as defined by the index terms assigned to the item.

With the advent of electronic holdings of items, it is possible to perform automatic clustering of the items. The techniques described for the clustering of terms in Sect. 6.2.2.1 through 6.2.2.3 also apply to item clustering. Similarity between documents is based upon two items that have terms in common versus terms with items in common. Thus, the similarity function is performed between rows of the item matrix. Using Fig. 6.2 as the set of items and their terms and similarity equation:

$$\text{SIM}(\text{Item}_i, \text{Item}_j) = \sum (\text{Term}_{i,k})(\text{Term}_{j,k})$$

as $k$ goes from 1 to 8 for the eight terms, an Item-Item matrix is created (Fig. 6.9). Using a threshold of 10 produces the Item Relationship matrix shown in Fig. 6.10.

**Fig. 6.9** Item/Item matrix

|        | Item 1 | Item 2 | Item 3 | Item 4 | Item 5 |
|--------|--------|--------|--------|--------|--------|
| Item 1 |        | 11     | 3      | 6      | 22     |
| Item 2 | 11     |        | 12     | 10     | 36     |
| Item 3 | 3      | 12     |        | 6      | 9      |
| Item 4 | 6      | 10     | 6      |        | 11     |
| Item 5 | 22     | 36     | 9      | 11     |        |

**Fig. 6.10** Item relationship matrix ,

|        | Item 1 | Item 2 | Item 3 | Item 4 | Item 5 |
|--------|--------|--------|--------|--------|--------|
| Item 1 |        | 1      | 0      | 0      | 1      |
| Item 2 | 1      |        | 1      | 1      | 1      |
| Item 3 | 0      | 1      |        | 0      | 0      |
| Item 4 | 0      | 1      | 0      |        | 1      |
| Item 5 | 1      | 1      | 0      | 1      |        |

Using the Clique algorithm for assigning items to classes produces the following classes based upon Fig. 6.10:

Class 1 = Item 1, Item 2, Item 5
Class 2 = Item 2, Item 3
Class 3 = Item 2, Item 4, Item 5

Application of the single link technique produces:

Class 1 = Item 1, Item 2, Item 5, Item 3, Item 4

All the items are in this one cluster, with Item 3 and Item 4 added because of their similarity to Item 2. The Star technique (i.e., always selecting the lowest non-assigned item) produces:

Class 1 = Item 1, Item 2, Item 5
Class 2 = Item 3, Item 2
Class 3 = Item 4, Item 2, Item 5

Using the String technique and stopping when all items are assigned to classes produces the following:

Class 1 = Item 1, Item 2, Item 3
Class 2 = Item 4, Item 5

In the vocabulary domain homographs introduce ambiguities and erroneous hits. In the item domain multiple topics in an item may cause similar problems. This is especially true when the decision is made to partition the document space. Without precoordination of semantic concepts, an item that discusses "Politics" in "America" and "Economics" in "Mexico" could get clustered with a class that is focused around "Politics" in "Mexico."

Clustering by starting with existing clusters can be performed in a manner similar to the term model. Let's start with item 1 and item 3 in Class 1, and item 2 and item 4 in Class 2. The centroids are:

Class 1 = 3/2, 4/2, 0/2, 0/2, 3/2, 2/2, 4/2, 3/2
Class 2 = 3/2, 2/2, 4/2, 6/2, 1/2, 2/2, 2/2, 1/2

| Fig. 6.11 Item clustering with initial clusters | | Class 1 | Class 2 | Assign |
|---|---|---|---|---|
| | Item 1 | 33/2 | 17/2 | Class 1 |
| | Item 2 | 23/2 | 51/2 | Class 2 |
| | Item 3 | 30/2 | 18/2 | Class 2 |
| | Item 4 | 8/2 | 24/2 | Class 2 |
| | Item 5 | 31/2 | 47/2 | Class 2 |

The results of recalculating the similarities of each item to each centroid and reassigning terms is shown in Fig. 6.11.

Finding the centroid for Class 2, which now contains four items, and recalculating the similarities does not result in reassignment for any of the items.

Instead of using words as a basis for clustering items, the Acquaintance system uses n-grams (Damashek-95, Cohen-95). Not only does their algorithm cluster items, but when items can be from more than one language, it will also recognize the different languages.

## 6.4   Hierarchy of Clusters

Hierarchical clustering in Information Retrieval focuses on the area of hierarchical agglomerative clustering methods (HACM). The term agglomerative means collecting in a mass. When applied to clustering, the goal is to create a hierarchy of clusters where the higher level clusters represent the contents of the lower level clusters. There are two approaches to create the hierarchy of clusters. In one approach you start at the bottom level of items and continually combine them in clusters and combine the clusters into higher level of clusters. This is usually referred to as bottom up hierarchical clustering. Divisive is the term applied to starting with a single cluster and breaking it down into smaller clusters. This is referred to as top down hierarchical clustering. The objectives of creating a hierarchy of clusters are to:

- Reduce the overhead of search
- Provide for a visual representation of the information space
- Expand the retrieval of relevant items.

Search overhead is reduced by performing top-down searches of the centroids of the clusters in the hierarchy and trimming those branches that are not relevant. This top down search approach can reduce recall and cause relevant items to be missed (discussed in greater depth in Sect. 6.6).

It is difficult to create a visual display of the total item space. Use of dendograms along with visual cues on the size of clusters (e.g., size of the ellipse) and strengths of the linkages between clusters (e.g., dashed lines indicate reduced similarities) allows a user to determine alternate paths of browsing the database (see Fig. 6.12). The dendogram allows the user to determine which clusters to be reviewed are likely to have items of interest. Even without the visual display of the hierarchy, a

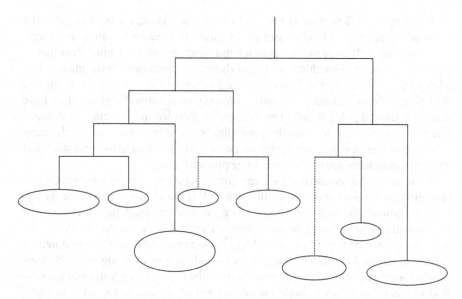

**Fig. 6.12** Dendogram

user can use the logical hierarchy to browse items of interest. The user can increase the specificity of items by going to children clusters or by increasing the generality of items being reviewed by going to a parent cluster.

A user, once having identified an item of interest via a search, can request to see other items in a cluster that the item is in. This is analogous to going to a library and looking at other books in the proximity of the book you are interested in.

Most of the existing HACM approaches can be defined in terms of the Lance-Williams dissimilarity update formula (Lance-66). It defines a general formula for calculating the dissimilarity D between any existing cluster $C_k$ and a new cluster $C_{i,j}$ created by combining clusters $C_i$ and $C_j$.

$$D(C_{i,j}, C_k) = \alpha_i D(C_i, C_k) + \alpha_j D(C_j, C_k) + \beta D(C_i, C_j)$$
$$+ \gamma |D(C_i, C_k) - D(C_j, C_k)|$$

By proper selection of $\alpha$, $\beta$, and $\gamma$, the current techniques for HACM can be represented (Frakes-92). In comparing the various methods of creating hierarchical clusters Voorhees and later El-Hamdouchi and Willet determined that the group average method produced the best results on document collections (Voorhees-86, El-Hamdouchi-89).

The similarity between two clusters can be treated as the similarity between all objects in one cluster and all objects in the other cluster. Voorhees showed that the similarity between a cluster centroid and any item is equal to the mean similarity between the item and all items in the cluster. Since the centroid is the average of all items in the cluster, this means that similarities between centroids can be used to calculate the similarities between clusters.

The techniques described in Sect. 6.2 created independent sets of classes. The automatic clustering techniques can also be used to create a hierarchy of objects (items or terms). The automatic approach has been applied to creating item hierarchies more than in hierarchical statistical thesaurus generation. In the manual creation of thesauri, network relationships are frequently allowed between terms and classes creating an expanded thesaurus called semantic networks. Hierarchies have also been created going from general categories to more specific classes of terms. The human creator ensures that the generalization or specification as the hierarchy is created makes semantic sense. Automatic creation of a hierarchy for a statistical thesaurus introduces too many errors to be productive.

A cluster can be represented by a category label if the clusters were monolithic (membership is based upon a specific attribute). If the cluster is polythetic, generated by allowing for multiple attributes (e.g., words/concepts), then it can best be represented by using a list of the most significant words in the cluster. An alternative is to show a two or three-dimensional space where the clusters are represented by clusters of points. Monolithic clusters have two advantages over polythetic (Sanderson-99): how easy it is for a user to understand the topic of the cluster and the confidence that every item within the cluster will have a significant focus on the topic. For example, YAHOO is a good example of a monolithic cluster environment.

Sanderson and Croft proposed the following methodology to building a concept hierarchy. Rather than just focusing the construction of the hierarchy, they looked at ways of extracting terms from the documents to represent the hierarchy. The terms had the following characteristics:

- Terms had to best reflect the topics
- A parent term would refer to a more general concept then its child
- A child would cover a related subtopic of the parent
- A directed acyclic graph would represent relationships versus a pure hierarchy.
- Ambiguous terms would have separate entries in the hierarchy for each meaning.

As a concept hierarchy, it should be represented similar to WordNet (Miller-95) which uses synonyms, antonyms, hyponym/hypernym (is-a/is-a-type-of), and meronym/holonym (has-part/is-a-part-of). Some techniques for generating hierarchies are Grefenstette's use of the similarity of contexts for locating synonyms (Grefenstette-94), use of key phrases (e.g., "such as", "and other") as an indicator of hyponym/hypernym relationships (Hearst-98), use of head and modifier noun and verb phrases to determine hierarchies (Woods-97) and use of a cohesion statistic to measure the degree of association between terms (Forsyth-86). Sanderson and Croft used a test based upon subsumption. It is defined given two terms X and Y, X subsumes Y if:

$$P(X/Y) \geq 0.8, \ P(Y/X) < 1.$$

X subsumes Y if the documents which Y occurs in are almost (0.8) a subset of the documents that X occurs in. The factor of 0.8 was heuristically used because an absolute condition was eliminating too many useful relationships. X is thus a parent of Y.

The set of documents to be clustered was determined by a query and the query terms were used as the initial set of terms for the monolithic cluster. This set was expanded by adding more terms via query expansion using peudorelevance feedback (Blind feedback, Local Context Analysis) which is described in Chap. 5. They then used the terms and the formula above to create the hierarchies.

## 6.4.1 Automatic Hierarchical Cluster Algorithms

The generation of hierarchical clusters starts after the techniques in Sect. 6.2 have been applied and there is an initial set of clusters. The algorithms recursively focus on the question of which two clusters to combine given the current set of clusters. The combination process will generate an unbalanced tree that represents the final set of items. In each iteration the number of clusters that need to be considered will be reduced by one cluster. There are four techniques that will be presented for combining clusters. As with the options presented in Sect. 6.2, the techniques tradeoff complexity of computation versus creation of better clusters. The first two techniques called single link and complete link graphically are similar to the single link and clique techniques presented previously.

The first technique is call Single Link and it uses as its basis for determining the similarity between two clusters comparing the similarity between one item from each cluster. That item selected will be the item that has the most similarity (least distance) from any of the items in the other cluster. Thus the two items selected will generate the maximum similarity or minimum distance measure. Once all of the values have been generated, then the maximum similarity (minimum distance) between any two of the current set of clusters will determine the next two clusters to combine. This is similar to Kruskal's algorithm for minimum spanning trees except the order of combination is important in defining the hierarchy generated.

The Complete Link technique is similar in doing the calculations from one item from each cluster. In this case the items selected are the item from each cluster that has the minimum similarity (maximum distance) to calculate the value used for those two clusters. This defines an outer limit and all other item pairs will be more similar.

Ward's Method (Ward-63) chooses the minimum square Euclidean distance between points (e.g., centroids in this case) normalized by the number of objects in each cluster. He uses the formula for the variance I, choosing the minimum variance:

$$I_{i,j} = \left( (m_i m_j) / (m_i + m_j) \right) d_{i,j}^2$$
$$d_{i,j}^2 = \sum_{k=1} \left( x_{i,k} - x_{j,k} \right)^2$$

where $m_i$ is the number of objects in $Class_i$ and $d_{i,j}^2$ is the squared Euclidean distance. The process of selection of centroids can be improved by using the reciprocal nearest neighbor algorithm (Murtagh-83, Murtagh-85). A simpler algorithm can be used where just the centroids are used in determining the similarity between existing clusters. This is known as the Average Link process. In both approaches the maximum similarity or minimum distance between two clusters is used as the value to decide which clusters to combine. In the average link process using the centroids is the same as calculating the similarity (or distance) from every item in one cluster with every item in the other cluster.

The final technique is Group Average clustering. Group average extends the Average Link clustering to also considering items with each cluster. Thus group average clustering calculates the similarity between all items both between clusters and within each cluster. This will assure that the two clusters that are combined will produce the tightest coupled new cluster where the distances between the centroid and each item in the new cluster is less than any other cluster combination. Figure 6.13 shows graphically all four techniques. The Average Link is shown versus Ward's minimum variance.

Comparing the four different hierarchical clustering techniques helps understand how they are used. The Single Link process does not promise tightly couple clusters but is far more likely than the other techniques to combine clusters producing less tightly coupled clusters since the only metric used is the best case between one item from each cluster. Rather than clusters that tend to be more circular you are apt to get clusters that are ellipsoidal. There are efficient techniques that can be implemented to use this technique and it does not require a cluster centroid to be calculated and recalculated thus avoiding changing the similarity matrix. The Complete Link method uses the items that are least similar and thus all of the items will have a similarity less than that value. This will tend to create more tightly bounded

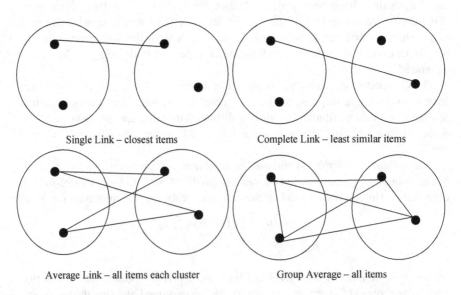

Single Link – closest items         Complete Link – least similar items

Average Link – all items each cluster         Group Average – all items

**Fig. 6.13** Types of hierarchical clustering

clusters. Ward's method that combines the clusters that minimizes the within cluster sum of the squares distance should create more symmetric clusters that will have a good representative centroid for the items in the cluster. The group average link method will generate clusters whose tightness is between the single link and complete link methods. It requires a lot of computation to calculate cluster similarities during each iteration.

An example of applying the different hierarchical clustering techniques based upon the following document—document similarity matrix:

|      | D1 | D2 | D3 | D4 | D5 | D6 | D7 | D8 | D9 | D10 | D11 | D12 |
|------|----|----|----|----|----|----|----|----|----|-----|-----|-----|
| D1   |    | 7  | 16 | 15 | 14 | 14 | 9  | 7  | 0  | 4   | 2   | 7   |
| D2   | 7  |    | 8  | 12 | 3  | 18 | 6  | 17 | 1  | 4   | 1   | 1   |
| D3   | 16 | 8  |    | 18 | 6  | 16 | 0  | 8  | 3  | 5   | 2   | 1   |
| D4   | 15 | 12 | 18 |    | 6  | 18 | 6  | 9  | 9  | 5   | 6   | 7   |
| D5   | 14 | 3  | 6  | 6  |    | 6  | 9  | 3  | 2  | 8   | 3   | 5   |
| D6   | 14 | 18 | 16 | 18 | 6  |    | 2  | 16 | 9  | 3   | 6   | 7   |
| D7   | 9  | 6  | 0  | 6  | 9  | 2  |    | 3  | 11 | 6   | 12  | 16  |
| D8   | 7  | 17 | 8  | 9  | 3  | 16 | 3  |    | 0  | 0   | 5   | 9   |
| D9   | 0  | 1  | 3  | 9  | 2  | 6  | 11 | 0  |    | 12  | 6   | 11  |
| D10  | 4  | 4  | 5  | 5  | 8  | 3  | 6  | 0  | 12 |     | 6   | 19  |
| D11  | 2  | 1  | 2  | 6  | 3  | 6  | 12 | 5  | 5  | 6   |     | 11  |
| D12  | 7  | 1  | 1  | 7  | 5  | 7  | 16 | 9  | 11 | 19  | 11  |     |

And given the following four existing clusters the different techniques will be applied to combine the existing clusters to new clusters. Two iterations will be demonstrated:

CL1 = D1, D3, D4
CL2 = D2, D6, D8
CL3 = D5, D7, D12
CL4 = D9, D10, D11

Single Link—Join clusters with the highest similarity weights

D10 & D12 have similarity 19 thus in the first iteration join Cluster 3 and Cluster 4

CLNew1 = D5, D7, D9, D10, D11, D12
CL1 = D1, D3, D4
CL2 = D2, D6, D8

D4 & D6 have similarity 18 Join thus in the second iteration join Cluster 1 and Cluster 2 (note other 18 weights are within the same clusters (e.g., D3 and D4, D2 and D6))

**CLNew1 = D5, D7, D9, D10, D11, D12**
**CLNew2 = D1, D2, D3, D4, D6, D8**

Complete Link—Join Clusters with the Lowest Weights

D2 & D9 have similarity of 1 thus in the first iteration join Cluster 2 and Cluster 4 (Note: D2 also has similarity of 1 with D11 and D12 and D3 has similarity of 1 with D12, thus CL2 and CL3 or CL1 and CL3 could have been selected)

**CLNew1 = D2, D6, D8, D9, D10, D11**
CL1 = D1, D3, D4
CL3 = D5, D7, D12

D3 & D12 have similarity of 1 thus in second iteration join Cluster 1 and Cluster 3 (NOTE: D2 and D12 have similarity of 1 thus CLNEW1 could have been combined with CL3)

**CLNew1 = D2, D6, D8, D9, D10, D11**
**CLNew2 = D1, D3, D4, D5, D7, D12**

Average Link—Find average between Items in one cluster to items in another cluster

Average of C1 and C2 = $7+14+7+8+16+8+12+18+9 = 99/9$
Average of C1 and C3 = $14+9+7+6+0+1+6+6+7 = 56/9$
Average of C1 and C4 = $0+4+2+1+4+1+9+5+6 = 32/9$
Average of C2 and C3 = $3+6+1+6+2+7+3+3+9 = 40/9$
Average of C2 and C4 = $1+4+1+6+3+6+0+0+5 = 26/9$
Average of C3 and C4 = $2+8+3+11+6+12+11+19+11 = 83/9$
C1 and C2 have the highest average
**CLNew1 = D1, D2, D3, D4, D6, D8**
CL3 = D5, D7, D12
CL4 = D9, D10, D11
Average of ClNew1 and Cl3 = $(56+40)/18 = 5.333$
Average of ClNew1 and Cl4 = $(32+26)/18 = 3.2222$
Average of C3 and C4 = $2+8+3+11+6+12+11+19+11 = 83/9 = 9.222$
C3 and C4 have the highest average
**CLNew1 = D1, D2, D3, D4, D6, D8**
**CLNew2 = D5, D7, D9, D10, D11, D12**

Group Average Link—Find average between all items in 2 clusters

Average of C1 and C2 = $7+14+7+8+16+8+12+18+9+16+15+18+18+17+16 = 199/15$
Average of C1 and C3 = $14+9+7+6+0+1+6+6+7+9+16+15+18+9+5+16 = 144/15$
Average of C1 and C4 = $0+4+2+1+4+1+9+5+6+16+15+18+12+5+6 = 104/15$
Average of C2 and C3 = $3+6+1+6+2+7+3+3+9+18+17+16+9+5+16 = 121/15$
Average of C2 and C4 = $1+4+1+6+3+6+0+0+5+18+17+16+12+5+6 = 100/15$
Average of C3 and C4 = $2+8+3+11+6+12+11+19+11+9+5+16+12+5+6 = 136/15$

**Fig. 6.14** Clustering example

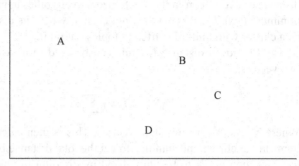

C1 and C2 have the highest average
**CLNew1 = D1, D2, D3, D4, D6, D8**
CL3 = D5, D7, D12
CL4 = D9, D10, D11

Average of ClNew1 and Cl3 = (199 + 14 + 9 + 7 + 6 + 0 + 1 + 6 + 6 + 7 + 3 + 6 + 1 + 6 + 2 + 7 + 3 + 3 + 9 + 9 + 5 + 16)/(36) = 9.0277
Average of ClNew1 and Cl4 = (199 + 0 + 4 + 2 + 1 + 4 + 1 + 9 + 5 + 6 + 1 + 4 + 1 + 6 + 3 + 6 + 0 + 0 + 5 + 12 + 5 + 6)/36 = 7.777
Average of C3 and C4 = 2 + 8 + 3 + 11 + 6 + 12 + 11 + 19 + 11 + 9 + 5 + 16 + 12 + 5 + 6/15 = 9.0666
C3 and C4 have the highest average (BARELY)
**CLNew1 = D1, D2, D3, D4, D6, D8**
**CLNew2 = D5, D7, D9, D10, D11, D12**

At any particular step in the merge process it's possible that suboptimal results could occur. Given four documents that you are starting to cluster shown in Fig. 6.14. There would be a tendency with most algorithms to combine the two closest items B and C into the next cluster created. But more optimal would be to combine D and C and A and B. Thus binary decisions at each step do not ensure an optimal final solution.

## 6.5 Measure of Tightness for Cluster

Given the different techniques to create clusters, a method is needed to determine how good the cluster is. The objective of clustering is to place similar items or words together. This allows a single representation for all the similar items reducing the complexity of representing a number of items individually. It also allows for determining new items to be retrieved when a user is looking at a particular item. Thus the goal of clustering is to get similar item together. But that is not always possible because many items discuss multiple topics and there may not be a best clustering allocation for an item. In addition the errors in the information retrieval process guarantee that there will be errors in clustering. Since the goal of a cluster is to place like items together then a measure of how good a cluster is can be based upon the distance of every item in the cluster from every other item. When that distance is a minimum then it will be a very tight cluster. When the distance is large then it will be a cluster with multiple different topics within it.

The Euclidean distance formula can be used to measure the distance between two vectors:

$$D(X_r, X_s) = \left( \sum (x_{i,r} - y_{i,s})^2 \right)^{1/2}$$

Where $X_r$ and $X_s$ are two item vectors. This is then calculated between all of the items in the cluster and summed to get the total distance between items in the cluster. This then needs to be normalized by dividing by the number of items in the cluster to get a normalized average distance value that is not dependent upon the number of items in the cluster and thus can be compared to other clusters. Thus the average distance for a cluster is:

$$\text{AVED} = \frac{1}{n} \sum_r \sum_s D(X_r, X_s)$$

The smaller the distance the more focused the items will be within the cluster on a topic.

## 6.6    Issues with Use of Hierarchical Clusters for Search

One special area of concern arises from search of clusters of terms that are stored in a hierarchical scheme. The items are stored in clusters that are represented by the centroid for each cluster. In Fig. 6.15, each letter at the leaf (bottom nodes)

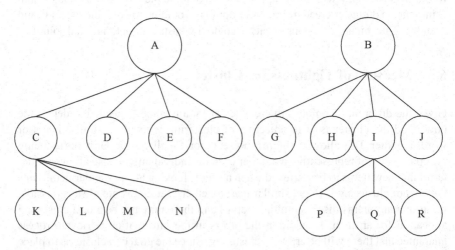

**Fig. 6.15** Item cluster hierarchy

represents an item (i.e., K, L, M, N, D, E, F, G, H, P, Q, R, J). The letters at the higher nodes (A, C, B, I) represent the centroid of their immediate children nodes. The hierarchy is used in search by performing a top-down process. The query is compared to the centroids "A" and "B." If the results of the similarity measure are above the threshold, the query is then applied to the nodes' children. If not, then that part of the tree is pruned and not searched. This continues until the actual leaf nodes that are not pruned are compared. The problem comes from the nature of a centroid which is an average of a collection of items (in Physics, the center of gravity). The risk is that the average may not be similar enough to the query for continued search, but specific items used to calculate the centroid may be close enough to satisfy the search. The risks of missing items and thus reducing recall increases as the standard deviation increases. Use of centroids reduces the similarity computations but could cause a decrease in recall. It should have no effect on precision since that is based upon the similarity calculations at the leaf (item) level.

## 6.7  Summary

With clustering there are now three different techniques that may appear to be overlapping capabilities. They are Categorization discussed in Chap. 3, Searching discussed in Chap. 5 and clustering discussed in this chapter. Clustering and categorization are very similar. The difference is that categorization is based upon training data for each category defined. Clustering is an unsupervised learning process that will logically organize a set of items into clusters based upon similarity. Some items may never be assigned to any category but typically every item will be assigned to a cluster, even if they are the only item in the cluster. Searching is like categorization in that there is a definition of the information that is being looked for. The difference is that categorization is based upon large free text examples and sometimes counter examples of what is being looked for. Queries are typically much shorter definitions and more poorly defined. In searching every item is assigned a similarity weight even if it is zero. The categorization is a classification process where a decision is made that an item is either assigned to the category or not.

Thesauri, semantic nets and item clusters are essential tools in Information Retrieval Systems, assisting the user in locating relevant items. They provide more benefit to the recall process than in improving precision. Thesauri, either humanly generated or statistical, and semantic nets are used to expand search statements, providing a mapping between the user's vocabulary and that of the authors. The number of false hits on non-relevant items retrieved is determined by how tightly coupled the terms are in the classes. When automatic techniques are used to create a statistical thesaurus, techniques such as cliques produce classes where the items are more likely to be related to the same concept than any of the other approaches. When a manually created thesaurus is used, human intervention is required to eliminate homonyms that produce false hits. A homonym is when a term has multiple, different meanings (e.g., the term field meaning an area of grass or an electromagnetic field). The longer (more terms) in the search statement, the less important the human intervention to eliminate homonyms. This is because items identified by the wrong interpretation of the homonym should have a low weight because the other search terms are not likely to be found in the item. When search statements are short, significant decreases in precision will occur if homonym pruning is not applied.

Item clustering also assists the user in identifying relevant items. It is used in two ways: to directly find additional items that may not have been found by the query and to serve as a basis for visualization of the Hit file. Each item cluster has a common semantic basis containing similar terms and thus similar concepts. To assist the user in understanding the major topics resulting from a search, the items retrieved can be clustered and used to create a visual (e.g., graphical) representation of the clusters and their topics (see Chap. 8 for examples). This allows a user to navigate between topics, potentially showing topics the user had not considered. The topics are not defined by the query but by the text of the items retrieved.

When items in the database have been clustered, it is possible to retrieve all of the items in a cluster, even if they were not identified by the search statement. When the user retrieves a strongly relevant item, the user can look at other items like it without issuing another search. When relevant items are used to create a new query, the retrieved hits are similar to what might be produced by a clustering algorithm. As with the term clustering, item clustering assists in mapping between a user's vocabulary and the vocabulary of the authors.

From another perspective term clustering and item clustering achieve the same objective even though they are the inverse of each other. The objective of both is to determine additional relevant items by a co-occurrence process. A statistical thesaurus creates a cluster of terms that co-occur in the same set of items. For all of the terms within the same cluster (assuming they are tightly coupled) there will be significant overlap of the set of items they are found in. Item clustering is based upon the same terms being found in the other items in the cluster. Thus the set of items that caused a term clustering has a strong possibility of being in the same item cluster based upon the terms. For example, if a term cluster has 10 terms in it (assuming they are tightly related), then there will be a set of items where each item contains major subsets of the terms. From the item perspective, the set of items that has the commonality of terms has a strong possibility to be placed in the same item cluster.

Hierarchical clustering of items is of theoretical interest, but has minimal practical application. The major rationale for using hierarchical clustering is to improve performance in search of clusters. The complexity of maintaining the clusters as new items are added to the system and the possibility of reduced recall are examples of why this is not used in commercial systems. Hierarchical thesauri are used in operational systems because there is additional knowledge in the human generated hierarchy. They have been historically used as a means to select index terms when indexing items. It provides a controlled vocabulary and standards between indexers.

## 6.8    Exercises

1. If clustering has been completed on two different domains. Discuss the impact of merging the domains into a single cluster for both term clustering and item clustering. What factors will affect the amount of work that will be required to merge the clusters together? (HINT: consider the steps in clustering)
2. Which of the guidelines and additional decisions can be incorporated in an automatic statistical thesaurus construction program? Describe how they would be implemented and the risks with their implementation. Describe your justification for the guidelines and exercises selected that cannot be automated.
3. Prove that a term could not be found in multiple clusters when using the single link technique.
4. Describe what effect increasing and decreasing the threshold value has on the creation of classes and under what condition you would make the change.
5. Given the following Term-Term matrix:

|     | T1 | T2 | T3 | T4 | T5 | T6 | T7 | T8 | T9 |
|-----|----|----|----|----|----|----|----|----|----|
| T1  |    | 14 | 9  | 0  | 3  | 0  | 12 | 0  | 16 |
| T2  | 14 |    | 0  | 6  | 4  | 0  | 14 | 0  | 11 |
| T3  | 9  | 0  |    | 12 | 7  | 4  | 1  | 0  | 14 |
| T4  | 0  | 6  | 12 |    | 3  | 0  | 14 | 9  | 8  |
| T5  | 3  | 4  | 7  | 3  |    | 12 | 6  | 16 | 0  |
| T6  | 0  | 0  | 4  | 0  | 12 |    | 9  | 2  | 9  |
| T7  | 12 | 14 | 1  | 14 | 6  | 9  |    | 0  | 12 |
| T8  | 0  | 0  | 0  | 9  | 16 | 2  | 0  |    | 8  |
| T9  | 16 | 11 | 14 | 8  | 0  | 9  | 12 | 8  |    |

   a. Determine the Term Relationship matrix using a threshold of 10 or higher
   b. Determine the clusters using the clique technique
   c. Determine the clusters using the single link technique
   d. Determine the clusters using the star technique where the term selected for the new seed for the next star is the smallest number term nor already part of a class.
   e. Discuss the differences between the single link, the clique and the star clusters. What are the characteristics of the items that would suggest which technique to use?

6. a. Using the document/document relationship matrix for similarity values and the starting point of the following 4 cluster, combine the clusters until you get to 2 clusters using the four HACM techniques described in the book (Single link, complete link, average link (not Wards method) and group average link)

       CL1 = D1, D3, D4
       CL2 = D2, D6, D8
       CL3 = D5, D7, D12
       CL4 = D9, D10, D11

b. Trade off the use of Single link, complete link, Wards method and group average link techniques in creating a hierarchical cluster set. Which one gives the
best and which one gives the worst clusters and why

|      | D1 | D2 | D3 | D4 | D5 | D6 | D7 | D8 | D9 |
|------|----|----|----|----|----|----|----|----|----|
| D1   |    | 7  | 16 | 15 | 14 | 14 | 9  | 7  | 0  |
| D2   | 7  |    | 8  | 12 | 3  | 18 | 6  | 17 | 1  |
| D3   | 16 | 8  |    | 18 | 6  | 16 | 0  | 8  | 3  |
| D4   | 15 | 12 | 18 |    | 6  | 18 | 6  | 9  | 9  |
| D5   | 14 | 3  | 6  | 6  |    | 6  | 9  | 3  | 2  |
| D6   | 14 | 18 | 16 | 18 | 6  |    | 2  | 16 | 9  |
| D7   | 9  | 6  | 0  | 6  | 9  | 2  |    | 3  | 11 |
| D8   | 7  | 17 | 8  | 9  | 3  | 16 | 3  |    | 0  |
| D9   | 0  | 1  | 3  | 9  | 2  | 6  | 11 | 0  |    |
| D10  | 4  | 4  | 5  | 5  | 8  | 3  | 6  | 0  | 12 |
| D11  | 2  | 1  | 2  | 6  | 3  | 6  | 12 | 5  | 5  |
| D12  | 7  | 1  | 1  | 7  | 5  | 7  | 16 | 9  | 11 |

7. Will the clustering process always come to the same final set of clusters no matter what the starting clusters? Explain your answer.
8. Can statistical thesaurus generation be used to develop a hierarchical cluster representation of a set of items? Discuss the value of creating the hierarchy and how
you would use it in a system.
9. What is the effect of clustering techniques on reducing the user overhead of finding relevant items.

# Chapter 7
# Information Presentation

## 7.1 Information Presentation Introduction

Once a search has been completed the system has identified a "hit list" of items in ranked order based upon the most likely to be relevant. The next step is to present the information to the user. The presentation has a significant impact on the user's ability to find the information they are looking for. There are two stages for information presentation. The first is how the hit list is presented so the user can determine if it may contain potential information to answer their information need. The second is how individual items are presented to the user from which they will look for specific information. There are a few scenarios where the hit list presentation could answer the user's question without the need to look at the individual items—but this is the exception case.

There are multiple techniques applicable to each of the stages based upon what information a user is looking for. But in all cases the goal is to leverage off the humans ability to visually process information to optimize the presentation to assist in identifying the needed information. Historically the primary presentation has been a linear list of potential information. For users in the 1980s and 1990s that was adequate because their experience followed that paradigm. But in the 2000s with the availability of sophisticated virtual games, the Internet and communications devices the users are expecting more sophisticated presentation methods. In all cases the goal is to organize the information's presentation to allow the user to detect patterns that help focus on the most likely location for the information of potential interest.

## 7.2 Presentation of the Hits

The hit list contains the items of potential interest. What is less obvious is how long the hit list is. Most systems display the hit list as a sequential list of hits and the user at most reviews the first two pages of hits (20–30 hits). The system will display a count of the total number of hits. In most systems they have not been uniquely iden-

G. Kowalski, *Information Retrieval Architecture and Algorithms,*
DOI 10.1007/978-1-4419-7716-8_7, © Springer Science+Business Media, LLC 2011

tified but instead the total hit count is an estimate is created based upon the subset of hits identified for actual display.

Looking at textual items there are four major organizations that can be used to display the hit list, each satisfying a different information need. The first is the sequential list that is in ranked order based upon the users query and a confidence level (weight). It is the most common hit display. The next is a cluster visualization that quite often is hierarchical in nature (see HACM from Chap. 6). A network display is used when entities are identifiable and the relationships are the goal. Less often used is a time line display.

## 7.2.1  Sequential Listing of Hits

The details on how the weights are calculated are discussed in Chap. 5. This display is the most common display because it is the easiest to present. The display of each hit can be broken down into three major subcomponents, each of which is designed to help the user decide if they want to select and display that hit. The first line of the hit is the "title". This is usually extracted from the Title of the page that is being referenced or the title of the item. The next part is the "snippet" that is text that comes from that hit item (e.g., web page) that is designed to provide the semantic information to help the user understand what the item is about. The simplest snippet is text taken the first few sentences of the item or if there is a metadata Description tag to use that information. If there specific zones such as an "Abstract" zone that also could be used. The advantage to this definition of a snippet is that it is static and thus can be predefined allowing for faster display of the Hit list. The snippet can come from anywhere in the document. A more focused solution will have the snippet come from specific sentence fragments that the search term(s) was found. This could lead to many different possible snippets that could be extracted. Using the weights of the hit terms and proximity of the hit terms within text segments (possible snippets) can help in determining which snippets to display. The length of the snippet needs to be limited because the longer the snippet the fewer hits can be displayed on a display screen. Ideally the snippet would include a summarization focusing on the information need (query) of the item but that is unrealistic. Text summarization is discussed in Sect. 7.3.2 where the difficulties are described. In all cases if any of the user's search terms are in the displayed text they are usually highlighted to draw attention to them. The final most critical part of the hit listing is a link to the item.

Once past the basic hit list display data there is optional data that may be displayed based upon how complex the search engine and system is? In general, it's specific data that is related to the nature of the particular item being displayed. For example if the item being displayed is recognized with an entity type (one of the advantages of doing entity identification) that suggests it has a physical location and if the address is available—links are provided to a map showing where it is located. If the item is a company links could be provided to show the stock value of the company. The goal of this process is to not only present the user with adequate information to understand what the link to the item will likely return but also provide links to other information that frequently is of interest when looking for an item. Thus, the rationale behind showing a link to the map for an address of a business is that quite often the users real information need is for where a company is located but their search query may only have the company name in it.

A sequential listing of hits is most useful when a user is looking for a specific fact or gathering background on a very focused topic. Given the specificity of the topic and that the user wants some very focused data, the sequential ranked presentation presents the information in an optimum organized format. The user will either find the one or two items it will take to answer their question in the first few pages or find additional terms to try a new query and find the information. The nature of this search is that the user does not need to have an overview of many items to help in locating the information needed.

## 7.2.2   Cluster View

In some cases the user is looking to understand a more broad topical area. It could be an area that is new to the user or it could by its nature be a more general focus. In this case a sequential list of items will never satisfy the real information need. It is too focused on individual items when the user needs to understand a more general view of the information to help in focusing on the specific information they need. For example if the user wants to understand how to invest money, a query on money investment brings up 27,000,000 hits and a number of articles on "investing money". The individual items may be useful in starting to get a background but they may never present the scope of the information available in the system on this topic.

An alternative approach is to present a visualization of all of the hits or large representative sample. To do this a clustering algorithm would be applied to the hits (possibly a hierarchical clustering approach) and then the clusters would be presented in a graphical interface to the user. The clusters would have labels that would in effect be categorizing the different topics that are part of the more general search. The key to this interface is the ability to provide a meaningful name to the clusters. The user would then be able to focus on the individual clusters looking in more depth on the clusters within the first set of clusters (if hierarchical clustering is used) and eventually look at specific items of interest.

This type of an interface is typically not provided because of the significant overhead in dynamically clustering the hits from a search. In many cases the cluster software will be an additional application and the user can request that the hits be exported to that package where the clustering takes place. This is quite often limited to hundreds of thousand hits (e.g., In-Spire from PNNL see its Theme View). A two or three dimensional display is quite often used with the heights or densities of the display indicating topical areas. In a 2-dimension display (e.g., scattergram) the density of points indicate topical areas where each point represents another item.

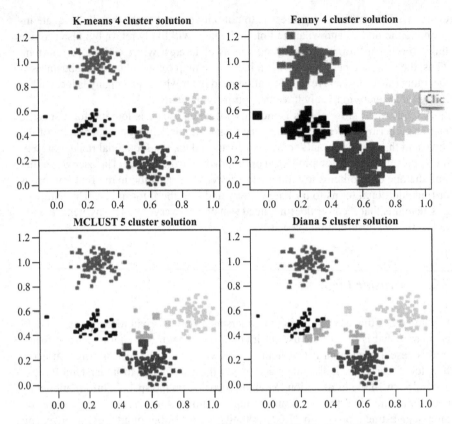

**Fig. 7.1** Example of clustering scattergram. (Courtesy of Pacific Northwest National Laboratory from their web site)

For example in Fig. 7.1 there are some examples of a scatter gram where you can see by the densities the number of items that are discussing the different topics. In addition for this example the size of the point for each item indicates the confidence level that it is associated with cluster. The user can then focus on the overall set of topical areas and then investigate which ones most closely map to the users information need. The second example in Fig. 7.2 shows a 3-dimensional visualization. In this case each topic is associated with each of the three dimensional "hills" in the picture. In addition the height and size of each hill indicates how many items are associated with that area.

Filtering and zooming are the most important parts for an interface such as this. Zooming follows the general rule of visualization design where the more general higher level information visualization is presented first and then the user can "zoom in" or focus on particular parts of the display to expand the details for that segment. The other important capability is filtering. This allows a user to specify some criteria that they want to be removed from the current display. This allows filtering out

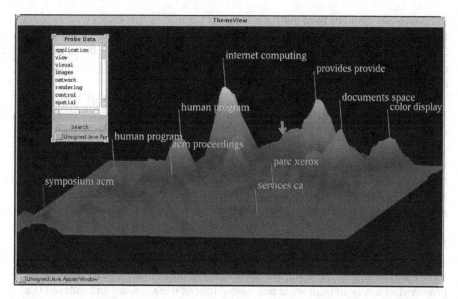

**Fig. 7.2** Example of theme view 3-dimensional display. (Courtesy of Pacific Northwest National Laboratory from their web site)

items that may be confusing the display and not helping the user to find the desired information. For example filtering out information of foreign currency exchange could reduce the complexity of a scattergram on investments. Quite often a time filter is also very useful where items older than a certain date can be filtered out. This can change the display from an overall graphical view of a topical area to just the most recent information on a topical area.

One of the challenges in creating a cluster view is how to name the clusters. The simplest technique is to find the highest weighted terms that are found across the cluster and then use the top few words as a label for the cluster. This can lead to errors when the cluster is representing a large concept whose label is not frequently found in the specific processing tokens of the items in the cluster. Another approach is to try and abstract out the cluster name. For example one approach could take clusters as the input and generates appropriate labels for the clusters using a reference database. The objective is to take the highest weighted terms and then look up the different word senses for those words and also look for more abstract concepts that the words are part of. Then based upon the set of words that come from the look-up a weighting algorithm can be used to select the most important labels to be associated with the clusters. This helps in consolidating synonyms or near synonym words into a single word representation and allows the cluster names to come from words that are not in the cluster. If the cluster is a hierarchical cluster structure then the process works the same except the children labels can be inherited to the parent clusters and merged into a higher cluster label. The advantage of working with a Natural Language Processing indexing scheme is that it will provide additional information that could be used in determining the name to be associated with a cluster. In this case the part of speech and usage of the words could be an additional weighting factor in determining the weight of individual words in labeling the cluster. For example a Subject would have a lot more weight that a word that is an adjective or direct object in use.

In many cases clustering software starts with a reprocessing of the original items to create an index more optimized for the performing the clustering and manipulating the display of the cluster. That is why there are limits placed on the number of items clustered (i.e., in the tens to hundreds of thousands). Clustering is very different than indexing data for a query in that the final goal is a visual presentation of all of the data to assist the user in better understanding the overall information content of all of the data. In clustering the original concepts of applying Ziph's Law to reduce the complexity of the index re-emerges as a viable constraint. Ziph's Law says the frequency of occurrence of words in a set of text follows and exponential rule where a small percentage of terms are found very frequently and a very large number of terms are only found a few times in the text. When computer computation resources was limited many years ago that was proposed as a way to limit what processing tokens were created and indexed (i.e., eliminating the high frequency and low frequency words). When the goal is to create a visualization of a large number of items that rule currently applies. High frequency words that are found in most of the items blur the differences between items and do not help in clustering where the objective is to show the unique general topics of the items. The low frequency words that are only found in a few items does not help in clustering in that they only help define single items that will be at the edges or standing alone in a cluster space. When indexing for clustering it's possible to reduce the dimensionality (i.e., number of processing tokens) that are kept and used in the clustering from millions down to hundreds to a few thousands without seriously degrading the information value of the cluster display. The goal is to select those words that provide the best discrimination value to help in defining the clusters. This is usually a few thousands terms that are primary needed to represent the major concepts across a corpora. That does not mean that all terms are not kept for "filtering" the current or new set of items that are used in creating the cluster display. But when that subset of items is selected the reduced index can then be used to create the new clusters. In creating the processing tokens for the clustering quite often units other than individual words are used. Thus the system may also treat multiple words or even sentences as a unit to index to help in the clustering. In a sense this approach is driving more towards the idea of "concept indexing" such as use of Latent Semantic Indexing as a way to reduce the dimensionality of the original set of items to hundreds of processing tokens that represent the concepts in the items.

Once the reduced set of processing tokens is defined then Luhn's concept of co-occurrence of processing tokens with the same items suggesting those items are talking about the same concept applies. As discussed in Chap. 6 there are significant performance issues when trying to do the clustering using the full set of $term_i$ and $term_j$ co-occurrence. That is why the K-means algorithm (i.e., starting with an initial set of clusters and then reassigning items to that set in an iterative process) is often applied to define the clusters.

Once the clusters have been determined then there is the issue of mapping the clusters to a 2-dimensional or 3-dimensional representation that can be shown on visualization. One of the common ways of doing that is using Principal Component Analysis (PCA). It can reduce the n-dimensional processing token space into a few dimensions for display. It dates back to 1901 when it was first introduced by Karl Pearson. It uses orthogonal vector decomposition of the multivariate data. These are called "principal components" and is accomplished by applying single value decomposition of the data matrix (see Latent Semantic Indexing in Chap. 4). By choosing the top 2 or 3 variables it provides a "shadow" of the higher n-dimension space into a 2 or 3-dimension space which can then be used to create the display. PCA is mathematically defined as an orthogonal linear transformation that transforms the data to a new coordinate system such that the greatest variance by any projection of the data comes to lie on the first coordinate (called the first principal component), the second greatest variance on the second coordinate, and so on. PCA is theoretically the optimum transform for given data in least squares terms (Jolliffe-2002). In PCA you are applying Singular Value Decomposition (SVD) on the covariance matrix. The original matrix is changed into a new matrix by subtracting the mean from the elements (new matrix has zero mean). Next the covariance matrix is found by multiplying $1/(n-1)$ times the original matrix and its transpose. SVD is then applied to the new matrix. Then as described in Chap. 4 just the top "k" rows are kept which then define the dimensions that are displayed.

## 7.2.3 Network View

The network view of a hit list is the best display of search results where the user is looking for relationships between entities. Notice in this case individual hits are not the basic unit of representation but typically entities that are found in the hit items. The number and specific hit items are just evidence to support the links (relationships) between the entities. The existence of a relationship is identified within an item. An example would be if a user wants to see what companies would be effected if the General Motors Corporation (GMC) car company goes bankrupt. The system is trying to determine relationships between GMC and other companies. The result would be a multinode network where each node represents a company or subnetwork of companies and the links indicate a relationship between the companies. There could be associative relationships where one company is dependent upon GMC and another company is dependent upon that company. This is one of the examples where part of the user's information need could be answered by the display which should be displayed in a network graph form. Figure 7.3 shows what a network graph might look like for this information need. The network graph representation summarizes the specific examples the system has determined to suggest relationships. The width of the connecting lines indicates the confidence level of

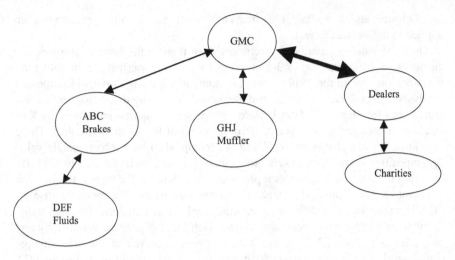

**Fig. 7.3** Network diagram example

that connection. By clicking on any of the lines the system would display all of the specific items that went into defining that line. In this example there are two nodes that really represent additional lower level networks (e.g., dealers and Charities). Clicking on either of those nodes would expand out the all of the sub-nodes in that node (e.g., list of all dealers and their links to each other and GMC). The algorithms to determine the relationships will likely contain errors in accuracy due to the challenges in Information retrieval that have been discussed throughout this book. The network graph should be looked at another way of organizing the hits, but for the user to make an accurate decision the user needs to review the items that led to the parts of the graph the user feels is important. In this case the hit items are associated with the lines between the nodes where a relationship was determined from the text of the item. But the real information is between the entities and the network graph that shows the relationships.

There are many different algorithms that can be used in determining that two entities are related by an item. The simplest technique is to use the concept of co-occurrence that has been used in many previous algorithms. The idea is that if two entities co-occur in many items then those two entities may be related. A weighting algorithm is:

$$\text{Link Weight}\left(\text{Entity}_i, \text{Entity}_j\right) = N * \sum \left(WT_{Ei} * WT_{Ej}\right)$$

where N is a normalization constant and $WT_{Ei}$ is the term frequency weight of the entity within the item. The term frequency is based upon the fully normalized occurrence count of the entity within the item versus just the specific name variation of the entity as entered by the user. If entity normalization (see Chap. 3) is not available for that specific entity then just the entered term would be counted.

The formula above can be adjusted to have more semantic strength in the possibility of the two entities being related by adding a proximity constraint to when the system counts an occurrence of the two entities being in the item that leads to the $WT_{Ei}$ value. Thus a proximity constraint that Term for Entity$_i$ and the term representing Entity$_j$ must be within "m" units of each other before it will count towards a linkage can be applied. In this case "units" could be words, sentences, paragraphs or any other meaningful measure.

The statistical approach introduces errors in that the co-occurrence does not guarantee the semantic relationship between the entities just their existence. A more sophisticated approach would use either the existence of "cue words" or natural language processing to increase the recognition of the strength between the entities when found in an item. "Cue words" are words that are chosen because they indicate the likelihood of what something is about. One of the first uses for "cue words" was in detecting sentiment analysis about products on the Internet. Sentiment analysis is the ability for web crawlers to understand the tone, be it positive or negative, of conversations on the Internet For example Coca Cola might want to see what the "Buzz" is about their latest flavor. Rather than doing a telephone survey they hire a company to crawl and detect when that product is being discussed in a chat room or blogs and what is being said about it. To detect the sentiment a set of "cue" words are used to determine if the discussion is positive or negative. This is easier than trying to do full linguistic analysis. Selection of cue words can be tricky. For example the word "worse" would usually imply a negative. Thus someone might have written "New Coke is the worse drink I have had". But in the sentence is "I want New Coke in the worse way" it is indicating a positive. The selection of the right list of "cue words" for a particular relationship and then looking for their presence can help identify better linkages.

The best solution, but most complex, is to do full linguistic analysis on the sentences where the entity words occur to be sure that the linkage is warranted and the strength of it. This is the least likely to have errors but is most complex and difficult to provide unless the system is already a natural language index system.

The final product once the link analysis has been performed is a network diagram that has the entities of interest as the nodes and the links as lines between the nodes. Ideally the strength of the link should be indicated in some way by different representations of the line (e.g., width of the line). The user may have their information need filled by just seeing the network graph. But the network graph is another way of showing a hit list. The hits are the items that contributed to the creation of the connecting lines. The user should have the capability to click on a line and see the items that contributed towards creation of that link. The user can then display the individual items to see exactly what information was in the item that suggested the relationship. As with clusters a network graph can be very dense and difficult to understand. Thus as with clusters the users need the capability to filter some of the nodes out of the display and to zoom in and navigate around the network. Zooming in will allow expansion of parts of the network that may be hidden when shown in the context of the complete network.

## 7.2.4   *Timeline Presentation*

Although not as common as the above three presentations, an additional way of showing the hits from a search in some instances can be a time line (actually date/ time but it is generalized to just "timeline" even though most presentations are date oriented rather than time within date). In the right circumstances this can significantly reduce the users time in finding the information needed. The trouble with ranked hit lists is that the hits are weighted by similarity to the search in ranked order, but time is not typically a factor in that display. Thus if the highest weighted information is years old it will be presented first. The most recent information may be presented way down the list. GOOGLE accounts for this in their advanced search where the user can constrain the results list to a date range and then the ranking occurs for the hits within that range. That is equivalent to searching the "citation metadata" of an item (e.g., publish date) along with the normal text relevance weighted search. When the user is looking for a specific question then time may not be as important as similarity to the search. But in some cases the user is interested in more recent information or how a topical area grew over time. There are two possible date/times of interest. The first is when a particular item was published. The second is when information the item discusses (semantics of the item). Originally when GOOGLE first experimented with this concept on their experimental web site they had a more generalized view of the data. For example if you searched on Automobile view: timeline example you will see a time line with the hits on the time line (see Fig. 7.4). As with any visualization you can zoom in on a part of the time line and have it expanded out in greater detail.

Eventually the business decision of what timeline aspect is most interesting by GOOGLE led them to focus the time line on news rather than letting it be too generic. This then lead to GOOGLE News Timeline option made available on April 20, 2009 (http://newstimeline.googlelabs.com/) and search on a news story (example is crash of Air France Plane). It presents news stories based upon that as a search. You will notice there are false hits on other airline crashes since this is a ranked retrieval system (see Fig. 7.5).

Central to display of a timeline presentation is the extraction of date and time information in an item as additional metadata to be used in creating the display. This may sound simple but the goal is to extract the date/time that is relevant to the semantics of the item and not date/time relative to its publication (or at least keep that as a different time data set). There are many different formats for date and time along with textual definitions (e.g., last week, last month, a year ago) all of which need during ingest to be mapped to a single entity class and process able format. As with all of the other displays this is just a different way of organizing the hits to help the user find the information they are interested in. The "drilling" down on the time line will eventually lead to the links to specific items for the user to view. Some of the aspects of the design of a timeline view to help the user are:

- Time (i.e., date/time) spans should be hierarchical in display in that larger time windows are first displayed and then the user can "drill down" to more detailed time periods

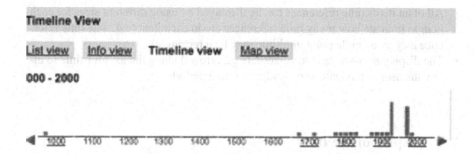

**Fig. 7.4** Original GOOGLE time line capability

**Fig. 7.5** GOOGLE news timeline

- All of an items time references can be displayed by using different sizes for each item to indicate how many time references are in each item (e.g., one time reference may be a single point, multiple may be a rectangle)
- The display needs simple navigation (e.g., arrows) along the axis for time to allow the user to navigate to new adjacent time periods.

## 7.3    Display of the Item

Eventually the user has to look at the original item to find the specific information they need along with the context around it. This requires the user to look at each item. Techniques that help the user in finding the information they are potentially interested in the item can also save the total time to find the information needed.

### 7.3.1    Indicating Search Terms in Display

Display of the item can also influence how much time it takes a user to locate the information he is interested in. In particular the user wants to be able to quickly locate the text(s) in the item that was the basis behind its retrieval. This has historically been accomplished via highlighting the search terms within the text of the item. Highlighting has been experimented with using colors for the different search terms but that can cause difficulties with users that have color recognition problems and are thus not generally usable by all. The most common technique is to highlight/bold the search terms in the text.

For short items that are only a couple of paragraphs long, highlighting is sufficient and lets the user to quickly focus on the areas of potential interest. But when an item is many pages long then other techniques can add significantly more insight to the user than just highlighting. One technique that helps the user in quickly orienting his focus is to display in a vertical display along either edge of the item what search terms are found in which lines of text. Thus the user can quickly scroll down through the item seeing which search term(s) are found together and helping in doing a first level scan to decide where to read in more detail. This technique shows how the information presentation can leverage off of the users visual ability to scan to reduce the time it takes to locate potential information of value.

Also with long items where not all of the search terms are on the viewable screen, the ability to jump from the current position to the next occurrence of a specific search term or any of the search terms also is very beneficial to the user. This is made more powerful if the user can select (filter) in deciding which search terms will be highlighted/jumped between.

But the real challenge is in knowing which search terms contributed most to the retrieval of that item and being able to indicate that information to the user. Quite often a user wants to refine their search to get better results. Knowing which search terms have been causing the current retrieval set lets them how best to modify their search. This becomes very difficult because the ranking algorithms do not lend themselves to understanding the contribution of individual terms to an items retrieval. Even given that information there is a complex human factors question on how to display that information to the user so they can take an action to improve their search based upon the presentation.

## 7.3.2   Text Summarization

Indicating important terms in items help the user focus on the parts of the item that are most likely to be of value to the users information need. The nature of most items on a particular topic is that there will be significant redundancy in each item describing the same basic facts before it expands upon those facts. A user in trying to answer their information need spends a lot of time redundantly reading information they are already aware of. In many cases they will not find any new information in the items they review.

The solution to this problem is text summarization. Examples of summaries that are often part of any item are titles, table of contents, and abstracts with the abstract being the closest to a summarization of the important ideas in an item. The abstract can be used to represent the item for search purposes or as a way for a user to determine the utility of an item without having to read the complete item. There are two classes of text summarization with the first being to summarize the text within an item eliminating redundancy and focusing on the most important information. The second level is to summarize text between multiple items. Summarization of the item could significantly save the user time in understanding the information in the item. If the summaries were made short enough they could be used as the snippet in the hit list, reducing further the need for a user to open a complete item to see if it has information of value. Another factor that can be used in summarization is if the goal is to summarize the complete item or if the summarization should be focused around the topics indicated by the terms in the users query.

The summarization process is typically done in three steps. First potential material within the item is identified that is important. Next the material is compressed to eliminate redundancy. Finally it is paraphrased to make it continuous and readable. The simplest summarization can be extracts of phrases, sentences or even paragraphs of an item. The more complex summarizations are a compiled abstract that eliminates redundancy and summarizes the item. There are two ways of approaching the summarization process. The first is to create a summarization of the item (or items) based upon the content in the item. An alternative is to focus the summarization on the parts of the item that are related to the query. Summarizations can be either "extract" based or "abstract" based. Extracts are identifying textual units within an item (e.g., sentences) that have high information value and extracting and concatenating them Abstract based requires text understanding because it merges ideas into a new textual descriptor. Endres-Niggenger in their analysis discovered that users sometimes prefer extract based summaries which allow the user to merge the specifics into an abstract over system generated abstracts that may tend to diffuse the information in the summary.

Luhn was one of the first to propose automated methods for summarization. He proposed that the frequency of a word in an item indicates the word may be about a topic within an item. Clusters of frequent words within a sentence would indicate that sentence would be a good summarizing sentence for the item. He also felt this should be adjusted by the frequency of the word in the database (e.g., similar to the concept of inverse document frequency but based upon term frequency in database not document frequency). It is not feasible to automatically generate a coherent narrative summary of an item with proper discourse, abstraction and language usage (Sparck Jones-93). Restricting the domain of the item can significantly improve the quality of the output (Paice-93, Reimer-88). The more restricted goals for much of the research is in finding subsets of the item that can be extracted and concatenated (usually extracting at the sentence level) and represents the most important concepts in the item. There is no guarantee of readability as a narrative abstract and it is seldom achieved. It has been shown that extracts of approximately 20% of the complete item can represent the majority of significant concepts (Morris-92). Different algorithms produce different summaries. Just as different humans create different abstracts for the same item, automated techniques that generate different summaries does not intrinsically imply major deficiencies between the summaries.

Another historical method for extraction is based upon the work of Edmundson which uses position in the text. The idea is that important sentences occur in specific locations. Thus the position of the sentence in a paragraph and the position of the paragraph in the overall text can be used to determine what sentences to extract as summary sentences. The position is not universal but is dependent upon the type of an item it is. For example news items have the important sentences in the beginning. Scientific items tend to have them at the end. In addition to using the position, the Title of an item attempts to describe what the item's core idea is. Thus any sentences where major words from the title are found should be weighted heavier. Finally there are "cue" words/phrases as discussed earlier that are indicative of a good summary sentence. Some examples of them are: "In summary", "we have shown that" and "the goal of this". Using the above factors and assigning weights to them it's possible to assign weights to sentences to determine which sentences to extract.

There is no overall theoretic basis for the approaches, leading to many heuristic algorithms. Kupiec et al. are pursuing statistical classification approach based upon a training set reducing the heuristics by focusing on a weighted combination of criteria to produce "optimal" scoring scheme (Kupiec-95). They selected the following five feature sets as a basis for their algorithm:

- Sentence Length Feature that requires sentence to be over five words in length
- Fixed Phrase Feature that looks for the existence of phrase "cues" (e.g., "in conclusion")
- Paragraph Feature that places emphasis on the first ten and last five paragraphs in an item and also the location of the sentences within the paragraph
- Thematic Word Feature that uses word frequency
- Uppercase Word Feature that places emphasis on proper names and acronyms.

As with previous experiments by Edmundson, Kupiec et al. discovered that location based heuristics gives better results than the frequency based features (Edmundson-69).

Extraction is simple, but the problem is how to link extracted sentences and make them one single and meaningful summary. Abstraction is another main method used for summarization, and it is the main method human using. The special characteristic is of the abstraction method is that it will include the sentences the original text does not have. In order to build abstraction, people or machines need to understand the original text. Abstraction method has higher intelligence than extraction method, and it is also more difficult and complicated. Several commonly used abstraction methods are: the model method, the term rewrite method, the event relation method, and the concept stage method.

Text summarization is the process of condensing a source text while preserving its information content and maintaining readability. The main difference between automatic and human-based text summarization is that humans can capture and convey subtle themes that permeate documents, whereas automatic approaches have a large difficulty to do the same. Nonetheless, as the amount of information available in electronic format continues to grow, research into automatic text summarization has taken on renewed interest.

One of the major new forums for presenting the latest techniques and comparing how well a text summarization approach works is in the Text Summarization Track of the Text Analysis Conference sponsored yearly by the National Institute of Standards and Technology (NIST) which provides problem definitions and a ground truth test data set to apply techniques to and compare results (http://www.nist.gov/tac).

In most cases, passage and sentence similarity analysis is performed along with computing a significance value for each. Similar passages can be condensed to one extract. In particular a sentence or passage that is closest to the centroid of a cluster of similar sentences/passages is a candidate to be selected for the summary. When going across multiple documents and additional rule such as sentences that are most similar to the item and most dissimilar to sentences already selected for the summary also help in selecting the correct sentence (Goldstein et al.-2000). The more complex approaches will attempt to understand the text to a deeper level than statistical. They will use syntactic parsers and semantic analysis. There are many dictionaries/thesaurus that can help support this process by looking up words of interest. Some examples are WordNet (started in 1985), which has parts of speech and limited semantic network relationships. ConceptNet from MIT Media Labs tries to merge more of a common sense understanding of ideas with a natural language processing approach. FrameNet from Berkley contains more in depth linguistic knowledge that can be used in understanding text.

## 7.4   Collaborative Filtering

Collaborative filtering is another mechanism to help users in determining how to find information. The technique is based upon other users who have similar needs and what information path they followed to answer their question. It also includes feedback from other users as well as what actions they took. This is sometimes referred to as collective intelligence where enough samples can be used in determining a consensus decision.

In collaborative filtering the system predicts what a user is interested in based upon historical data it has collected on other users. When enough different previous user reactions are used the prediction accuracy improves. Thus a comparison is made of the current state and attributes of the current user with a similar state and attributes of previous users to predict the most likely next information item will be of interest. This often referred to as passive filtering.

An alternative approach looks at specific entities and looks for users interested in those entities and other entities. In this case users share their evaluation on specific entities that can be used in the estimation process. It then predicts if a user is interested in specific entities—what other entities they are likely also to be interested in. For example if a user indicates a wine they are interested in, the system can predict other wines they may be interested in based upon previous users interested in that wine. This is referred to as active filtering. The active filtering can be on specific web pages (e.g., user ranking of them) or of a specific item—such as the wine example.

One approach is memory based reasoning where the system tries to recognize examples from the past that equate to the current information need. The technical approach is divided into two major steps. The first is a prediction of what might be of value to the user who has the information need. The second is generation of a recommendation list for the user. In the memory based approach the system looks at all of the other previous users of the system to determine users similar to the current user. Then based upon that set of users and the current state and attributes the system predicts the top n likely items of interest. This is also called nearest neighbor or user based collaborative filtering. User based correlation uses Pearson correlation while item based collaborative filtering uses adjusted cosine similarity (http://delab. csd.auth.gr/~apostol/pubs/webmine2006.pdf.).

This is not related to search but more an augmentation to search or just browsing. A user once they start looking at an item could either go back to hit list to see next item or the system could recommend where to go to next (navigation aide).

The concept is collecting usage patterns by users of the system can recommend for new users what information is of value. An earlier example already discussed was the page rank formula that suggested that the importance of a web page is based upon how much other pages (i.e., other users) link to that page.

There are two approaches to collecting collaborative filtering data: user centric and data centric. User centric asks users to tell the system what they like. The system then looks across large number of users for data they entered and when new user is interested in one thing the system can suggest additional answers based upon the model it has built for similar users. Data centric takes each entity as a point and then sees what else users are interested in that are at that entity or page. Thus the system can keep track of where users go next given a page. Or the system can track what else a user buys when they buy one item. Based upon another user reaching that page/item the system can recommend where to go next. It is based upon either users wanting to share information or passive filtering where the users allow the system to keep track of their clicks.

## 7.4.1 Page Ranking as Collaborative Filtering

A special case of collaborative filtering that is the Page ranking algorithm this was the original basis of the GOOGLE search system. The algorithm is named after Larry Page who developed it as part of his doctorial program at Stanford University. The concept was that any web page has an information value based upon how many other pages reference it. This is a passive form of collaborative filtering in that aggregate actions of other users accumulate to determine the value of a particular item. Thus a page gets a value based upon its popularity or how much it's an authority based upon how many other pages reference it.

A simple view of the approach is to just count the number of "in-links" from other pages to a page to determine its value. The next level of complexity is saying that not only the in-links but the page rank value of the pages that link to it should also be a factor. Thus if a page is pointed to by a number of other pages of high value it should get a higher page rank than a page with the same number of in-links from pages with lower weights. An additional refinement in determining the value of the "out-links" from a page is the number of out-links from a page. Some pages are just references to lots of other pages and thus they do not have substantive information. Those links will be of less value than links from textual pages that are talking about particular topics. This leads to the following formula for Page Rank (A):

$$PR(A) = \sum_{D_i} \frac{PR(D_i)}{C(D_i)}$$

where $PR(D_i)$ is the page rank for page $D_i$ and $C(D_i)$ is the number of outlinks for page $D_i$. Since each pages rank value can effect the rank values of other pages, the analysis process is an iterative process until the values stabilize. The trouble with this process is that pages that have no inlinks would have a page rank of zero. To account for this and have some flexibility in weighting the page ranks, another factor called a dampening factor is added. The dampening factor is "d" and the formula for page rank now becomes:

$$PR(A) = (1 - d) + d \sum_{D_i} \frac{PR(D_i)}{C(D_i)}$$

A typical value for d is 0.85.

Another similar approach is called HITS. HITS is a little more dynamic in that it is used to rank a hit list. It divides pages into pages that are pointed to by a number of pages—called authorities—and pages that have a number of out-links called "hubs" This leads to algorithms defining "strong authorities" that is pointed to by a number of "hubs" and a hub that points to many "strong authorities" is a "popular hub". This more a social networking approach to a number of items.

## 7.5 Multimedia Presentation

One of the challenges in working with multimedia is how to create an interface to enter searches and how to display the results. The methodologies vary based upon the modality of the multimedia as discussed in Chap. 1. The user expects to have a combination of structured search and multimedia search in the basic search capability. The structured search is against the citation metadata that describes the multimedia item. For example, the user expects to be able to include in his searches constraints on the hit list by date ranges, file names and source information when its available (e.g., what TV source that video indexing is from). Given the complexity of multimedia search earlier search systems did not provide direct search of the multimedia. Instead they indexed the text around the link to the multimedia, the file names associated with multimedia objects and when the user entered a textual query that was the index that was searched. This section focuses on when the actual multimedia is searched.

Following the format of Chap. 4 on indexing multimedia by addressing each modality separately, the presentations will be addressed in a similar order.

### 7.5.1  Audio Presentation

Chapter 4 discussed the indexing techniques applied against audio sources. In most cases what is of interest is what is being spoken in audio sources (i.e., transcribing the spoken words into text). But in addition there is other metadata that can be found such as speaker identification and other special identified sounds can be recognized (e.g., music, explosions). But typically the special identified sounds need to be strained before the audio is indexed to be included in the index of the audio sources.

When the speech in the audio is being searched (the most common case) the speech is being transcribed into text typically in Unicode. The text is then indexed using the text indexing algorithms discussed for normal textual items. Since the index is a textual index the user interface can also be textual. That is, the user enters a textual search and it is run against the index. The interface for search creation is a standard textual user interface. For the other identified sounds or for locating a specific person leveraging off speaker identification, the interface is mainly textual. The one exception is when a user is searching for music. In that case the interface can allow the user to play some music and the system will take that audio input and search on it. The user will inform the system they are ready to search for music and then immediately play the music to be searched. The interactive interface is more typical than the user pointing to previously stored audio file to use as the query. Although that approach would also be technically feasible if desired. One of the first major uses for this type searches was to validate that commercials were played the number of times their contract required on radio and television by monitoring a broadcast source.

The place where the interfaces begin to take on special characteristics is on display of the search results. Since there is a direct correlation between the transcribed text and the original audio, both are used in the results GUI. The results can be ordered by ranking and could even be displayed using clustering techniques because the index is textual for the case of transcribed text from Automatic Speech Recognition (ASR) indexing. If phonetic indexing is used then only ranking is available because there are no semantic units (words) that could be clustered. The ranking is modified to be based upon the phonetic search. In the case of ASR, when a linear hit list is displayed, the system can create "snippets" of the transcribed text to be included in the hit list. When phonetic search (or special sound search) is used, the system can only provide the file name of the original source and an offset into it. Thus the latter ASR approach allows contextual information of the transcribed words around the hit term to be used by the user to understand the context of the search hits especially useful when homonyms are the search term (e.g., blew versus blue).

A major new capability in the GUI is when a user selects a specific item to be opened for detailed review. In the case of phonetic search when a specific item is opened the system knows the locations of all the found search terms. Thus the system can allow a user to jump from one term to another and play the audio at that point. Actually systems start playing the audio slightly before the hit point to let the user get orientated on the audio. When the audio has been transcribed then there is a complete textual item that can be displayed. But the textual item is mapped to the original audio source (i.e., each word in the transcription has the offset of where it occurred in the audio). In this case when the textual item is displayed there is also an associated multimedia audio player that is synchronized with the textual item. All of the search terms in the textual item can be highlighted to allow the user to quickly focus on where in the transcription the hit words were found. The user then has the option of looking at the context of each hit location and validating if that might be the information they are looking for. For example the words "plane" and "plain" are phonetically identical but the other words in the context will disambiguate if an aeroplane, a woodworking tool or descriptive adjective is being spoken. Since the speech to text process is errorful (at best in the 90% accuracy but often more in the 75–80% accuracy) the user will in many cases need to play the original source to be sure they are getting the correct information. This is accomplished by using the offset of every transcribed word to the location in the audio for that word. When the user clicks on the highlighted search term in the transcribed text (or any word in the transcribed text) the system can start to play the audio just before when that word was spoken. At that point the user can use the playback controls of the multimedia audio player to control the playback (e.g., pause, restart, speed up playback, slow down playback, etc). Since there is a direct linkage between the transcribed text and the audio, as the user is playing the audio the system can highlight each transcribed word as it's being played (highlighting the text is synchronized with the audio playback). For places where the textual word was not recognized or there is no text in the audio, the highlighting freezes in the transcribed text until the next transcribed word is played.

When speaker identification is also available the textual interface will partition the words spoken into which speaker (or indicating an unknown speaker) is saying the words. When you are processing an original textual item (not multimedia) there are many syntactical and formatting cues in the textual item on what is being described and they are used by the user to find information of value. In audio transcription those cues are not in the audio but have to be, where possible, extrapolated from the audio—which means there will be errors in those cues. The most significant ones are sentence boundaries and capitalization. Capitalization is useful to help the user identify if a person is being discussed or just a noun or other descriptive word (e.g., "Bush" versus "bush"). Sentence boundaries help in understanding breaks that separate the context from one idea to the next idea in the next sentence. Systems attempt to identify sentence boundaries in audio by looking for pauses that often come as a person switches from one sentence to another. Capitalization is much harder but for example when letters are spoken versus words it is typically an acronym for an organization and thus should be capitalized. Also in the original training of the speech to text system the training data is appropriately capitalized and that capitalization carries over to the dictionary associated with the ASR process. So for example even if "ASR" was not part of the training data the system would capitalize it. In addition a proper name like Italy would be transcribed with a capital letter.

Many systems are starting to cascade additional processing capabilities on the transcribed text. In particular machine translation has been applied to the transcribed text to change from a news program in a language a user does not understand to a news program in the user's native language. This process introduces a third "associatively" linked item. There is the original audio along with the multimedia player for it. There is the transcribed text along with links from each word in the transcribed text to the original audio. There is now a machine translation of the transcribed text that is produced (directly associated) with the transcribed text but is also associatively linked to the original audio. Translation is typically not done on a word by word basis but is applied to a sentence or a phrase. The translated text is not a positional word for word correlation to the original transcribed text. Thus the relative time links in the translated text to the audio are not to the word level but the start of each translated sentence/phrase. All of the words in a translated segment will point to the same audio positioning start point in the audio file at just before the beginning of the translated segment. If during playback of the audio the translated text is synchronized and highlighted with the audio playback, it will be more a step function on highlighting the text where a phrase will be statically highlighted until the first word in the next phrase is reached. See Sect. 7.5.3 on video to see an example of audio transcription applied to television news audio.

### 7.5.2 Image Item Presentation

The presentation for search of audio demonstrated close parallel to textual presentations because the audio was converted to text and systems can leverage off the textual options. When considering image search those options do not exist to the same degree. As noted in the introduction to this section historically the multimedia image was not indexed. Instead the text associated with the image was indexed. This allows for a simple user interface that is textual in nature. The user can type in a search statement on what they want to see and the system will search the indexed text associated with images and return in a ranked list the possible hits. Since the user goal is to find an image, typically a thumbnail of the image is presented to the user in the sequential ranked hit list. Figure 7.6 is from a simple GOOGLE search which also shows additional filtering options that can be used to get more precise results.

Google search is primarily focused on text associated with the image. But GOOGLE does allow filtering on specific characteristics of an image or categorizations that they have preprocessed the image to belong to. For example, you can filter on image size, colors or if the image is of a face, clip art, photo or line drawing.

The goal in the information retrieval system is to index the semantics of the image and not just the text associated with the image. The search interface must allow a user to identify an image to be searched to find other images like it. In addition to identifying an image another critical aspect of defining the search is to be able to select a subset of the displayed image as the search image versus the total image. That

**Fig. 7.6** Google image search results page

can significantly increase the accuracy of the search and save the user significant time. Without the capability to "rubber band" via a box in the image thereby defining a subset of an image, the user would need to use a multimedia edit tool to "crop" the original image to define a new image of exactly what they want to search for.

In addition to the image to be used as the query, the user should also be able to adjust parameters on how important characteristics of the image are to increase the precision. For example the user should be able to specify how import color is to the search. If I am searching for a car and the image I have is for a red car, it would be useful to indicate to the system that I am more interested in the shape of the object—a car—then finding images that have a lot of red in them. The specific attributes that the user can tune will be specific to what the attributes from the image are indexed. Since the search process of images will be significantly more likely to return erroneous images, another option is to specify a threshold that defines the minimum required relevancy of search hits—if they want any hit or those with a high correlation to the search image. This is useful in reducing the size of the hit file and the overhead of creating the display page (e.g., the time to create the hit display page). Figure 7.7 is from the PixLogic system and shows one approach to the search user interface. It shows how to "rubber band" around just the burning car to make the image search more focused on it. It has thresholds for color, the importance of shape, foreground, background and color as well as a setting for confidence level. On the left hand side it's possible to specify multiple images and include Boolean logic between them. When an "and" is specified between two images in a search it means that the indexable attributes from both images are treated as if they were all

**Fig. 7.7** Image search interface

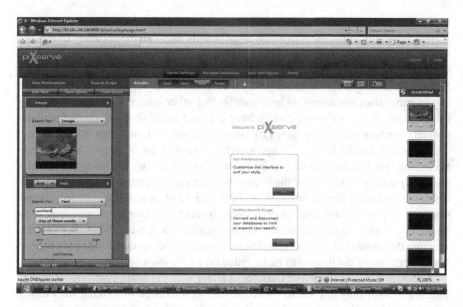

**Fig. 7.8** Image and text search

from a single image and those attributes are used in the search process against the attributes associated with other images. Unless the confidence level is set to high the system will return images that have subsets of the attributes. It is not a "strict" AND in the Boolean sense where a returned hit must have all of the specifications in it. The capability of adding logic to image searchable features can be seen clearer in Fig. 7.8 where search for text within the image is also added to the query frame.

Imbedded within an image there are also additional artifacts that by them selves can be segmented and made searchable. The segmentation (just identifying that portion of the image with the artifact) will increase the accuracy and processing of the artifact. The best example is text that is imbedded within the image. The text within an image should not be searched using the same algorithms that objects within an image are searched for. Instead the text within an image can easily be identified and then it should be searchable where the user enters a textual query. The technologies to make the text searchable are discussed in Chap. 4 (e.g., optical character reading, text image segmentation). But the presentation interface should allow the user to enter text to be found as text within the image. That should be part of an overall search statement that should allow both text in images as well as objects to be part of the query specification. An example of that more complex search statement is shown for PixLogic in Fig. 7.8 the search is looking for a car accident as an image and where there is text on the image with the word accident (e.g., subtitled news displays).

Another artifact that can be separately identified in an image with focused indexing is logos. They are very useful in identifying some aspects of the topic within an image. In this case the user should be able to present a logo looking for images that have that logo. In addition to artifacts such as they discussed there are other objects that might have an importance to a set of users that focused attempts of uniquely identifying them within an image may significantly improve the accuracy of a users search. For example identifying maps within an image or where they are the image or wiring diagrams (these have a lot in common in terms of image characteristics) could be useful allowing a user to specify they want to search to find that specific generic object rather than presenting an image an finding other image of a map and finding other images like it. This would again have a textual interface where the list of these special objects would be available that a user could select from as part of their query.

The search results from an image search is a ranked list of images and as mentioned the standard presentation is by showing the title (e.g., file name) of the image along with a thumbnail of the image. When a user selects a particular image to display from the hit list the image should come up in its own display window. Some non-critical but useful display operations associated with display of an image is to be able to "zoom" in on a portion of the image to see it in more detail. But the one function that is needed when displaying an image is to select that image (or a rubber banded portion of the image) to be included on a follow-on search.

Although a sequential list of the images along with the name associated with the image is one display approach. Since the user is interested in looking for images a more dense display where only the thumbnails are displayed getting as many as possible on the display page. This will allow the user to quickly scan the thumbnail search results for the images they are looking for. The human visual system can process a lot of image very quickly and is optimized to do that looking for the real "information need" of the user. A characteristic of this display that is useful is the ability to define the size of the thumbnails—making them all larger will make them easier to recognize but have fewer per display page while smaller has the opposite effect. Figure 7.9 from PiXlogic shows how multiple search hits can be displayed more effectively than a sequential display.

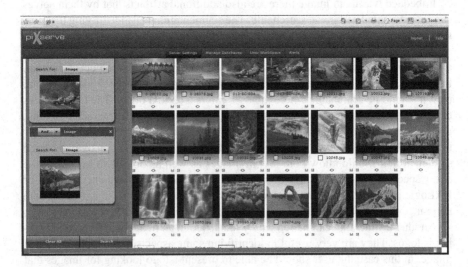

**Fig. 7.9** Display of maximum number of thumbnails

Another query interface is being tested by GOOGLE is their GOGGLE interface for cell phones (http://www.google.com/mobile/goggles/#dc=gh0gg). The idea is that everyone has cell phones. To define the query the user would use the video/image capture capability of the cell phone to define what they are searching for. GOOGLE would then provide them information about what the image defines. Examples would be if the image was a wine label or some other product label the system could return all the information it knows about that product. If the image is of a street or historic site then the system would show maps of where you are at or explain what the historic site is back to the sender. Thus instead of a traditional client the interactive interface is the smaller portable device the users have with them.

## 7.5.3 Video Presentation

As mentioned in Chap. 4 on indexing, a video is really a combination of both an audio track and an image track. When looking to the search entry and results displays for a video, all of the discussions and the results presentations discussed in the last two sections (audio and image) are applicable and both could be combined in the same query. In addition to those there are additional tracks of information that are correlated to relative time within the video. In particular there is closed captioning and teletext that could also be available an indexed. They would add additional text entry aspects for the search. The query generation display would have areas for search entry for images to be searched as frames within the video as well as textual entry to search the audio transcription, machine translation (if available), text on the images and closed captioning/teletext.

The search results options would be similar to image search except the thumbnail would be associated with the first frame in the video that satisfied the image search. The thumbnail would also be point to a video that would be opened in a video player when selected. If only an image search was entered, then the thumbnail only display would be optimum displaying as many different hit videos as possible on the display screen. It there was an associated text aspect to the search then snippets could also be displayed to help indicate the context of some of the text that satisfied the query.

When considering textual searches if the user opens the item, the full text can be displayed with the hit terms highlighted. When an image is part of the search a different strategy is needed in generating the display of a particular video item. When an item is opened up then what is displayed would be the thumbnails of all of the scenes within that video that satisfied the query. Thus, for video there is a two tiered display process. The thumbnail representing the hit of a video item would be the thumbnail of the scene that has the highest weight for that item. But when the item is opened the thumbnails for all of the hit scenes would be displayed along with an indication of the confidence level of that scene matching the search image. The risk associated with this display hierarchy is that the highest ranked scene that is used in the hit list might be a non-relevant frame. A lower weighted frame could satisfy the user's information need but the user would never know and skip over that item. This is similar to when a user looking at a textual snippet thinks the item is not relevant when there could be lower weighted relevant information in an item. Clicking on any of the thumbnails representing hits would start the video item from playing at that offset within the item.

Since the multimedia item is now a video there is an additional search option available where the search query is a video clip. The concept is that the user is trying to find where a video clip or subsets of a search video clip are found within the video item database. This is a more complex search because it is possible that part of the search video is found in the video item as well as the entire search video clip. When a specific video item is opened the video search clip needs to be mapped to the locations within the video item that satisfy some or the entire video clip. One approach to displaying that information is to have a linear line representing the search video clip and another line representing the video item and showing mapping to segments within the video item that satisfy some or all of the video clip.

Since a lot of video (e.g., television) has an audio track the speech to text (ASR) capabilities described for audio sources also apply to video items like television news. The Broadcast Monitoring System (BMS) from BBN Technologies provides an example how there is correlation between the transcribed text and audio (in this case television video/audio combination). In addition to transcribing the audio track of the news the BMS system also uses Language Weaver to translate the transcribed text. The goal of the BMS is to provide a mechanism to monitor live TV and via a "watch list" (think of it like an "alert profile") of terms let the user know whenever anything of importance is happening. Figure 7.10 from the BMS system shows an example of how a user interface displays all three; audio (or in their case video from which audio is transcribed), the audio transcription (Arabic in this example) and the machine translation.

The display not only displays the translation along with the original audio transcribed text vernacular, it synchronizes the play of the video with the text being displayed. By clicking on any word, in the transcribed text or machine translation,

**Fig. 7.10** BMS results display

the video will automatically start playing at that location. The BMS also does entity identification on the transcribed text and machine translation. It identifies people, places and organizations in different colors to make it easier for users to locate them in the text. As the video plays the current word being spoken is also highlighted.

The translated text is also searchable but if the transcribed text is 85–95% accurate the translated text will be significantly less than that based upon the impact of the mis-recognized words in the transcription process. But errors in the transcription process and the translation process may not have a direct correlation to inaccuracy in the search process. Most of the words in text are not ever searched on. What are typically searched on are names and other descriptive words that tend to be long in nature. The speech to text process tends to be more accurate for longer words with more of the errors being on shorter words. If the longer words are transcribed correctly they will have a stronger likelihood to be translated correctly. The initial goal of the speech to text and machine translation process is to create the index to the original multimedia object not as a replacement for it. Thus the cascading errors in the process may not have as significant effect on overall user search performance as indicated by the accuracy of each step. That being said the ultimate vision would be if both processes could be accurate enough to be directly usable in addition to the multimedia object.

## 7.6   Human Perception and Presentation

The primary focus on Information Retrieval Systems has been in the areas of indexing, searching and clustering versus information display. This has been due to the inability of technology to provide the technical platforms needed for sophisticated display, academic's focusing on the more interesting algorithmic based search aspects of information retrieval, and the multi-disciplinary nature of the human-computer interface (HCI). The core technologies needed to address sophisticated information visualization have matured, supporting productive research and implementation into commercial products. The commercial demand for these technologies is growing with availability of the "information highway." System designers need to treat the display of data as visual computing instead of treating the monitor as a replica of paper. Functions that are available with electronic display and visualization of data that were not previously provided are (Brown-96):

- modify representations of data and information or the display condition (e.g., changing color scales)
- use the same representation while showing changes in data (e.g., moving between clusters of items showing new linkages)
- animate the display to show changes in space and time
- enable interactive input from the user to allow dynamic movement between information spaces and allow the user to modify data presentation to optimize personal preferences for understanding the data.
- Create hyperlinks under user control to establish relationships between data

If information retrieval had achieved development of the perfect search algorithm providing close to 100% precision and recall, the need for advances in information visualization would not be so great. But reality has demonstrated in TREC and other information forums that advancements are not even close to achieving this goal. Thus, any technique that can reduce the user overhead of finding the needed information will supplement algorithmic achievements in finding potential relevant items. Information Visualization addresses how the results of a search may be optimally displayed to the users to facilitate their understanding of what the search has provided and their selection of most likely items of interest to read. Visual displays can consolidate the search results into a form easily processed by the user's cognitive abilities, but in general they do not answer the specific retrieval needs of the user other than suggesting database coverage of the concept and related concepts.

The theoretical disciplines of cognitive engineering and perception provide a theoretical base for information visualization. Cognitive engineering derives design principles for visualization techniques from what we know about the neural processes involved with attention, memory, imagery and information processing of the human visual system. By 1989 research had determined that mental depiction plays a role in cognition that is different from mental description. Thus, the visual representation of an item plays as important a role as its symbolic definition in cognition.

Cognitive engineering results can be applied to methods of reviewing the concepts contained in items selected by search of an information system. Visualization can be divided into two broad classes: link visualization and attribute (concept) visualization. Link visualization displays relationships among items. Attribute visualization reveals content relationships across large numbers of items. Related to attribute visualization is the capability to provide visual cues on how search terms affected the search results. This assists a user in determining changes required to search statements that will return more relevant items.

### 7.6.1  Introduction to Information Visualization

The beginnings of the theory of visualization began over 2,400 years ago. The philosopher Plato discerned that we perceive objects through the senses, using the mind. Our perception of the real world is a translation from physical energy from our environment into encoded neural signals. The mind is continually interpreting and categorizing our *perception* of our surroundings. Use of a computer is another source of input to the mind's processing functions. Text-only interfaces reduce the complexity of the interface but also restrict use of the more powerful information processing functions the mind has developed since birth.

Information visualization is a relatively new discipline growing out of the debates in the 1970s on the way the brain processes and uses mental images. It required significant advancements in technology and information retrieval techniques to become a possibility. One of the earliest researchers in information visualization was Doyle, who in 1962 discussed the concept of "semantic road maps" that could provide a user a view of the whole database. The road maps show the items that are related to a specific semantic theme. The user could use this view to focus his query on a specific semantic portion of the database. The concept was extended in the late 1960s, emphasizing a spatial organization that maps to the information in the database. It implemented a non-linear mapping algorithm that could reveal document associations providing the information required to create a road map or spatial organization.

In the 1990s technical advancements along with exponential growth of available information moved the discipline into practical research and commercialization. Information visualization techniques have the potential to significantly enhance the user's ability to minimize resources expended to locate needed information. The way users interact with computers changed with the introduction of user interfaces based upon Windows, Icons, Menus, and Pointing devices (WIMPs). Although movement in the right direction to provide a more natural human interface, the technologies still required humans to perform activities optimized for the computer to understand. A better approach was stated by Donald A. Norman (Rose-96):

> ... people are required to conform to technology. It is time to reverse this trend, time to make technology conform to people

Norman stresses that to optimize the user's ability to find information, the focus should be on understanding the aspects of the user's interface and processing of information which then can be migrated to a computer interface (Norman-90).

Although using text to present an overview of a significant amount of information makes it difficult for the user to understand the information, it is essential in presenting the details. In information retrieval, the process of getting to the relevant details starts with filtering many items via a search process. The result of this process is still a large number of potentially relevant items. In most systems the results of the search are presented as a textual list of each item perhaps ordered by rank. The user has to read all of the pages of lists of the items to see what is in the Hit list. Understanding the human cognitive process associated with visual data suggests alternative ways of presenting and manipulating information to focus on the likely relevant items. There are many areas that information visualization and presentation can help the user:

1. reduce the amount of time to understand the results of a search and likely clusters of relevant information
2. yield information that comes from the relationships between items versus treating each item as independent
3. perform simple actions that produce sophisticated information search functions.

A study was performed by Fox et al. using interviews and user task analysis on professionals in human factors engineering, library science, and computer science to determine the requirements to optimize their work with documents

(Fox-93b). Once past the initial requirement for easy access from their office, the researchers' primary objective was the capability to locate and explore patterns in document databases. They wanted visual representations of the patterns and items of interest. There was a consistent theme that the tools should allow the users to view and search documents with the system sensitive to their view of the information space. The users wanted to be able to focus on particular areas of their interest (not generic system interest definitions) and then easily see new topical areas of potential interest to investigate. They sought an interface that permits easy identification of trends, interest in various topics and newly emerging topics. Representing information in a visual mode allows for cognitive parallel processing of multiple facts and data relationships satisfying many of these requirements.

The exponential growth in available information produces large Hit files from most searches. To understand issues with the search statement and retrieved items, the user has to review a significant number of status screens. Even with the review, it is hard to generalize if the search can be improved. Information visualization provides an intuitive interface to the user to aggregate the results of the search into a display that provides a high-level summary and facilitates focusing on likely centers of relevant items. The query logically extracts a virtual workspace (information space) of potential relevant items which can be viewed and manipulated by the user. By representing the aggregate semantics of the workspace, relationships between items become visible. It is impossible for the user to perceive these relationships by viewing the items individually. The aggregate presentation allows the user to manipulate the aggregates to refine the items in the workspace. For example, if the workspace is represented by a set of named clusters (name based upon major semantic content), the user may select a set of clusters that defines the next iteration of the search.

An alternative use of aggregates is to correlate the search terms with items retrieved. Inspecting relevant and non-relevant items in a form that highlights the effect of the expanded search terms provides insights on what terms were the major causes for the results. A user may have thought a particular term was very important. A visual display could show that the term in fact had a minimal effect on the item selection process, suggesting a need to substitute other search terms.

Using a textual display on the results of a search provides no mechanism to display inter-relationships between items. For example, if the user is interested in the development of a polio vaccine, there is no way for a textual listing of found items to show "date" and "researcher" relationships based upon published items. The textual summary list of the Hit file can only be sorted via one attribute, typically relevance rank.

Aspects of human cognition are the technical basis for understanding the details of information visualization systems. Many techniques are being developed heuristically with the correlation to human cognition and perception analyzed after the techniques are in test. The commercial pressures to provide visualization in delivered systems places the creativity under the intuitive concepts of the developer.

## 7.6.2   Cognition and Perception

The user-machine interface has primarily focused on a paradigm of a typewriter. As computers displays became ubiquitous, man-machine interfaces focused on treating the display as an extension of paper with the focus on consistency of operations. The advent of WIMP interfaces and simultaneous parallel tasks in the user work environment expanded the complexity of the interface to manipulate the multiple tasks. The evolution of the interface focused on how to represent to the user what is taking place in the computer environment. The advancements in computer technology, information sciences and understanding human information processing are providing the basis for extending the human computer interface to improve the information flow, thus reducing wasted user overhead in locating needed information. Although the major focus is on enhanced visualization of information, other senses are also being looked at for future interfaces. The audio sense has always been part of simple alerts in computers. Illegal inputs are usually associated with a beep, and more recently users have a spectrum of audio sounds to associate with everything from start-up to shut down. The sounds are now being replaced by speech in both input and output interfaces. Still in the research arena is the value of using audio to encapsulate information (e.g., higher pitch as you move through an information space plus increased relevance). The tactile (touch) sense is being addressed in the experiments using Virtual Realty (VR). For example, VR is used as a training environment for areas such as medical procedures where tactile feedback plays an increasing role. Olfactory and taste are two areas where practical use for information processing or computer interfaces in general has yet to be identified. For Information Retrieval Systems, the primary area of interest is in information visualization.

### 7.6.2.1   Background

A significant portion of the brain is devoted to vision and supports the maximum information transfer function from the environment to a human being. The center of debates in the 1970s was whether vision should be considered data collection or also has aspects of information processing. In 1969 Arnheim questioned the then current psychological division of cognitive operations of perception and thinking as separate processes (Arnheim-69). Until then perception was considered a data collection task and thinking as a higher level function using the data. He contended that visual perception includes the process of understanding the information, providing an ongoing feedback mechanism between the perception and thinking. He further expanded his views arguing that treating perception and thinking as separate functions treats the mind as a serial automata (Arnheim-86). Under this paradigm, the two mental functions exclude each other, with perception dealing with individual instances versus generalizations. Visualization is the transformation of information into a visual form which enables the user to observe and understand the information. This concept can be extended where the visual images provide a fundamentally different way to understand information that treats the visual input not as discrete facts but as an understanding process. The Gestalt psychologists postulate that the mind follows a set of rules to combine the input stimuli to a mental representation that differs from the sum of the individual inputs (Rock-90):

Proximity          nearby figures are grouped together

Similarity         similar figures are grouped together

Continuity         figures are interpreted as smooth continuous patterns rather than discontinuous concatenations of shapes (e.g., a circle with its diameter drawn is perceived as two continuous shapes, a circle and a line, versus two half circles concatenated together)

Closure            gaps within a figure are filled in to create a whole (e.g., using dashed lines to represent a square does not prevent understanding it as a square)

Connectedness      uniform and linked spots, lines or areas are perceived as a single unit

Shifting the information processing load from slower cognitive processes to faster perceptual systems significantly improves the information-carrying interfaces between humans and computers (Card-96). There are many ways to present information in the visual space. An understanding of the way the cognitive processes work provides insights for the decisions on which of the presentations will maximize the information passing and understanding. There is not a single correct answer on the best way to present information.

### 7.6.2.2   Aspects of the Visualization Process

One of the first-level cognitive processes is preattention, that is, taking the significant visual information from the photoreceptors and forming primitives. Primitives are part of the preconscious processes that consist of involuntary lower order information processing (Friedhoff-89). An example of this is the ease with which our visual systems detect borders between changes in orientation of the same object. In Fig. 7.11 the visual system detects the difference in orientations between the left and middle portion of the figure and determines the logical border between them. An example of using the conscious processing capabilities of the brain is the detection of the different shaped objects and the border between them shown between the left side and middle of the Fig. 7.11. The reader can likely detect the differences in the time it takes to visualize the two different boundaries.

This suggests that if information semantics are placed in orientations, the mind's clustering aggregate function enables detection of groupings easier than using different objects (assuming the orientations are significant). This approach makes maximum use of the feature detectors in the retina.

The preattentive process can detect the boundaries between orientation groups of the same object. A harder process is to identify the equivalence of rotated objects. For example, a rotated square requires more effort to recognize it as a square. As we

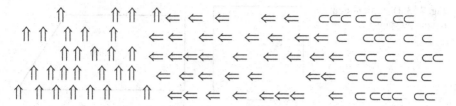

**Fig. 7.11** Preattentive detection mechanism

migrate into characters, the problem of identification of the character is affected by rotating the character in a direction not normally encountered. It is easier to detect the symmetry when the axis is vertical. Figure 7.12 demonstrates these effects.

Another visual factor is the optical illusion that makes a light object on a dark background to appear larger than if the item is dark and the background is light. Making use of this factor suggests that a visual display of small objects should use bright colors. An even more complex area is the use of colors. Colors have many attributes that can be modified such as hue, saturation and lightness. Hue is the physiological attribute of color sensation. Saturation is the degree to which a hue is different from a gray line with the same lightness, while lightness is the sensation of the amount of white or black. Complementary colors are two colors that form white or gray when combined (red/green, yellow/blue). Color is one of the most frequently used visualization techniques to organize, classify, and enhance features (Thorelli-90). Humans have an innate attraction to the primary colors (red, blue, green and yellow), and their retention of images associated with these colors is longer. But colors also affect emotion, and some people have strong aversion to certain colors. The negative side of use of colors is that some people are color blind to some or many colors. Thus any display that uses colors should have other options available.

Depth, like color, is frequently used for representing visual information. Classified as monocular cues, changes in shading, blurring (proportional to distance), perspective, motion, stereoscopic vision, occlusion and texture depict depth. Most of the cues are affected more by lightness than contrast. Thus, choice of colors that maximizes brightness in contrast to the background can assist in presenting depth

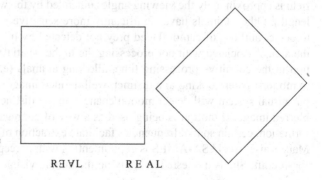

**Fig. 7.12** Rotating a square and reversing letters in "REAL"

**Fig. 7.13** Distortions of a
regular polygon

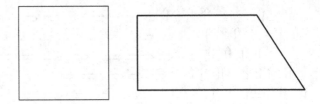

as a mechanism for representing information. Depth has the advantage that depth/
size recognition are learned early in life and used all of the time. Gibson and Walk
showed that six-month-old children already understand depth suggesting that depth
may be an innate concept (Gibson-60). The cognitive processes are well developed,
and the use of this information in classifying objects is ubiquitous to daily life. The
visual information processing system is attuned to processing information using
depth and correlating it to real world paradigms.

Another higher level processing technique is the use of configural aspects of a
display (Rose-95). A configural effect occurs when arrangements of objects are presented to the user allowing for easy recognition of a high-level abstract condition.
Configural clues substitute a lower level visual process for a higher level one that
requires more concentration (see preattentive above). These clues are frequently
used to detect changes from a normal operating environment such as in monitoring an operational system. An example is shown in Fig. 7.13 where the sides of a
regular polygon (e.g., a square in this example) are modified. The visual processing
system quickly detects deviations from normally equally sized objects.

Another visual cue that can be used is spatial frequency. The human visual and
cognitive system tends towards order and builds a coherent visual image whenever
possible. The multiple spatial channel theory proposes that a complex image is constructed from the external inputs, not received as a single image. The final image is
constructed from multiple receptors that detect changes in spatial frequency, orientation, contrast, and spatial phase. Spatial frequency is an acuity measure relative to
regular light-dark changes that are in the visual field or similar channels. A cycle is
one complete light-dark change. The spatial frequency is the number of cycles per
one degree of visual field. Our visual systems are less sensitive to spatial frequencies of about 5–6 cycles per degree of visual field (NOTE: one degree of visual
field is approximately the viewing angle subtended by the width of a finger at arms
length). Other animals have significantly more sensitive systems that allow them
to detect outlines of camouflaged prey not detected by humans until we focus on
the area. Associated with not processing the higher spatial frequencies is a reduction in the cognitive processing time, allowing animals (e.g., cats) to react faster
to motion. When looking at a distinct, well defined image versus a blurred image,
our visual system will detect motion/changes in the distinct image easier than the
blurred image. If motion is being used as a way of aggregating and displaying information, certain spatial frequencies facilitate extraction of patterns of interest. Dr.
Mary Kaiser of NASA-AMES is experimenting with perceptually derived displays
for aircraft. She is interested in applying the human vision filters such as limits of

spatial and temporal resolution, mechanisms of stereopsis, and attentional focus to aircraft (Kaiser-96).

The human sensory systems learn from usage. In deciding upon visual information techniques, parallels need to be made between what is being used to represent information and encountering those techniques in the real world environment. The human system is adept at working with horizontal and vertical references. They are easily detected and processed. Using other orientations requires additional cognitive processes to understand the changes from the expected inputs. The typical color environment is subdued without large areas of bright colors. Thus using an analogous situation, bright colors represent items to be focused on correlating to normal processing (i.e., noticing brightly colored flowers in a garden). Another example of taking advantage of sensory information that the brain is use to processing is terrain and depth information. Using a graphical representation that uses depth of rectangular objects to represent information is an image that the visual system is used to processing. Movement in that space is more easily interpreted and understood by the cognitive processes than if, for example, a three-dimensional image of a sphere represented a visual information space.

In using cognitive engineering in designing information visualization techniques, a hidden risk is that "understanding is in the eye of the beholder." The integration of the visual cues into an interpretation of what is being seen is also based upon the user's background and context of the information. The human mind uses the latest information to assist in interpreting new information. If a particular shape has been representing important information, the mind has a predisposition to interpret new inputs as the same shape. For example, if users have been focusing on clusters of items, they may see clusters in a new presentation that do not exist. This leads to the question of changing visualization presentations to minimize legacy dispositions. Another issue is that our past experiences can affect our interpretation of a graphic. Users may interpret figures according to what is most common in their life experiences rather than what the designer intended.

## 7.7  Summary

Search algorithms are very important in information retrieval because they define the subset of the database that will be displayed to the user and the ranked order of what is most likely to be of interest. Just as important to the user finding what they are looking for is how the information is presented. In some cases the standard linear ranked list is sufficient for the user to locate a few items on a particular topic. But when the user is looking for a more exhaustive set of information or trying to understand the different subtopics of information on a particular problem other presentation techniques such as clustering is the best methodology to help the user to navigate to the needed information. Although the more sophisticated methods for information visualization require significant more computer resources, advances in hardware performance and software architecture are making their common use possible over the next few years. The end result will be to marry the advances in searching with sophisticated results presentation allowing the user to leverage off their minds ability to absorb and assess patterns and specific information in more complex displays resulting on detection of their needed information faster and more comprehensive.

Text summarization techniques also hold significant promise in eliminating the redundancy of information within and especially between hits allowing the user to focus on the specific new facts rather than having to reread the same data over many times to detect one new piece of information.

Information presentation for multimedia searching is still in its infancy as is generally providing search of multimedia items. But there is tremendous pressure on developing information retrieval technologies in this area as cell phones and other Personal Digital Assistants become common place.

## 7.8   Exercises

1. What are the technical issues with providing clustering presentation with every search? Is there some preprocessing approach that could make such a presentation more realistic?
2. In order to do timeline presentation what information is needed? How would that information be determined?
3. Use the autosummarize capability in MS Word against a textual item you have. How well did it work. Search the Internet for other sites that allow you to submit text to be summarized and look at those results. What seems to work and what are the inherent limits in text summarization.
4. Expand the discussion on text summarization to when you are summarizing across multiple items. What functions and capabilities are essential in the display of the summarized information to assist the user in validating the results and feeling confident about its completeness?
5. What are the basic limitations and difficulties in a user generating a search and getting results back from an image or video image search? What unique functions need to be provided to allow the user to validate the results of their search (map their search to each result returned) and to enhance the search to make it more precise?

# Chapter 8
# Search Architecture

## 8.1 Index Search Optimization

Search as described so far in Chap. 5 is based upon the concept that a user enters a query and the system returns a ranked list of hits based upon a similarity measure between the users search and weights of the processing tokens in the index. This suggests the final result will be a sorted ranked list of hits where any item whose relevance weight is above zero will be in the ranked list. This then creates Hit lists of potentially hundreds of thousands to millions of hits. When the results of the search are being used for viewing by the searcher we know that the user seldom looks at hits one more than the first 2 or at most three pages of hits. Thus the user is only really concerned with less than 1% of the top hits. Historically search systems have taken advantage of that fact by having an internal threshold set and when the number of hits that have been discovered reaches that threshold the system stops the query and returns those hits (e.g., Retrievalware system). The designers felt that the user would never really know that the very best hit may not be in the hit list and thus there is likely sufficient information to make the user feel comfortable that the system worked. There are many design solutions that can use that a user only views a few hit pages and leverage off returning to the user the most likely top "n" hits but not guarantee it and reduce the computation load on executing the search. This does fall down a little when the goal of the search is to deliver the hit list to a visualization system that will use most of the hits (at least in the hundreds of thousands) to create a visualization of the search results. But this is the exception case in current systems. A number of these techniques have been described in Manning et. al. book on Information retrieval (Manning-2008). Even though the techniques described below limit the calculations needed to crate the Hit list, the systems will use an approximation estimate formula to estimate how many hits they would expect to be from searching the complete database. Thus the "total hit" count is really an estimate with the system really only having a small subset of those hits actually identified. But since the user can only go one linear list page of hits at a time there is no mechanism for the user to get to hit 1,000,000 without paging through lots of hit pages.

G. Kowalski, *Information Retrieval Architecture and Algorithms*,
DOI 10.1007/978-1-4419-7716-8_8, © Springer Science+Business Media, LLC 2011

## 8.1.1  Pruning the Index

Most systems already make a simplification assumption and retrieve only the inversion lists for the search terms in the query. This focuses the search on the user supplied search terms but does mean that other terms in the documents that have the users search terms can not be used to find additional relevant items. This will maximize precision at the expense of recall. The problem of mismatch of vocabulary described as one of the major issues in getting complete search results is ignored in this approach. If the goal is for even higher reduction in analysis the system can limit the relevance calculations to only those items that have all of the search terms in them.

An additional technique leverages off of the fact that we are only interested in the most relevant hits which will come from a similarity measure. Thus items with low relevance weights for a particular search term will not likely be in the final top portion of a returned hit list. Thus when the inversion list is being merged in the similarity calculations, values in the index list below a certain threshold can be treated as if they were zero and skipped over. This significantly reduces the number of similarity calculations that need to be performed.

The above assumes the inversion lists are sorted by Item ID. But since the goal is to find the highest weighted items a better sort to early find the most similar items would be by weight. Unfortunately this can then randomly place the item IDs in the inversion lists. By having the order in this fashion a particular inversion list can stop being processed after the top weighted items rather than going through the complete list. But if the goal is to just get the top few items for the first few pages of hits this technique will more quickly find those items with minimal processing.

## 8.1.2  Champion Lists

The concept of champion lists is based upon the approach of only analyzing the highest ranked items that the inversion lists that are typically sorted by unique item ID. The system normally has to go through the complete inversion list to find the items that have the highest weights to be used in the actual calculation. In this approach there is a "champion" inversion list created that is a subset of the original inversion list that only has items in it where the weight of the processing token exceeds a threshold. The threshold can vary by inversion list and be based upon the weights in that inversion list (basically taking the top "n" percent of the items in the list with highest weights).

The search is then executed against the champion lists rather than the full inversion lists. The challenge is to find that percentage of high weighted items that you want to keep in each inversion list to be sure that when the similarity calculations are complete that there will be sufficient hits returned. Although by having the complete inversion lists available, if there are too few hits found in the champion lists because there are very few documents that all of the search terms, the system can then process that query against the full lists. This can be enhanced further because the system getting to the full inversion lists would have first processed the search against the champion list. Instead of keeping the full inversion list all of the entries from the champion list could be deleted thus reducing the calculation to only items not already addressed in the champion list analysis.

In the current search systems in addition to weights associated with specific processing tokens (terms) in items, there is sometimes a weight assigned to each item in terms of its potential value (e.g., the GOOGLE link analysis). This value is also used in determining which items to be retrieved and the ranked order of the list. In a sense this is another weighting factor on the weights of the processing tokens in an item based upon the likely importance of that item. Thus instead of the inversion list only containing the weight of a term in a document using the weighting formulas previous discussed (e.g., inverse document frequency), the value in the inversion list could also be biased by the potential importance weight for the item. This runs a significant computation risk because the weights of the relative importance of each item can initially vary based upon changes in the system until it stabilizes which would mean that the inversion lists (even the champion lists) would be changing as new data enters the system for existing values in the inversion lists. Ideally the goal is to have the inversion lists for the already ingested items in the system not change until the item is deleted. This then suggests that the weights for the items need to be kept separate from the inversion lists for newer items and only added to the inversion lists after they have stabilized. After that only when there is a significant change to an item would it is necessary to update the inversion list or just keep a smaller list of those modified items to be dynamically adjusted for.

## 8.2 Text Search Optimization

The basic concept of a text scanning system is the ability for one or more users to enter queries, and the text to be searched is accessed and compared to the query terms. When all of the text has been accessed, the query is complete. One advantage of this type architecture is that as soon as an item is identified as satisfying a query, the results can be presented to the user for retrieval. Figure 8.1 provides a diagram

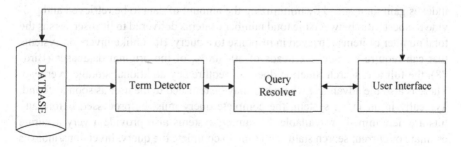

**Fig. 8.1** Text streaming architecture

of a text streaming search system. The database contains the full text of the items. The term detector is the special hardware/software that contains all of the terms being searched for and in some systems the logic between the items. It will input the text and detect the existence of the search terms. It will output to the query resolver the detected terms to allow for final logical processing of a query against an item. The query resolver performs two functions. It will accept search statements from the users, extract the logic and search terms and pass the search terms to the detector. It also accepts results from the detector and determines which queries are satisfied by the item and possibly the weight associated with hit. The Query Resolver will pass information to the user interface that will be continually updating search status to the user and on request retrieve any items that satisfy the user search statement. The process is focused on finding at least one or all occurrences of a pattern of text (query term) in a text stream. It is assumed that the same alphabet is used in both situations (although in foreign language streamers different encodings may have to be available for items from the same language such as in Cyrillic). The worst case search for a pattern of $m$ characters in a string of $n$ characters is at least $n - m + 1$ or a magnitude of $O(n)$ (Rivest-77). Some of the original brute force methods could require $O(n * m)$ symbol comparisons (Sedgewick-88). More recent improvements have reduced the time to $O(n + m)$.

In the case of hardware search machines, multiple parallel search machines (term detectors) may work against the same data stream allowing for more queries or against different data streams reducing the time to access the complete database. In software systems, multiple detectors may execute at the same time.

There are two approaches to the data stream. In the first approach the complete database is being sent to the detector(s) functioning as a search of the database. In the second approach random retrieved items are being passed to the detectors. In this second case the idea is to perform an index search of the database and let the text streamer perform additional search logic that is not satisfied by the index search (Bird-78, Hollaar-79). Examples of limits of index searches are:

- search for stop words
- search for exact matches when stemming is performed
- search for terms that contain both leading and trailing "don't cares"
- search for symbols that are on the interword symbol list (e.g., " , ;)

The major disadvantage of basing the search on streaming the text is the dependency of the search on the slowest module in the computer (the I/O module). Inversions/indexes gain their speed by minimizing the amount of data to be retrieved and provide the best ratio between the total number of items delivered to the user versus the total number of items retrieved in response to a query. But unlike inversion systems that can require storage overheads of 50–300%, of the original databases (Bird-78), the full text search function does not require any additional storage overhead. There is also the advantage where hits may be returned to the user as soon as found. Typically in an index system, the complete query must be processed before any hits are determined or available. Streaming systems also provide a very accurate estimate of current search status and time to complete the query. Inversions/indexes also encounter problems in fuzzy searches ($m$ of $n$ characters) and imbedded string query terms (i.e., leading and trailing "don't care", see Chap. 1). It is difficult to locate all the possible index values short of searching the complete dictionary of possible terms. Most streaming algorithms will locate imbedded query terms and some algorithms and hardware search units will also perform fuzzy searches. Use of special hardware text search units insures a scalable environment where performance bottlenecks can be overcome by adding additional search units to work in parallel of the data being streamed.

Many of the hardware and software text searchers use finite state automata as a basis for their algorithms. A finite state automata is a logical machine that is composed of five elements:

**I**     a set of input symbols from the alphabet supported by the automata
**S**     a set of possible states
**P**     a set of productions that define the next state based upon the current state and input symbol
$S_0$     a special state called the initial state
$S_F$     a set of one or more final states from the set **S**

A finite state automata is represented by a directed graph consisting of a series of nodes (states) and edges between nodes represented as transitions defined by the set of productions. The symbol(s) associated with each edge defines the inputs that allow a transition from one node $S_i$ to another node $S_j$. Figure 8.2a shows a finite state automata that will identify the character string CPU in any input stream. The automata is defined by the automata definition in Fig. 8.2b.

The automata remains in the initial state until it has an input symbol of "C" which moves it to state $S_1$. It will remain in that state as long as it receives "C"s as input. If it receives a "P" it will move to $S_2$. If it receives anything else it falls back to the initial state. Once in state $S_2$ it will either go to the final state if "U" is the next symbol, go to $S_1$ if a "C" is received or go back to the initial state $S_0$ if anything else is received.

It is possible to represent the productions by a table with the states as the rows and the input symbols that cause state transitions as each column. The states are representing the current state and the values in the table are the next state given the particular input symbol.

## 8.2.1   Software Text Search Algorithms

In software streaming techniques, the item to be searched is read into memory and then the algorithm is applied. Although nothing in the architecture described above prohibits software streaming from being applied to many simultaneous searches against the same item, it is more frequently used to resolve a particular search against a particular item. The best example is searching an item before display to highlight the search query terms in the text. Four algorithms associated with soft-

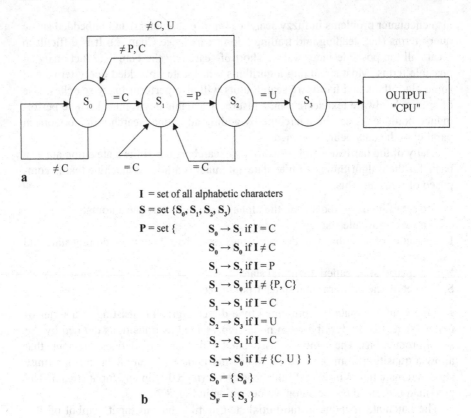

**Fig. 8.2  a** Finite state automata. **b** Automata definition

ware text search are discussed as examples on software text searching optimization: the brute force approach, Knuth-Morris-Pratt, Boyer-Moore, and Rabin-Karp. Of all of the algorithms, Boyer-Moore has been the fastest requiring at most $O(n+m)$ comparisons (Smit-82). Knuth-Pratt-Morris and Boyer-Moore both require $O(n)$ preprocessing of search strings (Knuth-77, Boyer-77, Rytter-80).

The Brute force approach is the simplest string matching algorithm. The idea is to try and match the search string against the input text. If as soon as a mismatch is detected in the comparison process, shift the input text one position and start the comparison process over. The expected number of comparisons when searching an input text string of $n$ characters for a pattern of $m$ characters is (Baeza-Yates-89):

$$N_c = \frac{c}{c-1}\left(1 - \frac{1}{c^m}\right)(n - m + 1) + O(1)$$

where $N_c$ is the expected number of comparisons and $c$ is the size of the alphabet for the text.

The Knuth-Pratt-Morris algorithm made a major improvement in previous algorithms in that even in the worst case it does not depend upon the length of the text pattern being searched for. The basic concept behind the algorithm is that whenever a mismatch is detected, the previous matched characters define the number of characters that can be skipped in the input stream prior to starting the comparison process again. For example given:

| Position | | 1 | 2 | 3 | 4 | 5 | 6 | 7 | 8 |
|---|---|---|---|---|---|---|---|---|---|
| Input Stream | = | a | b | d | a | d | e | f | g |
| Search Pattern | = | a | b | d | f | | | | |

When the mismatch occurs in position 4 with an "f" in the pattern and a "b" in the input stream, a brute force approach may shift just one position in the input text and restart the comparison. But since the first three positions of the pattern matched (a b d), then shifting one position can not find an "a" because it has already been identified as a "b". The algorithm allows the comparison to jump at least the three positions associated with the recognized "a b d". Since the mismatch on the position could be the beginning of the search string, four positions can not be skipped. To know the number of positions to jump based upon a mismatch in the search pattern, the search pattern is pre-processed to define a number of characters to be jumped for each position. The Shift Table that specifies the number of places to jump given a mismatch is shown in Fig. 8.3. In the table it should be noted that the alignment is primarily based on aligning over the repeats of the letters "a" and "ab". Figure 8.4 provides an example application of the algorithm (Salton-89) where S is the search pattern and I is the input text stream.

Boyer-Moore recognized that the string algorithm could be significantly enhanced if the comparison process started at the end of the search pattern processing right to left versus the start of the search pattern. The advantage is that large jumps are possible when the mismatched character in the input stream does not exist in the search pattern which occurs frequently. This leads to two possible sources of determining how many input characters to be jumped. As in the Knuth-Morris-Pratt technique any characters that have been matched in the search pattern will require

| Position in pattern | pattern character | length previous repeating substring | number of input characters to jump |
|---|---|---|---|
| 1 | a | 0 | 1 |
| 2 | b | 0 | 1 |
| 3 | c | 0 | 2 |
| 4 | a | 0 | 4 |
| 5 | b | 1 | 5 |
| 6 | c | 2 | 6 |
| 7 | a | 3 | 3 |
| 8 | c | 4 | 3 |
| 9 | a | 0 | 8 |
| 10 | b | 1 | 8 |

**Fig. 8.3** Shift characters table

| P | 1 | 2 | 3 | 4 | 5 | 6 | 7 | 8 | 9 | 10 | 11 | 12 | 13 | 14 | 15 | 16 |
|---|---|---|---|---|---|---|---|---|---|----|----|----|----|----|----|----|
| S | a | b | c | a | b | c | a | c | a | b |    |    |    |    |    |    |
| I | b | a | b | c | b | a | b | c | a | b | c | a | a | b | c | a |
|   | ↑ |   |   |   |   |   |   |   |   |   |   |   |   |   |   |   |

mismatch in position 1 shift one position

| P | 1 | 2 | 3 | 4 | 5 | 6 | 7 | 8 | 9 | 10 | 11 | 12 | 13 | 14 | 15 | 16 |
|---|---|---|---|---|---|---|---|---|---|----|----|----|----|----|----|----|
| S |   | a | b | c | a | b | c | a | c | a | b |    |    |    |    |    |
| I | b | a | b | c | b | a | b | c | a | b | c | a | a | b | c | a |
|   |   |   |   |   | ↑ |   |   |   |   |   |   |   |   |   |   |   |

mismatch in position 5, no repeat pattern, skip 3 places

| P | 1 | 2 | 3 | 4 | 5 | 6 | 7 | 8 | 9 | 10 | 11 | 12 | 13 | 14 | 15 | 16 |
|---|---|---|---|---|---|---|---|---|---|----|----|----|----|----|----|----|
| S |   |   |   |   | a | b | c | a | b | c | a | c | a | b |    |    |
| I | b | a | b | c | b | a | b | c | a | b | c | a | a | b | c | a |
|   |   |   |   |   | ↑ |   |   |   |   |   |   |   |   |   |   |   |

mismatch in position 5, shift one position

| P | 1 | 2 | 3 | 4 | 5 | 6 | 7 | 8 | 9 | 10 | 11 | 12 | 13 | 14 | 15 | 16 |
|---|---|---|---|---|---|---|---|---|---|----|----|----|----|----|----|----|
| S |   |   |   |   | a | b | c | a | b | c | a | c | a | b |    |    |
| I | b | a | b | c | b | a | b | c | a | b | c | a | a | b | c | a |
|   |   |   |   |   |   |   |   |   |   |   |   |   | ↑ |   |   |   |

mismatch in position 13, longest repeating pattern is "a b c a" thus skip 3

| P | 1 | 2 | 3 | 4 | 5 | 6 | 7 | 8 | 9 | 10 | 11 | 12 | 13 | 14 | 15 | 16 |
|---|---|---|---|---|---|---|---|---|---|----|----|----|----|----|----|----|
| S |   |   |   |   |   |   |   |   | a | b | c | a | b | c | a | b |
| I | b | a | b | c | b | a | b | c | a | b | c | a | a | b | c | a |

alignment after last shift

**Fig. 8.4** Example of Knuth-Morris-Pratt algorithm

an alignment with that substring. Additionally the character in the input stream that was mismatched also requires alignment with it's next occurrence in the search pattern or the complete pattern can be moved. This can be defined as:

- ALGO$_1$—on a mismatch, the character in the input stream is compared to the search pattern to determine the shifting of the search pattern (number of characters in input stream to be skipped) to align the input character to a character in the search pattern. If the character does not exist in the search pattern then it is possible to shift the length of the search pattern matched to that position.
- ALGO$_2$—on a mismatch occurs with previous matching on a substring in the input text, the matching process can jump to the repeating occurrence in the pattern of the initially matched subpattern—thus aligning that portion of the search pattern that is in the input text.
- Search Pattern = abcabcacab

Upon a mismatch, the comparison process can skip the MAXIMUM (ALGO$_1$, ALGO$_2$). Figure 8.5 gives an example of this process. In this example the search pattern is (a b d a a b) and the alphabet is (a, b, c, d, e, f) with $m = 6$ and $c = 6$.

| Position | 1 | 2 | 3 | 4 | 5 | 6 | 7 | 8 | 9 | 10 | 11 | 12 | 13 |
|---|---|---|---|---|---|---|---|---|---|---|---|---|---|
| Input Stream | f | a | b | f | a | a | b | b | d | a | b | a | b |
| Search Pattern | | | a | b | d | a | a | b | | | | | |
| | | | | ↑ | | | | | | | | | |

**a**

| Position | 1 | 2 | 3 | 4 | 5 | 6 | 7 | 8 | 9 | 10 | 11 | 12 | 13 |
|---|---|---|---|---|---|---|---|---|---|---|---|---|---|
| Input Stream | f | a | b | f | a | a | b | b | d | a | b | a | b |
| Search Pattern | | | | | | a | b | d | a | a | b | | |
| | | | | | | | | | ↑ | | | | |

**b**

| Position | 1 | 2 | 3 | 4 | 5 | 6 | 7 | 8 | 9 | 10 | 11 | 12 | 13 | 14 | 15 |
|---|---|---|---|---|---|---|---|---|---|---|---|---|---|---|---|
| Input Stream | f | a | b | f | a | a | b | b | d | a | b | d | a | a | b |
| Search Pattern | | | | | | | | | | a | b | d | a | a | b |

**c**

**Fig. 8.5** Boyer-Moore algorithm. **a** Mismatch in position 4: $ALGO_1 = 3$, $ALGO_2 = 4$, thus skip 4 places. **b** Mismatch in position 9: $ALGO_1 = 1$, $ALGO_2 = 4$ thus skip four places. **c** New aligned search continues with a match

The comparison starts at the right end of the search pattern and works towards the start of the search pattern. In the first comparison (Fig. 8.5a) the mismatch occurs in position 4 after matching on positions 7, 6, and 5. $ALGO_1$ wants to align the next occurrence of the input text stream mismatch character "f" which does not exist in the search pattern thus allowing for a skip of three positions. $ALGO_2$ recognizes that the mismatch occurred after 3 previous search pattern characters had matched. Based upon the pattern stream it knows that the subpattern consisting of the first three characters (a b) repeats in the first two positions of the search pattern. Thus given a mismatch in position 4, the search pattern can be moved four places to align the subpattern consisting of the first two characters (a b) over their known occurrence in positions 6, and 7 in the input text. In the next comparison (Fig. 8.5b) there is a mismatch in position 9. The input character that mismatched is a "d" and the fewest positions to shift to align the next occurrence of a "d" in the search pattern over it is one position. The analysis for $ALGO_2$ is the same as before. With the next jump of four positions, the two patterns will match.

The original Boyer-Moore algorithm has been the basis for additional text search techniques. It was originally designed to support scanning for a single search string. It was expanded to handle multiple search strings on a single pass (Kowalski-83). Enhanced and simplified versions of the Boyer-Moore algorithm have been developed by many researchers (Moller-Nielsen-84, Iyengar-80, Commentz-Walter-79, Baeza-Yates-90, Galil-79, Horspool-80).

A different approach that has similarity to n-grams and signature files defined in Chap. 4 is to divide the text into *m*-character substrings, calculate a hash function (signature) value for each of the strings (Harrison-71). A hash value is calculated for the search pattern and compared to that of the text. Karp and Rabin discovered an efficient signature function to calculate these values; $h(k) = k \bmod q$, where q is a large prime number (Karp-87). The signature value for each location in the text which is based upon the value calculated for the previous location. Hashing functions do not guarantee uniqueness. Their algorithm will find those positions in the text of an item that have the same hash value as the search pattern. But the actual text must then be compared to ensure there is a match. Detailed implementation of the Karp-Rabin algorithm is presented by Baeza-Yates (Baeza-Yates-92). In his comparison of all of the algorithms on a search of 1000 random patterns in random text, the Horspool simplification of the Boyer-Moore algorithm showed the best execution time for patterns of any length. The major drawback of the Boyer-Moore class of algorithms is the significant preprocessing time to set up the tables. Many of these algorithms are also implemented with hardware.

## 8.2.2   Hardware Text Search Systems

### 8.2.2.1   History

Software text search is applicable to many circumstances but has encountered restrictions on the ability to handle many search terms simultaneously against the same text and limits due to I/O speeds. One approach used in the 1980s and 1990s that off loaded the resource intensive searching from the main processors was to have a specialized hardware machine to perform the searches and pass the results to the main computer which supported the user interface and retrieval of hits. Since the searcher is hardware based, scalability is achieved by increasing the number of hardware search devices. The only limit on speed is the time it takes to flow the text off of secondary storage (i.e., disk drives) to the searchers. By having one search machine per disk, the maximum time it takes to search a database of any size will be the time to search one disk. In some systems, the disks were formatted to optimize the data flow off of the drives. Another major advantage of using a hardware text search unit is in the elimination of the index that represents the document database. Typically the indexes are 70% the size of the actual items. Other advantages are that new items can be searched as soon as received by the system rather than waiting for the index to be created and the search speed is deterministic. Even though it may be slower than using an index, the predictability of how long it will take to stream the data provides the user with an exact search time. As hits as discovered they can immediately be made available to the user versus waiting for the total search to complete as in index searches.

Figure 8.6 represents hardware as well as software text search solutions. The algrithmetic part of the system is focused on the term detector. There have been three approaches to implementing term detectors: parallel comparators or associative memory, a cellular structure, and a universal finite state automata (Hollaar-79).

Specialized hardware that interfaces with computers and is used to search secondary storage devices was developed from the early 1970s with the most recent

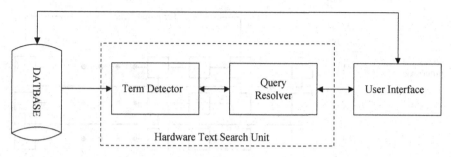

**Fig. 8.6** Hardware text search unit

product being the Parasel Searcher (previously the Fast Data Finder). The need for this hardware was driven by the limits in computer resources. The typical hardware configuration is shown in Fig. 8.6 in the dashed box. The speed of search is then based on the speed of the I/O.

One of the earliest hardware text string search units was the Rapid Search Machine developed by General Electric (Roberts-78). The machine consisted of a special purpose search unit where a single query was passed against a magnetic tape containing the documents. A more sophisticated search unit was developed by Operating Systems Inc. called the Associative File Processor (AFP) (Bird-77). It is capable of searching against multiple queries at the same time. Following that initial development, OSI, using a different approach, developed the High Speed Text Search (HSTS) machine. It uses an algorithm similar to the Aho-Corasick software finite state machine algorithm except that it runs three parallel state machines. One state machine is dedicated to contiguous word phrases (see Chap. 2), another for imbedded term match and the final for exact word match. In parallel with that development effort, GE redesigned their Rapid Search Machine into the GESCAN unit. TRW, based upon analysis of the HSTS, decided to develop their own text search unit. This became the Fast Data Finder which is now being marketed by Parasal. All of these machines were based upon state machines that input the text string and compared them to the query terms.

The GESCAN system uses a text array processor (TAP) that simultaneously matches many terms and conditions against a given text stream the TAP receives the query information from the users computer and directly access the textual data from secondary storage. The TAP consists of a large cache memory and an array of four to 128 query processors. The text is loaded into the cache and searched by the query processors (Fig. 8.7). Each query processor is independent and can be loaded at any time. A complete query is handled by each query processor. Queries support exact term matches, fixed length don't cares, variable length don't cares, terms may be restricted to specified zones, Boolean logic, and proximity.

A query processor works two operations in parallel; matching query terms to input text and Boolean logic resolution. Term matching is performed by a series of character cells each containing one character of the query. A string of character cells is implemented on the same LSI chip and the chips can be connected

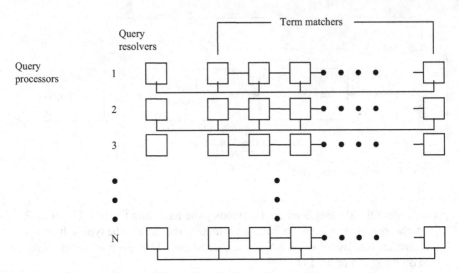

**Fig. 8.7** GESCAN text array processor

in series for longer strings. When a word or phrase of the query is matched, a signal is sent to the resolution sub-process on the LSI chip. The resolution chip is responsible for resolving the Boolean logic between terms and proximity requirements. If the item satisfies the query, the information is transmitted to the users computer. The text array processor uses these chips in a matrix arrangement. Each row of the matrix is a query processor in which the first chip performs the query resolution while the remaining chips match query terms. The maximum number of characters in a query is restricted by the length of a row while the number of rows limit the number of simultaneous queries that can be processed.

Another approach for hardware searchers is to augment disc storage. The augmentation is a generalized associative search element placed between the read and write heads on the disk. The content addressable segment sequential memory (CASSM) system (Roberts-78) uses these search elements in parallel to obtain structured data from a database. The CASSM system was developed at the University of Florida as a general purpose search device (Copeland-73). It can be used to perform string searching across the database. Another special search machine is the relational associative processor (RAP) developed at the University of Toronto (Schuster-79). Like CASSM performs search across a secondary storage device using a series of cells comparing data in parallel.

The Fast Data Finder (FDF) is the most recent specialized hardware text search unit still in use in many organizations. It was developed to search text and has been used to search English and foreign languages. The early Fast Data Finders consisted of an array of programmable text processing cells connected in series forming a pipeline hardware search processor (Mettler-93). The cells are implemented using a VSLI chip. In the TREC tests each chip contained 24 processor cells with a typical system containing 3600 cells (the FDF-3 has a rack mount configuration with 10,800 cells). Each cell will be a comparator for a single character limiting the total number of characters in a query to the number of cells. The cells are interconnected with an 8-bit data path and approximately 20-bit control path. The text to be searched passes through each cell in a pipeline fashion until the complete database has been searched. As data is analyzed at each cell, the 20 control lines states are modified depending upon their current state and the results from the comparator. An example of a Fast Data Finder system is shown in Fig. 8.8. A cell is composed of both a register cell (Rs) and a comparator (Cs). The input from the Document database is controlled and buffered by the microprocess/memory and feed through the comparators. The search characters are stored in the registers. The connection between the registers reflect the control lines that are also passing state information.

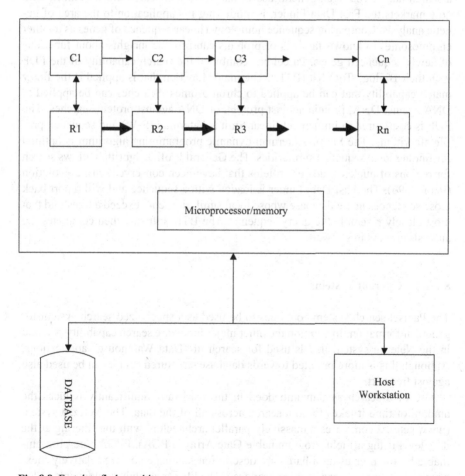

**Fig. 8.8** Fast data finder architecture

Groups of cells are used to detect query terms, along with logic between the terms, by appropriate programming of the control lines. When a pattern match is detected, a hit is passed to the internal microprocessor that passes it back to the host processor, allowing immediate access by the user to the Hit item. The functions supported by the Fast data Finder are:

- Boolean Logic including negation
- Proximity on an arbitrary pattern
- Variable length "don't cares"
- Term counting and thresholds
- fuzzy matching
- term weights
- numeric ranges

The expense and requirement that the complete database be streamed to complete a search has discouraged general use of hardware text search units. Paracel, who now markets the Fast Data Finder, is modifying it's application to the area of genetic analysis. Comparing sequence homology (linear sequence of genes as another chromosome) to known families of proteins can provide insights about functions of newly sequenced genes. Parcel has combined the search capability of the FDF with their Biology Tool Kit (BTK). The major function that is applied is the fuzzy match capability that can be applied to chromosomes. Searches can be applied to DNA against DNA, protein against protein, or DNA against protein searches. The FDF is configured to implement linear Smith-Waterman (S-W) and sequence-profile algorithms. The Smith-Waterman dynamic programming algorithm is optimal for finding local sequence similarities. The General Profile algorithm allows search for regions of nucleic acids or proteins that have been conserved during evolution (Paracel-96). The Fast Data Finder is loaded with a sequence and will report back those sequences in the database whose local similarity score exceed a threshold that most closely resemble the query sequence. The BTK software then completes the analysis process in software.

### 8.2.2.2   Current Systems

The Parasel search system continues to be used as a specialized search system for genetic information. In addition the other major hardware search capability is found in the Netezza system that is used for search in "Data Warehouse" applications. Although this is more oriented towards database structured data it can be used also against free text.

Use of a search system imbedded in the hardware significantly reduces the amount of time it takes to do a search across all of the data. The Netezza system (www.netezza.com) uses a massively parallel architecture with the filtering at the disk level using a Field Programmable Gate Array (FPGA). FPGAs are programmable by the user using a hardware description language and are relatively inexpensive because they can be mass produced. The FPGAs contain components called "logic blocks" whose connections can be defined using simple logic gates like AND OR and XOR. These are used in lieu of the traditional disk controller chips and can be programmed with the search logic. Thus each node in the parallel processing architecture consists of the FPGA along with the storage on the disk (e.g., 400 GB). These are also called snippet processing units (Sups). For example a rack of equipment can hold 112 of these units all executing the query in parallel. The results of the processing are then sent to a host server to aggregate the results of the parallel processing. Thus the search process is running in parallel at the storage level rather than at the server level.

## 8.3  GOOGLE Scalable Multiprocessor Architecture

Although GOOGLE was founded on a research project that focused on using link analysis between Internet web pages to influence the ranking of search results, GOOGLES other major contribution to the evolution of search systems was in the architecture they developed to allow GOOGLE to provide fast response time against very large data sets and also allowed for their link analysis to occur inexpensively. Until GOOGLE most systems used very large processors and in some cases parallel processors (e.g., Alta Vista) to perform search and functions like link analysis. The GOOGLE approach was to use inexpensive commodity type processors in large numbers by developing a file system and software development methodology that allowed easy distribution of functions across many processors. In addition the system had to be made fault tolerant thereby allowing failures of a subset of the processors without effecting the operation taking place. This approach is becoming common place when information retrieval systems are being used against very large databases of text and/or multimedia information.

GOOGLE developed many capabilities that are used in their overall architecture. They knew they were going against massive data sets and those data sets would have to be redundantly stored to allow for the parallel search of them and the capability to recover from a failure. Thus they developed the GOOGLE File System (GFS). The GOOGLE file system started with an earlier concept called BigFiles that was part of the original research effort at Stanford University that laid the groundwork for the GOOGLE system. The characteristic of an information retrieval system is that most data is relatively static. That is the data seldom is updated. Once written it may have a very long life before it is deleted. But the data is very large and thus large chunks of storage need to be managed. This lead to the concept of "chunks" where 64 MB fixed size chunks of data which can be redundantly stored on multiple nodes, called chunk servers. The more often a chunk is accessed the more it will be replicated thus allowing for parallel access by many parallel processing nodes. There is a Master node that keeps the metadata on the chunk servers keeping track of what are the current operational chunk servers and what files are on them. Chunk servers can fail but then the MASTER Node can route data requests to the other replicated servers. Rather than trying to synchronize the metadata knowledge on the Master Node with what is on the Chink Servers, the Master Node queries the Chunk servers which provide both a health check and an update of what is currently on the server.

GOOGLE Web Servers (GWS) are the commodity search servers. A query is first processed and via the Domain Name Server (DNS) an initial load balancing take place to determine which GOOGLE Processing center the query should go to. Once at a processing center the query is then distributed to multiple GWS to process the search. That is because each GWS has a subset of the index to process against a query (called an index shard) and those GWS can be replicated so there is a possible pool of servers to process subsets of the index. Each GWS goes to the Master Node to get a list of the chunk servers that contain the index to be searched. The results of the search are an initial rank list of document IDs of potential hits for the query.

The document IDs are then passed to Document Servers that manage access to the documents. The final document may still be at the web site it was found at or cached locally in the file system. But sufficient information is kept on the document servers and file system to create the "snippet" that will be used in displaying the list of hits. The Document servers will determine the Title, a query weighted summary snippet and the URL that will be used by the user to retrieve the complete document. The architecture of the document servers is similar to the web servers in that there will be a large number of servers that will be randomly handling a subset of the document set (shards) and they will use the file system to get where to go to get the data to process. Like the index there are multiple copies of the documents from the Web that GOOGLE caches locally. Figure 8.9 shows the architecture.

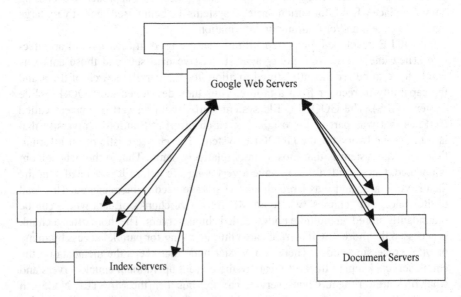

**Fig. 8.9** Google architecture

Creating applications that can execute on a distributed architecture could also be a difficult task. That is because the applications need to be easy to be replicated to multiple servers for processing and then have a mechanism to collect the results from the individual instances and consolidate them into a single answer. Google developed a programming model that allows for simple creation and execution of applications in a distributed environment against large data sets. The model is called MapReduce. The programmer first defines a "map" application that will work against a key/value pair and will generate an intermediate key/value pairs as output. Then there is a "reduce" function that takes all of the intermediate values associated with the same intermediate key and merges them. This architecture was based upon and an enhancement of the map and reduce primitives in the LISP language and other functional languages. Programs written using this model can easily and automatically be distributed across a large cluster of servers. This model also allows for easy re-execution if a particular server fails.

The architecture concepts of General file System (BigTables) and MapReduce were implemented in a Java software framework called Hadoop. It allows applications to be developed that can be executed as a distributed application on thousands of nodes and pedabytes of data. It is an Apache project (*hadoop.apache.org*) that is developed and being used by many contributors including Yahoo that uses it extensively in their system. The framework was initially developed by Doug Cutting who got the name from his child's stuffed elephant.

## 8.4  Summary

Text search techniques using text scanning have played an important role in the initial development of Information Retrieval Systems. In the 1970s and 1980s they were essential tools for compensating for the insufficient computer power and for handling some of the more difficult search capabilities such as imbedded character strings and fuzzy searches. They currently play an important role in word processor systems (e.g., the Find function) and in Information Retrieval Systems for locating offensive terms (e.g., imbedded character strings) in the dictionary. The need for specialized hardware text search units to directly search the data on secondary storage has diminished with the growth of processing power of computers.

With the significant decrease in costs of computers and the introduction of using large numbers (in the hundreds of thousands) of inexpensive appliance processors to execute searches against very large databases in the terabytes and pedabytes ranges, the need for hardware solution has given way to scalable software solutions. But even in the scalable domain when the system is exposed to the Internet with thousands of searches per second, massive parallelism still has a high cost. Thus optimization techniques to reduce the resources need to complete any query still is needed. Leveraging off the fact that only a very small subset of hit items are ever viewed and those are just the top hit items, redesign of inversion lists can significantly reduce the resources to provide the user with the initial hit list.

## 8.5   Exercises

1. Trade off the use of hardware versus software text search algorithms citing advantages and disadvantages of each in comparison to the other.
2. Construct finite state automata for each of the following set of terms:

   a. BIT, FIT, HIT, MIT, PIT, SIT
   b. CAN, CAR, CARPET, CASE, CASK, CAKE
   c. HE, SHE, HER, HERE, THERE, SHEAR

   Be sure to define the three sets I, S, and P along with providing the state drawing (e.g., see Fig. 8.2).
3. Use the Boyer-Moore text search algorithm to search for the term FANCY in the text string FANCIFUL FANNY FRUIT FILLED MY FANCY.

   a. Show all of the steps and explain each of the required character shifts.
   b. How many character comparisons are required to obtain a match?
   c. Compare this to what it would take using the Knuth-Pratt-Morris algorithm (you do not have to show the work for the KMP algorithm).

# Chapter 9
# Information System Evaluation

## 9.1 Introduction to Information System Evaluation

Interest in the evaluation techniques for Information Retrieval Systems has significantly increased with the commercial use of information retrieval technologies in the everyday life of the millions of users of the Internet. Until 1993 the evaluations were done primarily by academicians using a few small, well known corpora of test documents or even smaller test databases created within academia. The Cranfield model created at the Cranfield Institute for Information Retrieval Evaluation was one of the earliest structured approaches to evaluating information retrieval and still continues in TREC and other evaluation platforms. This model incorporates a test collection of documents, a set of test queries and, for each query, a set of judgments about whether each document in the collection is relevant or not relevant to that query. The evaluations focused primarily on the effectiveness of search algorithms. The Cranfield test collection (see below description of the data set) was one of the primary evaluative data sets until TREC.

The next major improvement in information retrieval evaluation started with the creation of the annual Text Retrieval Evaluation Conference (TREC) sponsored by the Defense Advanced Research Projects Agency (DARPA) and the National Institute of Standards and Technology (NIST) which changed the standard process of evaluating information systems. TREC conferences have been held every year, starting from 1992, usually in the Fall months. The conference provides multiple ground truth databases consisting of gigabytes of test data, search statements and the expected results from the searches to academic researchers and commercial companies for testing of their systems. This has placed a standard baseline into comparisons of algorithms. Although there is now a standard database, there is still debate on the accuracy and utility of the results from use of the test corpus. In the last few years new organizations in Europe and the Far East have been created leveraging off the techniques created by TREC to sponsor their own focused conferences to evaluate the technologies they consider of prime importance. Many of the test datasets are now commercially available so that anyone can acquire them and use them in evaluating new algorithms and products they are creating.

G. Kowalski, *Information Retrieval Architecture and Algorithms,*
DOI 10.1007/978-1-4419-7716-8_9, © Springer Science+Business Media, LLC 2011

In recent years the evaluation of Information Retrieval Systems and techniques for indexing, sorting, searching and retrieving information have become increasingly important. This growth in interest is due to two major reasons: the growing number of retrieval systems being used and additional focus on evaluation methods themselves. The Internet is an example of an information space (infospace) whose text content is growing exponentially along with products to find information of value. Information retrieval technologies are the basis behind the search of information on the Internet. In parallel with the commercial interest, the introduction of a large standardized test databases and a forum for yearly analysis via TREC and other conferences has provided a methodology for evaluating the performance of algorithms and systems. There are many reasons to evaluate the effectiveness of an Information Retrieval System:

- To aid in the selection of a system to procure
- To monitor and evaluate system effectiveness
- To evaluate the system to determine improvements
- To provide inputs to cost-benefit analysis of an information system
- To determine the effects of changes made to an existing information system.

From an academic perspective, measurements are focused on the specific effectiveness of a system and usually are applied to determining the effects of changing a system's algorithms or in comparing algorithms among systems. When evaluating systems for commercial use measurements are also focused on availability and reliability. In an operational system there is less concern over 55% versus 65% precision than 99% versus 89% availability. For academic purposes, controlled environments can be created that minimize errors in data. In operational systems, there is no control over the users and care must be taken to ensure the data collected are meaningful.

The most important evaluation metrics of information systems (i.e., precision and recall) will always be biased by human subjectivity. This problem arises from the specific data collected to measure the user resources in locating relevant information. Metrics to accurately measure user resources expended in information retrieval are inherently inaccurate. A factor in most metrics in determining how well a system is working is the relevancy of items. Relevancy of an item, however, is not a binary evaluation, but a continuous function between an item's being exactly what is being looked for and it being totally unrelated. It is the middle area rather than the two extremes where disagreement between users on an items relevancy occurs. To discuss relevancy, it is necessary to define the context under which the concept is used. From a human judgment standpoint, relevancy can be considered:

Subjective     depends upon a specific user's judgment
Situational    relates to a user's requirements
Cognitive      depends on human perception and behavior
Temporal       changes over time
Measurable     observable at a points in time

The subjective nature of relevance judgments has been documented by Saracevic and was shown in TREC-experiments (Harman-95, Saracevic-91). In TREC-2 and

TREC-3, two or three different users were given the same search statement and the same set of possible hits to judge as relevant or not. In general, there was a unanimous agreement on 70–80% of the items judged by the human. Even in this environment (i.e., where the judges are not the creators of the query and are making every effort to be unbiased) there is still significant subjective disagreement on the relevancy of some of the items. In an operational environment, each user has his own understanding of the requirement and the threshold on what is acceptable. Based upon his cognitive model of the information space and the problem, the user judges a particular item. Some users consider information they already know to be non-relevant to their information need. For example, a user being presented with an article that the user wrote does not provide "new" relevant information to answer the user's query, although the article may be very relevant to the search statement. Also the judgment of relevance can vary over time. Retrieving information on an "XT" class of PCs is not of significant relevance to personal computers in 2010, but would have been valuable in 1992. Thus, relevance judgment is measurable at a point in time constrained by the particular users and their thresholds on acceptability of information.

Another way of specifying relevance is from information, system and situational views. The information view is subjective in nature and pertains to human judgment of the conceptual relatedness between an item and the search. It involves the user's personal judgment of the relevancy (aboutness) of the item to the user's information need. When reference experts (librarians, researchers, subject specialists, indexers) assist the user, it is assumed they can reasonably predict whether certain information will satisfy the user's needs. Ingwersen categorizes the information view into four types of "aboutness" (Ingwersen-92):

| | |
|---|---|
| Author Aboutness | determined by the author's language as matched by the system in natural language retrieval |
| Indexer Aboutness | determined by the indexer's transformation of the author's natural language into a controlled vocabulary they use to index the document |
| Request Aboutness | determined by the user's or intermediary's processing of a search statement into a query |
| User Aboutness | determined by the indexer's attempt to represent the document according to presupposition about what the user will want to know |

Thus the information view suggests how the relevancy of an item is determined can be from the perspective of the creator (author) of an item and the vocabulary and concepts they use in the original writing of an item, from an professional indexer (or automated indexing process) and how it maps what the author wrote to the searchable terms extracted from the items, from the specific information need specified at retrieval time thus limited to how that information need is specified, or from what the user really wants not constrained by how they expressed it in their information need statement.

The system view is more technical in nature and ignores the subtle definition of relevance and looks only at the match between query terms and words within an item. It can be objectively observed, manipulated and tested without relying on human judgment because it uses metrics associated with the matching of the query to the item. The semantic relatedness between queries and items is assumed to be inherited via the index terms that represent the semantic content of the item in a consistent and accurate fashion. Other aspects of the system view are presented in Sect. 9.2.

The situation view pertains to the relationship between information and the user's information problem situation. It assumes that only users can make valid judgments regarding the suitability of information to solve their information need. The information and situation views are refered to as relevance and pertinence respectively. Pertinence can be defined as those items that satisfy the user's information need at the time of retrieval. The TREC-evaluation process uses relevance versus pertinence as its criteria for judging items because pertinence is too variable to attempt to measure in meaningful items (i.e., it depends on each situation).

Although relevancy is the central metric to evaluate a system upon, it is also the least specific to determine. Relevancy can only be defined in the terms of human judgment. That is why in the evaluation process an "information need" is specified rather than a specific search statement. This allows the required human evaluators to have a conceptual basis to do their relevancy judgments. No two users will read the same information need statement and end up coming to the same decisions on relevancy of the items they look at. And yet the goal of an information system is to satisfy the user and thus needs to be judged on what the user considers is correct. But even though there is no one correct answer to what items satisfy an information need, most users will agree on 70–80% of the items that are relevant and most of the items that are not relevant. Although not perfect this level agreement is sufficient for the purpose of evaluating information systems. In general the evaluation is either to compare how different systems work or the impact of an improvement to a specific system. The relevancy judgments will in general not impact the final tradeoff comparison since they will affect all the systems equally.

It's possible to measure the amount of agreement (or disagreement) between users on relevancy using a mathematical technique called Cohen's Kappa coefficient. It's a statistical measure of inter-evaluator agreement. It takes into consideration the probability there is agreement because of chance as well as agreement because the raters came to the same conclusion. Some researchers believe that the assumptions in the Kappa coefficient produce an overly conservative result. The measure is of the agreement between two evaluators who each classify N items into C mutually exclusive categories. In this case there will be N items placed in one of 2 categories (relevant or non-relevant). The formula is:

$$\kappa = \frac{\Pr(a) - \Pr(e)}{1 - \Pr(e)}$$

In this formula Pr(a) is the observed agreement between evaluators and PR(e) is the hypothetical probability of chance agreement. Kappa will take a value between

0 and 1 where 1 means there is total agreement and zero means there is no agreement. Pr(a) is known for any judging by comparing the results list. If you take the position that the probability of chance agreement is purely random then Pr(e) will be 0.5 (50%). But it really is not purely chance because the evaluators are working from the same information need statement. Thus some form of a marginal statistic is used to determine Pr(e). Typically a Kappa value between 0.4 and 0.6 is considered moderate agreement and 0.6–0.8 is substantial agreement. Above 0.8 is almost perfect agreement. Typically evaluations from TREC type conferences with full time evaluators is within the moderate range tending towards the 0.8 value.

The process of evaluating an information retrieval system starts with a collection of items, the information retrieval capability(s) and a "ground truth" data set satisfying a number of information needs. The ground truth data set is the set of relevant items that should be found based upon the information need. The expense and challenge is in determining this set. In some cases two sets of known relevant items are needed. The second set is needed as a training set when a categorization system is being evaluated. The training set must be representative and it is used to train the categorization algorithm. Then the evaluation is run against the ground truth test data set. Techniques are discussed in Sect. 9.2. An information need is used rather than a query because a query is too constraining and there are many ways of developing a query based upon a particular information system characteristics to find items on the information need. One thing that has been shown is that the evaluation results are very query specific. Thus around 50 different information needs are needed to ensure that the results are not biased by the search set. A lot of evaluation is needed to develop the relevant items for each of the 50 information needs. There are a number of existing data sets with queries and ground truth already defined for them. The largest are the data sets from the TREC. The following is a list of some of the more major test data sets available. There are always more being developed, quite often focused on a particular information retrieval problem.

- Cranfield collection: Is one of the oldest collections that were manually generated in the late 1950s. It contains 1,398 abstracts of aerodynamics journal articles and a set of 255 queries and relevance judgments across the complete database.
- Text Retrieval Conference (TREC) has many different data sets developed by the National Institute of Standards and Technology (NIST) over the 17 years the conference has been running. The most used data sets are for the ad hoc search tracks of TREC 1 to TREC 8. The total of the data sets and evaluations is 1.9 million items typically from news media and 450 information needs (the concept of information needs) was formalized in the TREC conferences. Within this total set the latest subset of 528,000 news items and 50 information needs is the most highly used. TREC developed the technique of determining the set of relevant items by reviewing the top 100 items from each system and evaluating them. Thus the relevant ground truth is not against the entire database.

  - TREC wanted to evaluate search against large data sets (e.g., trying to relate closer to the Internet) and thus developed a collection of 25 million web pages (GOV2 dataset). This is one of the largest datasets that is available for use.

- NII Test Collection for IR Systems (NTCIR)—is a set of test databases based upon the TREC model but for the East Asian languages and focuses on cross language information retrieval. Their web site summarizes data available and conferences (http://research.nii.ac.jp/ntcir/data/data-en.html)
- FIRE—Forum for Information Retrieval Evaluation—is focused on the Indian subcontinent (i.e., Pakistan, Bangladesh, Nepal, Sri Lanka, Bhutan and India). It has the major languages such as Hindi and Bengali that are among the top ten most-spoken languages of the world. A large volume of Indian/language electronic documents are coming into existence. The Forum for Information Retrieval Evaluation (FIRE) is using a test corpus and evaluation forum for the languages of this area.
- Cross Language Evaluation Forum (CLEF)—concentrates on European languages and information retrieval issues that they are interested in. To get to their web site for the latest evaluations and data sets go to: http://clef-campaign.org/ One of the areas that CLEF is pursuing is XML search. The have a test collection (consisting of 12,000 XML documents with about 500 MB of data).
- Reuters—developed the best test data sets for classification (categorization) information retrieval techniques. The data was originally collected and labeled by Carnegie Group, Inc. and Reuters, Ltd. in the course of developing the CONSTRUE text categorization system. In 2000, Reuters Ltd. made available a large collection of Reuters News stories for use in research and development of natural language processing, information retrieval, and machine learning systems. This corpus, known as "Reuters Corpus, Volume 1" or RCV1, is significantly larger than the older, well-known Reuters-21578 collection heavily used in the text classification community. The newer data available is:
- Reuters Corpus, Volume 1, English language, 1996-08-20 to 1997-08-19. This is distributed on two CDs and contains about 810,000 Reuters, English Language News stories. It requires about 2.5 GB for storage of the uncompressed files.
- In addition because of interest in non-English Corpus and there is a database (RCV-2) of non-English Language News stories covering the period 20 August 1996–19 August 1997. This is distributed on one CD and contains over 487,000 Reuters News stories in thirteen languages (Dutch, French, German, Chinese, Japanese, Russian, Portuguese, Spanish, Latin American Spanish, Italian, Danish, Norwegian, and Swedish). These stories are contemporaneous with RCV1, but some languages do not cover the entire time period.
- In Fall of 2004, NIST took over distribution of RCV1 and any future Reuters Corpora. You can now get these datasets by sending a request to NIST.
- Newsgroup—The 20 Newsgroups data set is a collection of approximately 20,000 newsgroup documents, partitioned across 20 different newsgroups. Each newsgroup corresponds to a different category.
- Linguistic Data Consortium (LDC)—(http://www.ldc.upenn.edu/). The Linguistic Data Consortium is an open consortium of universities, companies and government research laboratories. It creates, collects and distributes speech and text databases, lexicons, and other resources for research and development purposes. The University of Pennsylvania is the LDC's host institution. The LDC

was founded in 1992 with a grant from the Advanced Research Projects Agency (ARPA), and is partly supported by grant IRI-9528587 from the Information and Intelligent Systems division of the National Science Foundation. It has many different documented data sets in speech to text and other areas that can be used in testing new technologies.

## 9.2 Measures Used in System Evaluations

To define the measures that can be used in evaluating Information Retrieval Systems, it is useful to define the major functions associated with identifying relevant items in an information system (see Fig. 9.1). Items arrive in the system and are automatically or manually transformed by "indexing" into searchable data structures. The user determines what his information need is and creates a search statement. The system processes the search statement, returning potential hits. The user selects those hits to review and retrieves the item. The item is reviewed to see if it has any needed information.

Measurements can be made on each step in this process. Measurements can be made from two perspectives: user perspective and system perspective. The user perspective was described in Sect. 9.1. The Author's Aboutness occurs as part of the system executing the query against the index. The Indexer Aboutness and User

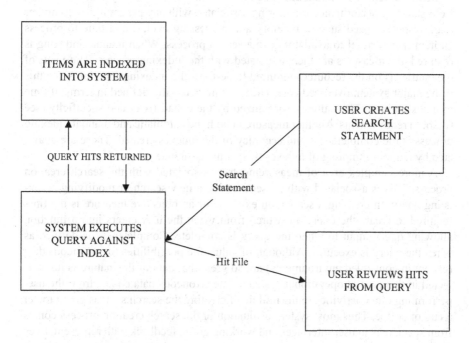

**Fig. 9.1** Identifying relevant items

Aboutness occur when the items are indexed into items are indexed into the system. The Request Aboutness occurs when the user creates the search statement. The ambiguities in the definition of what is relevant occur when the user is reviewing the hits from the query.

Typically, the system perspective is based upon aggregate functions, whereas the user perspective takes a more localized personal view. If a user's PC is not connecting to the system, then, from that user's view the system is not operational. From the system operations perspective, one user not having access out of 1,000 users still results in a 99.9% availability rate. Another example of how averaging distorts communications between the system and user perspective is the case where there are 150 students taking six courses. Assume there are 5 students in three of the courses and 45 students in the other three courses. From the system perspective there is an average of 25 students per instructor/course. For 10% of the students (15 students) there is a really good ratio of 10 students per instructor. But, 90% of the users (215 students) have a ratio of 45 students to one instructor. Thus most of the users may complain of the poor ratio (45 to one instructor) to a system person who claims it is really good (average of 25 to one instructor). Thus use of aggregate functions is useful but the technical person needs to be sure to place them in context of the user's perspective.

Techniques for collecting measurements can also be objective or subjective. An objective measure is one that is well-defined and based upon numeric values derived from the system operation. A subjective measure can produce a number, but is based upon an individual user's judgment.

Measurements with automatic indexing of items arriving at a system are derived from standard performance monitoring associated with any program in a computer (e.g., resources used such as memory and processing cycles) and time to process an item from arrival to availability to a search process. When manual indexing is required, the measures are then associated with the indexing process. The focus of the metrics is on the resources required to perform the indexing function since this is the major system overhead cost. The measure is usually defined in terms of time to index an item. The value is normalized by the exhaustivity and specificity (see Chap. 4) requirements. Another measure in both the automatic and manual indexing process is the completeness and accuracy of the indexes created. These are evaluated by random sampling of indexes by quality assurance personnel.

A more complex area of measurements is associated with the search creation process. This is associated with a user creating a new search or modifying an existing query. In creating a search, an example of an objective measure is the time required to create the query, measured from when the user enters into a function allowing query input to when the query is complete. Completeness is defined as when the query is executed. Although of value, the possibilities for erroneous data (except in controlled environments) are so great that data of this nature is not collected in this area in operational systems. The erroneous data comes from the user performing other activities in the middle of creating the search such as going to get a cup of coffee. Thus most system evaluation of the search creation process comes from specialists in user interfaces and working group feedback with representatives from the user population.

Response time is a metric frequently collected to determine the efficiency of the search execution. Response time is defined as the time it takes to execute the search. The ambiguity in response time originates from the possible definitions of the end time of a search. The beginning is always correlated to when the user tells the system to begin searching. The end time is affected by the difference between the user's view and a system view. From a user's perspective, a search could be considered complete when the first result is available for the user to review, especially if the system continues to have new items available whenever a user needs to see the next item. Thus from the user perspective the search is complete when the first display page of hits is shown. From a system perspective, system resources are being used until the search has determined all hits. To ensure consistency, response time is usually associated with the completion of the search. This is one of the most important measurements in a production system. Determining how well a system is working answers the typical concern of a user: "the system is working slow today."

It is difficult to define objective measures on the process of a user selecting hits for review and reviewing them. The problems associated with search creation apply to reviewing the results of a search. Using time as a metric does not account for reading and cognitive skills of the user along with the user performing other activities during the review process. Data are usually gathered on the search creation and Hit file review process by subjective techniques, such as questionnaires to evaluate system effectiveness.

In addition to efficiency of the search process discussed above, the most important evaluation factor is the quality of the search results which can be measured typically by precision and recall. Precision is a measure of the accuracy of the search process. It directly evaluates the correlation of the query to the database and indirectly is a measure of the completeness of the indexing algorithm. If the indexing algorithm tends to generalize by having a high threshold on the index term selection process or by using concept indexing, then precision is lower, no matter how accurate the similarity algorithm between query and index. Recall is a measure of the ability of the search to find all of the relevant items that are in the database. The following are the formulas for precision and recall:

$$Precision = \frac{Number\_Retrieved\_Relevant}{Number\_Total\_Retrieved}$$

$$Recall = \frac{Number\_Retrieved\_Relevant}{Number\_Possible\_Relevant}$$

where *Number_Possible_Relevant* is the number of relevant items in the database, *Number_Retrieved_Relevant* is the number of relevant items in the Hit file, and *Number_Total_Retrieved* is the total number of items in the Hit File. In controlled environments it is possible to get values for both of these measures and relate them to each other. Two of the values in the formulas, *Number_Retrieved_Relevant* and *Number_Total_Retrieved,* are always available. *Number_Possible-Relevant* poses a problem in uncontrolled environments because it suggests that all relevant items in the database are known. This was possible to manually determine with very small databases in some of the early experiments in information systems. To gain the insights associated with testing a search against a large database with millions of items makes collection of this data almost impossible. Two approaches have been suggested to estimate the total number of relevant items in a test data set. The first is to use a sampling technique across the database performing relevance judgments on the returned items. This would form the basis for an estimate of the total relevant items in the database (Gilbert-79). Using this approach a total number of relevant documents estimate is determined that is associated with the complete database being searched. This technique calculates an estimate of the number of relevant items but it does not determine what they are. Thus the denominator number is available but a human has to evaluate the returned results to determine which ones are relevant to figure out precision and recall.

The other technique is applicable when there are different search strategies to the same database for the same query. This is the case where you are testing multiple technologies in a conference situation such as TREC. An assumption is then made that an estimate of all the relevant items for evaluation purposes between the different search technologies can be defined as the summation of all of the relevant items returned by all of the search systems in the evaluation (Sparck Jones-75). In other words, the search results from all of the different search systems are placed in an aggregate set and the number of relevant items in that combined set of items is defined as the total relevant items in the data set for that query. Since ranking is part of the search approach—the most likely location for relevant items should be nearer the top of the ranked returned results. Thus the technique is to take the top "n" items from each search system and merge them. The majority of the hits are found across the results. This significantly reduces the number of items that need manual review for relevancy. At first TREC started with 150 items from each search system but then they dropped back to 100 not seeing that many more unique relevant items being found by using the larger data set. Each item in the aggregate list is reviewed by a human against the information need statement and is classified as either relevant or not relevant. Since the process provides a detailed list of items that are relevant, it is possible to use that list to evaluate the detailed performance of each search system. In this controlled environment it is possible to create Precision/Recall graphs by reviewing the Hit file in ranked order and recording the changes in precision and recall as each item is judged.

In an operational system it is unrealistic to calculate recall because there is no reasonable approach to determine *Number_Possible_Relevant*. It is possible, however to calculate precision values associated with queries, assuming the user provides relevance judgments. There is a pragmatic modification that is required to the precision formula denominator factor of *Number_Total_Retrieved*. The user cannot be forced to review all of the items in the Hit file. Thus, there is a likely possibility that there will be items found by the query that are not retrieved for review because the user stops review part way into the hit file. The adjustment to account for this operational scenario is to redefine the denominator to *Number_Total_Reviewed* versus *Number_Total_Retrieved*. Under this condition the Precision factor becomes the precision associated with satisfying the user's information need versus the precision of the query. If reviewing three relevant items satisfies the user's objective in the search, additional relevant items in a Hit file do not contribute to the objective of the information system. Thus precision can be defined as the total number of items the user looks at in order to find the number of relevant items the user needs. The other factor that needs to be accounted for is the user not reviewing items in the Hit file because the summary information in the status display is sufficient to judge the item is not likely to be relevant. Under this definition, precision is a more accurate measure of the use of the user's time. Any item in the hit list the user does not open for review has to be assumed to be non-relevant.

Precision recall graphs can be produced based upon the precision and recall values determined at specific hit file sizes (for example calculate precision and recall based upon the top 10 items, top 20 items, up to the top 100 items). The result is a very saw tooth looking graph. The graph can be made smoother by using interpolated precision. Recall can only increase as you retrieve more items as each point is determined in the graph (recall is only dependent upon the number of relevant items and will be either the same or higher as you retrieve more items). But precision can change in either direction being sensitive to the ratio of relevant and non-relevant items. Interpolated precision is where at each recall point in generating the graph the "highest" precision value at that point or any future point is selected for the precision at that point. The rationale is that is the precision goes up at a future point and the recall will also be going up that the user is interested in that point. Using this strategy, the precision value can only be either staying the same or decreasing as you look at future points in the graph. This eliminates the saw tooth nature and makes a more continuous looking graph that will go from the top right part of the graph to the bottom left in a decreasing plot.

In evaluating multiple systems it is difficult to compare how each does by trying to compare their precision/recall graphs. It is desirable to calculate a single value that can be used in comparing systems at recall levels. The value typically used is the F-measure which trades off precision versus recall and is adjustable. It calculates the weighted harmonic mean of the precision and recall:

$$F = \frac{1}{\alpha\frac{1}{p} + (1-\alpha)\frac{1}{r}} = \frac{(\beta^2+1)p*r}{C*p+r} \quad \text{where } \beta^2 = \frac{1-\alpha}{\alpha}$$

Where $\alpha$ is a value between 0 and 1. The standard F measure weights precision and recall equally and thus $\alpha = 1/2$ or $\beta = 1$. The typical formula for an F measure in information retrieval is:

$$F_1 = \frac{2*p*r}{p+r}$$

If it is desired to place more weight on precision then a value of $\beta < 1$ would be used. If the emphasis is on recall then a value of $\beta > 1$ is used. The harmonic mean is used instead of an arithmetic mean because recall is insensitive to the number of non-relevant items retrieved. Thus if you retrieved all of the items in the database the arithmetic mean would be 1/2 because you would have a value of 0 for precision and a value of 1 for recall. Let's use an example of a database with 2 relevant items and 100,000 total items. If all of the items were retrieved using the harmonic formula above the F score (measure) would be:

$$F_1 = \frac{2 * (2/100000) * (2/2)}{2/100000 + (2/2)} \approx 0.00004 \text{ or } 0.004\%$$

The F-score is far more representative of the effect of large retrievals and how it would be considered negative from a user's perspective. The harmonic mean tends to be closer to the smaller number when two numbers vary by a lot.

Although precision and recall formed the initial basis for measuring the effectiveness of information systems, they encounter mathematical ambiguities and a lack of parallelism between their properties (Salton-83). In particular, what is the value of recall if there are no relevant items in the database or recall if no items are retrieved (Fairthorne-64, Robertson-69)? In both cases the mathematical formula becomes 0/0. The lack of parallelism comes from the intuitiveness that finding more relevant items should increase retrieval effectiveness measures and decrease with retrieval of non-relevant items. Recall is unaffected when non-relevant items are retrieved. Another measure that is directly related to retrieving non-relevant items can be used in defining how effective an information system is operating. This measure is called Fallout and defined as (Salton-83):

$$Fallout = \frac{Number\_Retrieved\_Nonrelevant}{Number\_Total\_Nonrelevant}$$

where *Number_Total_Nonrelevant* is the total number of non-relevant items in the database. Fallout can be viewed as the inverse of recall and will never encounter the situation of 0/0 unless all the items in the database are relevant to the search. It can be viewed as the probability that a retrieved item is non-relevant. Recall can be viewed as the probability that a retrieved item is relevant. From a system perspective, the ideal system demonstrates maximum recall and minimum fallout. This combination implicitly has maximum precision. Of the three measures (precision, recall and fallout), fallout is least sensitive to the accuracy of the search process. The large value for the denominator requires significant changes in the number of retrieved items to affect the current value. Examples of precision, fallout and recall values for systems tested in TREC-4 are given in Sect. 9.3.

Another measure that seems to reflect how a particular search will perform across different databases and can be used for comparisons is the Mean Average precision (MAP). The MAP provides a single value estimate across all recall levels for a query averaged across all queries. It basically is applied to the top "n" items from a retrieved list. It only looks at the precision values for relevant items as they are found in the hit list. The non-relevant items are assumed to have a value of zero. The formula is:

$$MAP(Q_n) = \frac{1}{|Q_n|} \sum_{j=1}^{|Q_n|} \frac{1}{m_j} \sum_{k=1}^{m_j} P(I_{j,k})$$

Where $n$ is the number of queries in the $Q_n$ set of results. The $m_j$ is the number of relevant items for query $Q_j$ in the top items being retrieved. $P(I_{j,k})$ is the precision at the point for query $j$ when relevant item $k$ is found (the value is zero when the item is not relevant and does not effect the average). Since it is the average of all of the queries each query is weighted the same (although some queries—information needs are better than others). Different sets of queries produce significantly different MAP scores against a database. But the same set of queries tends to produce the same MAP scores no matter what database they run against.

There are other measures of search capabilities that have been proposed. A new measure that provides additional insight in comparing systems or algorithms is the "Unique Relevance Recall" (URR) metric. URR is used to compare more two or more algorithms or systems. It measures the number of relevant items that are retrieved by one algorithm that are not retrieved by the others:

$$\text{Unique\_Relevance\_Recall} = \frac{Number\_unique\_relevant}{Number\_relevant}$$

*Number_unique_relevant* is the number of relevant items retrieved that were not retrieved by other algorithms. When many algorithms are being compared, the definition of *uniquely* found items for a particular system can be modified, allowing a small number of other systems to also find the same item and still be considered unique. This is accomplished by defining a percentage ($P_u$) of the total number of systems that can find an item and still consider it unique. *Number_relevant* can take on two different values based upon the objective of the evaluation.

Using TNRR as the denominator provides a measure for an algorithm of the percent of the total items that were found that are unique and found by that algorithm. It is a measure of the contribution of uniqueness to the total relevant items that the algorithm provides. Using the second measure, TURR, as the denominator, provides a measure of the percent of total unique items that could be found that are actually found by the algorithm. Figure 9.2a, b provide an example of the overlap of relevant items assuming there are four different algorithms. Figure 9.2a gives the number of items in each area of the overlap diagram in Fig. 9.2b. If a relevant item is found by only one or two techniques as a "unique item," then from the diagram the following values URR values can be produced:

| Algorithm I | 6 unique items (areas A, C, E) |
| Algorithm II | 16 unique items (areas B, C, J) |
| Algorithm III | 29 unique items (areas E, H, L) |
| Algorithm IV | 31 unique items (areas J, L, M) |

$$\text{TNRR} = A + B + C + \cdots + M = 985$$

$$\text{TURR} = A + B + C + E + H + J + L + M = 61$$

| Algorithm | URR$_{TURR}$ | URR$_{TNRR}$ |
|---|---|---|
| Algorithm I | 6/985=0.0061 | 6/61=0.098 |
| Algorithm II | 16/985=0.0162 | 16/61=0.262 |
| Algorithm III | 29/985=0.0294 | 29/61=0.475 |
| Algorithm IV | 31/985=0.0315 | 31/61=0.508 |

VALUE                               INTERPRETATION

Total Number Retrieved            the total number of relevant items found by all
Relevant (TNRR)                   algorithms

Total Unique Relevant             the total number of unique items found by all
Retrieved (TURR)                   the algorithms

| A | B | C | D | E | F | G | H | I | J | K | L | M |
|---|---|---|---|---|---|---|---|---|---|---|---|---|
| 3 | 4 | 2 | 22 | 1 | 100 | 200 | 22 | 100 | 10 | 500 | 6 | 15 |

**a**

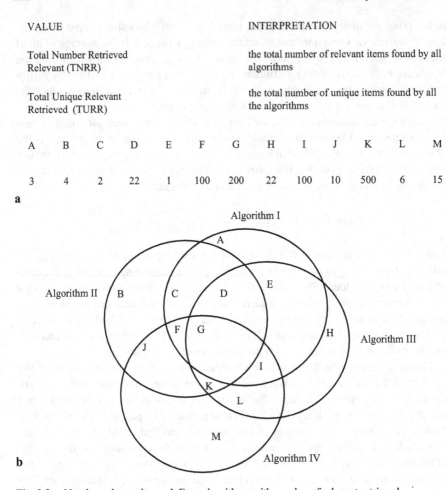

**b**

**Fig. 9.2 a** Number relevant items. **b** Four algorithms with overlap of relevant retrieved

The URR value is used in conjunction with Precision, Recall and Fallout to determine the total effectiveness of an algorithm compared to other algorithms. The $URR_{TNRR}$ value indicates what portion of all unique items retrieved by all of the algorithms was retrieved by a specific algorithm. The $URR_{TURR}$ value indicates the portion of possible unique items that a particular algorithm found. In the example, Algorithm IV found 50% of all unique items found across all the algorithms. The results indicate that if a user wanted to increase my recall by running two algorithms, the user would choose algorithm III or IV in addition to the algorithm with the highest recall value. Like Precision, URR can be calculated since it is based upon the results of retrieval versus results based upon the complete database. It assists in determining the utility of using multiple search algorithms to improve overall system performance.

When evaluating technologies where the users are not interested in high recall but are more interested in getting sufficient information to take action on (e.g., searches on the Web) what matters is the precision and recall on the top of the returned hit list. The average precision and other current evaluation measures are not robust to incomplete relevance judgments. There is a measure that is better when there is incomplete relevance information. The approach looks at evaluating a system on only the judged items. The evaluations discussed so far assume an estimate of the total number of relevant items is available to calculate the recall value. The preference measure that they proposed is a function of the number of times judged non-relevant items are retrieved before relevant items. It is called bpref because it uses binary relevance judgments to define the preference relation. Binary relevance judgments obtain a large set of preferences since the number of non-relevant judgments plus the number (N) of relevant judgments (R) yield N*R preferences. Since the bpref measure could be sensitive to the absolute number of nonrelevant items the measure uses the number of non-relevant between relevant items as a basis. Bpref is a function of how frequently relevant items are retrieved before non-relevant items:

$$\text{Bpref} = \frac{1}{R} \sum_r 1 - \frac{|n_r|}{R}$$

Where R is the first R items judged as relevant so far and $r$ is the number of relevant items. The factor $n_r$ is the number of non-relevant items prior to the current relevant item from the start of the hit file. Non-judged items are not counted. As an example assume there are 12 items with 4 relevant its. The user has reviewed the first 9 items of which 2 items were not judged and D2, D5 and D9 are relevant:

D1
D2 relevant
D3 unjudged
D4
D5 relevant
D6
D7 unjudged
D8
<u>D9 relevant</u>
D10

$$\text{Bpref} = 1/3 \left[ (1 - 1/3) + (1 - 2/3) + (1 - 4/3) \right]$$

If the number of relevant items is very small there can be only one or two factors in the formula. To compensate for this condition they proposed adding an additional constant of 10 in the denominator and called the formula bpref-10.

Another approach to evaluating information retrieval systems eliminates the need for evaluators to judge the results and thus can be automated. In this case a number of known relevant items are introduced into the database. The measure that can be used in this scenario is called R-precision. The number of relevant items introduce is R and is known ahead of time. The top R items are reviewed. If there are $r$ relevant items in the top R items in the hit file then both the precision and recall both equal $r/R$. In a perfect system both will equal 1. R-precision is a single number on the precision recall curve. It has been shown to correlate well with the MAP measure.

Another measure that is oriented towards user satisfaction is the discounted cumulative gain (DCG). The measure looks at the position in the hit list for relevant items knowing the higher on the list the more valuable it is to the user. This is especially true for the internet where users only look at the first few pages of the hit list. The gain starts with higher values if the item is near the top of the hit list and decreases as you go down the hit list. The discounted cumulative gain is a modification of the earlier cumulative gain (CG) measure:

$$CG_l = \sum_{i=1}^{l} rel_i$$

Where $l$ is a rank position in the list $rel_i$ is the relevance at position $i$. But shifting the ordering of the items does not effect their relevance and thus not the CG value as long as they remain in the $l$ items. Position does not matter. The discounted cumulative gain where the position (i) is a factor is:

$$DCG_l = \sum_{i=1}^{l} \frac{2^{rel_i} - 1}{\log_2(1 + i)}$$

But this is affected by different length hit lists based upon different searches. To normalize the value across queries a normalizing factor is calculated by sorting the items by relevance which will produce the best DCG for an $l$. The DCG is divided by this ideal DCG value. This is also referred to as the Normalized discounted cumulative gain.

Other measures have been proposed for judging the results of searches (Keen-71, Salton-83):

Novelty Ratio:     ratio of relevant and not known to the user to total relevant retrieved
Coverage Ratio:    ratio of relevant items retrieved to total relevant by the user before the search
Sought Recall:     ratio of the total relevant reviewed by the user after the search to the total relevant the user would have liked to examine

In some systems, programs filter text streams, software categorizes data or intelligent agents alert users if important items are found. In these systems, the Information Retrieval System makes decisions without any human input and their decisions are binary in nature (an item is acted upon or ignored). These systems are called binary classification systems for which effectiveness measurements are created to determine how algorithms are working. One measure is the utility measure that can be defined as:

$$U = \alpha * (Relevant\_Retrieved) + \beta * (Non\text{-}Relevant\_Not\ Retrieved)$$

$$- \delta * (Non\text{-}Relevant\_\ Retrieved\ ) - \gamma * (Relevant\_Not\ Retrieved)$$

where $\alpha$ and $\beta$ are positive weighting factors the user places on retrieving relevant items and not retrieving non-relevant items while $\delta$ and $\gamma$ are factors associated with the negative weight of not retrieving relevant items or retrieving non-relevant items. This formula can be simplified to account only for retrieved items with $\beta$ and $\gamma$ equal to zero (Lewis-96). Another family of effectiveness measures called the E-measure that combines recall and precision into a single score was proposed by Van Rijsbergen (Rijsbergen-79).

## 9.3 Multimedia Information Retrieval Evaluation

There are some efforts at establishing ground truth and evaluation of multimedia search systems. But the difficulties of establishing a ground truth evaluation set for multimedia evaluations is significantly more difficult then establishing ground truth for textual systems in that it requires a lot more manual review of the multimedia to define the expected results where automated techniques were found to assist in reducing the amount of data to be reviewed and its focus for text.

Some of the earliest efforts for multimedia were not focused on the search of the multimedia as much as the conversion of the multimedia to a textual form (where possible) that could then have the standard text search techniques apply to it. There have been conferences and evaluations with ground truth examples for Optical Character Reading (OCR) or Optical Character Writing (OCW) that converts images with typed or written text into computer text. In the area of conversion of audio to Speech there was a series of conferences call HUB that focused on that technology. The Hub conferences eventually encountered the same issue as the TREC Ad Hoc search evaluations where the technologies had evolved using Hidden Markov Models and there was no significant improvement between yearly evaluations. The Hub program was replaced by the DARPA EARS (Effective, Affordable, Reusable Speech-to-Text) program that continues to develop robust speech recognition technology to address a range of languages and speaking styles. The results from the HUB conferences were used in TREC 6-8 on a Spoken Document Retrieval track evaluating how search technologies worked against the errorful transcribed audio. Most recently DARPA has focused on the GALE Program. The Global Autonomous Language Exploitation (GALE) program is designed to translate and understand foreign language material (e.g., television shows and newspapers) in near real time. The system automatically identifies important information and stores the results in a searchable database. In addition to speech to text, GALE's translation of structured speech and text (e.g., broadcast news and newswire) has improved to the point that it produces "edit-worthy" text (http://www.darpa.mil/ipto/programs/gale/gale.asp).

A lot of multimedia evaluation is done by individual organizations as they investigate different search technologies. There is one European group looking at the problem; CHORUS (Coordinated approach to the EurOpean effoRt on aUdio-visual Search engines). CHORUS started in November 2007. CHORUS is a Coordination

Action whose goal is to create the conditions of mutual information and cross fertilization between the projects that will run under Strategic objective 2.6.3 (Advanced search technologies for digital audio-visual content). CHORUS is setting up conferences and meetings to discuss how to approach evaluation and rating of multimedia search systems for Europe.

The longest running effort at multimedia formal evaluation has been by TREC that focuses on video. In 2001 TREC launched a track on information retrieval of digital video. By 2003 this track had become a major evaluation area as digital video became more prevalent and the track separated and became its own evaluation forum (TRECVid—http://www-nlpir.nist.gov/projects/trecvid). The earliest work focused on indexing the video which is one approach to defining a semantic representation of it. The index is against the continuous video stream and is associated with key frames extracted from the video similar to indexing images. The technology challenge is to develop algorithms to automatically detect semantic features in the video.

TRECVid 2006 had 160 h of ground truth TV news recording as a test data set. TRECVid has subsetted their evaluation into a number of different areas:

- Shot boundary detection is the process of dividing the video up into specific areas to be analyzed.
- Detection of important high level semantic concepts in the video—39 concepts have been identified that act as the ground truth information needs.
- 24 topics are identified typically for each yearly conference and the systems identify and extract the shots that best represent the topics. To identify the shot results the system can use only the topic definition, the can redefine the topic and finally the tester can interact with the system trying to find the best results (these options are similar to the original TREC evaluations).
- Redundancy and ad hoc retrieval is against raw footage that has not been processed to develop techniques for filtering out redundancy and detecting important scene data for product creation.

By the 2006 conference over 70 groups from 20 different countries and 380 researchers were participating in the conference. The shot boundary detection has significantly improved with current results showing over 90% precision and recall for hard cuts and 70% precision and recall for gradual transitions to new topics. Detecting semantic information in video is even more difficult than in text. The systems are performing more in the 50% range.

Another location for ground truth data is at Carnegie Mellon University where they have been creating the Large Analytics Library For Large Scale Concept Ontology For Multimedia (LIBSCOM) data sets. They have defined an ontology list of ideas and lower level terms describing the ideas which they are applying to collected video from YouTube. The goal is not to just provide data sets but also the tools that can be shared by users in creating additional datasets and expanding and maintaining the ontology used to describe the semantics in a video (http://www.lscom.org/index.html).

## 9.4 Measurement Example: TREC Evolution

Until the creation of the Text Retrieval Conferences (TREC) by the Defense Advance Research Projects Agency (DARPA) and the National Institute of Standards and Technology (NIST), experimentation in the area of information retrieval was constrained by the researcher's ability to manually create a test database. One of the first test databases was associated with the Cranfield I and II tests (Cleverdon-62, Cleverdon-66). It contained 1,400 documents and 225 queries. It became one of the standard test sets and has been used by a large number of researchers. Other test collections have been created by Fox and Sparck Jones (Fox-83, Sparck Jones-79). Although there has been some standard usage of the same test data, in those cases the evaluation techniques varied sufficiently so that it has been almost impossible to compare results and derive generalizations. This lack of a common base for experimentation constrained the ability of researchers to explain relationships between different experiments and thus did not provide a basis to determine system improvements (Sparck Jones-81). Even if there had been a better attempt at uniformity in use of the standard collections, all of the standard test sets suffered from a lack of size that prevented realistic measurements for operational environments.

The goal of the Text Retrieval Conference was to overcome these problems by making a very large, diverse test data set available to anyone interested in using it as a basis for their testing and to provide a yearly conference to share the results. There have been 17 TREC conferences since 1992, usually held in the Fall. During the first 8 TREC conferences, two types of retrieval were examined: "adhoc" query, and "routing" (dissemination). As experience has been gained from in the TREC conferences, the details and focus of the experiments have evolved. TREC-provides a set of training documents and a set of test documents, each over 1 GB in size. It also provides a set of training search topics (along with relevance judgments from the database) and a set of test topics. The researchers send to the TREC-sponsor the list of the top 200 items in ranked order that satisfy the search statements. These lists are used in determining the items to be manually reviewed for relevance and for calculating the results from each system. The search topics are "user need" statements rather than specific queries. This allows maximum flexibility for each researcher to translate the search statement to a query appropriate for their system and assists in the determination of whether an item is relevant.

Figure 9.3 describes the initial sources and the number and size of items in the test database (Harman-95). Figure 9.3 also includes statistics on the number of terms in an item and number of unique terms in the test databases. The database was initially composed of disks 1 and 2. In later TRECs, disk 3 of data was added to focus on the routing tests. Figure 9.3b includes in the final column the statistics for the Cranfield test collection. Comparing the Cranfield collection to the contents of disk 1 shows that the initial TREC-test database is approximately 200 times larger and the average length of the items is doubled. Also the dictionary size of unique words is 20 times larger. All of the documents are formatted in Standard Generalized Markup Language (SGML) with a Document Type Definition (DTD) included

| Collection Source | Size in MBytes | Mean Terms per record | Median Terms per record | Total Records |
|---|---|---|---|---|
| ZIFF (disk 3) | 249 | 263 | 119 | 161,021 |
| FR (1994) | 283 | 456 | 390 | 55,554 |
| IR Digest | 7 | 2,383 | 2,225 | 455 |
| News Groups | 237 | 340 | 235 | 102,598 |
| Virtual Worlds | 28 | 416 | 225 | 10,152 |

**a**

| Subset of collection | WSJ (disks 1&2) SJMN (disk 3) | AP | ZIFF | FR (disks 1&2) PAT (disk 3) | DOE | Cranfield test database |
|---|---|---|---|---|---|---|
| Size of Collection (Mbytes) | | | | | | |
| (disk 1) | 270 | 259 | 245 | 262 | 186 | 1.5 |
| (disk 2) | 247 | 241 | 178 | 211 | | |
| (disk 3) | 290 | 242 | 349 | 245 | | |
| Number of Records | | | | | | |
| (disk 1) | 98,732 | 84,678 | 75,180 | 25,960 | 226,087 | 1400 |
| (disk 2) | 74,520 | 79,919 | 56,920 | 19,860 | | |
| (disk 3) | 90,257 | 78,321 | 161,021 | 6,711 | | |
| Median Number Terms per record | | | | | | |
| (disk 1) | 182 | 353 | 181 | 313 | 82 | 79 |
| (disk 2) | 218 | 346 | 167 | 315 | | |
| (disk 3) | 279 | 358 | 119 | 2896 | | |
| Average Number of Terms per record | | | | | | |
| (disk 1) | 329 | 375 | 412 | 1017 | 89 | 88 |
| (disk 2) | 377 | 370 | 394 | 1073 | | |
| (disk 3) | 337 | 379 | 263 | 3543 | | |
| Total Number of Unique Terms | | | | | | |
| (disk 1) | 156,298 | 197,608 | 173,501 | 126,258 | | 8226 |

**b**

**Fig. 9.3 a** Routing test database. **b** TREC-training and adhoc test collection. (From TREC-5 conference proceedings)

for each collection allowing easy parsing. SGML is a superset of HTML and is one of the major standards used by the publishing industry.

It was impossible to perform relevance judgments on all of the items in the test databases (over 700,000 items) to be used in recall and fallout formulas. The option of performing a random sample that would find the estimated 200 or more relevant items for each test search would require a very large sample size to be manually analyzed. Instead, the pooling method proposed by Sparck Jones was used. The top 200 documents based upon the relevance rank from each of the researchers were pooled, redundant items were eliminated and the resultant set was manually reviewed for relevance. In general one-third of the possible items retrieved were unique (e.g., out of 3,300 items 1,278 were unique in TREC-1) (Harman-93). This ratio also been shown to be true in other experiments (Katzer-82). In TREC, each test topic was judged by one person across all of the possible documents to ensure consistency of relevance judgment.

The search Topics in the initial TREC-consisted of a Number, Domain (e.g., Science and Technology), Title, Description of what constituted a relevant item, Narrative natural language text for the search, and Concepts which were specific search terms.

The following describes the source contents of each of the disks shown in Fig. 9.3 available for TREC analysis:

Disk 1

| | |
|---|---|
| WSJ | Wall street journal (1987, 1988, 1989) |
| AP | AP Newswire (1989) |
| ZIFF | Articles from Computer Select disks (ZIFF-Davis Publishing) |
| FR | Federal Register (1989) |
| DOE | Short Abstracts from DOE Publications |

Disk 2

| | |
|---|---|
| WSJ | Wall Street Journal (1990, 1991, 1992) |
| AP | AP Newswire (1988) |
| ZIFF | Articles from Computer Select disks (ZIFF-Davis Publishing) |
| FR | Federal register (1988) |

Disk 3

| | |
|---|---|
| SJMN | San Jose Mercury News (1991) |
| AP | AP Newswire (1990) |
| ZIFF | Articles from Computer Select disks (ZIFF-Davis Publishing) |
| PAT | U.S. Patents (1993) |

Precision and recall were calculated in the initial TREC. To experiment with a measure called Relative Operating Characteristic (ROC) curves, calculation of Probability of Detection (same as recall formula) and calculation of Probability of False Alarm (same as Fallout) was also tried. This use of a set of common evaluation formulas between systems allows for consistent comparison between different executions of the same algorithm and between different algorithms. The results are represented on Recall-Precision and Recall-Fallout graphs (ROC curves). Figure 9.4 shows how the two graphs appear. The x-axis plots the recall from zero to 1.0 based upon the assumption that the relevant items judged in the pooling technique account for all relevant items. The precision or fallout value at each of the discrete recall values is calculated based upon reviewing the items, in relevance rank score order, that it requires to reach that recall value. For example, assume there are 200 relevant items. A particular system, to achieve a recall of 40% (0.4) requiring retrieval of 80 of the relevant items, requires retrieving the top 160 items with the highest relevance scores. Associated with the Precision/Recall graph, for the x-axis value of 0.4, the y-axis value would be 80/160 or 0.5. There are sufficient sources of potential errors in generating the graphs, that they should only be used as relative comparisons between algorithms rather than absolute performance indicators. It has been proven they do provide useful comparative information.

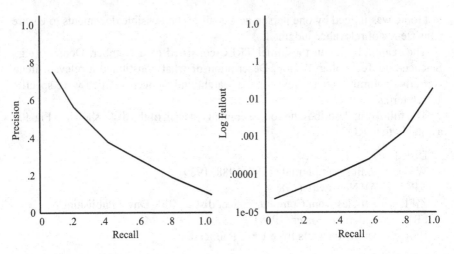

**Fig. 9.4** Examples of TREC-result charts

In addition to the search measurements, other standard information on system performance such as system timing, storage, and specific descriptions on the tests are collected on each system. This data is useful because the TREC-objective is to support the migration of techniques developed in a research environment into operational systems.

The results from each conference have varied based upon understanding from previous conferences and new objectives. A general trend has been followed to make the tests in each TREC-closer to realistic operational uses of information systems.

TREC-1 (1992) was constrained by researchers trying to get their systems to work with the very large test databases. TREC-2 in August 1993 was the first real test of the algorithms which provided insights for the researchers into areas in which their systems needed work. The search statements (user need statements) were very large and complex. They reflect long-standing information needs versus adhoc requests. By TREC-3, the participants were experimenting with techniques for query expansion and the importance of constraining searches to passages within items versus the total item. There were tradeoffs available between manual and automatic query expansion and the benefits from combining results from multiple retrieval techniques. Some of the experiments were driven by the introduction of shorter and less complex search statements. The "concept" field, which contained terms related to the query that a user might be expected to be aware of, was eliminated from the search statements. This change was a major source for the interest into query expansion techniques. TREC-4 introduced significantly shorter queries (average reduction from 119 terms in TREC-3 to 16 terms in TREC-4) and introduced five new areas of testing called "tracks" (Harman-96). The queries were shortened by dropping the title and a narrative field, which provided additional description of a relevant item.

The multilingual track expanded TREC-4 to test a search in a Spanish test set of 200 MB of articles from the "El Norte" newspaper. The interactive track modified the previous adhoc search testing from a batch to an interactive environment. Since there are no standardized tools for evaluating this environment, the TREC-5 goals included development of evaluation methodologies as well as investigating the search aspects. The database merging task investigated methods for merging results from multiple subcollections into a single Hit file. The confusion track dealt with corrupted data. Data of this type are found in Optical Character Reader (OCR) conversion of hardcopy to characters or speech input. The database for TREC-had random errors created in the text. Usually in real world situations, the errors in these systems tend not to be totally random but bursty or oriented towards particular characters. Finally, additional tests were performed on the routing (dissemination) function that focused on three different objectives: high precision, high recall and balanced precision and recall. Rather than ranking all items, a binary text classification system approach was pursued where each item is either accepted or rejected (Lewis-96, Lewis-95).

Insights into the advancements in information retrieval can be gained by looking at changes in results between TRECs mitigated by the changes in the test search statements. Adhoc query results from TREC-1 were calculated for automatic and manual query construction. Automatic query construction is based upon automatic generation of the query from the Topic fields. Manual construction is also generated from the Topic field manually with some machine assistance if desired. There was very little difference in the results between manual construction of a query and automatic construction.

By TREC-3 and TREC-4 the systems were focusing on how to accommodate the shorter queries. It is clear that if the shorter queries had been executed for TREC-1, the results would have been worse than those described. Figures 9.5 and 9.6 show

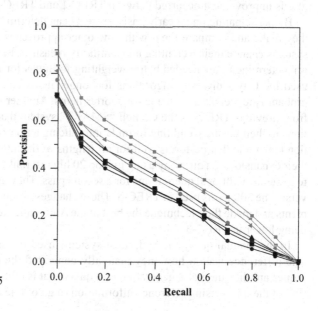

**Fig. 9.5** Automatic AdHoc query results from TREC-3 and TREC-4. (From TREC-5 conference proceedings)

**Fig. 9.6** Manual AdHoc
query results from TREC3
and TREC4. (From TREC-5
conference proceedings)

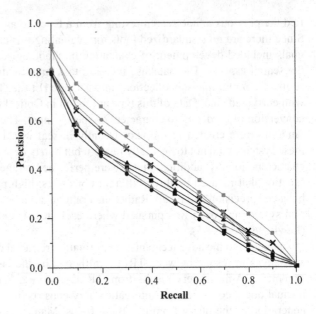

the precision recall results for Automatic and Manual adhoc searches for TREC-3
and TREC-4 (Harman-96). The significant reduction in query size caused even the
best algorithms shown in the figures to perform worse in TREC-4 than in TREC-3.

Even though all systems experienced significant problems when the size of the
queries was reduced, a comparison with TREC 1 results shows a significant improvement in the Precision/Recall capabilities of the systems. A significant portion
of this improvement occurred between TREC-1 and TREC-2.

By participating on a yearly basis, systems can determine the effects of changes
they make and compare them with how other approaches are doing. Many of the
systems change their weighting and similarity measures between TRECs. INQUE-
RY determined they needed better weighting formulas for long documents so they
used the City University algorithms for longer items and their own version of a
probabilistic weighting scheme for shorter items. Another example of the learning
from previous TRECs is the Cornell "SMART" system that made major modifications to their cosine weighting formula introducing a non-cosine length normalization technique that performs well for all lengths of documents. They also changed
their expansion of a query by using the top 20 highest ranked items from a first pass
to generate additional query terms for a second pass. They used 50 terms in TREC-4
versus the 300 terms used in TREC-3. These changes produced significant improvements and made their technique the best in the Automatic Adhoc for TREC-4 versus
being lower in TREC-3.

In the manual query method, most systems used the same search algorithms.
The difference was in how they manually generated the query. The major techniques are the automatic generation of a query that is edited, total manual generation of the query using reference information (e.g., online dictionary or thesaurus)

and a more complex interaction using both automatic generation and manual expansion.

When TREC-introduced the more realistic short search statements, the value of previously discovered techniques had to be reevaluated. Passage retrieval (limiting the similarity measurement to a logical subsets of the item) had a major impact in TREC-3 but minimal utility in TREC-4. Also more systems began making use of multiple algorithms and selecting the best combination based upon characteristics of the items being searched. A lot more effort was spent on testing better ways of expanding queries (due to their short length) while limiting the expanded terms to reduce impacts on precision. The automatic techniques showed a consistent degradation from TREC-3 to TREC-4. For the Manual Adhoc results, starting at about a level of 0.6, there was minimal difference between the TRECs.

The multilingual track expanded between TREC-4 and TREC-5 by the introduction of Chinese in addition to the previous Spanish tests. The concept in TREC-5 is that the algorithms being developed should be language independent (with the exception of stemming and stopwords). In TREC-4, the researchers who spent extra time in linguistic work in a foreign language showed better results (e.g., INQUERY enhanced their noun-phrase identifier in their statistical thesaurus generator). The best results came from the University of Central Florida, which built an extensive synonym list. In TREC-5 significant improvements in precision were made in the systems participating from TREC-4. In Spanish, the Precision-Recall charts are better than those for the Adhoc tests, but the search statements were not as constrained as in the ad hoc. In Chinese, the results varied significantly between the participants with some results worse than the adhoc and some better. This being the first time for Chinese, it is too early to judge the overall types of performance to be expected. But for Spanish, the results indicate the applicability to the developed algorithms to other languages. Experiments with Chinese demonstrates the applicability to a language based upon pictographs that represent words versus an alphabet based language.

The results in TREC 8, held in November 1999 did not show any significant improvement over the best TREC 3 or TREC 4 results for automatic searching. The manual searching did show some improvement because the user interaction techniques are improving with experience. One participant, Readware, did perform significantly better than the other participants. By TREC 8 highest Mean Average Precision scores were the standard in creating the comparative diagrams and tables.

By TREC 8 many of the major participants that had been submitting systems to TREC evaluations for many years and the NIST evaluators came to the conclusion that there were not any additional major improvements in searching that was being seen each year for the Ad Hoc search task. Most participants were just using the same system as the previous year to satisfy the requirement for an ad hoc run. Cornel showed this by looking at the results from their SMART system over the last 8 years of TRECs. They took their systems each year and ran the different query sets from all of the TRECs against them to normalize the results between years. Keep in mind retrieval effectiveness has always shown a dependency on the specific test query sets used as discussed previously. There system is representative of other

**Fig. 9.7** TREC 8 recall/
precision graph top eight
automatic short ad hoc runs.
(From TREC-8 conference
proceedings)

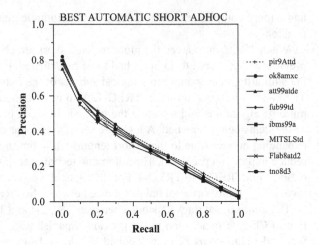

**Fig. 9.8** TREC 8 recall/
precision graph top 5 manual
ad hoc runs. (From TREC-8
conference proceedings)

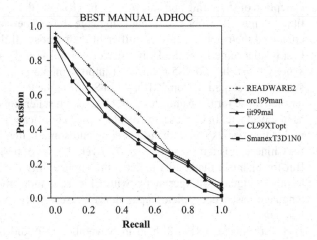

systems and they clearly showed that the system results had leveled off. Thus the
Ad Hoc search track ended with TREC 8 and Figs. 9.7 and 9.8 show what can be
expected for searching.

The major new change with TREC 8 was the introduction of the Question/Answer track. The goal of the track is to encourage research into systems that return
answers versus lists of documents. The user is looking for an answer to an information need and does not want to have to browse through long items to locate the
specific information of interest.

The experiment was run based upon 200 fact based short answer questions. The
participants returned a ranked list of up to five document-id/string location pairs
for each query. The strings were limited to either 50 or 250 characters. The answers were judged based upon the proposed string including units if asked for (e.g.,
world's population) and for famous objects answers had to pertain to that specific
object.

Most researchers processed the request using their normal search algorithms, but included "blind feedback" to increase the precision of the higher ranked hits. Then techniques were used to parse the returned document around the words that caused the hit using natural language techniques to focus on the likely strings to be returned. Most of the participants only tried to return the 250-character string range.

The TREC-series of conferences have achieved their goal of defining a standard test forum for evaluating information retrieval search techniques. It provides a realistic environment with known results. It has been evolving to equate closer to a real world operational environment that allows transition of the test results to inclusion of commercial products with known benefits. By being an open forum, it has encouraged participation by most of the major organizations developing algorithms for information retrieval search.

## 9.5  Summary

Evaluation of Information Retrieval Systems is essential to understand the source of weaknesses in existing systems and trade offs between using different algorithms. The standard measures of Precision, Recall, and Fallout have been used for the last 25 years as the major measures of algorithmic effectiveness. Some of the more recent evaluation formulas such as MAP and bpref are establishing new ways of describing information retrieval system performance. With the insertion of information retrieval technologies into the commercial market and ever growing use on the Internet, other measures will be needed for real time monitoring the operations of systems. One example was given in the modifications to the definition of Precision when a user ends his retrieval activity as soon as sufficient information is found to satisfy the reason for the search.

The measures to date are optimal from a system perspective, and very useful in evaluating the effect of changes to search algorithms. What are missing are the evaluation metrics that consider the total information retrieval system, attempting to estimate the system's support for satisfying a search versus how well an algorithm performs. This would require additional estimates of the effectiveness of techniques to generate queries and techniques to review the results of searches. Being able to take a system perspective may change the evaluation for a particular aspect of the system. For example, assume information visualization techniques are needed to improve the user's effectiveness in locating needed information. Two levels of search algorithms, one optimized for concept clustering the other optimized for precision, may be more effective than a single algorithm optimized against a standard Precision/Recall measure.

In all cases, evaluation of Information Retrieval Systems will suffer from the subjective nature of information. There is no deterministic methodology for understanding what is relevant to a user's search. The problems with information discussed in Chap. 1 directly affect system evaluation techniques in Chap. 9.

Users have trouble in translating their mental perception of information being sought into the written language of a search statement. When facts are needed, users are able to provide a specific relevance judgment on an item. But when general information is needed, relevancy goes from a classification process to a continuous function. The current evaluation metrics require a classification of items into relevant or non-relevant. When forced to make this decision, users have a different threshold. These leads to the suggestion that the existing evaluation formulas could benefit from extension to accommodate a spectrum of values for relevancy of an item versus a binary classification. But the innate issue of the subjective nature of relevant judgments will still exist, just at a different level.

Research on information retrieval suffered for many years from a lack of large, meaningful test corpora. The Text REtrieval Conferences (TRECs), sponsored on a yearly basis, provides a source of a large "ground truth" database of documents, search statements and expected results from searches essential to evaluate algorithms. It also provides a yearly forum where developers of algorithms can share their techniques with their peers. That model has been proliferated to many other similar organizations around the world each developing more sophisticated evaluation data sets focused on more specific information retrieval problems. More recently, developers are starting to combine the best parts of their algorithms with other developers' algorithms to produce an improved system.

The weakest area in information retrieval evaluation is in the area of multimedia information retrieval. There are not any large ground truth databases that have been made for evaluation purposes. Creating such databases against multimedia is far more complex and manually intensive then creating similar databases against textual items. The definition of relevancy is less well defined in this area.

## 9.6  Exercises

1. What are the problems associated with generalizing the results from controlled tests on information systems to their applicability to operational systems? Does this invalidate the utility of the controlled tests?
2. What are the main issues associated with the definition of relevance? How would you overcome these issues in a controlled test environment?
3. What techniques could be applied to evaluate each step in Fig. 11.1?
4. Consider the following table of relevant items in ranked order from four algorithms along with the actual relevance of each item. Assume all algorithms have highest to lowest relevance is from left to right (Document 1 to last item). A value of zero implies the document was non-relevant).

| Document | 1 | 2 | 3 | 4 | 5 | 6 | 7 | 8 | 9 | 10 | 11 | 12 | 13 | 14 |
|---|---|---|---|---|---|---|---|---|---|---|---|---|---|---|
| Algo 1 | 1 | 0 | 0 | 1 | 1 | 1 | 0 | 0 | 1 | 1 | 0 | 0 | 1 | 1 |
| Algo 2 | 0 | 1 | 1 | 0 | 1 | 1 | 1 | 0 | 0 | 1 | 1 | 0 | 1 | 1 |
| Algo 3 | 0 | 1 | 0 | 0 | 1 | 1 | 1 | 1 | 1 | 0 | 1 | 1 | 1 | 1 |
| Actual | 1 | 1 | 1 | 1 | 0 | 0 | 1 | 1 | 1 | 0 | 0 | 1 | 1 | 1 |

| Document | 15 | 16 | 17 | 18 | 19 | 20 | 21 | 22 | 23 | 24 | 25 | 26 | 27 |
|---|---|---|---|---|---|---|---|---|---|---|---|---|---|
| Algo 1 | 1 | 0 | 0 | 1 | 1 | 1 | 0 | 0 | 1 | 1 | 0 | 0 | 1 |
| Algo 2 | 0 | 1 | 1 | 0 | 1 | 1 | 1 | 0 | 0 | 1 | 1 | 0 | 1 |
| Algo 3 | 0 | 1 | 0 | 0 | 1 | 1 | 1 | 1 | 1 | 0 | 1 | 1 | 1 |
| Actual | 1 | 1 | 1 | 1 | 0 | 0 | 1 | 1 | 1 | 0 | 0 | 1 | 1 |

    a. Calculate and graph precision/recall for all the algorithms on one graph.
    b. Calculate and graph fallout/recall for all the algorithms on one graph
    c. Calculate the MAP value for each algorithm
    d. Calculate the Bpref at 20 items.
    e. Calculate the DCG at 10 items.
    f. What is the F-measure at item 20.

5. What is the relationship between precision and TURR.

# Bibliography

Aalbersberg-92 – Aalbersberg, I., "Incremental Relevance Feedback", In Proceedings of the Fifteenth Annual ACM SIGIR Conference on Research and Development in Information Retrieval, 1992, pages 11–22.

Adams-92 – Adams, E. S., "A Study of Trigrama and Their Feasibility as Index Terms in a Full Text Information Retrieval System", D.Sc. dissertation, The George Washington University, 1992.

Adamson-74 – Adamson, G. and J. Boreham, "The Use of an Association Measure Based on Character Structure to Identify Semantically Related Pairs of Words and Document Titles", *Information Storage and Retrieval*, #10, 1974, pages 253–260.

Ahlberg-94 – Ahlberg, C. and B. Shneiderman, "Visual Information Seeking: Tightly Coupling of Dynamic Query Filters with Starfield Displays", In Proceedings of CHI'94, April 1994, Boston, MA, pages 313–317 and 479–480.

Ahlberg-95 – Ahlberg, C. and E. Wistrand, "IVEE: An Information Visualization and Exploration Environment", In Proceedings of Information Visualization Symposium, in Gersho, N. and G. Eick (eds.), *IEEE CS Press*, Los Alamitos, CA, 1995, pages 66–73. (also URL http://www. cs.chalmers.se/SSKKII/software.html, current November 21, 1996).

Aho-75 – Aho, A. V. and M. Corasick, "Efficient String Matching: An Aid to Bibliographic Search", *Communications of the ACM*, Vol. 18, No. 6, June 1975, pages 333–340.

Aitchison-72 – Aitchison, J. and A. Gilchrist, "Thesaurus Construction—A Practical Manual", London, ASLIB, 1972.

Allan-95 – Allan, J., "Automatic Hypertext Construction", Technical Report TR95-1414, Department of Computer Science, Cornell University, New York, February 1995.

Allan-96 – Allan, J., "Incremental Relevance Feedback for Information Filtering", In Proceedings of the Nineteenth Annual ACM SIGIR Conference on Research and Development in Information Retrieval, ACM, New York, 1996, pages 270–278.

Angell-83 – Angell, R., Freund, G. and P. Willett, "Automatic Spelling Correction Using a Trigram Similarity Measure", *Information Processing and Management*, Vol. 19, No. 4. 1983, pages 255–261.

Apte-94 – Apte, C., Damerau, F. and S. Weiss, "Towards Language Independent Automated Learning of Text Categorization Models", In Proceedings of the Seventeenth Annual ACM SIGIR Conference on Research and Development in Information Retrieval, ACM, New York, 1994, pages 23–30.

Arnheim-69 – Arnheim, R., "Visual Thinking", University of California Press, 1969.

Arnheim-86 – Arnheim, R., "New Essays on the Psychology of Art", California Press, 1986.

Avram-75 – Avram, H. D., "MARC: Its History and Implications", Washington, Library of Congress, 1975.

Bach-96 – Bach, J., Fuller, C., Gupta, A., Hampapur, A., Horowitz, B., Humphrey, R. and R. Jain, "The Virage Image Search Engine: An Open Framework for Image Management", SPIE, *Storage and Retrieval for Still Images and Video Databases*, Vol. 2670, 1996, pages 76–87.

Baeza-Yates-89 – Baeza-Yates, R., "String Searching Algorithms Revisited", in *Workshop in Algorithms and Data Structures*, in Dehne F., Sack J. and N. Santoro (eds.), Springer Verlag *Lecture Notes on Computer Science*, Ottawa, Canada, 1989, pages 332–347.

Baeza-Yates-90 – Baeza-Yates, R. and M. Regnier, "Fast Algorithms for Two Dimensional and Multiple Pattern Matching", in Second Scandinavian Workshop in Algorithmic Theory, SAT'90, in Karlsson R. and J. Gilbert (eds.), *Lecture Notes in Computer Science*, 447, 1990, pages 332–347.

Baeza-Yates-92 – Baeza-Yates, R., "String Searching Algorithms", in *Information Retrieval Data Structures & Algorithms*, Prentice Hall, New Jersey, 1992, pages 219–237.

Baeza-Yates-92a – Baeza-Yates, R. and G. Gonnet, "A New Approach to Text Searching", *Communications of the ACM*, Vol. 35, No. 10, October 1992, pages 74–82.

Barry-94 – Barry, C., "User Defined Relevance Criteria: An Exploratory Study", *Journal of the American Society for Information Science*, Vol. 45, No. 3, April 1994, pages 149–159.

Bazzi-98 – Bazzi, I., LaPre, C., Makhoul, J. and R. Schwartz, "A Script-Independent Methodology for Optical Character Recognition", *Pattern Recognition*, Vol. 31, No. 9, 1998, pages 1285–1294.

Belkin-87 – Belkin, N. J. and W. B. Croft, "Retrieval Techniques", In Williams, M. (ed.), *Annual Review of Information Science and Technology*, Elsevier Science Publishers, New York, 1987, pages 109–145.

Belkin-89 – Belkin, N. and W. Croft, "Retrieval Techniques", in *Annual Review of Information Science and Technology*, Elsevier Science publishers, New York, 1989, pages 109–145.

Bernstein-84 – Bernstein T. M., "The Careful Writer by Theodore M. Bernstein", NY, Atheneum, 1984, pages 366–367.

Bergman-2001 – Bergman, M., "The Deep Web: Surfacing Hidden Value". *The Journal of Electronic Publishing*, 2001, 7(1), http://www.press.umich.edu/jep/07-01/bergman.html.

Berra-89 – Berra, P., Ghafoor, A., Mitkas, P., Marcinkowski, S. and Guizani, "Optical Searching", *IEEE Transactions on Knowledge and Data Engineering*, No. 1, 1989, pages 111–132.

Bikel-97 – Bikel, D., Miller, S., Schwartz, R. and R. Weischedel, "Nymble: A High-Performance Learning Name Finder", Fifth Conference on Applied Natural Language Processing, (published by ACL), 1997, pages 194–201.

Bird-77 – Bird, R., Tu, J. and R. Worthy, "Associative Parallel Processors for Searching Very Large Textual Databases", In Proceedings of Third Non-Numeric Workshop, Syracuse, NY, May 1977, pages 8–16.

Bird-78 – Bird, R., Newsbaum, J. and J. Trefftzs, "Text Files Inversion: An Evaluation", In Proceedings of the Fourth Workshop on Computer Architecture for Non-Numeric Processing, Syracuse, NY, August 1–4, 1978, pages 42–50.

Bird-79 – Bird, R. M. and J. Tu, "Associative Crosspoint Processor System", U.S. Patent, 4, 152, 762, May 1, 1979.

Blum-97 – Blum, T., Keislaer, D., Wheaton, J. and E. Wold, "Audio Databases with Content-Based Retrieval". In Maybury M. T. (ed.), *Intelligent Multimedia Information Retrieval*, 1997, pages 113–135.

Broder et al.-1997 – Broder, A., Glassman S., Manasse M. and G. Zweig, "Syntactic Clustering of the Web", In Proceedings of WWW6 '97, pages 391–404. Elsevier Science, April 1997.

Boyer-77 – Boyer, R. S. and S. Moore, "A Fast String Matching: An Aid to Bibliographic Search", *Communications of the ACM*, Vol. 20, No. 10, October 1977, pages 762–772.

Brookstein-78 – Brookstein, A., "On the Perils of Merging Boolean and Weighted Retrieval Systems", *Journal of the ASIS*, Vol. 29, No. 3., May 1978, pages 156–158.

Brookstein-80 – Brookstein, A., "Fuzzy Requests: An Approach to Weighted Boolean Searches", *Journal of the ASIS*, Vol. 31, No. 4, July 1980, pages 240–247.

Brookstein-95 – Brookstein, A., Klein, S. T. and T. Raita, "Detecting Content Bearing Words by Serial Clustering—Extended Abstract", SIGIR'95, In Proceedings of the Eighteenth Annual

International ACM SIGIR Conference on Research and Development in Information Retrieval, Seattle Washington, July 1995, pages 319–327.

Brown-96 – Brown, J. R. and N. Gershon, "The Role of Computer Graphics and Visualization in the GII", *Computer Graphics and Applications*, Vol. 16, No. 2, March 1996, pages 61–63.

Buckley-94 – Buckley, C., Salton, G. and J. Allan, "The Effect of Adding Relevance Information in a Relevance Feedback Environment", In Proceedings of the Seventeenth Annual ACM SIGIR Conference on Research and Development in Information Retrieval, ACM, New York, NY, 1994, pages 293–300.

Buckley-95 – Buckley, C., Salton, G., Allan, J. and A. Singhal, "Automatic Query Expansion Using SMART: TREC 3". In Harman D. K. (ed.), Overview of the Third Text Retrieval Conference (TREC-3), pages 69–79, NIST Special Publication 500-225, April 1995.

Buckley-96 – Buckley, C., Singhal, A., Mitra, M. and G. Salton, "New Retrieval Approaches Using SMART: TREC 4", in publishing of the Fourth Text Retrieval Conference (TREC-4), NIST Special Publication, 1996.

Bush-45 – Bush, V., "As We May Think", *Atlantic Monthly*, 176, July 1945, pages 101–108.

Bush-67 – Bush, V. (ed.), "Science Is Not Enough", William Morrow and Co. Reprinted in Nyce, J. M. and P. Kahn (eds.), *From Memex to Hypertex: Vannevar Bush and the Mind's Machine*, Academic Press, 1991, pages 197–216.

Caid-93 – Caid, W., Gallant, S., Hecht-Nielsen, R., Carlton, J., Pu Qing, K. and D. Sudbeck, "HNC's MatchPlus System", The First Text Retrieval Conference (TREC-1), NIST Special Publication 500-207, NIST, Gaithersburg, MD, March 1993, pages 107–111.

Callan-94 – Callan, J. P., "Passage-Level Evidence in Document Retrieval". In Proceedings of the Seventeenth Annual International ACM SIGIR Conference on Research and Development in Information Retrieval, pages 302–310, Dublin, Ireland, 1994. ACM.

Callan and Yang-2005 – Callan J. and H. Yang, Near Duplicate Detection for eRule making, http://www.cs.cmu.edu/~callan/Papers/dgo05-huiyang.pdf, February 2010.

Can-95 – Can, F., Fox, E., Snaverly, C. and R. France, "Incremental Clustering for Very Large Document Databases: Initial MARIAN Experience", *Information Systems*, 84, 1995, pages 101–114.

Card-96 – Card, K., "Visualizing Retrieved Information: A Survey", *IEEE Computer Graphics and Applications*, Vol. 16, No. 2, March 1996, pages 63–67.

Card-96a – Card, K., Robertson, G. G. and W. York, "The Web Book and the Web Forager: An Information Workspace for the World Wide Web", CHI 96, ACM Conference on Human Factors in Software, ACM Press, New York, 1996.

Catarci-96 – Catarci, T., "Interaction with Databases", *Computer Graphics and Applications*, Vol. 16, No. 2, March 1996, pages 67–69.

Chalmers-92 – Chalmers, M. and P. Chitson, "Bead: Explorations in Information Retrieval", In Proceedings of SIGIR 92, Copenhagen, Denmark, June 1992, pages 330–337.

Cho et. al-99 – Cho, J., N. Shivakumanar and H. Garcia-Molina, "Finding Replicated Web Collections", In Proceedings of the ACM SIGMOD Conference of Data Management, 1999, pages 355–366.

Chowdhurry et. al.-2002 – Chowdhury, A., Frueder O., Grossman D. and M. McCabe, "Collection Statistics for Fast Duplicate Document Detection", ACM Transcations on Information Systems, 20(2), 2002, pages 171–191.

Chuah-97 – Chuah, M., Roth, S. and S. Kerpedjiev, "Sketching, Searching, and Customizing Visualizations: A Content Based Approach to Design Retrieval". In Maybury M. T. (ed.), *Intelligent Multimedia Information Retrieval*, 1997. AAAI/MIT Press, pages 83–111.

Cleverdon-62 – Cleverdon, C. W., "Report on the Testing and Analysis of an Investigation into the Comparative Efficiency of Indexing Systems", College of Aeronautics, Cranfield, England, 1962.

Cleverdon-66 – Cleverdon, C. W., Mills, J. and E. Keen, "Factors Determining the Performance of Indexing Systems", Vol. 1: Design, Vol. 2: Test Results, slib Cranfield Research Project, Cranfield, England, 1966.

CNRI-97 – http://www.andle.net/docs/overview.html (current Jan 7, 1997)

Cohen-95 – Cohen, J., "Highlights: Language and Domain Independent Automatic Indexing Terms for Abstracting", *Journal of the American Society for Information Science*, Vol. 46, No. 3, 1995, pages 162–174.

Commentz-Walter-79 – Commentz-Walter, B., "A String Matching Algorithm Fast on the Average", in ICALP, *Lecture Notes in Computer Science*, 71, 1979, pages 118–132.

Conrad and Schriber-2004 – Conrad, J. and C. Schriber, "Constructing a Text Corpus for Inexact Duplicate Detection", In Proceedings of ACM SIGIR'04, Sheffield, South Yorkshire, UK. July 25–29, 2004.

Cooper-73 – Cooper, W., "On Selecting a Measure of Retrieval Effectiveness", *Journal of the American Society for Information Science*, 24, 1973, pages 87–100.

Cooper-78 – Cooper, W. and M. Maron, "Foundations of Probabilistic and Utility-Theoretic Indexing", *Journal of the Association for Computing Machinery*, No. 25, 1978, pages 67–80.

Cooper-94 – Cooper, W., "The Formalism of Probability Theory in IR: A Foundation or an Encumbrance", In Proceedings of the Seventeenth Annual ACM-SIGIR Conference, in Bruce Croft, W. and C. J. van Rijsbergen (eds.), Springer-Verlag, London, 1994, pages 242–247.

Cooper-94a – Cooper, W., Chen, A. and F. Gey, "Full Text Retrieval Based on Probabilistic Equations with Coefficients Fitted by logistic Regression", In Proceedings of the Second Text Retrieval Conference (TREC-2), NIST publication, 1994, pages 57–66.

Copeland-73 – Copeland, G., Lipovski, C. and S. Y. Su, "The Architecture of CASSM: A Cellular System for Non-Numeric Processing", In Proceedings of the First Annual Symposium on Computer Architecture, ACM, New York, December 1973, pages 121–125.

Crew-67 – Crew, B. and M. Gunzburg, "Information Storage and Retrieval", U.S. Patent 3, 358, 270, December 12, 1967.

Croft-77 – Croft, W. B., "Clustering Large Files of Documents Using the Single Link Method", *Journal of the ASIS*, Vol. 28, No. 6, November 1977, pages 341–344.

Croft-79 – Croft, W. B. and D. J. Harper, "Using Probabilistic Models of Document Retrieval without Relevance Information", *Documentation*, Vol. 3, No. 4, 1979, pages 285–295.

Croft-83 – Croft, W. B., "Experiments with Representation in a Document Retrieval System", *Information Technology: Research and Development*, Vol. 2, No. 1, 1983, pages 1–21.

Croft-94 – Croft, W. B., Callan, J. and J. Broglio, "Trec-2 Routing and Ad Hoc Retrieval Evaluation Using the INQUERY System", in The Second Text Retrieval Conference (TREC-2) Proceedings, NIST publications, 1993.

Cullum-85 – Cullum, J. K. and R. Willoughby, "Lanczos, Algorithms for Large Symmetric Eigenvalue Computations", Vol. I Theory, (Chapter 5), Birkhauser, Boston, MA, 1985.

Cutting-90 – Cutting D. and J. Pedersen, "Optimization for Dynamic Inverted Index Maintenance." Paper presented at Thirteenth International Conference on Research and Development in Information Retrieval, Brussels, Belgium.

Damashek-95 – Damashek, M., "Gauging Similarity with n-grams: Language Independent Categorization of Text", *Science*, Vol. 267, February 10, 1995, pages 843–848.

Damerau-64 – Damerau, F. J., "A Technique for Computer Detection and Correction of Spelling Errors", *Communications of the ACM*, Vol. 7, No. 3, March 1964, pages 171–176.

Dawson-74 – Dawson J., "Suffix Removal and Word Conflation" ALLC Bulletin, Michelmas, 1974, pages 33–46.

Deerwester-90 – Deerwester, S., Dumais, S., Furnas, G., Landauer, T. and R. Harshman, "Indexing by Latent Semantic Analysis", *Journal for the American Society for Information Science*, Vol. 41, No. 6, 1990, pages 391–407.

Dempster-77 – Dempster, A., Laird, N. and D. Rubin, "Maximum Likelihood from Incomplete Data via the EM Algorithm", *Journal of Royal Statistical Society*, B 39, 1977, pages 1–38.

Dennis-68 – Dennis, S. F., "The Design and Testing of a Fully Automated Indexing-Searching System for Documents Consisting of Expository Text", *Informational Retrieval: A Critical Review*. In Schecter, G. (ed.), Thompson Book Company, Washington D.C., 1967, pages 67–94.

Deppisch-86 – Deppisch, U., "S-Tree: A Dynamic Balanced Signature Index for Office Retrieval", In Proceedings of ACM Conference on Research and Development in Information Retrieval, Pisa, Italy, September 1986, pages 77–87.

Dumais-93 – Dumais, S., "Latent Semantic Indexing and TREC-2", in The Second Text Retrieval Conference (TREC-2) Proceedings, NIST publications, 1993, pages 105–115.

Dumais-95 – Dumais, S., "Latent Semantic Indexing: TREC-3 Report". In Harman, D. K. (ed.), Overview of the Third Text Retrieval Conference (TREC-3), NIST Special Publication 500-225, April 1995, pages 219–230.

Edmundson-69 – Edmundson, H., "New Methods in Automatic Abstracting", Journal of the ACM, Vol. 16, No. 2, April 1969, pages 264–285.

El-Hamdouchi-89 – El-Hamdouchi, A. and P. Willet, "Comparison of Hierarchic Agglomerative Clustering Methods for Document Retrieval", Computer Journal, 32, 1989, pages 220–227.

Fairthorne-64 – Fairthorne, R. A, "Basic Parameters of Retrieval Tests", In Proceedings of 1964 Annual Meeting of the American Documentation Institute, Spartan Books, Washington, 1964, pages 343–347.

Fairthorne-69 – Fairthorne, R. A., "Empirical Hyperbolic Distributions for Bibliometric Description and Prediction", International ACM SIGIR Conference: Research and Development in Information Retrieval, June 5–7, 1985.

Faloutsos-85 – Faloutsos, C., "Access Methods for Text", ACM Computing Surveys, Vol. 17, No. 1, March 1985, pages 49–74.

Faloutsos-87 – Faloutsos, C. and S. Christodoulakis, "Description and Performance Analysis of Signature File Methods", ACM TOOIS, Vol. 5, No. 3, 1987, pages 237–257.

Faloutsos-88 – Faloutsos, C. and R. Chan, "Fast Text Access Methods for Optical and Large Magnetic Disks: Designs and Performance Comparison", In Proceedings of Fourteenth International Conference on VLDB, Long Beach, CA, August 1988, pages 280–293.

Faloutsos-92 – Faloutsos, C., "Signature Files", in Frakes, W. B. and R. Baeza-Yates (eds.), Information Retrieval Data Structures & Algorithms, Prentice Hall, New Jersey, 1992, pages 44–65.

Feiner-90 – Feiner, S. and C. Beshers, "World Within Worlds: Metaphors for Exploring N-dimensional Virtual Worlds", UIST 94, ACM Symposium on User Interface Software, ACM Press, New York, 1990, pages 76–83.

Flickner-97 – Flickner, M., Sawhney, H., Niblack, W., Ashley, J., Huang, Q., Dom, B., Gorkani, M., Hafner, J., Lee, D., Petkovic, D., Steele, D. and P. Yanker, "Query by Image and Video Content: The QBIC System". In Maybury M. T. (ed.), Intelligent Multimedia Information Retrieval, 1997, pages 7–22.

Forsyth-86 – Forsyth, R. and R. Rada, "Adding an Edge". In Machine Learning: application in expert systems and information retrieval, Ellis Horwood Ltd., 1986, pages 198–212.

Foster-80 – Foster, M. and H. Kung, "Design of Special Purpose VLSI Chips: Examples and Opinions", In Proceedings of the Seventh Annual Symposium on Computer Architecture, May 1980, published as SIGARCH Newsletter, Vol. 8, No. 3, pages 300–307.

Fox-83 – Fox, E. A., "Characteristics of Two New Experimental Collections in Computer and Information Science Containing Textual and Bibliographic Concepts", Technical Reports TR 83-561, Cornell University: Computing Science Department, 1983.

Fox-86 – Fox, E. A. and S. Sharat, "A Comparison of Two Models for Soft Boolean Interpretation in Information Retrieval", Technical Report TR-86-1, Virginia Tech, Department of Computer Science, 1986.

Fox-93a – Fox, E. A., "Sourcebook on Digital Libraries: Report for the National Science Foundation", Technical Report TR-93-95, Computer Science Department, VPI&SU, Blacksburg, VA, 1993 (http://fox.cs.vt.edu/DLSB.html).

Fox-93b – Fox, E., Hix, D., Nowell, L., Brueni, D., Wake, W., Heath, L. and D. Rao, "Users, User Interfaces and Objects: Envision, a Digital Library", Journal of the American Society for Information Science, Vol. 44, No. 5, 1993, pages 480–449.

Fox-96 – Fox, E. A. and G. Marchionini (eds.), In Proceedings of the First ACM International Conference on Digital Libraries, ACM, New York, NY, 1996.

Frakes-92 – Frakes, W. B. and R. Baeza-Yates, Information Retrieval Data Structures & Algorithms, Prentice Hall, New Jersey, 1992.

Frieder et al.-2009 – Frieder, O., Urbain J. and N. Goharian, "Passage Relevance Models for Genomics Search", BMC Bioinformatics, 10(suppl. 3):S3 doi: 10.1186/1471-2105-10-S#-S3, 2009.

Friedman-89 – Friedman, J., "Regularized Discriminant Analysis", *Journal of the American Statistical Association*, Vol. 84, No. 405, 1989, pages 165–175.

Friedhoff-89 – Friedhoff, R. M. and W. Benzon, *The Second Computer Revolution: Visualization*, Harry N. Adams, Inc., New York, 1989.

Fuhr-89 – Fuhr, N., "Optimum Polynomial Retrieval Functions Based on the Probability Ranking Principle", *ACM Transactions on Information Systems*, Vol. 7, No. 3, 1989, pages 183–204.

Fung-95 – Fung, R. and B. Del Favero, "Applying Baysian Networks to Information Retrieval", *Communications of the ACM*, Vol. 58, No. 3, March 1995.

Furui-2000 – Furui, S., Ohtsuki, K. and Z. P. Zhang, "Japanese Broadcast News Transcription and Information Extraction". In Maybury M. T. (ed.), *News On Demand. Communications of the ACM*, Vol. 43, No. 2, pages 71–75, 2000.

Furuta-89 – Furuta, R., Plaisant, C. and B. Shneiderman, "Automatically Transforming Regularly Structured Text Into Hypertext", *Electronic Publishing*, Vol. 2, No. 4, December 1989, pages 211–229.

Galil-79 – Galil, Z., "On Improving the Worst Case Running Time of the Boyer-Moore String Matching Algorithm", CACM, 22, 1979, pages 505–608.

Garcia et al.-2008 – Garcia-Molina, H., Menestrina, D., Su, Qi, Whang, S. and J. Widom, "SWOOSH: A Generic Approach to Entity Resolution", *VLDB Journal*, 2008.

Gauvain-2000 – Gauvain, J. L., Lamel, L. and G. Adda, "Transcribing Broadcast News for Audio and Video Indexing". In Maybury M. T. (ed.), *News On Demand*, 2000. *Communications of the ACM*, Vol. 43, No. 2:64–70.

Gildea-99 – Gildea, D. and T. Hofmann, "Topic based language models using EM", In Proceedings of the Sixth European Conference on Speech Communications and Technology (EUROSPEECH), 1999.

Gnanadesikan-79 – Gnanadesikan, R., "Methods for Statistical Data Analysis of Multivariate Observations", Wiley, New York, 1979.

Gershon-95 – Gershon, N. D., "Moving Happily Through the World Wide Web", *Computer Graphics and Applications*, Vol. 16, No. 2, March 1996, pages 72–75.

Gershon-95a – Gershon, N. D. and S. G. Eick, "Visualization's New Tack: Making Sense of Information", *IEEE Spectrum*, Vol. 32, No. 11, November 1995, pages 38–56.

Gey-94 – Gey, F., "Inferring Probability of Relevance Using the Method of Logistic Regression", In Proceedings of the Seventeenth Annual ACM-SIGIR Conference. In Bruce Croft, W. and C. J. van Rijsbergen. (ed.), Springer-Verlag, London, 1994, pages 222–241.

Gibson-60 – Gibson, E. and R. Walk, "The Visual Cliff", *Scientific American*, April 1960, pages 140–148.

Gilbert-79 – Gilbert, H. and K. Sparck Jones, "Statistical Bases of Relevance Assessments for the Ideal Information Retrieval Test Collection", Computer Laboratory, University of Cambridge, BL R and D Report 5481, Cambridge, England, March 1979.

Goldstein et al.-2000 – Goldstein, J., Mittal, V., Carbonell, J. and M. Kantrowitz, "Multidocument Summarization by Sentence Extraction", ANLP/NAACL 2000 Workshop on summarization, Vol. 4, 2000.

Gonnet-92 – Gonnet, Gaston, Baeza-Yates, R. and T. Snider, "New Indices for Text: Pat Trees and Pat Arrays", in Frakes, W. B. and R. Baeza-Yates (eds.), *Information Retrieval Data Structures & Algorithms*, Prentice Hall, New Jersey, 1992, pages 66–81.

Gordon-91 – Gordon, M. D. and P. Lenk, "A Utility Theoretic Examination of the Probability Ranking Principle in Information Retrieval", *Journal of the American Society for Information Science*, No. 42, 1991, pages 703–714.

Gordon-92 – Gordon, M. D. and P. Lenk, "When is the Probability Ranking Principle Suboptimal", *Journal of the American Society for Information Science*, No. 43, 1992, pages 1–14.

Greffenstette-94 – Greffenstette, G., "Explorations in Automatic Thesaurus Discovery", Kluwer Academic Publishers, 1994.

Grossman and Frieder-2004 – Grossman, D. and O. Frieder, Information Retrieval Algorithms and Heuristics, Springer, 2004, page 204.

Gustafson-71 – Gustafson, R. A., "Elements of the Randomized Combinatorial File Structure", ACM SIGIR, Proceedings of the Symposium on Information Storage and Retrieval, University of Maryland, April 1971, pages 163–174.

Hagler-91 – Hagler, R., "The Bibliographic Record and Technology", *American Library Association*, Chicago, Illinois, 1991.

Hahn-94 – Hahn, Harley and R. Stout, "The INTERNET Complete Reference", McGraw-Hill, Berkley, CA., 1994, pages 476–477.

Hafer-74 – Hafer, M. and S. Weiss, "Word Segmentation by Letter Successor Varieties," *Information Storage and Retrieval*, Vol. 10, 1974, pages 371–385.

Halasz-87 – Halasz, F., Moran, T. P. and R. H. Trigg, "Notecards in a Nutshell", In Proceedings ACM CHI+GI'87, Toronto, Canada, 5–9 April 1987, pages 45–52.

Harrison-71 – Harrison, M., "Implementation of the Substring Test by Hashing", *CACM*, Vol. 14, 1971, pages 777–779.

Harman-86 – Harman, D., "An Experimental Study of Factors Important in Document Ranking", ACM Conference on Research and Development in Information Retrieval, Pisa, Italy, 1986.

Harman-91 – Harman, D., "How Effective is Suffixing?", *Journal of the American Society for Information Science*, Vol. 42, No. 1, 1991, pages 7–15.

Harman-93 – Harman, D., "Overview of the First Text Retrieval Conference (TREC-1)", The First Text Retrieval Conference (TREC-1), NIST Special Publication 500-207, NIST, Gaithersburg, MD, March 1993, pages 1–20.

Harman-95 – Harman, D., "Overview of the Third Text Retrieval Conference (TREC-3)". In Harman, D. K. (ed.), Overview of the Third Text Retrieval Conference (TREC-3), pages 1–19, NIST Special Publication 500-225, April 1995.

Harman-96 –Harman, D., "Overview of the Fourth Text Retrieval Conference (TREC-4)", paper to be included in the Overview of the Fifth Text Retrieval Conference (TREC-5), NIST Special Publications.

Harper-78 – Harper, D. J. and C. J. van Rijsbergen, "An Evaluation of Feedback in Document Retrieval Using Co-Occurrence Data", *Journal of Documentation*, Vol. 34, No. 3, 1978, pages 189–216.

Harper-80 – Harper, D. J., "Relevance Feedback in Automatic Document Retrieval Systems: An Evaluation of Probabilistic Strategies", Doctoral Dissertation, Jesus College, Cambridge, England.

Hasan-95 – Hasan, M. Z., Mendelzon, A. O. and D. Vista, "Visual Web Surfing with Hy+", In Proceedings of CASCON'95, Toronto, 1995, pages 218–227.

Haskin-83 – Haskin, R. and L. Hollaar, "Operational Characteristics of a Hardware-based Pattern Matcher", *ACM Transactions Database*, Vol. 8, No. 1, 1983.

Hearst-96 – Hearst, M. and J. Pedersen, "Reexamining the Cluster Hypothesis: Scatter/Gather on Retrieval Results", In Proceedings of the Nineteenth Annual ACM SIGIR Conference on Research and Development in Information Retrieval, ACM, New York, NY, 1996, pages 76–83.

Hearst-98 – Hearst, M. A., "Automated Discovery of WordNet Relations", in WordNet: An electronic lexical database. In Fellbaum, C. (ed.), MIT Press, 1998.

Heilmann-96 – Heilmann, K., Kihanya, D., Light, A. and P. Musembwa, "Intelligent Agents: A Technology and Business Application Analysis", http://www.mines.u-nancy.fr/~gueniffe/CoursEMN/I31/heilmann/heilmann.html.

Hemmje-94 – Hemmje, M., Kunkel, C. and A. Willett, "CyberWorld—A Visualization User Interface Supporting Full Text Retrieval", In Proceedings of the Seventeenth Annual ACM SIGIR Conference on Research and Development in Information Retrieval, ACM, New York, NY, 1994, pages 249–259.

Hendley-95 – Hendley, R. J. et al., "Narcissus: Visualizing Information", In Proceedings Information Visualization Symposium 95, in Gershon, N. and S. G. Eick (eds.), *IEEE CS Press*, Los Alamitos, CA, 1995, pages 90–96.

Herlocker-99 – Herlocker, J., Konstan, J., Borchers, A. and J. Riedi, "An Algorithmic Framework for Performing Collaborative Filtering", In Proceedings of the Twenty-second Annual ACM SIGIR Conference on Research and Development in Information Retrieval, 1999, pages 230–237.

Hindle-90 – Hindle, D., "Noun Classification From Predicate Argument Structures", In Proceedings of Twenty-eighth Annual Meeting of the ACL, 1990, pages 268–275.

Hinton-84 – Hinton, G. E., "Distributed Representations", Technical Report CMU-CS-84-157, Carnegie-Mellon University, Department of Computer Science.

Hofmann-99 – Hofmann, T., "Latent Class Models for Collaborative Filtering", In Proceedings of the Sixteenth International Joint Conference on Artificial Intelligence (IJCAI), 1999.

Hollaar-79 – Hollaar, L., "Text Retrieval Computers", *IEEE Computer*, Vol. 12, No. 3, March 1979, pages 40–50.

Holaar-84 – Hollaar, L. and R. Haskin, "Method and System for Matching Encoded Characters", U.S. Patent, 4, 450, 520, May 22, 1984.

Hollaar-92 – Hollaar, L., "Special Purpose Hardware for Information Retrieval", *Information Retrieval Data Structures & Algorithms*, Prentice Hall, New Jersey, 1992, pages 443–458.

Horspool-80 – Horspool, R., "Practical Fast Searching in Strings", *Software-Practice and Experience*, Vol. 10, 1980, pages 501–506.

Hosmer-89 – Hosmer, D. and S. Lemeshow, "Applied Logistic Regression", Wiley, New York, 1989.

Howard-81 – Howard, R. A. and J. E. Matheson, "Influence Diagrams", *Readings on the Principles and Applications of Decision Analysis*, in Howard, R. A. and J. E. Matheson (eds.), *Strategic Decision Group*, Menlo Park, CA, 1981, pages 721–762.

Hull-94 – Hull, D., "Improving Text Retrieval for the Routing Problem Using Latent Semantic Indexing", In Proceedings of the Seventeenth Annual ACM SIGIR Conference on Research and Development in Information Retrieval, ACM, New York, NY, 1994, pages 282–289.

Hull-95 – Hull, D., "Information Retrieval Using Statistical Classification", Ph.D. Thesis, Stanford University, 1995.

Hull-96 – Hull, D., Pedersen, J. and H. Schutze, "Method Combination for Document Filtering", In Proceedings of the Nineteenth Annual ACM SIGIR Conference on Research and Development in Information Retrieval, ACM, New York, NY, 1996, pages 279–287.

Huffman-95 – Huffman, S. and M. Damashek, "Acquaintance: A Novel Vector Space N-Gram Technique for Document Categorization". In Harman, D. K. (ed.), Overview of the Third Text Retrieval Conference (TREC-3), NIST Special Publication 500-225, April 1995, pages 305–310.

Hyland-99 – Hyland, R., Clifton, C. and R. Holland, "Geonode: Visualizing News in Geospatial Context", 1999. AFCEA Federal Data Mining Symposium. Washington, DC.

Hyman-82 – Hyman, R., "Shelf Access in Libraries", Chicago, ALA, 1982.

Hyman-89 – Hyman, R. J., "Information Access", American Library Association, Chicago, 1989.

Ide-69 – Ide, E., "Relevance Feedback in an Automatic Document Retrieval System", Report No. ISR-15 to National Science Foundation from Department of Computer Science, Cornell University.

Ide-71 – Ide, E., "New Experiments in Relevance Feedback", *The SART Retrieval System*, in Salton, G. and N. J. Englewod (eds.), Prentice-Hall, 1971, pages 337–354.

IETF-96 – "Uniform Resource Names, a Progress Report", in the February 1996 issue of *D-Lib Magazine*.

Ingwersen-92 – Ingwersen, P., *Information Retrieval Interaction*, ISBN:0-947568-54-9, London, England, 1992.

Iyengar-80 – Iyengar, S. and V. Alia, "A String Search Algorithm", *Applied Mathematics and Computation*, Vol. 6, 1980, pages 123–131.

Jing-94 – Jing, Y. and B. Croft, "An Association Thesaurus for Information Retrieval", In Proceedings of RIAO, 1994, pages 146–160.

Jolliffe-2002 – Jolliffe, I. T., "Principal Component Analysis", Series: Springer Series in Statistics, 2nd ed., Springer, NY, 2002, XXIX, 487 page 28 illus.

Johnson-91, Johnson, "Tree Maps, A Space Filling Approach to the Visualization of Hierarchical Information Structures", IEEE Visualization '91 Conference Proceedings, *IEEE Computer Society Press*, Los Alamitos, CA, 1991, pages 284–291.

Jones-97 – Jones, G., Foote, J., Spärck Jones, K. and S. Young, "The Video Mail Retrieval Project: Experiences in Retrieving Spoken Documents". In Maybury M. T. (ed.), *Intelligent Multimedia Information Retrieval*, 1997, pages 191–214.

Jones-71 – Jones, K. Sparck, *Automatic Keyword Classification for Information Retrieval*, Buttersworths, London, 1971.

Kanuango et al.-2002 – Kanuango, T., D. Mount, N. Netanyahu, C. Piatko, R. Silverman and A. Wu, Annual Symposium on Computational Geometry, Proceedings of the Eighteenth annual symposium on Computation Geometry, Barcelona Spain, 2002, pages 10–18.

Kaiser-96 – Kaiser, M. K., http://vision.arc.nasa.gov/AFH/Brief/Vision.S.T./Perceptually.T.html, as of November 2, 1996.

Karp-87 – Karp, R. and M. Rabin, "Efficient Randomized Pattern Matching Algorithms", *IBM Journal of Research and Development*, Vol. 31, 1987, pages 249–260.

Kaskiel-97 – Kaskiel, M. and J. Zobel, "Passage Retrieval Revisited", In Proceedings of the Twentieth Annual ACM SIGIR Conference on Research and Development in Information Retrieval, 1999, ACM Press, pages 178–185.

Katzer-82 – Katzer, J., McGill, M., Tessier, J., Frakes, W. and P. Gupta, "A Study of the Overlap Among Document Representations", *Information Technology: Research and Development*, Vol. 1, No. 2, 1982, pages 261–274.

Keen-71 – Keen, E., "Evaluation Parameters", *The SMART Retrieval System—Experiments in Automatic Document Processing*. In Salton, G. (ed.), Prentice-Hall, Inc., Englewood, New Jersey, 1971, Chapter 5.

Kellog-96 – Kellog, R. and M. Subhas, "Text to Hypertext: Can Clustering Solve the Problem in Digital Libraries", In Proceedings of the First ACM International Conference on Digital Libraries. In Fox, E. and G. Marchionini (eds.), March 1996, pages 144–148.

Knaus-95 – Knaus, D., Mittendorf, E., Schauble, P. and P. Sheridan, "Highlighting Relevant Passages for Users of the Interactive SPIDER Retrieval System", The Fourth Text Retrieval Conference (TREC-4), NIST Special Publication 500-236, NIST, Gaithersburg, MD, November 1995, pages 233–244.

Kowalski-83 – Kowalski, G., "High Speed Multi-Term String Matching Algorithms", Dissertation for Doctor of Science, The George Washington University, May 1983.

Kracsony-81 – Kracsony, P., Kowalski, G. and A. Meltzer, "Comparative Analysis of Hardware versus Software Text Search", Information Retrieval Research. In Oddy, R. N. (ed.), 1981, pages 268–309.

Knuth-77 – Knuth, D. E., Morris, J. and V. Pratt, "Fast Pattern Matching in Strings", *SIAM Journal of Computing*, Vol. 6, No. 2, June 1977, pages 323–350.

Kretser-99 – Kretser, O. and A. Moffat, "Effective Document Presentation with a Locality Based Similarity Heuristic", In Proceedings of the Twenty-second Annual ACM SIGIR Conference on Research and Development in Information Retrieval, 1999, pages 113–120.

Krohn-95 – Krohn, U., "Visualization of Navigational Retrieval in Virtual Information Spaces", In Proceedings of the Workshop on New Paradigms in Information Visualization and Manipulation, Baltimore, MD, 1995, pages 26–32.

Krovetz-93 – Krovetz, R., "Viewing Morphology as an Inference Process", In Proceeding of the ACM-SIGIR Conference on Research and Development in Information Retrieval, 1993, pages 191–202.

Kstem-95 – Information from the Kstem.doc File Distributed with INQUERY Search System", *Applied Computing Systems Institute of Massachusetts, Inc* (ACSIOM), 1995.

Kubala-97 – Kubala, F., Imai, T., Makhoul, J., Nguyen, L. and R. Schwartz, "A Maximum Likelihood Model for Topic Classification of Broadcast News", Proceedings Eurospeech'97, Rhodes, Greece, 1997, pages 1455–1458.

Kubala-99 – Kubala, F., Colbath, S., Liu, D. and J. Makhoul, "Rough'n'Ready: A Meeting Recorder and Browser", June 1999. Article No. 7 in Mills, K. (ed.), *ACM Computing Surveys*, Vol. 31, No. 2.

Kubala-2000 – Kubala, F., Colbath, S., Liu, D., Srivastava, A. and J. Makhoul, "Integrated Technologies for Indexing Spoken Language". In Maybury, M. T. (ed.), Special Section on *News On Demand, Communications of the ACM*, Vol. 43, No. 2, pages 48–56, 2000.

Kubala-98 – Kubala, F. et al., "The 1997 Byblos System Applied to Broadcast News Transcription", In Proceedings of the DARPA Broadcast News Transcription and Understanding Workshop, Lansdowne, VA, February 1998.

Kupiec-95 – Kupiec, J., Pedersen, J. and F. Chen, "A Trainable Document Summarizer", In Proceeding of the eighteenth Annual International ACM SIGIR Conference on Research and Development in Information Retrieval, 1995, pages 68–74.

Kunze-95 – Kunze, J. J. and R. P. C. Rodgers, "Z39.50 in a Nutshell", *Lister Hill National Center for Biomedical Communications*, National Library of Medicine, July 1995.

Kwok-95 – Kwok, K. and L. Grunfeld, "TREC-3 Ad-Hoc Routing Retrieval and Thresholding Experiments using PIRCS". In Harman, D. K. (ed.), Overview of the Third Text Retrieval Conference (TREC-3), NIST Special Publication 500-225, April 1995, pages 247–255.

Kwok-96 – Kwok, K. and L. Grunfeld, "TREC-4 Ad-Hoc Routing Retrieval and Filtering Experiments Using PIRCS", in Harman, D. K. (ed.), Overview of the Fourth Text Retrieval Conference (TREC-4), NIST, 1996.

Lamping-95 – Lamping, J., Rao, R. and P. Pirolli, "A Focus + Context Technique Based on Hyperbolic Geometry for Visualizing Large Hierarchies", in CHI 95, Proceedings of ACM Conference on Human Factors in Computing Systems, ACM Press, New York, 1995, pages 401–408.

Lance-66 – Lance, G. N. and W. Williams, "A General Theory of Classificatory Sorting Strategies. 1. Hierarchical Systems", *Computer Journal*, Vol. 9, 1966, pages 373–380.

Lawrence-99 – Lawrence, S. and L. Giles, "Accessibility and Distribution of Information on the Web", *Nature*, 1999, pages 107–109.

Lawrence and Giles-2000 – Lawrence S. and L. Giles, "Accessibility of Information on the Web", *Intelligence*, 2000, 11(1): pages 32–39.

Lee-85 – Lee, D. L., "The Design and Evaluation of a Text Retrieval Machine for Large Databases", Ph.D. Thesis, University of Toronto, September 1985.

Lee-90 – Lee, D. L. and F. Lochovsky, "HYTREM—A Hybrid Text-Retrieval Machine for Large Databases", *IEEE Transactions on Computers*, Vol. 39, No. 1, 1990, pages 111–123.

Lee-88 – Lee, W. C. and E. A. Fox, "Experimental Comparison of Schemes for Interpreting Boolean Queries", Virginia Tech M.S. Thesis, Technical Report TR-88-27, Department of Computer Science, 1988.

Lee-89 – Lee, D. L. and C. W. Leng, "Partitioned Signature Files: Design and Performance Evaluation", *ACM Transactions on Information Systems*, Vol. 7, No. 2, 1989, pages 158–180.

Leek-99 – Leek, T., Miller, D. and R Schwartz, "A Hidden Markov Model Information Retrieval System", In Proceedings of the Twenty-second Annual ACM SIGIR Conference on Research and Development in Information Retrieval, 1999, pages 214–221.

Lehnert-91 – Lehnert, W. and B. Sundheim, "A Performance Evaluation of Text-Analysis Technologies", *AI Magazine*, Vol. 12, No. 3, Fall 1991, pages 81–93.

Lewis-92 – Lewis, D., "An Evaluation of Phrasal and Clustered Representations on a Text Categorization Task", In Proceedings of the Fifteenth Annual ACM SIGIR Conference on Research and Development in Information Retrieval, 1992, pages 37–50.

Lewis-94 – Lewis, D. and W. Gale, "A Sequential Algorithm for Training Text Classifiers", In Proceedings of the Seventeenth Annual ACM SIGIR Conference on Research and Development in Information Retrieval, ACM, New York, NY, 1994, pages 11–22.

Lewis-94a – Lewis, D. and M. Ringuette, "A Comparison of Two Learning Algorithms for Text Categorization", in Symposium on Document Analysis and Information Retrieval, University of Las Vegas, 1994.

Lewis-95 – Lewis, D., "Evaluating and Optimizing Autonomous Text Classification Systems", in Fox, E., Ingwersen, P. and R. Fidel (eds.), SIGIR'95: Proceedings of the Eighteenth Annual International ACM SIGIR Conference on Research and Development in Information Retrieval, ACM, New York, 1995, pages 246–254.

Lewis-96 – Lewis, D., "The TREC-4 Filtering Track", paper to be included in the Overview of the Fifth Text Retrieval Conference (TREC-5), NIST Special Publications.

Liddy-93 – Liddy, E. D. and S. H. Myaeng, "DR-LINK's Linguistic-Conceptual Approach to Document Detection", The First Text Retrieval Conference (TREC-1), NIST Special Publication 500-207, NIST, Gaithersburg, MD, March 1993, pages 113–129.

Lin-88 – Lin, Z. and C. Faloutsos, "Frame Sliced Signature Files", CS-TR-2146 and UMI-ACS-TR-88-88, Department of Computer Science, University of Maryland, 1988.

Lin-91 – Lin, X., Liebscher and G. Marchionini, "Graphic Representation of Electronic Search Patterns", Journal of American Society for Information Science, Vol. 42, No. 7, 1991, pages 469–478.

Lin-92 – Lin, X., "Visualization for the Document Space", In Proceedings of Visualization'92, Boston, MA, October 1992, pages 274–281.

Lin-96 – Lin, Xia, "Graphical Table of Contents", In Proceedings of the First ACM International Conference on Digital Libraries, in Fox, E. and G. Marchionini (eds.), March 1996, pages 45–53.

Lochbaum-89 – Lochbaum, K. E. and L. A. Streeter, "Comparing and Combining the Effectiveness of Latent Semantic Indexing and the Ordinary Vector Space Model for Information Retrieval", Information Processing and Management, Vol. 25, No. 6, 1989, pages 665–676.

Lovins-68 – Lovins, J. B., "Development of a Stemming Algorithm", Mechanical Translation and Computational Linguistics, Vol. 11, No. 1–2, 1968, pages 22–31.

Lennon-81 – Lennon, M. D., Pierce, D., Tarry, B. and P. Willett, "An Evaluation of Some Conflation Algorithms for Information Retrieval", Journal of Information Science, Vol. 3, 1981, pages 177–183.

Levine-94 – Levine, J. R. and C. Baroudi, "The Internet for Dummies", IDG Books, San Mateo, CA, 1994, pages 261–262.

Luhn-58 – Luhn, H. P., "The Automatic Creation of Literature Abstracts", IBM Journal of Research and Development, Vol. 2, No. 2, April 1958, pages 159–165.

Mandala-99 – Mandala, R., Tokunaga, T. and H. Tanaka, "Combining Evidence from Different Types of Thesaurus for Query Expansion", In Proceedings of the Twenty-second Annual ACM SIGIR Conference on Research and Development in Information Retrieval, 1999, pages 191–197.

Mani-97 – Mani, I., House, D., Maybury, M. and M. Green, "Towards Content-Based Browsing of Broadcast News Video". In Maybury M. T. (ed.), Intelligent Multimedia Information Retrieval, 1997, pages 241–258.

Marchionini-88 – Marchionini, G. and B. Shneiderman, "Finding Facts vs. Browsing Knowledge in Hypertext Systems", Computer, January 1988, pages 70–80.

Maron-60 – Maron, M. E. and J. L. Kuhns, "On Relevance, Probabilistic Indexing, and Information Retrieval", Journal of ACM, 1960, pages 216–244.

Masand-92 – Masand, B., Linoff, G. and D. Waltz, "Classifying News Stories Using Memory Based Reasoning", In Proceedings of the Fifteenth Annual ACM SIGIR Conference on Research and Development in Information Retrieval, 1992, pages 59–65.

Maybury-97 – Maybury, M. T. (ed.), Intelligent Multimedia Information Retrieval, 1997. AAAI/MIT Press. (http://www.aaai.org:80/Press/Books/Maybury2/)

Maybury-97 – Maybury, M., Merlino, A. and D. Morey, "Broadcast News Navigation Using Story Segments", 1997. ACM International Multimedia Conference, Seattle, WA, November 8–14, pages 381–391.

Maybury-2000 – Maybury, M. T. (ed.), "News On Demand". Communications of the ACM, Vol. 43, No. 2, February 2000, pages 33–34.

Maybury-98 – Maybury, M. T. and W. Wahlster, (eds.) Readings in Intelligent User Interface, 1998. Morgan Kaufmann Press. (http://www.mkp.com/books_catalog/1-55860-444-8.asp)

Mayper-80 – Mayper, V., Nagy, A., Bird R., Tu J. and L. Michaels, "Finite State Automation with Multiple State Types", U.S. Patent 4, 241, 402, December 23, 1980.

McIllroy-82 – McIlroy, M. D., "Development of a Spelling List", IEEE Transaction on Communications, Vol. Com-30, 1982, pages 91–99.

McCullagh-89 – McCullagh, P. and J. Nelder, "Generalized Linear Models", chapter 4, pages 101–123, Chapman and Hall, 2nd ed., 1989.

McCulloch-43 – McCulloch, W. and W. Pitts, "A Logical Calculus of the Ides Immanent in Nervous Activity", Bulletin of Mathematical Biophysics, No. 5, 1943, pages 115–137.

Merlino-99 – Merlino, A. and M. Maybury, "An Empirical Study of the Optimal Presentation of Multimedia Summaries of Broadcast News", In Mani, I. and M. Maybury (eds.), *Automated Text Summarization*, MIT Press, pages 391–401.

Mettler-93 – Mettler, M., "Text Retrieval with the TRW Fast Data Finder", The First Text Retrieval Conference (TREC-1), NIST Special Publication 500-207, NIST, Gaithersburg, MD, March 1993, pages 309–317.

Miike-94 – Miike, S., Itoh, E., Ono, K. and K. Sumita, "A Full Text Retrieval System with a Dynamic Abstract Generation Function", In Proceedings of the Seventeenth Annual ACM SIGIR Conference on Research and Development in Information Retrieval, ACM, New York, NY, 1994, pages 152–161.

Miller-95 – Miller, G. A., "WordNet: A Lexical Database for English", in Communications of the ACM, 38(11), 1995, pages 39–41.

Minker-77 – Minker, J., "Information Storage and Retrieval—A Survey and Functional Description", SIGIR Forum, *Association for Computer Machinery*, Vol. 12, No. 2, Fall 1977, pages 1–108.

Minsky-69 – Minsky, M. and S. Papert, Perceptrons, "An Introduction to Computational Geometry", MIT Press, Cambridge, MA, 1969.

Mitkas-89 – Mitkas, P., Berra, P. and P. Guilfoyle, "An Optical System for Full Text Search", In Proceedings of SIGIR 89.

Mittendorf-99 – Mittendorf, E. and P. Schauble, "Document and Passage Retrieval Based on Hidden Markov Models", Twenty-second International Conference on Research and Development in Information Retrieval, 1994, pages 318–327.

Moller-Nielsen-84 – Mollier-Nielsen, P. and J. Staunstrup, "Experiments with a Fast String Searching Algorithm", *Information Processing Letters*, Vol. 18, 1984, pages 129–135.

Mooers-49 – Mooers, C., "Application of Random Codes to the Gathering of Statistical Information", Bulletin 31, Zator Co., Cambridge, MA, 1949.

Morris-75 – Morris, R. and L. Cherry, "Computer Detection of Typographical Errors", *IEEE Transactions on Professional Communications*, Vol. 18, No. 1, March 1975, pages 54–56.

Morris-92 – Morris, A., Kasper, G. and D. Adams, "The Effects and Limitations of Automated Text Condensing on Reading Comprehension Performance", *Information Systems Research*, March 1992, pages 17–35.

Mukherjea -95 – Mukherjea, S. and J. D. Foley, "Visualizing the World Wide Web with Navigational View Builder", *Computer Networks and ISDN Systems*, Vol. 27, 1995, pages 1075–1087.

Multimedia Manager: Professional Edition for OS/2 & DB2/2 Brochure, IBM.

Munzer-95 – Munzer, T. and P. Burchard, "Visualizing the Structure of the World Wide Web in 3D Hyperbolic Space", The Geometry Center, University of Minnesota, 1995. (see http://www.geom.umn.edu/docs/research/webviz/ current November 1996).

Murtagh-83 – Murtagh, F., "A Survey of Recent Advances in Hierarchical Clustering Algorithms", *Computer Journal*, Vol. 26, 1983, pages 354–359.

Murtagh-85 – Murtagh, F., "Multidimensional Clustering Algorithms", Vienna: Physica-Verlag (COMP-STAT Lectures 4), 1985.

Nelson-65 – Nelson T., "A File Structure for the Complex, the Changing, the Indeterminate", In Proceedings of the ACM Twentieth National Conference, 1965, pages 84–100.

Nelson-74 – Nelson, T., "Computer Lib/Dream Machine", 1st ed., Self-Published in 1974 (revised edition published by Microsoft Press in 1987).

Niblack-93 – Niblack, W., Barber, R. et al., "The QBIC Project: Querying Images by Content Using Color Texture and Shape", SPIE, Vol. 1908, Storage and Retrieval for Image and Video databases, 1993, pages 173–187.

Niblack-93-95 – Niblack, W. and R. Jain, (eds. 1993, 1994, 1995), In Proceedings of IS&T/SPIE. Conference on Storage and Retrieval for Image and Video Databases I, II, and III, Vol. 1908, 2185, and 2420. Bellingham, WA: SPIE.

Nordlie-99 – Nordlie, R., "User Revealment—A Comparison of Initial Queries and Ensuing Question Development in Online Searching and in Human Reference Interactions", In Proceedings of the Twenty-second Annual ACM SIGIR Conference on Research and Development in Information Retrieval, 1999, pages 11–18.

Norman-90 – Norman, D. A., "Why Interfaces Don't Work", *The Art of Human Computer Interface Design*. In Laurel, B. (ed.), Addison Wesley, 1990, pages 209–219.

Norris-69 – Norris, D. M., "A History of Cataloguing and Cataloguing Methods 1100–1850", (1939; reprint ed., Detroit: Gale, 1969).

Nowell-96 – Nowell, L., France, R., Hix, D., Heath, L. and E. Fox, "Visualizing Search Results: Some Alternatives to Query-Document Similarity", In Proceedings of the Nineteenth Annual ACM SIGIR Conference on Research and Development in Information Retrieval, ACM, New York, NY, 1996, pages 66–75.

Olsen-93 – Olsen, K. A. et. al., "Visualization of a Document Collection: the VIBE System", *Information Processing and Management*, Vol. 29, No. 1, 1993, pages 69–81.

ORION-93 – ORION White Paper, Wide-Area Information Server (WAIS) Evaluation, Orion Scientific, Inc., 1993.

Paice-84 – Paice, C., "Soft Evaluation of Boolean Search Queries in Information Retrieval Systems", *Information Technology, Research and Development Applications*, Vol. 3, No. 1, 1983, pages 33–42.

Paice-90 – Paice, C., "Another Stemmer", *ACM SIGIR Forum*, Vol. 24, No. 3, 1990, pages 56–61.

Paice-93 – Paice, C. and P. Jones, "The Identification of Important Concepts in Highly Structured Technical Papers", in the Sixteenth Annual International ACM SIGIR Conference on Research and Development in Information Retrieval, ACM Press, June 1993, pages 69–78.

Paice-94 – Paice, C., "An Evaluation Method for Stemming Algorithms", In Proceedings of the Seventeenth Annual International ACM-SIGIR Conference, Springer-Verlag, London, 1994, pages 42–50.

Paracel-96 – "Biology Tool Kit Software Manual", Revision 1, Paracel Inc., Pasadena, CA.

Pearl-88 – Pearl, J., "Probabilistic Reasoning in Intelligent Systems", Morgan Kaufmann, San Mateo, CA, 1988.

Pentlan-94 – Pentland, A., Picard, R. and S. Sclaroff, "Photobook: Tools for Content Based Manipulation of Image Databases", SPIE, Vol. 2185, Storage and Retrieval for Image and Video Databases, 1994, pages 34–47.

Pentland-97 – Pentland, A., "Machine Understanding of Human Behaviour". In Maybury M. T. (ed.), *Intelligent Multimedia Information Retrieval*, 1997, pages 175–188.

Picard-97 – Picard, J. *Affective Computing*. 1997, Cambridge: MIT Press.

Peterson-80 – Peterson, J. L., "Computer Programs for Detecting and Correcting Spelling Errors", *Communications of the ACM*, Vol. 23, No. 12, December 1980, pages 676–687.

Pirolli-96 – Pirolli, P., Schank, P., Hearst, M. and C. Diehl, "Scatter/Gather Browsing Communicates the Topic Structure of a Very Large Text Collection", In Proceedings of the ACM SGCHI Conference on Human Factors in Computing Systems, Vancouver, WA, May 1996.

Porter-80 – Porter, M. F., "An Algorithm for Suffix Stripping", *Program*, Vol. 14, No. 3, 1980, pages 130–137.

Pratt-42 – Pratt, F., "Secret and Urgent", *Blue Ribbon Books*, Garden City, NJ, 1942, page 50.

Rabiner-89 – Rabiner, L., "A Tutorial on Hidden Markov Models and Selected Applications in Speech Recognition", In Proceedings of the IEEE, Vol. 77, No. 2., February 1989, pages 257–285.

Rather-77 – Rather, L., "Exchange of Bibliographic Information in Machine Readable Form", *Library Trends*, Vol. 25, January 1977, pages 625–643.

Rearick-91 – Rearick, T., "Automating the Conversion of Text into Hypertext", in Berk E. and J. Devlin (eds.), *Hypertext/Hypermedia Handbook*, MacGraw-Hill Inc., New York, 1991, pages 113–140.

Reimer-88 – Reimer, U. and U. Hahn, "Text Condensation as Knowledge Base Abstraction", in IEEE Conference on AI Applications, 1988, pages 338–344.

RetrievalWare-95 – CONQUEST Software Manual, The ConQuest Semantic Network, 1995.

Ribeiro-96 – Ribeiro, B. and R. Muntz, "A Belief Network Model for IR", In Proceedings of the Nineteenth Annual ACM SIGIR Conference on Research and Development in Information Retrieval, ACM, New York, NY, 1996, pages 253–260.

Rivest-77 – Rivest, R., "On the Worst-Case Behaviour of String Searching Algorithms", *SIAM Journal on Computing*, Vol. 6, 1977, pages 669–674.

Rivlin-2000 – Rivlin, Z. et al., "MAESTRO: Conductor of Multimedia Analysis Technologies", 2000. In Maybury, M. T. (ed.), Communications of the ACM: *Special Issue of News on Demand*, Vol. 43, No. 2, pages 57–63, 2000.

Rijsbergen-79 – van Rijsbergen, C. J., *Information Retrieval*, 2nd ed., Buttersworths, London, 1979.

Roberts-78 – Roberts, D. C., "A Specialized Computer Architecture for Text Retrieval", Fourth Workshop on Computer Architecture for Non-Numeric Processing, Syracuse, NY (published as SIGIR Vol. 13, No. 2: SIGARCH Vol. 7, No. 2; and SIGMOD Vol. 10, No. 1), pages 51–59.

Roberts-79 – Roberts, C. S., "Partial-Match Retrieval via the Method of Superimposed Codes", In Proceedings of IEEE, Vol. 67, No. 12, 1979, pages 1624–1642.

Robertson-69 – Robertson, S. E., "The Parametric Description of Retrieval Tests, Part I: The Basic Parameters", *Journal of Documentation*, Vol. 25, No. 1, March 1969, pages 1–27.

Robertson-76 – Robertson, S. E. and K. Spark Jones, "Relevance Weighting of Search Terms," *Journal of American Society for Information Science*, Vol. 27, No. 3, 1976, pages 129–146.

Robertson-77 – Robertson, S. E., "The Probability Ranking Principle in IR", *Journal of Documentation*, No. 33, 1977, pages 294–304.

Robertson-93 – Robertson, G. G., "Information Visualization Using 3-D Interactive Animation", *Communications of the ACM*, Vol. 36, No. 4, April 1993, pages 57–71.

Rocchio-71 – Rocchio, J. J., "Relevance Feedback in Information Retrieval". In Salton, G. (ed.), *The SMART Retrieval Storage and Retrieval System*, Prentice Hall, Inc., Englewood Cliffs, NJ, Prentice Hall, Inc., 1971, pages 313–323.

Rock-90 – Rock, I and S. Palmer, "The Legacy of Gestalt Psychology", *Scientific American*, December 1990, pages 84–90.

Rose-95 – Rose, R. (ed.), "P1000 Science and Technology Strategy for Information Visualization", Version 1.6, August 1995.

Rose-96 – Rose, R. (ed.), "P1000 Science and Technology Strategy for Information Visualization", Version 2, 1996.

Roseler-94 – Roseler, M. and D. Hawkins, "Gent Agents: Software Servants for an Electronic Information World (and More!)", *ONLINE*, July 1994, pages 19–32.

Ruge-92 – Ruge, G., "Experiments on Linguistically Based Term Associations", *Information Processing and Management*, Vol. 28, No. 3, 1992, pages 317–332.

Rumelhart-95 – Rumelhart, D., Durbin, R., Golden, R. and Y. Chauvin, "Learning Internal Representation by Error Propagation", in *Back-propagation: Theory, Architectures and Applications*, Lawrence Erlbaum, Hillsdale, NJ, 1995.

Rumelhart-95a – Rumelhart, D., Durbin, R. Golden, R. and Y. Chauvin, "Backpropagation: The Basic Theory", in *Back-propagation: Theory, Architectures and Applications*, Lawrence Erlbaum, Hillsdale, NJ, 1995.

Rush-71 – Rush, J., Salvador, R. and A. Zamora, "Automatic Abstracting and Indexing II, Production of Indicative Abstracts by Application of Contextual Inference and Syntactic Coherence Criteria", *Journal of the ASIS*, Vol. 22, No. 4., 1971, pages 260–274.

Rytter-80 – Rytter, W., "A Correct Preprocessing Algorithm for Boyer-Moore String Searching", *SIAM Journal on Computing*, Vol. 9, No. 3, August 1980, pages 509–512.

Sacks-Davis-83 – Sacks-Davis, R. and K. Ramamohanarao, "A Two Level Superimposed Coding Scheme for Partial Match Retrieval", *Information Systems*, Vol. 8, No. 4, 1983, pages 273–280.

Sacks-Davis-87 – Sacks-Davis, R., Kent, A. and K. Ramamohanarao, "Multikey Access Methods Based on Superimposed Coding Techniques", *ACM Transactions on Database Systems*, Vol. 12, No. 4, pages 655–696.

Salton-68 – Salton, G., "Automatic Information Organization and Retrieval". New York: McGraw-Hill, 1968.

Salton-72 – Salton G., "Experiments in Automatic Thesaurus Construction for Information Retrieval", *Information Processing 71*, North Holland Publishing Co., Amsterdam, 1972, pages 115–123.

Salton-73 – Salton, G. and C. S. Yang, "On the Specification of Term Values in Automatic Indexing", *Journal of Documentation*, Vol. 29, No. 4, pages 351–372.

Salton-75 – Salton, G., "Dynamic Information and Library Processing", Prentice-Hall, Inc., Englewod, New Jersey, 1975.

Salton-83 – Salton, G. and M. McGill, "Introduction to Modern Information Retrieval", McGraw-Hill, 1983.

Salton-83a – Salton, G. E., Fox, E. A. and H. Wu, "Extended Boolean Information Retrieval", *Communications of the ACM*, Vol. 26, No. 12, 1983, pages 1022–1036.

Seybold-94 – Seybold, 1994. IBM Unleashes QBIC Image-Content Search, The Seybold Report on Desktop Publishing, September 12, 1994, pages 34–35.

Salton-88 – Salton, G. and C. Buckley, "Term-Weighting Approaches in Automatic Text Retrieval," *Information Processing and Management*, Vol. 24, No. 5, pages 513–523.

Salton-89 – Salton, G. E., *Automatic Text Processing*, Addison-Wesley, Reading, MA, 1989, pages 260–265.

Sanderson-99 – Sanderson, M. and B. Croft, "Deriving Concept Hierarchies From Text", In Proceedings of the Twenty-second Annual ACM SIGIR Conference on Research and Development in Information Retrieval, 1999, pages 206–213.

Saracevic-91 – Saracevic, T., "Individual Differences in Organizing, Searching and Retrieving Information", ASIS'91: Proceedings of the American Society for Information Science (ASIS) Fifty-Fourth Annual Meeting, Vol. 28, 1991, pages 82–86.

Saracevic-95 – Saracevic, T., "Evaluation of Evaluation in Information Retrieval", In Proceeding of the Eighteenth Annual International ACM SIGIR Conference on Research and Development in Information Retrieval, 1995, pages 138–145.

Schamber-90 – Schamber, L., Eisenberg, M. and M. Nilan, "A Re-examination of Relevance: Toward a Dynamic, Situational Definition", *Information Processing and Management*, Vol. 26, No. 6, 1990, pages 755–776.

Schek-78 – Schek, H. J., "The Reference String Indexing Method", Research Report, IBM Scientific Center, Heidelberg, Germany, 1978.

Schuegraf-76 – Schuegraf, E. J. and H. S. Heaps, "Query Processing in a Retrospective Document Retrieval System That Uses Word Fragments as Language Elements", *Information Processing and Management*, Vol. 12, No. 4, 1976, pages 283–292.

Schuster-79 – Schuster, S., Nguyen, H., Ozkarahan, E. and K. Smith, "RAP2—An Associative Processor for Databases and Its Application", *IEEE Transactions on Computers*, Vol. C-28, No. 6., June 1979, pages 446–458.

Schutze-95 – Schutze, H., Hull, D and J. Pedersen, "A Comparison of Classifiers and Document Representations for the Routing Problem", Proceedings of the Eighteenth Annual International ACM SIGIR Conference on Research and Development in Information Retrieval, Seattle Washington, July 1995, pages 229–237.

Sedgewick-88 – Sedgewick, R., *Algorithms*, 2nd ed., Addison-Wesley, 1988.

Shannon-51 – Shannon, C. E., "Predication and Entropy of Printed English", *Bell Technical Journal*, Vol. 30, No. 1, January 1951, pages 50–65.

Singhal-95 – Singhal, A., Salton, G., Mitra, M. and C. Buckley, "Document Length Normalization", Technical Report TR95-1529, Cornell University, 1995.

Singhal-99 – Singhal, A. and F. Pereira, "Document Expansion for Speech Retrieval", In Proceedings of the Twenty-second Annual ACM SIGIR Conference on Research and Development in Information Retrieval, 1999, pages 34–41.

Smit-82 – Smit, G., "A Comparison of Three String Matching Algorithms", *Software: Practice and Experience*, Vol. 12, 1982, pages 57–66.

Sparck Jones-71 – Sparck Jones, K., *Automatic Keyword Classification for Information Retrieval*, Buttersworths, London, 1971.

Sparck Jones-75 – Sparck Jones, K. and C. van Rijisbergen, "Report on the Need for and Provision of an 'Ideal' Information Retrieval Test Collection", *British Library Research and Development Report 5266*, Computer Laboratory, University of Cambridge, England, 1975.

Sparck Jones-79 – Sparck Jones, K. and C. A. Webster, "Research in Relevance Weighting", *British Library Research and Development Report 5553*, Computer Laboratory, University of Cambridge, 1979.

Sparck Jones-81 – Sparck Jones, K., "Information Retrieval Experiment", Butterworths, London, England, 1981.

Sparck Jones-93 – Sparck Jones, K., "Discourse Modelling for Automatic Summarizing", Technical Report 29D, Computer Laboratory, University of Cambridge, 1993.

Spoerri-93 – Spoerri, A., "Visual Tools for Information Retrieval", In Proceedings of IEEE Symposium on Visual Languages, IEEE CS Press, Los Alamitos, CA, 1993, pages 160–168.

Stirling-77 – Stirling, K. H., "The Effect of Document Ranking on Retrieval System Performance: A Search for an Optimal Ranking Rule", Ph.D. Thesis, University of California, Berkley, 1977.

Sundheim-92 – Sundheim, B. M., "Overview of the Fourth Message Understanding Evaluation and Conference", In Proceedings Fourth Message Understanding Conference (MUC), Morgan Kaufmann Publishers, Inc., 1992, pages 3–21.

Thesuarus-93 – "Microsoft Word Version 6.0a", 1983–1994 Microsoft Corporation, Thesaurus, Soft-Art Inc., 1984–1993.

Thorelli-62 – Thorelli, L. E., "Automatic Correction of Errors in Text", *BIT*, Vol. 2, No. 1, 1962, pages 45–62.

Thorelli-90 – Thorelli, L. G. and W. J. Smith, "Using Computer Color Effectively", Prentice Hall, 1990.

Tong-94 – Tong, R. and L. Appelbaum, "Machine Learning for Knowledge Based Document Routing", in The Second Text Retrieval Conference (TREC-2) Proceedings, NIST publications, 1993, pages 253–264.

Turner-95 – Turner, F., "An Overview of the Z39.50 Information Retrieval Standard", UDT Occasional paper #3, National Library of Canada, July 1995.

Van Dam-88 – van Dam, A., "Hypertext'87 Keynote Address", *Communications of the ACM*, Vol. 31, No. 7, July 1988, pages 887–895.

Van Rijsbergen-79 – Van Rijsbergen, C. J., *Information Retrieval*, 2nd ed., Buttersworth, London, 1979, Chapter 3.

Veerasamy-96 – Veerasamy, A. and N. Belkin, "Evaluation of a Tool for Information Visualization of Information Retrieval Results", In Proceedings of the Nineteenth Annual ACM SIGIR Conference on Research and Development in Information Retrieval, ACM, New York, NY, 1996, pages 85–93.

Vickery-70 – Vickery, B. C., "Techniques of Information Retrieval", Archon Books, Hamden, Conn., 1970.

Visionics Corporation. Face It, Face Detector and Face Recognizer SDK http://www.faceit.com.

Voorhees-86 – Voorhees, E. M., "The Effectiveness and Efficiency of Agglomerative Hierarchic Clustering in Document Retrieval", Ph.D. Thesis, 1986, Cornell University.

Voorhees-93 – Voohrees, E. M., "Using WordNet to Disambiguate Word Senses for Text Retrieval", In Proceedings of the Sixteenth SIGIR, ACM, 1993, pages 171–180.

Voohrees-94 – Voohrees, E. M., "Query Expansion Using Lexical-Semantic Relations", In Proceedings of the Seventeenth SIGIR, ACM, 1994, pages 61–69.

Voorhees-96 – Voorhees, E. and P. Kantor, "TREC-5 Confusion Track", paper to be included in the Overview of the Fifth Text Retrieval Conference (TREC-5), NIST Special Publications.

Wactlar-2000 – Wactlar, H., Hauptmann, A., Christel, M., Houghton, R. and A. Olligschlaeger, "Complementary Video and Audio Analysis for Broadcast News Archives", 2000. In Maybury, M. T. (ed.), *Communications of the ACM*, Vol. 43, No. 2, pages 42–47.

Wade-89 – Wade, S. J., Willet, J. P. and D. Bawden, "SIBRIS: The Sandwich Interactive Browsing and Ranking Information System", *Journal of Information Science*, 15, 1989, pages 249–260.

Waibel-90 – Waibel, A. and K. Lee, (eds.), "Readings in Speech Recognition", Morgan Kaufmann, San Mateo, CA, 1990.

Waltz-85 – Waltz, D. L. and J. B. Pollack, "Massively Parallel Parsing: A Strongly Interactive Model of Natural Language Interpretation", *Cognitive Science*, Vol. 9, 1985, pages 51–74.

Wang-77 – Wang, C. H. C, Mitchell, P. C., Rugh, J. S. and B. W. Basheer, "A Statistical Method for Detecting Spelling Errors in Large Databases", IEEE Proceedings of the Fourteenth International Computer Society Conference, 1977, pages 124–128.

Wang-85 – Wang, Y. -C., Vandenthorpe, J. and M. Evans, "Relationship Thesauri in Information Retrieval", *Journal of American Society of Information Science*, 1985, pages 15–27, 1985.

Ward-63 – Ward, J. H., "Hierarchical Grouping to Optimize an Objective Function", *Journal of American Statistical Association*, Vol. 58, No. 301, 1963, pages 235–244.

Wayne-98 – Wayne, C., "Topic Detection & Tracking (TDT) Overview & Perspective", DARPA Broadcast News Transcription and Understanding Workshop, February 8–11, 1998, Lansdowne Conference Resort, Lansdowne, Virginia, http://www.nist.gov/speech/tdt98/tdt98.htm.

Wiederhold-95 – Wiederhold, G., "Digital Libraries, Value, and Productivity", *Communications of the ACM*, Vol. 38, No. 4, April 1995, pages 85–96.

Weiner-95 – Weiner, M. L. and E. D. Liddy, "Intelligent Text Processing and Intelligence Tradecraft", *Journal of the AGSI*, July 1995.

Whittaker-99 – Whittaker, S., Hirschberg, J., Choi, J., Hindle, D., Pereira, F. and A. Singhal, "SCAN: Designing and Evaluating User Interfaces to Support Retrieval From Speech Archives", In Proceedings of the Twenty-second Annual ACM SIGIR Conference on Research and Development in Information Retrieval, 1999, pages 26–33.

Wilkinson-95 – Wilkinson, R., "Effective Retrieval of Structured Documents", In Proceedings of the Seventh Annual International ACM SIGIR Conference on Research and Development in Information Retrieval, Dublin, Ireland, July 1994.

Wilkenson-95 – Wilkenson, R. and J. Zobel, "Comparison of Fragment Schemes for Document Retrieval". In Harman, D. K. (ed.), Overview of the Third Text Retrieval Conference (TREC-3), pages 81–84, NIST Special Publication 500-225, April 1995.

Willet-88 – Willet, P., "Recent Trends in Hierarchic Document Clustering: A Critical Review", *Information Processing and Management*, Vol. 24, No. 5, 1988, pages 577–597.

Wise-95 – Wise, J. A. et al., "Visualizing the Nonvisual: Spatial Analysis and Interaction with Information from Text Documents", In Proceeding of Information Visualization Symposium, IEEE Computer Society Press, Los Alamitos, CA, 1995, pages 51–58.

Woods-97 – Woods, W. A. (ed.), "Conceptual Indexing: A Better Way to Organize Knowledge", Sun Labs technical report: TR-97-61, Technical Reports, 901 San Antonio Road, Palo Alto, CA, 94303.

Wold-96 – Wold, E., Blum, T., Keislar, D. and J. Wheaton, "Content-Based Classification, Search, and Retrieval of Audio," *IEEE Multimedia Magazine*, Vol. 3, No. 3, 1996, pages 27–36. http://www.musclefish.com/crc/index.html.

Wu-92 – Wu, S. and U. Manber, "Fast Text Searching Allowing Errors", *Communications of the ACM*, Vol. 35, No. 10, October 1992, pages 83–89.

Xu-96 – Xu, J. and B. Croft, "Query Expansion Using Local and Global Domain Analysis", In Proceedings of the Nineteenth International Conference on Research and Development in Information Retrieval, Zurich, Switzerland, 1996, pages 4–11.

Yang-94 – Yang, Y., "Expert Network: Effective and Efficient Learning From Human Decisions in Text Categorization and Retrieval", In Proceedings of the Seventeenth Annual ACM SIGIR Conference on Research and Development in Information Retrieval, ACM, New York, NY, 1994, pages 13–22.

Yochum-85 – Yochum, J., "A High-Speed Text Scanning Algorithm Utilizing Least Frequent Trigraphs", IEEE Proceedings New Directions in Computing Symposium, Trondheim, Norway, 1985, pages 114–121.

Yochum-95 – Yochum, J., "Research in Automatic Profile Creation and Relevance Ranking with LMDS", In Harman, D. K. (ed.), Overview of the Third Text Retrieval Conference (TREC-3), NIST Special Publication 500-225, April 1995, pages 289–298.

Yu-86 – Yu, K., Hsu, S., Heiss, R. and L. Hasiuk, "Pipelined for Speed: The Fast Data Finder System", *Quest, Technology at TRW*, Vol. 9, No. 2, Winter 1986/1987, pages 4–19.

Zadeh-65 – Zadeh, L. A., "Fuzzy Sets", *Information and Control*, Vol. 8, 1965, pages 338–353.

Zamora-81 – Zamora, E. M, Pollack, J. J. and A. Zamora, "Use of Trigram Analysis of Spelling Error Detection", *Information Processing and Management*, Vol. 17, No. 6, 1981, pages 305–316.

Zaremba-95 – Zaremba, D., http://www.europe.digital.com/.i/info/DTJ102 /DTJ102sc.TXT, current as of November 21, 1996.

Ziph-49 – Ziph, G. K., *Human Behaviour and the Principle of Least Effort*, Adisson Wesley Publishing, Reading, MA, 1949.

Zizi-96 – Hascoet-Zizi, M. and N. Pediotakis, "Visual Relevance Analysis", In Proceedings of the First ACM International Conference on Digital Libraries, in Fox, E. and G. Marchionini (eds.), March 1996, pages 54–62.

Zloof-75 – "Query By Example", In Proceedings NCC 44, Anaheim, CA, AFIPS Press, Montvale, New Jersey, 1975.

Zobel-95 – Zobel, J., Moffat, A., Wilkenson, R. and R. Sacks-Davis, "Efficient Retrieval of Partial Documents", *Information Processing & Management*, 31(3), May 1995, pages 361–377.

# Index